UNFINISHED BUSINESS

UNFINISHED BUSINESS

ERITREA AND ETHIOPIA AT WAR

Edited by
**Dominique Jacquin-Berdal
and
Martin Plaut**

The Red Sea Press, Inc.
Publishers & Distributors of Third World Books

11-D Princess Road  P. O. Box 48
Lawrenceville, NJ 08648 Asmara, ERITREA

The Red Sea Press, Inc.
Publishers & Distributors of Third World Books

11-D Princess Road   **RSP**   P. O. Box 48
Lawrenceville, NJ 08648   Asmara, ERITREA

Copyright © 2005 Dominique Jacquin-Berdal and Martin Plaut
First Printing 2005

Book Design: 'Damola Ifaturoti
Cover Design: Roger Dormann

Library of Congress Cataloging-in-Publication Data

Unfinished business : Ethiopia and Eritrea at war / edited by Dominique Jacquin-Berdal and Martin Plaut.
    p. cm.
  Includes bibliographical references and index.
  ISBN 1-56902-216-X (cloth) -- ISBN 1-56902-217-8 (pbk.)
  1. Eritrean-Ethiopian War, 1998- I. Jacquin-Berdal, Dominique. II. Plaut, Martin.
  DT388.35.U54 2004
  963.07'2--dc22
                            2004021798

CONTENTS

Appendices

PREFACE

This book arose out of a desire to understand the war between Ethiopia and Eritrea. The conflict was, and in some ways remains, one of the strangest of modern times. A falling out of old friends and comrades, a welling up of old grievances and complex misunderstandings propelled the countries towards war. These factors combined with more readily understood components of international relations including economic interest, physical geography and the contest for political influence to ignite the conflict between them. That it should cost so many lives, result in such terrible suffering and disrupt so badly the development efforts of so many of the world's poorest people is a matter of enduring sadness.

Two points need to be made clear. Firstly, it is a matter of some regret that the chapter by Alexander Last from Eritrea is not matched by a similar account from Ethiopia. This was commissioned but unfortunately failed to materialise. Secondly, the United Nations maps presented at the end of the book were not provided to the editors by any of the authors of the individual chapters. Rather, they were discovered as the result of ordinary journalistic endeavour.

We would like to thank all the authors of the individual chapters for their contributions, revisions and patience, since this book (like too many before it) has taken longer than was originally anticipated.

We would also like to take this opportunity to thank our partners, Gillian Black and Mats Berdal, for their understanding and support. Without them this book would never have appeared. Finally we would like to thank our publisher, Kassahun Checole for his encouragement and commitment to this project.

Introduction -
The Eritreo-Ethiopian war
Dominique Jacquin-Berdal

'Absurd', 'senseless' and 'shocking'. These were some of the reactions elicited by the outbreak of hostilities between Ethiopia and Eritrea in May 1998. Dubbed 'the world's largest and deadliest conflict', the war claimed an estimated 70,000 to 100,000 casualties and displaced hundreds of thousands of peoples on both sides of the border. While such figures pale in comparison to those of the Rwandan genocide or the more recent estimates on the war in Congo, they are significant when considered alongside similar wars, that is: wars fought between states. And at a time when the prevailing view is that 'Clausewitzean' warfare is outmoded, the war between Ethiopia and Eritrea was indeed exceptional.

Departing from the pattern of warfare we have become accustomed to in the post-Cold War world, and this more particularly so in Africa where intra-state conflicts have been the norm, the Ethiopian-Eritrean war appeared to hark back to a bygone era. It displayed all the hallmarks of the most conventional interstate border confrontation and the tactics employed, in its initial stages at least, were such that comparisons to World War One's Western front were frequently made. Writing towards the end of the first year of war, Karl Vick thus commented:

> 'the battlefield recalls Flanders Fields. On the border between Ethiopia and Eritrea, battered trench lines overlook a no man's land strewed with shattered armor and the rotting corpses of soldiers mowed down by the hundreds in mid-charge.'[1]

Similarly, the Economist wrote:

> 'With both Ethiopia and Eritrea spending huge amounts on new weapons, many thought they would be fighting Africa's first high-tech war. In fact, it turned out to be something of a first-world-war

throwback, with human waves walking into banks of machinegun, tank and artillery fire.'[2]

But then, on 12 May 2000, the war took an unexpected and dramatic turn. Combining artillery fire with low-level aerial bombardment, Ethiopia's army launched a two-pronged attack on the strategically important town of Barentu, and successfully established itself well inside Eritrea's South-western territory. The following week, Ethiopian troops re-directed their efforts further East, and on 25 May, the Ethiopian flag was hoisted in Zalembessa. A few hours later, Eritrea's foreign ministry announced that Eritrea had "decided for the sake of peace, to accept the OAU's appeal for de-escalation" and "to redeploy its forces to the positions held before 6 May 1998." Eritrea's declaration, which fulfilled Ethiopia's foremost pre-condition for a cease-fire, a request it had issued from the start, was tantamount to a recognition of Addis Ababa's military victory. And the war was formally brought to an end on 12 December 2000, when the two parties signed the Algiers Peace treaty. But why did such full-scale inter-state conflict erupt? What role did the international community play in bringing it to an end? And, what impact has the war had on the two belligerent states and on the region more broadly? These are some of the questions the contributors to this volume have sought to address.

An interstate war

In a continent sadly better known for its relatively high incidence of civil wars[3], an armed conflict of the type and intensity as the one fought between Ethiopia and Eritrea is a rare occurrence. And, apart for the Ogaden war between Ethiopia to Somalia in 1977-78, and the war between Libya to Chad over the Aozou strip in 1987, the Ethiopian-Eritrean war of 1998-2000 is the only other interstate conflict that has been deemed to qualify as a full scale war in Africa since 1946.[4] Defined as a violent conflict between the armed forces of sovereign states, interstate war is usually understood to be, *pace* Clausewitz, as the continuation of policy by other means, a rational act waged to protect or advance the national interests of the state.[5] Within this framework, war can also be considered a potential, albeit extreme, mechanism for the resolution of conflicts between states that haven't been able to settle their differences through diplomatic means.[6]

Given the highly arbitrary way African boundaries were delineated by the colonial powers and their potentially contentious nature, the relative infrequency of full-fledged interstate war in Africa may seem particularly surprising. And, while some may have interpreted this as an indication of the strength of the Organisation of African Unity's (OAU) stance against any revision to the boundaries inherited upon achieving independence and thus as proof of the power of norms in the current international system, it is a doubtful explanation. There are numerous examples of states attempting to destabilise their neighbours, through the support of insurgencies or the establishment of proxies. And while not interstate wars in the strict sense of the term, these conflicts nonetheless reveal a pattern of international relations that is far from regulated and peaceful. This pattern of 'mutual intervention', to borrow Lionel Cliffe's terminology, is particularly prevalent in the Horn. And the fact that both Eritrea and Ethiopia appeared to resort to such tactics by supporting insurgencies that could undermine their opponent throughout the 1998-2000 war might even suggest that a pure Clausewitzian war it was not.

Nonetheless, while the case of Eritrea and Ethiopia may be exceptional in many respects, and most significantly in terms of the number of battle-related deaths incurred, it is by no means unique. In addition to the aforementioned cases over the Ogaden and the Aozou strip, there have been a number of border conflicts of differing intensity and duration, such as: the Algerian-Moroccan war of 1963, the dispute between Nigeria and Chad over lake Chad in 1983, or the conflict between Mauritania and Senegal which led to artillery fire exchange in January 1990. Also noteworthy is the Nigerian-Cameroon dispute over the Bakassi peninsula which led to border clashes and air strikes in 1978-79 and the more serious engagements of 1993-94. It may perhaps be significant to note here that the decision reached in 2002 by the International Court of Justice (ICJ), and which awarded the oil-rich peninsula to Cameroon, appears for the time being to be respected. Similarly, the five-day war between Mali and Burkina-Fasso over the Agacher strip in 1985 was successfully brought to halt by international pressure and the decision by the ICJ to partition the area between the two contenders. To these one may add: the dispute over the Dome Flore between Senegal and Guinea Bissau that led to minor skirmishes in 1991 and which appears to have been successfully resolved, as was the dispute between Eritrea and Yemen over the Hanish Islands. While full-fledged interstate warfare in Africa is therefore relatively rare, border disputes have been frequent. But why have the above listed wars not degenerated in the same way that the Eritrean-Ethiopian war did?

According to Anthony Clayton, the reason why many of the border conflicts that have erupted in Africa have not escalated into major war is that the belligerent states have had limited resources. Thus, the short-lived war between Mali and Burkina-Fasso 'only demonstrated the incapacity of the armies of impoverished African states to achieve decisive success.'[7] Ranked amongst the poorest countries in the world, neither Eritrea or Ethiopia would have been expected to have the resources to mount significant military operations, yet they did. That the two countries were governed by a leadership seasoned by more than two decades of war against Mengistu may account for their resolve and stamina. Whether Eritrea or Ethiopia were in a state of military preparedness that would have enabled anyone to foresee their bellicose intentions remains a contentious issue, military expenditure being in this regard an unreliable indicator. Yet, as Martin Plaut's detailed account of the war in this volume shows, neither side lost any time to built up its military capabilities. Revealing they had the financial resources to do so, both countries demonstrated an equal eagerness to spend on the weapons and combat aircraft that were readily available through official and less official global arms trade networks. Both were also able to promptly muster their own troops, a testimony perhaps to the organisational skills and discipline of their military. But, whereas Ethiopia was forced to mobilise manpower and increase the size of its army from 60 000 to 350 000, Eritrea was, despite its much smaller size, able to rely on the young men and women that had undergone obligatory military service. Rather than economic resources per se, military capability and readiness to fight may therefore account for why the war between Ethiopia an Eritrea reached the levels it did and lasted that long. And, while it is impossible to gauge the extent to which the war was supported by the populations within the two countries, the legitimacy of the war itself was never openly questioned, even by those who subsequently voiced their opposition to the governments in power. Still, the question of why the war erupted in the first place remains unanswered.

What causes war?

This question has exercised the minds of prominent thinkers throughout the centuries and generated a wealth of literature from different disciplines. Since the publication of Kenneth Waltz's seminal *Man, the State and War* in 1954, enquiries about the causes of war predominantly revolved around what is know as the levels of analysis debate. And depending on one's particular perspective, the origins of war were to be sought either in human nature, the particular type of state or in the anarchical structure of the international system, a system where states have to fend for themselves in a never-ending struggle for power and security.[8] But as the Cold War drew to an end, suggestions that the nature of war had changed prompted new lines of investigation. Previous models, steeped as they were in the history of the 19th and 20th centuries, were seen as unable to account for the causes of the 'new wars' that marred the contemporary international landscape. For many, violent conflict could no longer be described as the result of rational political calculations; wars were no longer fought between states, but within them. Some went as far as to suggest that a 'Coming Anarchy' loomed over the 21st century. Signalling a return to barbarism and to long repressed ancient tribal or ethnic hatreds, this appeared all too powerfully confirmed by Somalia, Yugoslavia, Liberia, Sierra Leone and the genocide in Rwanda.[9] But as ethnicity was establishing itself as the dominant paradigm in the study of conflict, a challenge was mounted by those who had uncovered the economic motivations behind the wanton violence.[10] And this is pretty much where the debate on the causes of war stands today. But how can this help us make sense of the case with which we are concerned here? To what extent can greed or grievance explain the outbreak of the war between Ethiopia and Eritrea?

The role played by ethnicity in this conflict is ambiguous. Since the leaders of Ethiopia and Eritrea are both ethnic Tigrayans and are even said to be cousins, ancient ethnic hatreds would not appear to be the answer. But if identity formation is understood not as a primordial given but as relatively flexible process, then its role in the conflict cannot altogether be discarded. While perhaps from a similar ethnic stock, Eritrean Tigrayans, or their leadership at least, have tended over that past few decades to distinguish themselves from their Ethiopian counterparts.[11] The fact that, at the onset of the conflict, Eritrea accused Ethiopia's Tigrayans of having irredentist ambitions which were allegedly revealed in the map issued by the local authorities in Mekele, shows how far the process of ethnic differentiation appears to have gone. More significantly, and discussed in greater detail by Martin Plaut, Richard Reid and Leenco Lata in this volume, is the degree to which their incompatible conceptions of nationhood have strained relations between the Eritrean People Liberation Front (EPLF) and the Tigrayan People Liberation Front (TPLF), even prior their accession to power. While the EPLF has sought to forge an Eritrean identity that overrides if not negates its multi-ethnic composition, the TPLF has on the contrary raised the saliency of ethnicity by establishing a federal system where its ethnically defined regions are given a right of self-determination up to secession. And if ethnicity, strictly speaking, was not responsible for the outbreak of the war, it is clear, as Richard Reid writes, that the 'question of "nationality" lay at the heart of the border issue'.

As with ethnicity, the role played by economic motives is also unclear. Badme, the border town over which the conflict erupted, is by all accounts nothing more than a barren piece of land with no know covetable resources that could justify its value and thus indicate the presence of economic motives. On the other hand, and as highlighted by David Styan's contribution in this volume, economic disagreements, while perhaps not directly responsible for its outbreak, are nonetheless fundamental to our understanding of the Ethiopian-Eritrean war and its prospects for resolution. The introduction by Eritrea, in November 1997, of its own currency the Nacfa not only expectedly affected the poorly institutionalised and unregulated economic relations between the two states, it suddenly also raised the saliency of their imprecise mutual boundary.

Interstate conflicts, as the previously listed examples show, are frequently initiated over territorial control and this, it would seem, more particularly so when the legal status of the boundary is in question.[12] By casting into doubt its territorial integrity, an ill-defined and porous boundary may appear to undermine the sovereignty of any state thus whishing to be considered in the international system. For a new state such as Eritrea, defining its boundaries is part and parcel of the process by which it asserts its sovereignty in the eyes of the world and in those of its population.[13] For an established state such as Ethiopia, whose geostrategic position and access to the sea were dramatically compromised by Eritrea's independence, any further territorial concessions would no doubt be interpreted as a sign of inherent weakness and add insult to injury. Although the fight over Badme may initially have been dismissed by many as nothing more than a pretext for a war whose causes ultimately lay elsewhere, its symbolic significance should not be discounted. Ethiopia's reaction to the decision delivered by the Boundary Commission has perhaps made this more obvious. Indeed, as noted by Martin Plaut, Richard Reid and Leenco Lata in this volume, the boundary's exact location was a subject of contention between the EPLF and the TPLF during the liberation struggle. And, as Gilkes argues here: 'The history of the boundaries of "Eritrea" goes far to provide an explanation for the problems that arose in the course of the 1990s'.

Outside intervention

The speed with which various member states and international organisations responded to the war between Ethiopia and Eritrea is noteworthy. Indeed, as John Prendergast and Philip Roessler's chapter shows, the United States reacted almost immediately, dispatching US Assistant Secretary of State for African Affairs, Susan Rice, and her team to Addis Ababa only days after the outbreak of violence. By the end of May 1998, the US-Rwandan diplomatic mission presented a proposal which was to provide the basis for the subsequent peace plans. After its meeting in Ouagadougou, Burkina Faso, in June 1998, the Organisation of African Unity (OAU) sent a high level delegation to Eritrea and Ethiopia. From then on, the OAU, working in close partnership with the US, the EU and the UN, would play a prominent role in the peace process and would draft the three documents upon which the war's end would be negotiated.[14]

The efforts deployed by Anthony Lake and Ahmed Ouyahia, respectively representing the US and Algeria (which had taken over the OAU's chairmanship in July 1999) must no doubt be commended. These were eventually to lead to the Algiers Peace Treaty of December 2000, whose signature by both Ethiopia and Eritrea signalled the end of the war. By then, the United Nations Mission in Ethiopia and Eritrea (UNME) was already under way. And in January 2001, the bulk of the 4,200 strong troop mandated by the UN Security Council was dispatched to the region. As discussed in Ian Martin's chapter, this was the first time the UN made use of the recently created rapid deployment force, the Stand-by High Readiness Brigade for UN Operations (SHIRBRIG). And although the UN's military involvement in African conflicts can be traced as far back as 1960, with the UN's first mission in Congo, this was also the first time its troops were mandated to monitor a cease-fire between two belligerent states. Yet its task was not made easier by this fact and the establishment and maintenance of the Temporary Security Zone has been riddled with problems. Nonetheless, UNMEE has successfully managed keep the combatants apart.

Although the peace process can be heralded as a model of how the UN can cooperate with a regional organisation such as the OAU, with the assistance of some the world's key member states, the role played by the international community in bringing the conflict to an end should not be overstated. It is after all important to recall that the war was effectively brought to an end, not through the use of third-party mediation, but because one of the sides decisively won the battle on the ground. So why was the international community, which has struggled to adapt to the changing patterns of warfare, unable to bring to a speedier end, let alone prevent, a war of the type for which its institutions were initially set up? It is true that the outbreak of the war took everyone by surprise. And while greater pressure, as suggested by Prendergast and Roessler, might have been put on Eritrea and Ethiopia to ensure that their mutual border be demarcated after Eritrea's independence in 1993, thereby preventing this issue at least from becoming a future *casus belli*, such foresight is seldom displayed in international relations. It is also true that the crisis in Kosovo preoccupied many at the time and paralysed UN activity. Yet, it must no doubt have been frustrating for those personally given the task to broker the peace, that the Security Council showed such reluctance to make full use of the instruments available in the UN Charter.

It was only on 17 May 2000, two years into the war and after Ethiopia launched its decisive attack on Barentu that the Security Council finally and unanimously adopted resolution 1298, which called for an arms embargo on Eritrea and Ethiopia.[15] Significantly, this was the first time such a measure was accompanied by a time limit. An apparent concession to France and Russia, the so-called sunset clause thus restricted the embargo's applicability to twelve months, after which the Security Council would have to decide whether or not to extend the measures for a further period. Since both Ethiopia and

Eritrea purchased significant amounts of military equipment soon after the war broke out, the imposition of an arms embargo in the early stages of the conflict would clearly have made a difference. And although the US backed various proposals for an arms embargo, it was unwilling to push the matter too far and jeopardise its relationship with Russia. The inability and unwillingness of the international 'community' to take any forceful action against Ethiopia and Eritrea, suggests that, while not directly responsible for the outbreak of the war, the international context was nevertheless a permissive condition for its unfolding.

The International response to a crisis such as the war between Ethiopia and Eritrea is clearly dependent on the calculations of its self-interested member states, particularly those who hold permanent seats on the UN Security Council. The US's prompt reaction to the conflict in the Horn must also be understood in this context. Following the Somalia debacle, it had been reluctant to intervene in Africa's conflicts. But soon thereafter, the threat of Islamic fundamentalism, replaced communism as the main focus of American foreign policy in the Horn of Africa. The war that erupted between Eritrea and Ethiopia was a significant blow to the US's policy of 'containment' towards Sudan.[16] It should also perhaps be remembered in this context that on August 29th 1998, that is only a few months after the outbreak of the Ethiopian-Eritrean war, the US bombed the Al-Shifa factory pharmaceutical plant outside Khartoum in response to the terrorist attacks on its embassies in Kenya and Tanzania. Similarly, the establishment of the American base in Djibouti was prompted by the tragic events of 11 September 2001 and by the possibility of military action in Iraq. The geostrategic significance of the Horn of Africa has thus once again been revealed, after the brief post-Cold War hiatus. Outside involvement in the region will only be incidentally motivated by what happens inside it. And, whether UNMEE is destined to become another UNFICYP, or its maintenance deemed too costly by the UN Security Council, will depend on the relevant powers's assessment of the potential wider security threats a resumption of hostilities may pose.

The War's impact

At the time of writing the situation that prevails can only euphemistically be described as one of 'neither war, nor peace'. All the more reason therefore to highlight the tremendous impact the 1998-2000 war between Ethiopia and Eritrea has had. And this is the focus of many of the contributions to the book.

To begin with, it has again to be restated, this was a very deadly war. The exact casualty figures will probably never be made public, but as Alex Last's vivid account all too tragically recounts this was a human carnage. Amongst those most directly affected by the war, are those ethnic communities that straddle the border: Kunama, Tigrayans, Saho, and Afars. These, as Patrick Gilkes aptly remarks, have been all too easily forgotten, not least by the Boundary Commission, with the consequences this may have on any long term prospects for peace. Moreover, and as has historically been the case in the region, conflict and famine go hand in hand. And as Philip White's incisive examination of the multiple linkages between the border war and food security reveals, their relationship was not only one of cause and effect, the war having been 'itself conditioned by food security considerations.' His analysis of the donor community's response to the crisis also shows that while the lessons from the Ethiopian famine of the mid-1980s may have been learned, they did not necessarily inform a more appropriate response. David Styan similarly describes the economic costs of the war on poverty-stricken Eritrea and Ethiopia in this volume. Not only did it disrupt the bilateral flows of trade and investment upon which the two countries are dependent, but the war and Ethiopia's mass expulsion of Ethiopians of alleged Eritrean descent has also brought to the fore the need to clarify the economic and legal status of the two countries' respective citizens. Indeed, as Styan makes clear in that chapter, any serious attempt to reach a long-lasting settlement in the region will depend on the restoration and enhancement of economic ties between Ethiopia and Eritrea.

Lionel Cliffe's chapter on the regional implications of the Eritrea-Ethiopia war and the chapter on Djibouti illustrate the many ways the war spilled over beyond the borders of the two states. Both protagonists provided support, in one form or another, to the warring sides within Somalia, thereby undermining the already fragile attempts to reach a peace is this conflict ridden country. Somaliland and Djibouti, on the other hand, benefited economically from the war, their ports having become Ethiopia's only access to the Sea. But while Somaliland successfully avoided some of the war's more pernicious effects and was able to keep a somewhat neutral position, Djibouti found itself in more delicate position. As Ethiopia and Eritrea sought to use their respective Afar minorities to destabilise their adversary, this affected Djibouti which also hosts members of this ethnic community. And although by the end of 1999, Eritrea and Djibouti resumed their diplomatic relations, in the intervening period, threats of a civil war in Djibouti seemed imminent.

Perhaps one of the more significant regional consequences of the war has been, as emphasised by Lionel Cliffe, Sudan's apparent diplomatic rehabilitation and the possibility of an end to its protracted civil war. As the alliance between Eritrea and Ethiopia broke down, Sudan's relations with its southern neighbours relaxed. Eritrea's previously acrimonious exchanges with Sudan were forgotten as soon as the war broke out and, by early 2000, full diplomatic relations were restored. Ethiopia and Sudan, which by contrast to Eritrea, had never totally severed their diplomatic links despite the strains caused by the Mubarak assassination attempt, have now developed a close partnership and, along with Yemen, have established an 'anti-Eritrean coalition', the Sanaa Alliance. Sudan's relations with the US have also much improved. While oil is no doubt a factor, the rapprochement was also brought about by Sudanese's successful attempts to assuage American security fears.

In addition to its effects on the populations of Ethiopia and Eritrea and on the region more broadly, the war also exacerbated divisions that had begun to emerge both within as well as between the governments of both countries. After triggering an initial 'rallying around the flag' reaction, the war quickly revealed the deep fissures that had started to fester inside the two governments, as Meles Zenawi and Isaias Afeworki found their authority more overtly challenged. The treatment of so-called 'dissidents' have been such that any lingering belief that these belonged to a new breed of African leaders has been cast aside. And this particularly so in the case of Eritrea, about which a formerly sympathetic foreign journalist has recently, albeit belatedly, written "Enough"![17] As revealed by Alex Last in Chapter 4, talks of a possible coup against Isaias were voiced as the war raged. Yet mounting opposition was not solely provoked by disagreement over the war's conduct. As the regime's authoritarian propensities surfaced, disillusionment replaced the post-independence honeymoon euphoria; and this, not merely from the regimes traditional foes but also and perhaps more significantly, from within Isaias's own party. As democracy appeared to recede into a distant future, former liberation fighters and members of the government began to feel increasingly alienated from and betrayed by their leadership. Similarly, and as described by Leenco Lata, divisions within the TPLF, notably over how the Ethiopian government should deal with Eritrea, became more manifest in the mid 1990s. Having shunned its previous alliance with the Oromo Liberation Front (OLF), the Ethiopian regime found its political base shrinking. Although Meles Zenawi may seem to have emerged victorious from these intra-party disputes, his position remains precarious. And, as his regime's domestic legitimacy is further questioned, it risks becoming overly reliant on foreign support, although no longer able to rely on its former alliance with Eritrea.

As indicated earlier, the outbreak of the war in May 1998 came as a surprise to most. Often considered as 'brothers in arms', the liberation movements that had come to power in Eritrea and Ethiopia were seen as the guarantors of peace in a formerly conflict ridden region of the world. Yet, as described by Leenco Lata, Richard Reid and Martin Plaut in Chapter One, relations between the EPLF and TPLF during the liberation struggle were not always as fraternal as frequently portrayed. And, as it transpires from their account, the seeds of the 1998-2000 war were most probably sown long before the movements came to power and the war eventually broke out. Whether these divisions could possibly have been overcome prior to 1998 can only remain the object of speculation. Yet, one thing seems clear today, it will take a long time for fences to be mended. Relations between the two governments remain tense and little progress has been made as far as re-establishing dialogue is concerned. Perhaps more damaging in the long-run is the extent to which the war seems to have also polarised public attitudes inside the two states. But neither government should find solace in the view that one of the outcomes of war is to reinforce nationalist feelings and thus consolidate statehood. As history reveals, war is only one of the factors, and not always a necessary one for that matter, that facilitate the process of state-making. More important is the extent to which the state and its representatives are perceived as legitimate by the people concerned. And, in this respect, there is still a lot of work to be done in Eritrea and Ethiopia.

CONCLUSION

While the war might have lasted much longer than it did had international involvement of the kind undertaken not occurred, it is also true that the decision reached by the Boundary Commission has not necessarily provided the basis for a lasting settlement. By allocating Badme to Eritrea, the Boundary Commission seems to have created, albeit unwittingly, an untenable situation. It is indeed a bitter irony for Ethiopia, that having won the war on the battlefield, it was to loose the peace in the courtroom. Moreover, its claim that its entry into war was prompted by Eritrea's invasion seems by the same token to have been rejected. Rather than signalling the beginning of an, albeit lengthy, peace process between Ethiopia and Eritrea, the Boundary Commission's decision to allocate Badme to Eritrea has brought the two countries closer to war. The international community is currently in a bind. It must on the one hand ensure that Ethiopia complies with the Border Commission's ruling, if the rule of law is to be upheld at the international level. Any concessions would risk setting a precedent and could thus potentially reopen disputes that have been settled through international arbitration, such as that between Eritrea and Yemen over the Hanish Islands, but perhaps, more significantly, that between Nigeria and Cameroon over the oil rich Bakassi peninsula. Yet, even if the current Ethiopian government were to concede and the demarcation of the border was to take place, there is such widespread opposition within Ethiopia, and in particular in the Tigray administration, to the Border Commission's decision, that the resumption of war seems all too likely. Another possible alternative would be for Eritrea to magnanimously cede Badme to Ethiopia. Although unlikely, this would in fact benefit Eritrea more than its current leaders may like to believe. For however strategically located the country may be, Isaias's attempts to cajole the Americans have not had the desired results. While international isolation may have been bearable during the war for liberation, Eritrea's leadership will find too soon that this is not a viable option for a poor sovereign state. Whether or not UNMEE's mandate is extended will depend on considerations outside regional dynamics, but if the peacekeeping force is withdrawn before any significant progress is made, it will once again be the people of Eritrea and Ethiopia that bear the brunt of what may ensue.

ENDNOTES

1   Vick, Karl, 'Old Tactics, New Arms, Lethal Result,' *Washington Post*, Sunday, March 12, 1999, p. A25.
2   The Economist March 13-19, 1999
3   SIPRI 2000 stated that Africa was the most conflict ridden region of the world
4   This is according to the dataset compiled by the Department of Peace and Conflict Research at Uppsala University, in which an armed conflict is considered a war when there are at least 1,000 battle-related deaths in that year. It might be noted that the Ogaden war, which is included above, and the Ugandan-Tanzanian war of 1979, which is not, are not considered in this dataset as interstate conflicts.
5   Carl Von Clausewitz, *On War*. Penguin Classics, 1982. Originally published in German in 1832.
6   Kalevi J. Holsti, *The State, War and the State of War*. Cambridge University Press, 1996.
7   Clayton, A., *Frontiersmen. Warfare in Africa since 1950*, UCL Press, 1999, p. 200.
8   Waltz, K, *Man, The State and War. A Theoretical Analysis*. Columbia University Press, New York, 1954.
9   See for example: Robert D. Kaplan, 'The Coming Anarchy', *Atlantic Monthly*, February 1994; and Jean-Christophe Rufin, *L'Empire et les nouveaux barbares: Rupture nord-sud*. J.-C. Lattès, Paris, 1991.
10   See for example: David Keen, *The Economic Functions of Civil War*. Oxford University Press, 1998; and Mats Berdal and David Malone (eds), *Greed and grievance: economic agendas in civil war*. Lynne Rienner Publishers, Boulder, Co., 2000.
11   Alemseged Abbay, *Identity Jilted or Re-Imagining Identity? The Divergent Paths of the Eritrean and Tigrayan Nationalist Struggles*, The Red Sea Press, 1998.
12   Kocs, Stephen A., 'Territorial disputes and Interstate War, 1945-1987', *The Journal of Politics*, Vol. 57, No. 1, February 1995, pp. 159-175.
13   Without prejudging who is responsible for the outbreak of the Ethiopian-Eritrean war, it may be recalled how Quincy Wright (1942) concluded his historical review of war, by suggesting that new nations are more likely than mature states to initiate wars. Such conclusion should of course only cautiously be accepted.
14, These are: The Framework for Agreement, the Modalities for Implementation and the Technical Arrangements, all included in the Annex to this volume.

15. While UN Security Resolution 1227 of 10 June 1999 'strongly urges all States to end immediate sales of arms and munitions to Ethiopia and Eritrea', the request was not implemented under Chapter 7, as it was under resolution 1298, and could thus not be considered an arms embargo as such.

16. In 1995, President Clinton authorized the transfer of $15 million in non-lethal defensive military assistance to Uganda, Ethiopia, and Eritrea 'to help these neighboring countries contain Sudanese-sponsored insurgencies'. Testimony of George E. Mosse, Assistant Secretary of State for African Affairs before the Subcommittee on Africa, *US Counterterrorism policy toward Sudan*, Senate Foreign Relations Committee, Washington, D.C., May 15, 1997.

17. Dan Connell, 'Enough! A Critique of Eritrea's Post-Liberation Politics', Paper presented at the *Eritrean Studies Association*, Boston, 1 November 2003.

Chapter 1

BACKGROUND TO WAR –

FROM FRIENDS TO FOES

Martin Plaut

INTRODUCTION

The war that broke out between Ethiopia and Eritrea on 6th May 1998, and was finally concluded by a peace treaty in the Algerian capital, Algiers, on 12th December 2000 can be summarised in a paragraph.

The neighbouring states, previously on good terms, were involved in a skirmish at the little known border town of Badme. The town lies in an inhospitable area towards the western end of the one thousand-kilometer border separating the two countries, not far from Sudan. The initial clash escalated dramatically. The conflagration spiraled out of control, and resulted in all-out war along the length of border. The international community, including the United States, Rwanda, the Organisation of African Unity, the United Nations and the European Union attempted to end the hostilities. They met with little success. Eritrea made initial gains on the battlefield, including taking Badme, but the frontlines soon solidified. After a month of fighting President Bill Clinton managed to persuade both sides to observe a temporary truce in order to allow further diplomatic efforts. However, these failed to bear fruit, and in February 1999 Ethiopia successfully re-captured Badme. Despite heavy fighting in May that year, Eritrea was unable to re-capture the area. For almost a year diplomats unsuccessfully sought to end the conflict. In May 2000 a frustrated Ethiopia launched its largest offensive of the war, breaking through Eritrean lines in the Western and Central sectors, and advancing deep into Eritrean territory. Having re-captured Badme and other land it had lost, and under considerable pressure from the international community, Ethiopia halted its advance and both sides signed a cease-fire on 18 June 2000. Six months later a final peace treaty was signed, with both countries agreeing to resolve the dispute through binding international arbitration.

These are the bare bones of this war – a conflict that cost as many as 100,000 lives, and resulted in over a million people being displaced. For two of the poorest countries in the world the economic costs were also immense. Yet the war remains something of a mystery to military analysts and historians. Despite being one of the bloodiest conflicts of the last decade of the twentieth century, involving over half a million troops, using some of the most sophisticated military technology, even the progress of the fighting is little understood.

At its outbreak the leaders of both countries professed ignorance as to its causes. Ethiopian Prime Minister Meles Zenawi told Ethiopian journalists on May 21st, 1998 that he had no satisfactory explanation for why relations had deteriorated so badly.

> "I really cannot make head or tail of this puzzling development. In fact I may have my own guesses, but they can not be satisfactory. As you all know there were certain misunderstandings between the two governments arising from measures taken after changes in currency on both sides. There were more or less certain misunderstandings even before this change, but it is very difficult for me to believe that the composite effect of all this would draw us into open conflict. That is why I still maintain I have no satisfactory answer for this baffling question." [1]

Eritrean President, Isaias Afwerki responded in similar terms when asked by a reporter from the Washington Post why he thought the conflict had come about. "It's very difficult to easily find an answer", he replied. [2]

It is, of course, possible to treat these replies with a fair degree of scepticism. Both leaders were attempting to explain why force had been unleashed with so little warning; why so much military muscle had been deployed over such an apparently insubstantial prize. But it may also be that both were numbed by the turn of events. It is certainly possible that they unleashed far more than either had bargained for, since the war ended an alliance that had put both men in their respective seats of power.

So why was there a war? As one writer suggested within months of the war beginning, the answer is anything but obvious. [3] "International wars are usually fought to acquire territory, to gain economic advantage, to overthrow a hated or dangerous neighbouring regime, for religious or ethnic reasons or in order to improve a country's position on a regional or international geostrategic chessboard." The complexity of the relations that brought about this war means that none of these appear to be provide satisfactory explanations on their own.

Before considering any other factor the idea that this was a struggle for Badme – the flash point that ignited this conflict— can be easily disposed of. This is what a visitor had to say about the town.

> "The focus of the conflict lies in the village of Badme, on the Mereb-Setit stretch" (of the frontier), "which is located 5km West of the internationally-recognised border, as calculated by GPS, and its surroundings, particularly to the South. This is a broken, stony table-land, with few wells, but which in lucky, rainier years can be persuaded, after the thorn-bush and prickly-pear have been cleared with a bulldozer, to produce a fair crop of cereals, such as sorghum or wheat. Badme itself, home to 300 families, is an unprepossessing element of human settlement – though that does not preclude the smiling welcome, with the traditional two glasses of tea, given to the occasional visitor. It is a dusty-one-street place, sited on a slight eminence, and consisting of crude huts, including the traditional conical *tukul*," (traditional hut) "interspersed with vegetation, a hamlet which nothing whatsoever – so the new cliché has it – predisposed it for its elevation overnight from total obscurity to the corridors of the Security Council.
>
> Badme is unlikely to detain the attention of the Ministry of Tourism, which is carrying out a national survey of tourist potential, for long. At one end of the 'town' as its former, Ethiopian administrators style it, a flagpole outside the only more modern house, on a small hill, indicates the office where the shooting incident which marked the start of hostilities took place."[4]

Ethiopian Prime Minister Meles Zenawi, made it clear that Badme itself was not the issue. "For us Badme is nothing, but the principle behind invading Badme is everything. For us, what is at stake in Badme is not a piece of real estate but a cardinal principle of international law." [5]

In fact anyone searching for a simple, easy to understand reason for the conflict is likely to end up confused and frustrated. This war had many causes; most of them intertwined. The history of Ethiopia, and the Horn of Africa, with its many disputes and diverse and overlapping ethnicities, religions and languages predisposes the region to conflicts. Unraveling the factors that contributed to the Ethiopia – Eritrea war is no easy task. Both sides are secretive by nature, and this impedes any investigation of these events. Both countries have long memories, and seldom forgive or forget past wrongs, whether real or imagined. At the same time issues that were important at one time were sometimes laid aside when there were more pressing issues at hand. There is no doubt that at times peace and harmony prevailed, and movements and individuals worked closely together. Indeed, ties were sealed in blood, as troops fought and died together to overthrow Mengistu Haile Mariam's dictatorship. In the end, however, the divisions that separated the two sides were allowed to fester.

No single issue caused this war. It was the outcome of years of suspicion and hostility that finally exploded into open conflict.

A troubled history

Until the end of the nineteenth century Ethiopia was rarely more than a loose confederation of kingdoms. The Ethiopian empire was alternatively dominated by Amhara or Oromo princes from the provinces of Gondar and Wollo in the centre of the country, or by Tigrean rulers from the northern region of Tigray, which at times included the Tigrinya speaking areas of what is now Eritrea. The empire's boundaries were fluid. When Tigrayan princes were in the ascendancy they extended their influence towards Eritrea's Red Sea Coast, exacting tribute from the Muslim lowland chiefs around Massawa or in the West. They brought Coptic Christianity to the Eritrean highlands, while the lowlands along the coast and towards the western border with Sudan remained Muslim.

In the sixteenth century the coastal plain of Eritrea became part of the Ottoman empire, though for most of the 17th and 18th centuries the rulers of the coast who were appointed by the Ottoman Pasha of Jeddah, sporadically acknowledging the overlordship of Tigray's rulers. As the Ottoman Empire declined, Egypt inherited its place along the Red Sea coasts, first taking over Massawa in the 1820's. In the 1870's, the Tigrean Emperor, Yohannis IV (1872 - 1889) defeated two Egyptian attempts to penetrate the Eritrean highlands. Subsequently he believed that in return for allowing the evacuation of Egyptian garrisons from Sudan after the rise of the Mahdi, he had British and Egyptian agreement to take over Massawa. In the event, Britain, worried about expanding French influence in Africa, encouraged Italy (which had laid claim to Assab in 1870) to take Massawa in 1885. Yohannis, rightly, felt betrayed, the more so as Italy promptly attempted to use the port as a base from which to extend its influence into Ethiopia. These hopes were dashed when the Italians were defeated in 1896 by Ethiopian forces of Emperor Menelik in the battle of Adua. The Italians accepted their reverse, and signed treaties with the Emperor in 1900, 1902 and 1908 establishing the border between their new colony of Eritrea and Ethiopia.

With the rise of fascism under Mussolini, Italy was determined to extend its presence in the Horn of Africa. In October 1935 Italy invaded Ethiopia. Despite the League of Nation's condemnation of the Italian action it was not until the outbreak of the Second World War that the world took a decisive stand against their aggression. By 1941 Emperor Haile Selassie had been returned to his throne by a combined force of British, South African, Indian and Sudanese troops fighting alongside Ethiopian patriots. While Ethiopia was independent once more, the international community was left with the problem of what to do with Eritrea, which was under temporary British Military Administration. It took until 1952 for the United Nations finally to decide that the territory should be federated with Ethiopia. There matters might have rested. However, the Emperor's absolutist rule alienated the Eritrean population by a series of decrees. These included outlawing the teaching of Eritrean languages, dismantling industries and removing them to Addis Ababa and repressing the trade union movement and political parties allowed under the British military administration.

By the early 1960's this repression was being met by armed resistance from the Eritrean Liberation Front. Despite this there was still considerable support inside Eritrea for unity with Ethiopia, particularly from among the Christian highlanders. In November 1962, after intense pressure from Addis Ababa, the federation was ended, and Eritrea was absorbed into Ethiopia. This served to spur on the opposition, led at first by the Eritrean Liberation Front (ELF), whose origins can partly be traced back to the Muslim League of the 1940's. It found most of its support from the Muslim community, although some Christian highlanders, including the future leader of Eritrea, Isayas Afeworki, were also drawn into membership. Disputes within the ELF, and particularly hostility towards Christian recruits, resulted in the formation of the Eritrean Peoples Liberation Front (EPLF) in the early 1970's. The EPLF rejected ethnic differences and stood for a secular and socialist state. An uneasy truce between the two ended in a bitter civil war that the EPLF finally won in 1981, forcing the ELF out of Eritrea.

Despite these divisions Ethiopia's campaign against Eritrean self determination did not go well. Discontent inside the Ethiopian army over the conduct of the war and the handling of a devastating famine, led to the overthrow of the Emperor in 1974. Haile Selassie was killed and his rule was replaced by a committee, the Dergue. In time this came under the dictatorial rule of Mengistu Haile Mariam. After initial discussions with the Eritreans failed, the war was continued and intensified. But the events of 1974 led to a second, equally important development. Students from Tigray, angered by the lack of development of their province, and building on the ancient claims of Tigray to be the centre of the Ethiopian state, launched their own campaign

5

to break Amhara rule. In 1975 the Tigray People's Liberation Front (TPLF) was formed, and began waging its own war against Addis Ababa.

Nationalism

On the face of it the EPLF and the TPLF had much in common, since they both opposed Ethiopian absolutism, whether exercised by Haile Selassie or Mengistu Haile Mariam. In reality, however, the forms of national identity that the two movements pursued, and in a sense embodied, were rather different. These factors contributed to the origins of the current conflict. The Eritreans saw their struggle as an anti-colonial movement designed to regain a lost political independence. The Tigrayan leadership, on the other hand, moved from a Tigrayan nationalism, to an acceptance that they were part of the Ethiopian empire. The TPLF came to see their rightful place as being at the heart of events in Ethiopia, as had occurred during the reign of the Tigrean Emperor, Johannes IV. They regarded the current regime as an oppressive state, which should be overthrown, although they reserved the right to self-determination up to and including independence.

Eritrean identity was more complex and more difficult to forge precisely because it reflected a more diverse population. Eritrea's 3.5 million people are divided between two major religions and speak nine different languages. The Christian agriculturalists of the central highlands share a common language, religion and ethnic background with the mainly Tigrinya speakers inside the Ethiopian region of Tigray, south of the Mereb river. Intermarriage between Tigrinya speakers of Eritrea and Tigray has traditionally been common. As an Eritrean put it in 1994, "Tigrayans are our brethren, part of our soul."[6] These areas had been part of the Ethiopian Empire; the mainly Muslim lowland pastoralists, on the other hand, who live to the West, North and East of the highlands, had little in common with them. The lowlanders support for the ELF was predominantly motivated by a sense of alienation from a highland government, speaking a different language and espousing a different religion. The first decade of the armed struggle, from 1961 to 1974 was largely confined to the Muslim lowlands, and driven more by this sense of alienation than a positive sense of Eritrean nationalism.

The EPLF attempted to mobilise Eritrean opinion irrespective of religion, but came up against considerable difficulties. Not all of the Christians in the highlands supported the cause of independence, and as late as 1982 some were still willing to act as armed militia for the Ethiopian administration. Outside the highlands, despite the terror employed by the Mengistu regime, a majority within the Kunama and the Afar people were at best ambivalent about the EPLF, while some actually supported continued unity with Ethiopia.

As a result the EPLF had to fight a vigorous campaign within its own community to win their support, or acquiescence.

While it recognised and even celebrated Eritrea's ethnic diversity, the EPLF resolutely refused to allow ethnicity to undermine its campaign for an independent state. This is not to suggest that ethnicity did not play any part in the Front's activities; great care was taken to represent the whole of the population within the leadership, even when they were not as well represented among its membership. The EPLF also spent a good deal of time and effort inculcating a wider sense of Eritrean identity in its new recruits.

For the TPLF mobilisation in Tigray was relatively simple, since it could call upon an existing concept of Tigrayan nationalism and a history of oppression common to all the areas in which it operated. They shared a common language, religion and mode of livelihood. The TPLF's activities were an attempt to end Amhara rule. In Tigrayan eyes the Amhara had usurped the traditional power base of Ethiopian society, and transferred it from the ancient Tigrayan capital of Axum to Addis Ababa. In its first political programme, released in 1976, the TPLF specified that it was fighting for the independence of Tigray from Ethiopia.[7] Shortly thereafter a TPLF congress repudiated the manifesto, but it was not publicly disowned for some time. This has been a recurrent issue for the movement, and has also been seized upon by its critics.

Since the TPLF's war aims, at least in the beginning, centred on achieving power in Tigray itself, its successes against the forces of the Dergue posed something of a problem for the movement, and led to considerable internal debate. Would the movement be satisfied with capturing Tigray, or would a hostile government in Addis Ababa require them to fight for the control of all Ethiopia? By early 1989 the TPLF exercised almost total control over the Tigrayan countryside, and was having increasing success against Ethiopian troops in garrisons across the province. In February 1989 TPLF forces, bolstered by an EPLF armoured brigade, took the area around Endaselasie, in western Tigray. Within two weeks garrisoned towns across the province were abandoned, sometimes without a fight.

The TPLF had achieved its initial objectives, and held most of Tigray. The question now was whether to press on to Addis Ababa. The movement had by this time established the Ethiopian People's Revolutionary Democratic Front (EPRDF), together with a number of other Ethiopian organisations, with the aim of taking power in Addis Ababa. Its leadership had ambitions to rule the whole of Ethiopia but were frustrated by many of its own supporters who, to use Lenin's famous phrase, voted with their feet. In 1990 some 10,000 TPLF fighters spontaneously returned home.[8] After months of protracted discussion the leadership managed to convince its followers that they should continue prosecuting the war. Tigrayan nationalism was, at least for the time being, to be subordinated within a wider Ethiopian identity.

The EPLF and the TPLF therefore relied upon completely different nationalisms. The Eritrean struggle, from 1961, generated a powerful sense of collective identity, as did the increasingly genocidal responses of the Dergue towards Tigrayans and Eritreans during the 1980s. It was nationalism forged in blood and with a clear objective in mind, namely an independent Eritrea.[9] Moreover, it was a nationalism that could justly claim that it was shaped by its own experience of colonialism. Italian rule had fashioned Eritrea just as other European colonisers had brought into being the other states of the continent, after the scramble for Africa at the end of the nineteenth century. Moreover, Italian colonialism had brought with it some of the benefits of European rule, in the shape of modern port facilities, roads and railways. The city of Asmara had developed into a pleasant town, with coffee shops, an opera house and fine government buildings. Eritrea also had political parties and a labour movement, neither of which were to be found across the border. By the time the Italians were driven out by the Allied forces in 1941, they left behind a far more developed state than the feudal empire that existed in Ethiopia.

The Tigrayans also had much to be proud of. They could hark back to past greatness, including the rule of the last "Tigrayan" emperor and to a history of rebellions against imperial rule. The most important of these was the "woyane" rebellion of 1943 against Haile Selassie, from which the TPLF took its inspiration. But while Eritrean nationalism was clearly associated with a nation state, Tigrayan nationalism played a difficult balancing act - at once recognising the aspirations of the Tigrayan people, but within the framework of the wider Ethiopian state. It was a problem that was to dog the relationship between the TPLF and the EPLF.

Co-operation and confrontation

Opposition to the dictatorial rule exercised from Addis Ababa temporarily united the two liberation movements, but divisions existed on a number of grounds, including ideology, strategy and tactics. Over time these grew in importance.

In 1974 as the founders of the TPLF were preparing to launch an armed struggle, they made contact with the Eritrean movements, an obvious source of assistance. They sought support from the EPLF, rather than the ELF. This was partly because another group of Tigrayans (The Tigray Liberation Front) had been established in 1972 – 73 and had formed a prior alliance with the ELF. From the EPLF the TPLF obtained promises of military training as well as arms, and, significantly, two EPLF veterans. They were Mahari Haile (who took the field name 'Mussie' and went on to be the first military commander) and Yemane Kidane (who took the name 'Jamaica') who is a member of the present Ethiopian government. The first group of TPLF trainees, twenty in all, was deployed to Eritrea at the same time.

This co-operation was fruitful and they learned much from the Eritreans. However, not all of it was to their liking. Ideology came to play a significant part in their differences. On the face of it both shared a Marxist analysis. In reality this was more of an impediment than a spur to unity. The EPLF's Marxism tended to be mainly 'third worldist' - long on anti-imperialist rhetoric and slogans. It considered the Soviet bloc 'strategic allies', even though they never received direct assistance from Moscow. States in the region that were close to the Soviets, like South Yemen provided some training and support in the initial stages. This disappeared after the Dergue seized power in 1974, since it had the backing of the Soviet Union.

The TPLF, on the other hand, was influenced by Maoism, and admired Albania as an example of an anti-Soviet socialist state. In the early 1980's Meles Zenawi rose to authority in the movement, and in 1984 the Marxist-Leninist League of Tigray (MLLT) was formed, as a vanguard party within the TPLF. The MLLT established links with what it saw as 'genuine' Eritrean Marxist groups, notably the Democratic Movement, later the Democratic Movement for the Liberation of Eritrea.[10] The Democratic Movement (itself a faction of the ELF which broke apart after its defeat by the EPLF in 1981) was allowed to continue to have bases in the Tigray region until about 1996, much to the annoyance of the EPLF.

The United States had openly backed the emperor, Haile Selassie, but his fall and the assumption of power by a military committee, known as the Dergue, led to a change in international support. Now it was Moscow, rather than Washington that backed the Ethiopian government. This tested the EPLF's ideological commitment to Marxism. However, the EPLF resisted labelling the Soviet Union as imperialist, realising that they might one day need its support as a permanent member of the Security Council if they were to facilitate the emergence of an independent Eritrea.[11] The Tigrayans had no such difficulties, and had no hesitation in condemning the Soviets as imperialist. Arcane as such arguments might now seem, they were an important source of friction between the two movements.[12]

Ideology was not the only issue to divide the movements. There was also the question of military tactics. While the TPLF's military strategy was one of mobile guerrilla warfare, the EPLF combined mobile with fixed positional warfare, based on a securely defended rear area. In this base area they established a considerable infrastructure, including schools, hospitals and workshops. As the Eritreans moved towards more conventional forms of warfare, the Tigrayans became increasingly critical of their tactics.

Matters came to a head during Ethiopia's 'Red Star' campaign of 1982. It was the most sustained offensive the government forces ever undertook and came within an ace of capturing the EPLF's base area, and with it Nakfa, the last town in rebel hands. Tigrayan fighters training with the EPLF were called upon to go into action, apparently without the permission of the TPLF Central Committee, who were furious at not being asked. After heroic efforts their combined forces just managed to repel the Ethiopian onslaught. Casualties were heavy, however, and the TPLF was deeply critical of the tactics employed by the EPLF, accusing them of moving too rapidly from guerrilla warfare to positional encounters with the enemy.

According to senior members of the TPLF, the Eritreans wanted TPLF fighters to remain in Eritrea to defend Eritrean positions. By this time, however, the TPLF leadership had become determined to overthrow the Dergue. Its strategy, therefore, was to make alliances with other Ethiopian opposition movements and to take the military struggle South to the gates of the capital. They therefore withdrew their fighters from Eritrea. This did nothing to endear them to their allies, but worse was to follow.

In the mid 1980's the simmering differences culminated in a major public row. Insults were exchanged. The TPLF defined the EPLF as "social imperialist". The EPLF in turn labelled the TPLF "childish". This row masked a serious theoretical difference with major political ramifications for the national question in Ethiopia.[13] The issue was which of its peoples had the right to self-determination up to, and including, secession. It had been a critical issue for the student radicals at Addis Ababa university in the 1960's and 1970's - many of whom went on to lead the Eritrean and Tigrayan liberation movements. The TPLF recognised Eritrea's unique status as a former colonial state. But they also came to promote the right to secession of the various nationalities within Ethiopia and - far more controversially - of those within Eritrea as well. During its exchange of polemics with the EPLF in 1986/87, the TPLF stated that "a truly democratic" Eritrea would have to respect "the right of its own nationalities up to and including secession". [14]

This appalled and infuriated the EPLF, which argued that it was precisely because Eritrea was a former colonial state that they had the right to independence. They argued that Ethiopian nationalities had a right to self-determination, but not to independence, as this was conditional on a colonial experience.[15] The EPLF was aware that any widening of the definition of self-determination to include independence for Ethiopian nationalities would detract from Eritrea's special status, as a colonially defined territory. Moreover, giving Eritrean nationalities the right to secede would also jeopardise Eritrea's future cohesion, not least because the Tigrayan and Afar peoples live on both sides of the border.

The TPLF argued that the EPLF's refusal to recognise the right of its own nationalities to secede was an example of its undemocratic nature. For this reason the TPLF regarded its relationship with the EPLF as tactical, rather than enduring, and consequently the TPLF provided support to other Eritrean movements, such as the Democratic Marxist League of Eritrea.

According to EPLF documents, the TPLF's flirtation with other movements came as a surprise and a disappointment and led to a rupture in their alliance.

> '...the TPLF had concluded that the EPLF was not a democratic organisation and that its relationship with the EPLF was "tactical". The EPLF had thought that its co-operation with the TPLF was genuine and not based on temporary tactical considerations. And so, when the TPLF's secret stand became public the EPLF realised its naiveté and although it did not regret its past actions, decided to break its relationship with the TPLF and not enter into polemics with it.' [16]

It was at this critical juncture, when relations were at their most difficult, that the movements sought to resolve the question of just where the border ran between Eritrea and Tigray. For a long time this had appeared of little real importance since both rebel groups ranged freely across the border, as did the Ethiopian army. Very little has been heard of the negotiations that took place in late 1984, but a founder member of the TPLF, Ghidey Zeratsion, has offered an insight into the negotiations. [17] He indicates why the issue became so critical for the Eritreans.

> "The border issue was raised for the first time at the meeting between the TPLF and EPLF in November 1984. At this meeting, the EPLF raised the issue and wanted to demarcate the boundary based on international agreements and documents. The areas under consideration were Badme, Tsorena-Zalambessa, and Bada. The TPLF agreed that there are areas between Ethiopia and Eritrea where they are not clearly demarcated. At the same time it argued that it was not prepared for such discussion and had not made documentary studies on the issue. Furthermore, the TPLF argued that it was not in a position to sign border agreements on behalf of Ethiopia because it did not have the legitimacy to do so. And hence, the TPLF proposed to maintain the existing administrative areas as they are and prepare the necessary documents for the final demarcation after

the fall of the Derg. The EPLF was convinced by the argument and both agreed to postpone the demarcation and maintain the existing administrative regions.
One may ask why the border issue was so important for EPLF while it was still trenched in the Sahel area?

The EPLF was very much constrained by its ability to get recruits for its army. It has been rounding up and forcefully recruiting people all over Eritrea. In such a situation, border areas like Badme were safe havens for people who wanted to escape recruitment. At the same time, there are a number of Eritreans living in these areas who were attractive for EPLF's quest of recruits. As a result, the EPLF was intruding these border areas and provoking a reaction from the TPLF. At one instant the two fronts were at the verge of war if the EPLF had not withdrawn. The EPLF could not afford to open another front while it was confined in the Sahel trenches by the Derg's army."[18]

By early 1985 relations between the two movements had become mired in distrust. As the relationship deteriorated the TPLF began providing assistance to Eritrean movements hostile to the EPLF. [19]

In June 1985 the EPLF decided to teach the TPLF a brutal lesson in power politics. The Eritreans cut the TPLF's supply lines to the Sudan that passed through their territory. [20] This was done at the height of one of the worst famine in modern times, denying Tigrayas access to food aid at a crucial juncture. Nothing was said publicly about the incident at the time, but it is not hard to imagine the animosity that it generated. The TPLF responded with characteristic efficiency, mobilising 100,000 peasants to build an alternative route through to Sudan that did not go via Eritrea.

While the EPLF leadership still refuses to speak about these events, Tigrayans recall it with great bitterness. As one put it: "...the EPLF behaviour was a savage act.....I do not hesitate to categorise it as a 'savage act'. It must be recorded in history like that!" [21]

Despite this rupture the imperatives of war continued to drive the two movements to co-operate with each other. By 1987 both Fronts had had considerable military success, but further advances required co-ordinated action. In April 1988, after four days of discussions in Khartoum, a joint statement was issued, indicating that their differences had been set aside. At the same time there was no suggestion that they had been resolved. This was a military pact, not an alliance of like-minded organisations — a point stressed by the TPLF's Yemane Kidane. The two fronts were not reconciled ideologically or politically: "Never, never. Only a military relationship. Ideologically never, politically never. We maintained our differences. So we always say it is a tactical relationship, not a strategic relationship. If they call it strategic, it is up to them." [22]

Military co-operation led to military success. By the time the Eritreans finally took Asmara in May 1991 and the Ethiopian rebels marched into Addis Ababa, supported by units of the EPLF, the movements had forged strong bonds.[23] Their members had fought side by side against appalling odds, while their leadership had come to know and rely upon one another, even if past differences had not been forgotten. Divisions remained, but there appeared every chance that these could be overcome, given the goodwill that existed. Agreements were made in 1991 and 1993 allowing the free movement of labour across their common border; for Eritrea's use of Ethiopian currency, the birr; for regulated Ethiopian use of the port of Assab to minimise the effects of its loss of a coastline, and so on. Above all, the TPLF honoured its promise to allow an Eritrean independence referendum in 1993, despite strong hostility from many sections of Ethiopian society. When the Ethiopian Prime Minister went to Asmara take part in the formal declaration of independence in late May 1993 in his capacity as an Ethiopian head of state Meles offered a warning to his audience. Although the speech made appealed for reconciliation it went on to call for both sides not to "scratch the wounds" of the past. At the time it struck an odd note, since both movements appeared firm comrades, having come through such difficult battles together. Nonetheless, the speech was well received in Asmara and relations between the two capitals appeared to be on a firm footing.

Indeed, co-operation between the two governing parties was so strong that a senior Eritrean could seriously look forward to the day when the two countries were united once more in a federal structure. [24] Extraordinary as such sentiments might seem today, they genuinely reflected the optimism of the time.

From the euphoria of liberation to a cooling of relations

Even at the moment of victory, cracks were appearing in the relationship. The EPLF expelled from its soil the Ethiopian army of occupation. It also insisted that tens of thousands of Ethiopian citizens, who had been involved in the Ethiopian administration, leave as well. Between 1991 and 1992 around 120,000 Ethiopians were forced to go, although a large number who had not participated in Addis Ababa's rule were allowed to stay. Some of those who were expelled had worked in Eritrea all their lives. Some knew no other home. One Ethiopian complained: 'The Eritrean soldiers told us we were strangers. But I was born in Eritrea like everyone else in my family.' [25] Many were not allowed to take their possessions when they left, and some had to abandon houses, businesses and cars.

13

The deportees included a significant number of Eritrean born women and children who had married or cohabited with civil servants and soldiers from other parts of Ethiopia. It was made clear that 'collaborators' of this kind were considered traitors, and some who were not expelled suffered social ostracism. The newly installed Ethiopian government neither officially complained, nor retaliated.[26] It continued to allow around half a million Ethiopians of Eritrean origin to live inside Ethiopia. Reportedly, the Eritrean community inside Addis Ababa had been one of the most reliable sources of intelligence for the Tigrayans and their allies when they took the capital.

The Ethiopian victory threw up its own difficulties. Eritrean support for the Tigrayans in capturing Addis Ababa was seen as a sign by many Ethiopians that the TPLF was in the EPLF's pocket. This was particularly strongly felt among Amhara, whom the Tigrayans displaced from power. Their accusation that Meles Zenawi was too pro Eritrean in his policies was a potential liability to the new Prime Minister. He could be seen as either failing to be robust enough in his defence of Ethiopian interests, or - from the perspective of the TPLF - insufficiently strong in prosecuting policies that favoured Tigray.

The question of secession, referred to above, also served to drive the movements apart, since their views of state administration were diametrically opposed. The new Ethiopian government reformed the state along ethnic lines. The constitution of 1995 allowed for 'a voluntary union of the nationalities of Ethiopia' which included the right to secession. [27] It was a position that was abhorrent to the EPLF.[28] By contrast, the Eritreans, building on their vision of their country as a product of colonialism, opted for a unitary state. The Eritrean constitution specifically forbids religious or ethnically based parties. In practice neither government tolerated much in the way of dissent. Political parties, other than the People's Front for Democracy and Justice - the successor to the EPLF - were not permitted to operate in Eritrea. In Ethiopia political parties were tolerated, but tightly controlled.

Despite these tensions the outward signs were that all was well between Addis Ababa and Asmara. Government delegations came and went, and life proceeded as normal. Yet relations between the governments of Ethiopia and Eritrea were not put upon the kind of solid footing that would stand the strains of office. Part of the problem was the fact that Eritrea achieved de facto independence in May 1991, but this was not formalised until May 1993. In the interim there were few official channels of communication. [29]

Even after 1993 the leaderships of the two victorious movements continued to treat relations between the two countries as if they were relations between liberation movements, or even between individuals. This may have been because both sides distrusted institutions, or because of a lack of experience of government structures. [30] Hence the bureaucratic infrastructure that should supports interstate relations was either not established or else sidelined. If President Isaias had a serious issue that he wished to raise concerning Ethiopia he simply contacted Prime Minister Meles Zenawi, and vice versa. The kind of institutional checks and balances that might have served as restraining influences on both leaders in democratic states were either poorly developed, or entirely absent.

This weakened the relations between the states in two crucial ways. Firstly, it left plenty of scope for misinterpretations and recriminations. Secondly, it meant that if the relationships between individuals broke down, there was no official position to fall back upon. Even when committees were established, they operated with such informality that when challenged by the critical events that led to the recent clashes, they failed to function effectively.

While the Eritreans and Tigrayans were coming to grips with the administration of their countries, events were taking place on their border. After 1991 a series of localised, small scale disputes took place in a number of locations. These were the sort of conflicts that flare up along any ill-defined border that is straddled by farming communities. Frequently these took place during the ploughing season, as farmers clashed over the exact boundaries of their fields. Eritrean farmers, living in border areas under Tigrayan administration, found themselves being penalised for infractions of Ethiopian laws. [31] In earlier times village elders would have sorted out these kinds of incidents, for in reality these were 'intra-village' disputes, rather than cross border conflicts. Traditional approaches to conflict-resolution were well established, tried and tested means of reducing tension. But since 1991 these methods had largely been abandoned in the border areas, and their place had been taken by government to government, or even party to party meetings. Low level discussions did take place between local officials in an attempt to resolve these matters, but to little avail. According to the Eritreans, no fewer than six such meetings took place between November 1993 and March 1996. [32]

When these talks failed to resolve matters a further series of discussions were held, this time involving senior party officials at a regional level. Again these failed to produce the desired results. Following a more serious conflict over the Bada area of southern Eritrea, President Isaias Afwerki wrote to Prime Minister Meles Zenawi on 25th of August 1997, proposing that a Joint Border Commission be established at governmental level. [33] Ethiopia presents a rather different picture of these events, maintaining that the initiative for establishing the Commission came from its side, following a deterioration in relations '...as a consequence of economic issues,...' [34]

The first meeting of the Commission took place in Asmara on 13th November 1997. The Eritrean side evidently pressed for a speedy resolution of the border issue, given the deteriorating situation on the ground. According to Ethiopia, a common understanding was reached at the meeting:

> "·To assign to a technical sub-committee drawn from both countries to examine the border question and to report to the commission to be formed.
> ·That each party should declare to the other side the list of its members to be represented in the sub-committee.
> ·That both sides respect the status quo and take measures to alleviate impending border disputes until such time that a lasting solution is attained." [35]

Despite this no further meeting took place until the 8th May 1998 with the Eritreans blaming Ethiopian procrastination for the delay.

In the meantime an apparently minor, unrelated event occurred that convinced the Eritreans that the Tigrayans were up to no good. The German government aid agency, the GTZ, operated in three regions of Ethiopia. Early in 1997 the Regional Education Board of Tigray approached the GTZ. They were asked to help fund the printing of a new map of Tigray for distribution to primary schools. The GTZ agreed and printed 1,000 maps with its logo on the bottom. The map turned out to be deeply controversial, for it portrayed the border with Eritrea in a completely new light. Several areas that had been the subject of the heated discussions between the two countries were now shown as being part of Tigray. For the Eritreans this was proof positive of the hostile intentions of the Tigrayans. Although it was the Tigrayan regional authority that undertook the printing, the Eritreans believed that this could not have taken place without the collusion of the government in Addis. Some interpreted it as the result of the long held TPLF dream of a 'Greater Tigray', that would encompass all Tigrean speakers, as outlined in the TPLF manifesto of 1976. [36]

The German government was horrified that they were caught up in this controversy, and came in for considerable criticism, both in the Horn of Africa and in the German parliament, where several MP's supported the Eritrean cause. The GTZ insisted that all it had done was to finance the project, and that they had no responsibility whatsoever for the map's contents, which was drawn up by the Ethiopian Mapping Authority.

It was against this background that a high level Eritrean delegation left Asmara on the 7th of May 1998 for a meeting of the Border Commission the following day. Led by Defence Minister Sebhat Efrem, it was en route to Addis Ababa when the incident at Badme took place. At first the clash was apparently not regarded as particularly serious, and the Commission's discussions proceeded according to plan. Both sides say the meeting on the 8th went well. According to the Ethiopians it was agreed that two members of the Commission would meet in Asmara in a month's time to hammer out an agreement and report back to the larger group. They say that it was further agreed that Eritrean armed units that had crossed into Ethiopian territory since May 6th would return to Eritrea and that the status quo ante would prevail until a final agreement had been reached. [37] When the meeting ended the Commission agreed to meet at 10.00 a.m. the following day. But when the Ethiopians arrived to pick up their guests, they discovered that the Eritreans had checked out of their hotel, and flown back to Asmara. In Ethiopian eyes this was a clear indication of a lack of good faith on the part of their guests.[38]

Economic relations deteriorate

Economics also helped to sour relations between the two states. Indeed, an examination of the economic issues is crucial to both the origins and implications of the conflict. In terms of origins, economics was the only sphere of public disagreement between the authorities prior to the outbreak of hostilities. Indeed, until then relations between the two countries appeared to be remarkably good, with economic co-operation reinforcing the political ties that had been forged during the years preceding the overthrow of the Dergue. Open animosity over bilateral trade relations surfaced in late 1997 following Eritrea's introduction of its new currency, the Nakfa. While apparently not a causal factor in the immediate crisis of mid-May, the new currency and ensuing dispute over trade relations had three consequences.

Firstly, the introduction of Eritrea's new currency necessitated a clear delineation of the border from mid-1997 in order to regulate cross border trade, taxation and foreign exchange flows. Secondly, the new currency prompted a dispute in late 1997 over the precise nature of post-Nakfa trade relations between Eritrea and Ethiopia, tarnishing relations between the two administrations. Thirdly, friction was exacerbated as the currency and trade dispute severely disrupted the flow of goods, remittances and labourers across the border, generating new political pressures on both governments. Taken together, these economic factors appear to have rekindled old animosities between the ruling groups of both countries, eroding their willingness to compromise or negotiate over disagreements.

The conflict's most significant short-term economic consequence was the suspension of all trade and communications links between Ethiopia and Eritrea. In December 1997, a de-facto, partial trade embargo was applied, largely at Asmara's instigation, following the dispute over the introduction of Eritrea's new currency. Nevertheless, normal air, road and telecommunications links remained open. It was only after the fighting at Badme, in mid-May 1998, that the rupture became total as the Ethiopian authorities suspended all links and halted the use of the ports of Massawa and Assab, for foreign trade, which has since been channelled via Djibouti.

Cultural factors

A number of factors came into play in this complex relationship that can broadly be called cultural. One could be described as a question of perception. The EPLF had given training and succour to the TPLF in its early stages, and tended to treat the movement as its 'younger brother'. Ordinary Tigrayans not involved in the politics of the Fronts also felt patronised by Eritreans. They had for many years taken low paid, low status jobs in Eritrea, as casual labourers and domestic servants. Tigrayans were denigrated as 'agame' - a term that implied that they were all uncouth peasants.[39] Most Tigrayan men working in Eritrea were hired as labourers. Some got work slaughtering farm animals, while others took up jobs such as woodcutters, potters and shepherds. Women were hired as waitresses, housemaids and washer-women. Many prostitutes in Asmara were Tigrayan. Eritreans, on the other hand, used their skills and capital to buy into or build up businesses in Ethiopia. Class, privilege, snobbery and envy were unspoken elements that ate away at the relationship between the Fronts.

A further issue that is easily ignored is the question of communication. Neither Ethiopians nor Eritreans are given to clear, open dialogue. Secrecy, always a necessity for guerrilla movements, was almost turned into a cult during the long years of fighting the Ethiopian government. Often this was required by the unfolding events. Eritreans, for example, insisted that all recruits take a nom de guerre, and forbade all discussion of family and origins. This was vital given that the entire Eritrean population numbered around three million people, and it would have been all too easy to extract information that might have endangered families still living behind enemy lines. But secrecy was not thrown off once the exigencies of war came to an end. While this cult of confidentiality may have served both movements well during the years of turmoil, it allowed for misunderstandings to multiply and for rumour to replace open debate that might have resolved genuine differences.

Finally there was the machismo that was an accretion of the long years of struggle. Both movements and both leaderships had been hardened by battle. They had developed a resolution that saw them through the most difficult of times. The Front inculcated in their members a determination to press ahead, no matter the cost. Anything less than a steely will was seen as a sign of weakness. This too militated against resolving differences through compromise.

None of these issues were insurmountable. Given time and patience they could and probably would have been resolved. But instead of eliminating their differences after they came to power in 1991 they were allowed to accumulate. Some analysts who knew both Fronts well warned that there could be trouble in store. John Young predicted as early as 1996 that "....political differences between the TPLF and the EPLF during their years of struggle will be reflected in their present and future relations, and as a result they may be far more problematic than is generally imagined." [40]

By mid-1998 old differences, compounded by fresh divisions and irritations, had turned former allies into bitter adversaries. [41]

ENDNOTES

1. Ethiopian television, Addis Ababa, Amharic 21 May, 1998. BBC Monitoring 22 May 1998
2. Washington Post, 17th June 1998.
3. Gerard Prunier. "The Ethio-Eritrean conflict: an essay in interpretation. November 1998. Writenet.
4. Margaret Fielding. "Bad times in Badme: bitter warfare continues along the Eritrea-Ethiopia border". *IBRU Boundary and Security Bulletin*, Spring 1999.
5. "Report of the meeting between Prime Minister Meles Zenawi and the OAU *Committee of Ambassadors* on the Peaceful Resolution of the conflict between Ethiopia and Eritrea. 20 July 1998." *Chronology of the Ethio-Eritrean Conflict and Basic Documents*, Walta Information Centre, Addis Ababa, 2001, p.153
6. Alemseged Abbay. *Identity Jilted or re-imagining identity?*, Red Sea Press, 1998, p. 151
7. John Young. *Peasant Revolution in Ethiopia*, Cambridge University Press, 1997, p. 99 - 100
8. John Young, The Tigray People's Liberation Front in: *African Guerrillas*, Christopher Clapham (ed.), James Currey, London 1998, p 48.
9. The difficulty for the EPLF was that the original cradle of the liberation movement was the Muslim pastoral areas to the north and west of Asmara. EPLF support came primarlily from the Kebessa, the central Tigrean inhabited Christian agricultural areas of Eritrea - Akele Guzai, Serae and Hamasien regions. These had previously been an integral part of Ethiopia, sharing culture, history, language, religion and ethnicity with Tigray. The people of the Kebessa were slow to support the independence struggle against the Ethiopian government. The major factor, in the end, was the failure of the Ethiopian regime to produce an acceptable administration. See Alemeseged Abbay, *Identity Jilted or re-imagining identity*, op cit. Tekeste Negash, *No medicine for the bite of a white snake: Notes on Nationalism and Resistance in Eritrea, 1890-1940*, University of Uppsala, 1986.
10. John Young. *Peasant Revolution in Ethiopia*, p. 157.
11. In August 1977, the EPLF summed up its position. 'The democratic forces of the Eritrean revolution led by the EPLF, while criticising and opposing the erroneous stands and baseless slanders of the socialist countries and democratic forces, have not wavered from its principled solidarity and alliances with these strategic friends.' 'The *present political situation*', Memorandum, August 1978. Selected Articles from EPLF publications (1973-1980), EPLF, May 1982, p. 44

12. See John Young, "The Tigray and Eritrean Liberation Fronts: a History of Tensions and Pragmatism". *Journal of Modern African Studies*, 34, 1. (1996) p. 115.
13. See Duffield, M and Prendergast, J. *Without Troops and Tanks, humanitarian intervention in Ethiopia and Eritrea.* Red Sea Press, 1994, p. 100.
14. Peoples Voice, 1986, Special Issue
15. *Adulis*, May 1985
16. *EPLF Political Report and NDP.* March 1987, pp. 148-9. Quoted in John Young, 'The Tigray and Eritrean Peoples Liberation Fronts: A history of tensions and pragmatism', *Journal of Modern African Studies*, 34,1.1996, p. 115.
17. Ghidey Zeratsion who a senior member of the TPLF until he left for Europe in 1987 when he fell out with the rest of the leadership. Some Ethiopians suggest that a deal between the TPLF and EPLF was concluded as early as 1977, but offer little explanation as to why conflict between the two movements continued long after that date. Belai Abbai, *Ethiopia betrayed: Meles and co. cede sovereign territory to Eritrea by secret agreements.* Unpublished paper.
18. Ghidey Zeratsion, *"The Ideological and Politial Causes of the Ethio-Eritrean War. An Insiders View."* Paper for the International Conference on the Ethio-Eritrean Crises, Amsterdam, July 24, 1999. Ghidey Zeratsion concludes:
    "To understand why the TPLF reacted violently to the intrusions, let us see what TPLF's policy was on the border issue (from my personal notes of the joint MLLT and TPLF leadership 03.01.1978 Ethiopian cal.). It states as follows (interpretation is mine):
    1. Our knowledge of the border issue between Eritrea and Tigray is not well supported by documents. The TPLF should make an endeavour to have a clear knowledge and understanding of the border.
    2. If the EPLF trespasses the present borders, even if we are not sure that the contested areas belong to Tigray, we will consider the EPLF as an aggressor and we will go to war.
    3. If the documents for demarcating the border areas, which now are under the Tigrean administration, prove the contrary we will consider them as a Tigrean territory because they have been under 'effective administration of Tigray'. The identity of a people is determined by the unity and common history created under the same administration. This type of areas, which are under the Tigrean adminis-tration (areas in Belesa- Muna and in Erob, which in the maps are shown within the boundaries of Eritrea) will be under common administration of TPLF and EPLF. If the EPLF rejects this and tries to administer it alone, we will consider the EPLF as an aggressor."
19. Ibid.
20. The Eritreans also shut down the TPLF's radio station which had been operating from EPLF controlled territory.
21. Tekleweini Assefa, Head of the Relief Society of Tigray, interviewed in Alemseged Abbay, *Identity jilted or re-imagining identity?*, Red Sea Press, 1998, p 129.
22. Yemane Kidane in Tekeste Negash and Kjetil Tronvoll, *Brothers at war: making sence of the Eritrean-Ethiopian War.* James Currey, Oxford, 2000, p. 20.
23. Even this co-operation could be a cause of friction. 'In the early years of its rule in

Addis Ababa, from 1991 to 1995, the TPLF was still dependent on its ally to keep the rather hostile Ethiopian political and military situation under control. To many non-Tigrayan Ethiopians the presence of Eritrean forces in Ethiopia during those years was resentful and a cause of discomfort.' Elias Habte Selassie. *The Ethiop-Eritrean Conflict: Its causes and consequences.* Life and Peace Institute, Nairobi, Kenya, unpublished paper, p. 4.

24. Amare Tekle (ed.), *Eritrea and Ethiopia, from conflict to co-operation*, Red Sea Press, 1994, p. 17.

25. *The Independent*, 25 July 1991.

26. Eritrean officials account for this by saying that this purging of agents of the former government was a strategy worked out with the TPLF, who carried out their own purge of Tigray.

27 J. Abbink, "Briefing: The Eritrea-Ethiopian Border Dispute", *African Affairs*, Vol. 97, 1998. p. 556

28. Negash and Tronvoll, op cit, p.15 – 16.

29. For example, it was only after 1993 that a Joint Ministerial Consultative Committee was established.

30. Ruth Iyob. The Ethiopian - Eritrean conflict: diasporic versus hegemonic states in the Horn of Africa, 1991 - 2000. *Journal of Modern African Studies*, 38, 4, p. 670

31. Ruth Iyob, *op cit.*, p. 665.

32. *A war without cause,* Network of Eritrean Professionals in Europe, London 1998, p. 5

33. *A war without cause,* op cit., p. 8.

34. *Ethiopian Foreign Ministry Statement*, August 12, 1998.

35. ibid.

36. *A war without cause*, op cit. pp. 10 – 11 Some Eritreans go further, arguing that the entire conflict was a deliberate attempt by the TPLF provoke a war so as to attain the long held goal of a Greater Tigray. This view portrays the TPLF as 'trapping' Eritrea into launching military retaliation after the initial clash in May 1998. Elias Habte Selassie, *The Ethio-Eritrean Conflict: its causes and consequences.* Life and Peace Institute, Nairobi, Kenya, unpublished paper, p. 7.

37. *Background to and Chronology of Events on the Eritrean Aggression against Ethiopia*, Ethiopian Ministry of Foreign Affairs, 24th June 1998.

38. Author's discussions with members of the Ethiopian government.

39. The term is derived from the name of one of the poorest areas of Tigray, which abuts onto Eritrea.

40. John Young, *op cit.*, 1996. p 120.

41. "The events of 6 May 1998, when armed Tigrayan and Eritrean units confronted each other in Badme, took place amidst a heightened sense of resentment by both Eritreans and northern Ethiopians. When the bullets were fired, they were not only a cause for future hostilities, but a tragic consequence of an ill-defined and misused alliance that had outgrown its wartime *raison-d'être*....As the border war escalated into aerial bombardments, mass deportations of civilians, and the massing of troops on the border, it became clear to observers, mediators and the world at large

that the old fraternal centre had not held, and that the alliance had ceased to exist."
Ruth Iyob op cit pp 675 – 676.

Chapter 2

'Ethiopians believe in God, Sha'abiya believe in mountains': the EPLF and the 1998-2000 war in historical perspective

Richard Reid

Introduction and overview

The 'quotation' in the main title of this chapter comes from a piece of graffiti scribbled by an Ethiopian soldier on a rocky outcrop at the side of the road out of Barentu, heading toward Agordat. It was daubed there in May 2000, when the Eritrean Defence Force – in this context representing the *Sha'abiya*, the traditional nickname for the Eritrean People's Liberation Front (EPLF) – had pulled out of Barentu and the western lowlands, and withdrawn back into the highlands in the face of an overwhelming Ethiopian offensive. The Eritreans accompanying the author back up to Asmara, following a trip to the former battle areas shortly after the ceasefire, found the slogan hilariously funny, and chuckled about it all the way into the highlands. The graffiti certainly seemed, at the time, to smack of angry frustration; and the image which the author's Eritrean companions conjured up was of a dusty, exhausted Ethiopian soldier shaking his fist helplessly at the vast highland plateau towering before him, as the Eritrean army stuck out a proverbial tongue from its lofty repose and silently mocked the aggressor. There may, indeed, be a grain of truth in this. But on reflection, the slogan actually speaks volumes about the troubled relationship between Ethiopia and Eritrea in recent years, and encapsulates the nature of conflict, state and society in the region, both historical and contemporary. In this scribbled statement, which perhaps caused as much mirth among the artist's Ethiopian companions as among the Eritreans who later gazed on it, we have nationhood, ideology, identity, and society evoked; and we have, in many ways, the definitive statement of the 1998-2000 war, insofar as it describes the Ethiopian sense of righteousness indignation on the one hand and, on the other, the simple but effective military device of 'strategic withdrawal' which kept Eritrean army and nation, ultimately, intact in those critical weeks in May and June 2000.

This chapter is concerned with the historical significance of the 1998-2000 war, with particular emphasis on the recent history of the EPLF. This war was, at the most fundamental level, about Eritrea; and it was about the EPLF, its vision of the region and of Eritrea, its structure and ideology, its interpretation of the past, and its relations with Ethiopia and more specifically with the Tigray People's Liberation Front (TPLF), the movement which assumed the dominant role in government in Addis Ababa at the same time as the EPLF took power in Asmara. It was a war which erupted with such apparent suddenness and violence that in its early stages the resultant smoke and ashes covered the lenses of the most powerful historical telescopes. When the air-borne debris had cleared, however, those telescopes began to refocus on the historical landscape of this troubled region in the attempt to spot the origins of this apparently unexpected and (it was widely held) pointless conflict. Various 'moments' through the 1990s were identified, as were pivotal points during the liberation struggle itself. The more powerful instruments could pick out landmarks in the region's deeper history, such as the 1940s, the period of the first organised Eritrean nationalism and on many levels the beginnings of the cycle of modern conflict; and even the late nineteenth century when 'Eritrea' was born, carved out of the northern mountain plateau and coastal lowlands by Italian colonialism, decapitating (as standard Ethiopianist historiography has it) the historic Ethiopian empire and (as Eritreans have it) creating one of the longest running vendettas in history.

There can be little doubt that the 1998-2000 war has deep roots, and there is no more effective way to examine these roots than to do so through the study of certain key aspects of the EPLF[1], and its relationship with Ethiopia in general and the TPLF in particular. Undoubtedly one of the most successful liberation movements anywhere in Africa – perhaps anywhere in the world – in the era of decolonisation from the 1950s onward, the EPLF fought for the independence of Eritrea from Ethiopia, the latter governed successively by the imperial *ancien regime* of Haile Selassie and, after 1974, by the Marxist-oriented *Dergue* (Amharic for 'committee') government. The entry of the army of the EPLF into Asmara in May 1991 crowned a landmark triumph in the history of remarkable military endeavours in general, and in the history of armed liberation struggle in particular. It was a victory which caught the imagination at the time, and is a victory which has if anything grown in stature since, in a number of ways, some less intellectually honest than others. With the increasing levels of interest – academic and otherwise – which Eritrea has attracted in the past few years, there has been among established scholars and niche-searching PhD candidates alike a desire to examine, explain and, in many cases, publicise this remarkable phenomenon encapsulated within the phrase 'Eritrean nationalism'. One of the basic premises of such interest is that 'Eritrean nationalism' has been given life and expression through the EPLF: this organisation is thus credited, directly or indirectly, not merely with military prowess but with the creation and shaping of the very society which it today governs[2]. This is undoubtedly hyperbole. Yet it is true that one of the most compelling aspects of the history of the EPLF is the degree to which it has attempted to reinvent and mould Eritrea, and Eritrea's modern history, in its own image. This dramatic and often painful process began on the mountainous battlefields of northern Eritrea; it has continued in the social setting, the political arena, and (though less obviously, perhaps) the academic world[3].

So far, so good; and had this piece been written in 1997, we would now proceed to an examination of the liberation war, outlining the movement's remarkable successes and placing due emphasis on the more recent 'challenges of independence', as they are so often termed. The history of the EPLF, however, cannot be studied without attempting to understand the 1998-2000 war, which was a defining moment for the movement as well as for Eritrea at large. It is a matter of debate whether we see the period of 1991-1998, after Marshal Foch in 1919, as a mere ceasefire for whom a further round of combat was inevitable. But that the 'new war' is fundamental to understanding the EPLF, and central to understanding how the movement has both envisaged and governed Eritrea, is obvious. Although initially characterised as a 'border dispute' – even while the term 'dispute' was clearly a massive understatement – the war came in time to be described by Eritreans as their 'second war of independence'. It was a defining moment for the EPLF as a government, in terms of both tactics and overall strategy, and of the need to rally a small population to an enormous cause. This is also true in terms of the directions which the government has taken since the ceasefire in 2000, a topic which is, however, somewhat outside the scope of this paper. It was also a cruel exposure of the realities of the relationships between the EPLF and the TPLF in particular, and between Eritrea and Ethiopia more generally. Those relationships, always problematic, had been forged in, and through, conflict, and the 'new war' can be seen to have been part of that long-term process.

Finally in this context, it should be pointed out that this chapter is not an attempt to provide a detailed study of either the EPLF or the TPLF as movements in themselves, their 'internal' histories. Neither was a monolith: they had their internal crises, shifts in direction, schisms over policy and strategy, leadership rivalries. This paper does not deal with these: we are here concerned, rather, with what the movements came to represent, how their particular standpoints and strategies engendered disagreements in the field of struggle, and how these disagreements in fact reflected deeper historical tensions across the region[4].

'Angels with dirty faces'?: the EPLF in war and peace

The EPLF emerged in the early 1970s as a rival to the original movement for Eritrean independence, the Eritrean Liberation Front (ELF). The EPLF expelled the ELF from the field of combat in the early 1980s following a period of civil war, becoming the sole movement inside Eritrea in the struggle for independence. The EPLF presented itself as the sole guardian of the Eritrean people's destiny, the keeper of the 'sacred flame', as it were, ideologically flexible (as it turned out), but with a powerful line in political purity. During the years of what is popularly known in Eritrea as 'the struggle', the EPLF espoused a people's war and social revolution, and indeed this went some way beyond mere rhetoric: literacy campaigns in rural areas, women's rights, and programmes for the improvement of health and sanitation, were applauded by those acquainted with the movement in the 1970s and 1980s. These are the aspects of the movement which have passed almost into the realm of 'legend' in contemporary Eritrea, creating a quasi-mythical aura around the memory and recollection of 'the struggle' and those who participated in it. Its leaders inspired understated (for almost everything in Eritrea is understated) hero-worship among that small handful of foreign writers and scholars concerned with the unfolding drama in what was then northern Ethiopia and in one way or another sympathetic to the Eritrean nationalist cause[5]. These were, as their opponents might have described them, 'liberation groupies' who were as extreme in their belief in the righteousness of EPLF aims and methodologies as were those, in the vast majority, who dismissed the movement contemptuously and invested their intellectual energy in the notion of a 'greater Ethiopia' for which an independent Eritrea was a cultural, geographical and historical illogic[6]. As for the movement itself, the proverbial stubbornness – or arrogance, according to its critics – of the leadership was born at least in part of the isolation of the northern mountains, the location of the movement's rear base from the end of the 1970s onward, giving rise to a unique miniature universe of hardship, sacrifice, total obedience and total control. These were critical to the movement's survival and eventual success; but at the same time the EPLF developed an essentially exclusivist ethos. As one veteran lamented to the author, 'we wanted to change them [on achieving independence]. But they have ended up changing us.' 'They', the people, were those on whose behalf, apparently, the struggle had been waged; but the paternalistic attitude is striking. 'They' were presumably not part of that struggle; 'they' would be led, mobilised, educated, 'changed'.

The period immediately following the achievement of independence was, on the whole, one of optimism and certainly self-belief. To a very great degree this was founded upon the sheer achievement of independence. The popular view of the EPLF was of a movement with few resources – the economic and financial situation of the country was dire – but little debt, and quite considerable political capital. However, if not everyone shared equally in the euphoria of liberation – and there were a few categories of 'dispossessed', many with little or no stake in the 'liberation system', both moral and institutional, created by military victory – then the problems which beset the movement in the years that followed were seized on enthusiastically by its critics. On the other hand these problems were explained away or justified by defenders (and the EPLF itself) with equal zeal. In many ways, the material problems of a devastated economic base in a country crippled by war were the least of the new government's worries, particularly when set alongside the deeper issues pertaining to the nation-building process. Problems with neighbours were alternately blamed on the EPLF's inherent aggression, or on long-standing issues concerning Eritrea and the wider region which required resolution; a troubled relationship with the donor community and NGOs great and small was evidence either of Eritrea's proud self-reliance or of the EPLF's arrogance and unreasonableness; lack of political freedom at home was either perfectly understandable in the context of the country's need for social and political discipline, or evidence of the movement's hardening authoritarianism and heightening paranoia.

While effective and ultimately successful in the field – and despite its many enemies, physical, moral and intellectual, it did achieve the victory which it set out to achieve – the EPLF has undoubtedly run into serious problems in recent years. But the most critical of these has been its relationship, and eventually its recent war, with Ethiopia. Understanding that relationship, therefore, is critical to understanding the 1998-2000 war as well as the EPLF itself; for despite the movement's professed isolationism, the EPLF has defined itself in many ways, and often involuntarily, vis-à-vis developments in Ethiopia. The ways in which the EPLF and the TPLF projected themselves, and how each projected the other, made for a profoundly troubled relationship throughout and beyond the era of liberation war. The effects of that relationship have been felt in both countries, but particularly acutely in Eritrea, owing to the country's smaller size and population and the relatively monolithic nature of its current political arena compared to Ethiopia (and indeed most other African states). Those effects can be seen in the way the EPLF invented and organised itself during the struggle; and in the formation of its political and social attitudes and philosophies in government since. It is not simply a matter of utilising the external enemy, the perennial bogeyman at the door, as the means to the end of internal control and discipline, although there is indeed much evidence for this; it goes deeper, right to the heart of what Eritrea actually *is*, has been, and might be in the future.

Dangerous liaisons in the arena of struggle

The EPLF was born in, was the product of, war. It forged, to a certain degree, its struggle – the tools, ideologies and visions of that struggle – in relative isolation from regional events and processes. Certainly, the 'isolation' tradition is strong in the EPLF itself, as the movement frequently recalls, for example, how it received little or no overseas aid, scarcely any foreign recognition, and was untainted by the cynical and corruptive machinations of global or even regional politics. The success of its 'revolution', by this view, was all the more remarkable because it was carried out 'alone'. The movement itself is, in other words, extremely proud of this 'tradition' of isolation. It forged itself in the unique crucible that was 'Eritrea', emphatically no more (this was *not* an 'Ethiopian' struggle, for example) and no less (it fought for complete sovereign independence of the *whole* of the Italian colonial territory of Eritrea). By its own account, the movement surveyed the historical problems which had beset the territory; interpreted (or diagnosed) these accordingly and appropriately; and went about carving out a revolution which would 'resolve' these problems and fulfil the territory's perceived destiny. Such clinical isolation, conducted in the virtual laboratory conditions of 'the Field', both physical and metaphorical, had important consequences for the evolution and ethos of the EPLF itself.

However, in reality, the EPLF cannot truly be understood in isolation: the movement itself, the struggle which it waged, and the paths taken by the government since, must be understood in terms of Eritrea's relationship with Ethiopia in general, and with Tigray and the TPLF in particular. Indeed, the deeper historical past also reveals this essential truth. That relationship served to shape the EPLF itself – despite, perhaps, the leadership's best intentions – during its struggle, and has served to define both the movement in power and the kind of state which Eritrea has become since independence. Further, it can be argued that the very ethos of isolationism so assiduously cultivated by the movement was itself a response to that ubiquitous and undeniable relationship, the 'isolationism' here being understood in the context that there

28

is something from which one wishes to be 'isolated', however unfeasibly. In the case of Eritrea and the EPLF, that 'something' was Ethiopia; and, in the end, the attempt at isolation has proved a resounding, and indeed tragic, failure, while the strategy itself was inconsistently and at times ineptly pursued. Indeed, we might take the argument further by suggesting that it was not simply the relationship itself which has been so profoundly influential in shaping both Eritrea and the EPLF, but the actual attempt to end that relationship, or at least to redefine it, insofar as it had hitherto been understood, to become 'isolated' from the very thing – the Ethiopian state, in all its many guises, and various physical and abstract manifestations – which had given it life. In this connection, it is worth noting that the EPLF had utilised, even in a sense embraced, a historically more 'distant' experience of colonial domination – the era of Italian imperialism – to lend weight to its arguments for legitimate sovereignty. This was precisely because, despite the movement's stated anti-colonialism, that particular experience had facilitated distance from Ethiopia.

Many of the disagreements between the movements – for example, those related broadly to ideology – were, after the fashion of revolutionary ideologues everywhere, frequently arcane and in any case largely meaningless. Few now recall the relevance of the Tigrayan predilection for Albanian socialism, or the Eritrean position on the Soviet Union. But other issues went to the heart of the historical relationship, which had their roots in an earlier era, but which were sharpened in the arena of ideological and nationalist struggle. From the late 1970s and through the 1980s, as in 1998, borders were an issue which represented something much larger, namely, nationality and identity. On one level, borders are by definition 'marginal'. They define the ragged edges of communities and polities and identities – ragged, that is, emotionally rather than strictly legally, although the latter sometimes follows from the former, and this appears to have been the case to some degree between Eritrea and Ethiopia. But they are also, in a sense, purely 'marginal' in terms of deeper issues and conflicts, physically distant from the core of international disagreements. Yet, on another level, borders also embody those disagreements, and are often the bloodiest manifestations of conditions at the heart. They are, at any rate, merely the points of contact in interstate conflict of this kind: they are the raw edges of history, lines of tension defined in another era, and often in another place. They are only 'causes' of war when the states involved permit them to be so; and the assumption must be that states only act in such a way when larger foreign policy (or indeed domestic policy) and wider strategic concerns dictate. According to this 'centrist' interpretation, borders have no 'life' of their own: they do not move except when they are pushed. And yet, according to another analysis, they can indeed have lives of their own, when they are the source of debate, competition or conflict among the very local communities defined by them. In dealing with the EPLF and the TPLF, we find both of these dynamics at work. Either way, borders very often reflect conditions at the centre, as well as responses *to* the centre; they can virtually *define* the state, at least in its most idealised form. In our context, it is worth observing that both the EPLF and the TPLF behaved like 'states' during the struggle, defined themselves as states-in-waiting. This had huge implications not only for the nature of struggle itself, but the nature of the post-war political settlement and relationship.

Problems over the exact location of borders pre-dated the liberation war. But for our purposes, it is worth noting that significant clashes were occurring between the TPLF and the ELF (not the EPLF) in the mid-1970s in the western lowlands between Eritrea and Tigray[7]. ELF claims over territory widely regarded as Tigrayan created further problems in an already problematic relationship with the Eritrean movement; perhaps reflecting its own relative weakness as a military and political force at that time, the TPLF played a waiting game[8], and it was only when the ELF were expelled from the area during the Eritrean civil war in the early 1980s that the TPLF regained control over much of this territory. But this was only the beginning. Through the early 1980s, borders were high on the agenda in exchanges between the TPLF and EPLF. The following EPLF statement on the matter, dating to the mid-1980s when relations between the movements had broken down, indicates the depth of the problem:

> In the period between 1979 and 1983, at different times the TPLF had caused many serious problems and tensions on the question of boundaries. The EPLF stated then that it was not the right time to raise such questions and that the colonial boundary was clear. However, the TPLF [continued to raise] the boundary issue by claiming the territory of the district of Badme, in the centre Tsorona, and in the south Bada, while the TPLF inhibited the EPLF's movement in and administration of those areas. Moreover, the TPLF [claimed that] Tigray had an outlet to the outside world through Dankalia.

The EPLF thus characterised the Tigrayans as 'expansionist'[9]. Almost certainly, the TPLF regarded the clarification of certain boundaries as a crucial step in the underpinning of Tigrayan 'national dignity', even as preparation for a Tigrayan nation-state should such an outcome become desireable. The movement stated that the issue would be resolved either by a democratic government or by an independent Tigrayan state[10]. Either way, it seems likely that it was to a very real degree a response to Eritrea's own tough position on 'national dignity' – namely, that the boundary was not up for discussion, and that any discussion was in itself compromising to Eritrean 'sovereignty'. The EPLF's own statement on this reveals something of a dilemma: 'it was not the right time' suggests an at least implicit recognition that borders did indeed deserve, at some point, to be negotiated; yet 'the colonial boundary was clear' is the final fall-back position, i.e. that there was nothing, in any case, to negotiate. In this sense do we see that borders reflected conditions at the heart, deeper relations between states-in-waiting. The TPLF, at this time, implicitly conceded the secondary nature of boundaries; but warned that negotiation was needed, and would come in the future, for although 'the Eritrean nation' was created through colonial boundary treaties between Menelik and the Italians, these borders were often not realised on the ground[11].

The question of 'nationality' lay at the heart of the border issue. While the Eritrean movement described its struggle as genuinely 'nationalist' and anti-colonial, and unambiguously sought complete independence for Eritrea, the TPLF had to decide whether it was an exclusively Tigrayan 'nationalist' movement, or the vanguard of a democratic Ethiopian revolution. Tigrayan nationalism, in its modern form, exhibited – in the mid- to late 1970s – signs of political confusion. Tigrayan nationalists represented an oppressed, marginalized part of Ethiopia, part of a system at the centre of which the province had once held sway. To be or not to be Ethiopian was the question now confronting them. The glories of the Emperor Yohannes and Ras Alula, at the centre of the Abyssinian tradition, had a powerful attraction; but the concept of a Tigrayan nation was an ideologically compelling one too[12]. (These were, in fact, historical heroes who served both purposes, for they were both Tigrayan nationalist icons and pan-Ethiopian champions.) In the end, they would claim their Abyssinian inheritance, and not reject the throne once it was clear that this was a prize which might be won. But what of the Eritreans? They could not be removed from the equation – indeed there is much to suggest that they were regarded as central to the entire calculation. The position of the EPLF was unequivocal: 'you fight for Ethiopia, and we'll fight for Eritrea'. For the EPLF, the figures of Yohannes and Alula were no shared historic and cultural icons to be embraced; these were Tigrayans who were not merely part of a pantheon of regional or ethnic champions, as they were for northern Abyssinian 'nationalists', but figures who had had designs on large parts of what would become Eritrea; and therefore, for the EPLF, Tigrayan nationalism was something to be wary of, even feared. The unequivocality of the Eritrean position likewise disconcerted the Tigrayan leadership. While it is possible that the TPLF initially imagined a future of trans-Mereb union – perhaps represented by Yohannes and Alula, but certainly on the grounds of perceived historical, cultural and linguistic links – they were swiftly divested of the notion. What it meant to be 'Eritrean' or 'Tigrayan' was misunderstood, at times wilfully, at others through genuine miscommunication, on either side.

In the end, the lure of pan-Ethiopia proved more powerful; but either way, it is unclear whether the Tigrayans were innocently aware of the offence which figures such as Yohannes might give to Eritreans, who perceived him in a somewhat different light. In the course of the dialogue between the movements – which so often had the appearance of two contemporaneous but wholly separate monologues – the TPLF appeared to reject the notion of 'multi-ethnic' struggle, and instead to articulate the idea that distinct peoples should fight their own wars of liberation. This implied criticism of EPLF strategy originated, perhaps, in the early TPLF formulation of the notion of a distinct Tigrayan and 'Tigrinya-speaking' identity, which linked the Eritrean highlands – the EPLF's heartlands – intrinsically with Tigray[13]. It later became more overt, as the TPLF depicted its own struggle as truly 'national' but as that of the EPLF as 'multi-national'. The peoples of Eritrea – an artificial colonial creation – had the right of secession from Eritrea and could not all be represented by the EPLF[14], which in any case (it was implied) represented a part of Eritrea which was firmly tied to Tigray, just as Tigray – a truly historic 'national' entity in a way that Eritrea could never claim to be – had the right of secession from Ethiopia. This, of course, went some way toward undermining the TPLF's own early professed support for the Eritrean cause and Eritrea's right to claim nationhood, a position to which, by the early 1990s, the movement had very publicly returned.

For its part, however, the EPLF was unbending: the TPLF must fight for Ethiopia (and indeed the EPLF rejected the concept of a 'Tigrayan nation' on economic, social and historical grounds[15], using the same arguments which had been used against Eritrean independence in the 1940s), the EPLF was fighting for all Eritreans. While the right of secession for 'internal nationalities' might apply to groups oppressed by undemocratic government, the principle of 'democratic unity' should take precedence over secession[16]. The EPLF was clearly determined – as it remains today – to put to rest any spectre of internal Eritrean disunity. In a curious way, perhaps, the EPLF was by default investing in the notion of a 'historic Ethiopia' – the bane of the Eritrean nationalist – on behalf of Tigray, as long as such a concept did not impinge on Eritrea. The disagreements between the leaders of Eritrea and Tigray on these issues did not bode well for future relations, because it was clear that any future Tigrayan-dominated Ethiopian government would be doubtful as to the actual legitimacy of Eritrea's entire struggle, as defined and controlled by the EPLF.

To a very real degree, the problematic relationship between Eritrea and Tigray, as represented by the EPLF and the TPLF, reflected the difficulties both sides had in defining themselves, although in the context of liberation war the Eritreans had, perhaps, a rather more straightforward task than the Tigrayans. For much of its early history, the TPLF had toyed with the idea of an independent Tigrayan republic, drawing – as the EPLF also did – on a selective interpretation of the past. But what exactly did the movement have in mind? Again, what was Tigray to be without Eritrea? Although the notion of Tigrayan independence was rejected by the EPLF, it seems possible to speculate that the TPLF had in fact originally envisaged, at least implicitly, some degree of unity with Eritrea. Talk of Tigrinya-speaking unity, noted earlier, was certainly strongly suggestive of this, and echoed similar ideas current in the 1940s[17]. Only some form of Tigray-Tigrinya unity would have justified the desire for an independent Tigray[18]. TPLF rhetoric supporting the Eritrean cause, while simultaneously claiming to have 'persuaded' the Ethiopian people of the righteousness of that cause, may also, in origin, have been part of the same thought—process. It seems possible to suggest that initially the TPLF had looked northward for its political destiny; the stance of the EPLF forced the Tigrayans to avert their gaze. The EPLF was clearly not interested, and effectively told the TPLF to look southward instead, to fight for Ethiopia, although it is also possible that the TPLF would have claimed the Ethiopian inheritance in any case, in the course of time. It is certainly the case that, as events proved, the Tigrayans proved themselves unable to resist that inheritance once it was within their grasp[19]. Once rebuffed by the Eritreans, the TPLF, already made conscious of the territorial vulnerability of Tigray through the activities of the ELF, began to insist on 'demarcation' of boundaries, an issue which was, and is, secondary to that of nationality and identity, issues which have more profoundly shaped the political destiny of the region. The nature of Eritrea's struggle, as represented by the EPLF, fundamentally altered that destiny: it was a rejection of everything that had come before, the carving of a new path in terms of regional identities.

CONCLUSION

The EPLF was, in many ways, the logical culmination of two centuries or more of war, and was both the heir to and the product of a regional culture of domination and hegemonic struggle. Much of that hegemonic struggle took place across the same areas brought to wider public attention during the 1998-2000 war. Like all historic junctions, the region of modern Eritrea has been a battleground for centuries, a frontline in the clash of cultures and civilisations, an arena of struggle and competition, of commercial as well as strategic value; the emergence of the EPLF, innovative and radical though in many ways the movement was, must be seen as a logical step in the attempt to force the historical endgame, to finally and unequivocally engender a 'definition' for Eritrea, while the 1998-2000 war was an uncomfortable reminder that the 'decisive moment' in that endgame was still some way off. The EPLF has not been able to bring it about, despite the clinical and frequently brutal nature of its strategy.

The 1998-2000 war was no isolated event. Rather, it stemmed from a history of complex and problematic relationships, and from the processes of definition and self-definition of the entities which went to war. Claims of surprise were disingenuous on both sides; but they can, perhaps, be forgiven for such secrecy, if not outright mendacity, both before and during the war itself, if only because the reality was too unpalatable to behold. And we are referring to the reality of the past, that is, rather than the myths and inventions (created for each other as well as for themselves) which have characterised the ethos of both movements. So there is God, and there are mountains. One represents belief in an ancient, semi-mythical history, investment in a historic 'idea', and an indignant, indeed holy, righteousness; the other represents an equally entrenched mental state and belief system, a moral as well as physical universe. One is Ethiopia, the holy land of almost Biblical stature, the great and ancient empire; the other is Eritrea, as represented by the EPLF, godless, rocky and Spartan. In the scenario under study, mountains are in abundance, and God is everywhere well represented; but the stereotypes tell us rather more about a region where movements and governments often believe a little too strongly in their own mythologies for the well-being of the peoples that they purport to represent.

ENDNOTES

1. There is a growing body of literature on the movement: Ruth Iyob, *The Eritrean Struggle for Independence: Domination, Resistance, Nationalism 1941-1993* (Cambridge, 1995), and D.Pool, *From Guerrillas to Government: the Eritrean People's Liberation Front* (Oxford, 2001), are among the best works at present. Somewhat less efficiently put together, but still useful on the details of the EPLF's political structure and military history, is R.Pateman, *Eritrea: Even the Stones are Burning* (Lawrenceville NJ, 2nd ed. 1998). D.Connell, *Against All Odds: a chronicle of the Eritrean revolution* (Lawrenceville NJ, 1997) remains one of the standard introductory works: what it lacks in scholarly rigour it makes up for as a very readable first-hand account.

2. It should, of course, be pointed out that the EPLF formally ceased to exist after 1994, when it became the People's Front for Democracy and Justice (PFDJ). The PFDJ, however, is basically the EPLF in everything but name.

3 The EPLF has since taken the battle to Eritrea's historic demons, seeking to slay the bogeymen of the country's complex past and in so doing create a 'new present'. It is not, perhaps, as yet clear whether the EPLF will embrace the same triumph on this front as it did when it pursued the Ethiopian army out of Eritrea in 1991; but the endeavour itself is, at the very least, worthy of future study.

4. See also my 'Old Problems in New Conflicts: some observations on Eritrea and its relations with Tigray, from liberation struggle to inter-state war', *Africa* (in press, 2003)

5. A good example is J.Firebrace, with S.Holland, *Never Kneel Down: Drought, Development and Liberation in Eritrea* (Trenton NJ, 1985).

6. See my 'The Challenge of the Past: the quest for historical legitimacy in independent Eritrea', *History in Africa*, 28 (2001)

7. Research and Documentation Centre, Asmara (hereafter RDC): Publications of the EPLF: 'The TPLF and the development of its relations with the EPLF' (c.1984), Acc. No. 05062/Rela/3, p.8; J.Young, 'The Tigray and Eritrean Peoples' Liberation Fronts: a history of tensions and pragmatisms', *Journal of Modern African Studies*, 34:1 (1996) p.106

8. RDC: Publications of the TPLF: 'The Eritrean Struggle, from Where to Where? An Assessment', (1985): Acc. No. Rela/10359, p.51

9. RDC Acc. No. 05062/Rela/3, pp.4, 13

10. RDC Acc. No. Rela/10359, p.81

11. ibid., pp.81-2

12. RDC Acc. No. 05062/Rela/3, pp.19-20; J.Young, *Peasant Revolution in Ethiopia: the Tigray People's Liberation Front* (Cambridge, 1997) p.99

13. RDC Acc. No. 05062/Rela/3, p.4

14. ibid., pp.20, 27

15. ibid., p.20

16. RDC Acc. No. Rela/10359, pp.161-2

17. See for example Alemseged Abbay, *Identity Jilted or Re-imagined Identity? The Divergent Paths of the Eritrean and Tigrayan Nationalist Struggle* (Lawrenceville, NJ, 1998), *passim*

18. P.Gilkes, 'Centralism and the PMAC', in I.M.Lewis (ed.), *Nationalism and Self-Determination in the Horn of Africa* (London, 1983) pp.205-6

19. Ruth Iyob, 'The Ethiopian-Eritrean Conflict: diasporic vs. hegemonic states in the Horn of Africa 1991-2000', *Journal of Modern African Studies*, 38:4 (2000) p.677; Young, 'The Tigray and Eritrean Peoples' Liberation Fronts', p.50

Chapter 3

ETHIOPIA: THE PATH TO WAR, AND THE CONSEQUENCES OF PEACE

Leenco Latta

"There will be justice in Athens when those who are not injured are as outraged as those who are."

Demosthenes

INTRODUCTION

The Ethiopia-Eritrea war of 1998 – 2000 originated from a discord between the closely related elite groups ruling the neighbouring states since 1991. The shock wave set off by the conflict's eruption then rippled throughout the Horn of Africa region raising the hopes of some actors and dashing those of others. The conflict ultimately rebounded on the inner most circles of the two ruling groups, seriously undermining the cohesion forged during the years of struggle, thereby highlighting one enduring feature of conflicts in the Horn of Africa. The region's inter-state and intra-state conflicts display a persistent tendency to seamlessly connect and to resonate with each other to a degree rarely witnessed elsewhere.

The Ethiopia-Eritrea conflict went further to demonstrate that even inter-elite and intra-elite relations are not immune from this enduring aspect of Horn conflicts. Furthermore, the outward and inward reverberation of the conflict's implications seems to indicate that the war's causations must have operated at the inter-state, intra-state, inter-group, intra-group and inter-personal locations.

These multiple sites can be further concretized as follows:

(1) trends in Ethiopia-Eritrea relations after 1991 (inter-state)
(2) unfolding societal relations within Ethiopia and Eritrea during the same time (intra-state)
(3) how the exercise of power after 1991 impacted on EPLF/TPLF relations and interactions (inter-group)
(4) the mood emerging within the Horn's Tigrinya-speaking community at large as well as within the two movements spawned by this community, i.e. the TPLF (and by extension its EPRDF coalition) and the EPLF and the TPLF (and by extension its EPRDF coalition) (intra-group) during the decade (inra-goup)
(5) the inter-personal relations between Eritrea's President Isaias Afewerki and Ethiopia's Prime Minister Meles Zenawi.

The eruption of open conflict between Ethiopia and Eritrea in the summer of 1998 took many students of Horn affairs by complete surprise. Once the conflict came into the open, however, there was a race to unravel its causes ultimately leading to the production of quite a significant body of literature. Most of the opinions expressed on the matter, however, are too propagandistic to deserve much attention.[1] Even the writings of relatively sober scholars often appeared focussed on vindicating the position of their favourite regime. Ruth Iyob, for example, attributes the war to newly independent Eritrea's defensive posture against Ethiopia's regional hegemonic ambitions.[2] To Patrick Gilkes, on the other hand, the pursuit of hegemonic ambitions by both sides was one of the factors that led to war.[3] Richard Trivelli traces the causes of the war to the distant and proximate history of the Tigrinya speaking community's identity differentiation as well as the political culture of the fronts that emerged from spawned by this community, i.e. the EPLF and TPLF.[4] The most comprehensive analysis of the conflict's causes and implications is the one offered by Tekeste Negash and Kjetil Tronvoll.[5] Elsewhere I use these opinions to draw my own conclusion that this conflict fits into neither the inter-state nor intra-state categories. And I list its stipulated causes as border disputes, economic issues, the divergence of the ideologies of the groups ruling the two states, differing visions and nature of state types, and the supposed contrast between authoritarianism in Eritrea and democracy in Ethiopia.[6]

In this essay I would have preferred to investigate the unfolding attitudinal and sentimental factors operating at the five interstices enumerated above and how these contributed to the outbreak of conflict. However, the highly secretive culture of the subjects renders such an attempt quite daunting. Furthermore, I am less informed about developments in Eritrea than I am about the unfolding mood within Ethiopia's societal and political groups. This forces me to concentrate on the Ethiopia side of developments and hope those aspects concerning Eritrea would be addressed in the companion contribution.

Hence, in this essay I look would be looking at the less tangible attitudinal and sentimental factors that operated at the following sites: at the following interfaces:

(1) trends in Ethiopia-Eritrea relations after 1991 (inter-state)
(2) unfolding relations between Ethiopia's political groups during the same time (intra-state)
(3) how the exercise of power after 1991 impacted on EPLF/TPLF relations and interactions (inter-group)
(4) the mood emerging within the TPLF and its EPRDF coalition (intra-group) during the decade
(5) the inter-personal relations between Eritrea's President Isaias Afewerki and Ethiopia's Prime Minister Meles Zenawi.

Due to the paucity of hard evidence, the following discussion will draw mostly on my personal knowledge supported by inferential data, where they are available, as well as clearly discernible trends. In addition, readers would realize that I do not give the border issue the importance usually ascribed to it. This is due to my conviction that the border was an issue only to the extent that it served two purposes. Its emotive value was useful for internal mobilization while its simplicity made the issue more attractive for international litigation.[7] Other than that, consistent with cases elsewhere, the border dispute was more of a convenient pretext than the single most important cause of the war.

1. The Emergence of Inter-state Relations

The Ethiopian Derg regime's overthrow by an alliance of liberation fronts (the EPLF, OLF, and TPLF) in late May 1991 occurred much more precipitously and with far fewer, less tumultuous, after effects than many expected. This can be put down to due to the following reasons. First, developments leading up to the end of the Cold War and the accompanying disengagement by the USSR from the Horn further exacerbated the Derg regime's steadily rising inability to dominate the state. Second, contact and dialogue between the Western powers and the major liberation fronts intensified, as the latter's victory started appearing increasingly imminent thus positively influencing morale. Third, the regime that took power in the Sudan in 1989 was willing to much more openly co-operate with the alliance, primarily to forestall its own defeat at the hands of the SPLA. Fourth, Somalia was in no position to take potentially complicating moves as it was steadily descending into chaos. Finally, the Derg regime had discredited itself and had weakened state institutions to such a degree that no successor could emerge from within its political or military establishments to continue the fight for keeping Ethiopia intact. Neither were other unionist elements in a position to do so by going beyond issuing empty ultimatums.

It was under these uniquely propitious circumstances that the Provisional Government of Eritrea (PGE) was installed in Asmara and the Transitional Government of Ethiopia (TGE) was constituted in the Ethiopian capital in the summer of 1991. Elaborating on the factors commonly shared by the former liberation fronts that then became state authorities need not detain us here, as they have been offered by others.[8] Hence, our focus here will be looking at the differing challenges confronting them subsequent to this change of status and how it impacted on their relations.

The peculiar challenge facing the Provisional Government of Eritrea (PGE) was governing a state lacking international recognition. On the other hand, there was no open internal challenge to the EPLF's prerogative of simply declaring itself as Eritrea's governing authority. Such a dispute was settled much earlier due to the EPLF's prior success in physically eliminating or expelling from Eritrea all other contenders thereby turning Eritrea into its exclusive domain. Under the circumstances prevailing then, none of the remnants of these forces was in a position to do much more than issuing protestations when the EPLF declared itself Eritrea's governing authority. The EPLF thus neither needed nor wanted consultation with (or the participation of) any other Eritrean political forces when declaring itself as the PGE. In addition, the EPLF's military and security capacity exceeded the requirements for controlling and ruling Eritrea thus enabling it to entertain the projection of its influence not only in Ethiopia but also elsewhere in Africa.

The situation prevailing in the rump Ethiopian state stood in stark contrast to these developments in Eritrea in a number of ways. Ethiopia's external legitimacy was in no doubt due to its stature as one of Africa's oldest internationally recognised states. Its internal legitimacy, however, was subject to other challenges besides the one successfully put up by the Eritreans. Perhaps the most decisive challenge was the one posed by the Oromo Liberation Front (OLF) which had the potential for mobilising more than 40% of Ethiopia's population. And contrary to that of the EPLF, the TPLF's military and security capacity appeared insufficient for containing even this challenge, let alone doing so while simultaneously facing possible resistance by the overthrown elite. Under the circumstance, the TPLF had to stick to two interrelated policy decisions in order to survive during its early days in power. Firstly, it had to preserve its alliance with the EPLF by very vocally endorsing

Eritrea's de facto independence. Secondly, it had to neutralise the challenge posed by the OLF and other nationalist elements by appearing to honour its decade-long advocacy of self-determination.

The upshot of this situation was that the TPLF, hence finding itself in no position to duplicate the EPLF's action of simply declaring itself as as the new Ethiopian government of Ethiopia, proceeded to invite the EPLF, the OLF and twenty other political organisations to the July 1991 Conference at which the TGE was constituted and Eritrea's separation officially endorsed. Constituting the TGE as a government representing the interests and identities of the country's numerous nations and nationalities was supposed to diminish the deficiency of Ethiopia's internal legitimacy. Those wishing to witness an end to Ethiopia's imperial structure expected that its internal and external legitimacy would thereafter come to rest on the respect of its component communities' right to self-determination. Otherwise they felt that the disjuncture between the internal and external legitimacy of the Ethiopian state and its officials was bound to continue.

The EPLF could not unilaterally advance Eritrea towards full independence, despite its ability to do so when declaring itself as Eritrea's governing authority. As has already been mentioned, Eritrea's *de facto* independence had been formally accepted by the TGE at the July 1991 Conference. The PGE's process of moving Eritrea towards full *de jure* independence, however, remained contingent on the continued goodwill of the Ethiopian authorities even after this initial positive gesture. International participation in the referendum that paved the way for the international recognition of Eritrea's independence would have been at least very problematic, if not outright impossible, in the absence of such co-operation. The internal and external stature of the force that constituted itself as the PGE thus also stood in stark contrast.

The totally new Eritrean state and an Ethiopian state being reconstituted on totally new basis thus started interacting with each other under these peculiar circumstances. The provisional regimes ruling these peculiar states had a mutual need of each other if they were to undo the deficiencies impacting on either their internal or external legitimacy. In the early post-victory days, however, an asymmetrical Eritrean involvement in Ethiopia's political affairs resulted from the invitations of both the OLF and TPLF, the main participants in the TGE. These two fronts, of course, drew the Eritreans deeper into Ethiopian politics in order to achieve diametrically opposite aims.

The OLF, along with the Ogadenis, the Sidamas, the Wallayitas, etc., wanted to realise the genuine reconfiguration of the Ethiopian state that would sufficiently satisfy the various people's quest for self-determination. Clashes between its troops and those of the TPLF erupted while the July Conference was still in session and continued without interruption. The OLF drew the

Eritreans deeper into Ethiopian politics by actively soliciting their mediation of these incessant clashes. It did so by signalling to the Eritrean leaders that averting the re-emergence of domination in Ethiopia would in the best interest of Eritrea as well.[9] The OLF counted on Eritrean awareness of the danger posed to Eritrea if domination relapses in Ethiopia. On the contrary, the TPLF needed "EPLF's support against the other Ethiopian resistance movements to stabilise the situation in Ethiopia and to gain and remain in control of the whole country."[10] As we will discuss later on, it too perhaps signalled to the Eritreans that its monopolisation of power would be in their best interest.

By late 1992 OLF leaders had reasons to feel that the EPLF had opted to bank on TPLF monopolisation of power in Ethiopia. This came about primarily due to occurrences at the last ditch PGE mediation of TPLF-OLF conflicts after the June 1992 failed district and regional elections. The composition and political orientation of the army emerged as the ultimate sticking point at these talks. Eritrean assurances had played a pivotal role in persuading the OLF to initially go along with the declaration of the TPLF army as Ethiopia's temporary defence force in 1991. However, this army's role in foiling the June 1992 elections had by then clearly demonstrated the negative implications of adopting the TPLF army as the country's temporary defence force. Its behaviour during the first set of elections had clearly pointed to the futility of all future electoral and other democratic exercises unless the composition and orientation of the military was fundamentally transformed. Thus, in the last round of talks in Asmara, the OLF strongly argued that all liberation armies are highly politicised and partisan and should therefore be demobilised and replaced by a new, non-partisan, more representative military.

Ironically, it was the PGE facilitators, President Isaias in particular, who dismissed all the alternatives presented by the OLF delegation even before the TPLF delegates aired their views. OLF delegates were surprised at this move and started questioning the motives of the Eritrean leadership. After the collapse of these talks, OLF involvement in Ethiopia-Eritrea contact and dialogue came to an end. The overall implication of this development will become clearer in the course of the next section.

Before taking up that topic we can summarise the peculiar manner of Eritrea's separation from Ethiopia as follows. Eritrea's breakaway did not fit into the Czech and Slovak "velvet divorce" as it resulted from a bitter and drawn out war. Neither did it fit into the more common highly acrimonious break up of states, as the new Ethiopian government was favourably disposed towards Eritrea's amicable separation. Even more unusually, the force ruling the smaller and new *de facto* state was seen (and saw itself) as the "senior brother" of the group that took control of the state from which Eritrea was breaking away. The state authorities of the new state were perceived as the most influential regional leaders, a view with which they too were comfortable. Surprisingly, the irony of the emerging situation, in which the tail was wagging the dog, struck very few observers as strange at the time. However, its inherent instability should have been obvious to any one willing to see it. As has happened in the history of the region time and again, in this case too there was a long time lag between cause and its effects.

2. Triangulation of Political Opinion in Ethiopia (Intra-state relations)

The above developments were unfolding at a time when political opinion in the rump Ethiopian state was steadily crystallising into three distinct camps. The first was constituted of members of the Amharic speaking elite, who were united in their almost unanimous opposition to not only Eritrea's separation but also the restructuring of the rump Ethiopian state. The second camp, embracing the Oromos, Ogadenis, Sidamas, etc., was united in the common aspiration of advancing the various people's genuine exercise of the right to self-determination. The third camp, embracing the TPLF and the coterie of surrogate organisations that it welded into its EPRDF alliance, stood in defence of the emerging order. Ethiopia-Eritrea relations of the time were interpreted in divergent ways by each of these three camps. Since the third camp's views will be the subject of a separate section, here we will focus on the views of only the first and second camps.

Members of the first camp were at the time trying to cope with the loss of power and pre-eminence. Excluded from the July conference and subsequent dealings, they suddenly found their role reduced to that of mere observers. They were at the time experiencing an acute feeling of despair, according to a commentator. He goes on to assert "In the course of 1992, the predominant mood among Ethiopians vacillated between defeatist apathy and desperado radicalism."[11] Meanwhile, they could take comfort in the fact that their worst nightmare, sustainable Oromo-Tigrean solidarity resulting from the OLF-TPLF alliance, was not about to become a reality. Their apprehensions were systematically being dispelled by the then daily clashes between the troops of the OLF and TPLF. Members of the first camp thus only needed to fan the on-going conflict by provoking, inciting or praising both sides to achieve total break-down in TPLF-OLF relations. Once the breakdown of relations led to OLF removal from the political process, members of this camp could then concentrate on subjecting TPLF-EPLF relations to similar manipulation.

One of the most common approaches that the Amharic elite adopted was ridiculing the TPLF regime as an agent of the Eritreans.[12] For example, a group writing in mid-1993, denigrated the TPLF as the EPLF's "surrogate."[13] The TPLF and EPLF were Ethiopia's co-rulers during the period prior to 1998 with the former serving as the latter's viceroy, according to another writer.[14] Meanwhile, members of this camp eagerly fanned any indication of discord marring EPLF/TPLF relations in order to bring about a total break-up. The row accompanying the introduction of the Eritrean currency (Nakfa) in 1997 brought members of this camp closer to achieving this aim than at any previous time. When the outbreak of hostilities became public barely a year later, the news was received with utter euphoria in this camp.

The Amhara elite thereafter did everything possible to entice the TPLF back into what they consider the authentic "Ethiopian nationalist" camp. They worked hard to persuade the TPLF to mend its "errant" ways by taking on the task of undoing Eritrea's separation. Exiles in the North America and Europe raised funds and travelled back home to publicly deliver the cheques. In their pronouncements during such events, they often alluded to the regime's re-incorporation in the "unionist" camp. The enhancement of "Ethiopian unity" that diplomats like to attribute to the outbreak of the war's outbreak was in fact nothing more than the outcome of these manoeuvrings. The fact that this tactic did perhaps contribute to rending in half the TPLF leadership is, however, rarely acknowledged. One of the resulting splinter groups was often described as being more "nationalist" vis-à-vis the Eritreans[15] and thus much more disposed to restoring the whole or parts of Eritrea to Ethiopia. The resulting weakening of the Ethiopian regime further enhanced the first camp's dreams of regaining the power and pre-eminence it lost to the alliance of the liberation fronts a decade earlier. It also raised the hopes of those wishing to promote the agenda of self-determination. We now turn our attention to the evolution of the second camp's mood during this period.

Members of the second camp share the common status of belonging to communities that were incorporated into the present Ethiopian state through a process of brutal conquest at the end of the 19th Century. They saw two possibilities resulting from the TPLF/EPLF capture of the Ethiopian capital in May 1991. First, they harboured palpable fear that this development could simply herald a new round of conquest, this time by the northernmost Abyssinians. Second, they also harboured the opposite hope that the implementation of the principles enshrined in the Transitional Charter could end Ethiopia's imperial system and thereby end their own status as its colonial subjects. The OLF's expression of cautious optimism[16] at the Charter's adoption was perhaps representative of the mood then prevailing. Prominent OLF personalities did not mince their words when concluding that the first scenario had resulted from the derailment of the promise to democratise the rump Ethiopian state.[17]

It should be pointed out that the second camp did not constitute a monolithic bloc. In fact other forces belonging to the second camp apparently viewed the OLF's close dealings with the TPLF and EPLF with some degree of suspicion when these were taking place. The views later aired by Asefa Chabo (a participant in the July Conference as the leader of the Omotic peoples) can be sited as an indicative case.[18] He believes that the three fronts had agreed to parcel Ethiopia among themselves even prior to the Derg's overthrow. According to him, the content of this secret agreement was: 1) Eritrea's independence, 2) the conversion of Ethiopia's southern regions into the second independent state of Oromia to be ruled by the OLF, and 3) the TPLF's installation as the master of what is left of the country. He believes the other members of the alliance needed the OLF only for the purpose of getting its backing for Eritrea's separation. Once it had played this role at the July Conference, the OLF could conveniently be be kicked out of the alliance, according to him. He then goes on to enumerate the factors that rendered war between even the remaining members of the alliance (i.e. EPLF and TPLF) inevitable. Among the factors he mentions is the alliance members' treatment of Ethiopia as their "common war booty" and the ensuing rivalry to get the lion's share. He concludes his analysis by celebrating the outbreak of hostilities in May 1998.[19]

Its hyperbolic delivery aside, this commentator's analysis is indicative of one emerging trend. The initial alliance involving the OLF, TPLF and EPLF was perhaps widely seen by members of the second camp as concerning strictly the guerrilla movements and as potentially targeting their societies. The alliance membership's reduction to the TPLF and EPLF after the OLF's removal produced another perception regarding the pre-1998 Eritrea-Ethiopia friendship. This friendship was widely resented as an unholy intra-Tigrinya alliance possibly targeting all other peoples. And the clearly discernible asymmetrical Eritrean involvement in Ethiopia's politics and economy served as further evidence for those perceiving the TPLF as an agent of the Eritreans. The asymmetrical Eritrean involvement in Ethiopia's affairs was resented by an increasing number of social sectors.[20] Hence, the eruption of hostilities between these two closely related groups was welcomed with the same level of consensus with which their alliance was resented. This trend has important implications for attitudes concerning future restoration of peace and friendship. Any move to achieve merely the revival of the kind of peace and friendship that prevailed in the pre-1998 period would likely be suspected and resented with a similar level of vehemence.

3. Inter-group Relations: the EPLF/TPLF Case

We now turn our focus onto EPLF/TPLF relations after they emerged as the dominant forces in the two neighbouring states. TPLF-EPLF relations have always been intriguing to observers. During the first decade of its existence (1975 – 84), the TPLF was commonly perceived as an EPLF agent operating south of the Ethiopia-Eritrea border. The TPLF started to throw off this image and to thus gain recognition as a distinct autonomous entity only after its dispute with the EPLF was made public in 1984. Its former image relapsed once again after it resumed co-operation with the EPLF in the late 1980s. The TPLF continued to be perceived as "the little brother" of the EPLF long after it took control of the larger state and consolidated its power. This happened to also be the image "favoured by the EPLF, which frequently portrayed itself as the dominant and leading political movement in the region."[21] The TPLF perhaps found humouring this EPLF self-perception pragmatic when the latter's backing was remained essential for its power consolidation.

TPLF reluctance to upset this EPLF self-image continued to persist even as its consolidation of power was nearing completion perhaps due to its pursuit of another agenda. This was the aim of enticing Eritrea back into some form of association with Ethiopia through various means. One of these was extending economic privileges to Eritrea and Eritreans in order to "induce or even force the Eritrean leadership to re-enter into some form of political union with Ethiopia."[22] The other was implicating Eritrea and Eritreans in its own tense relations with the rest of Ethiopian society so as to cement its alliance with them on the basis of the commonly shared feeling of insecurity. Adding the economic dimension to Eritrea's (and Eritreans') entanglement in TPLF military and security activities was adopted in order to heighten this common feeling.

The project of enticing Eritrea back into Ethiopia clearly contravened the Eritrean authorities' most cherished aspiration of turning their country into the quintessential nation-state with all the attributes of complete sovereignty and territorial integrity. The existence of this tension came into the open even as the Eritreans were celebrating the conclusion of the referendum. President Isaias was evidently cornered into publicly advocating confederation between Eritrea and Ethiopia in an interview with a journalist in the employ of the Ethiopian government.[23] Apparently this did not go down well in Eritrea where the President was soon after grilled on the wisdom of re-joining the former coloniser and enemy. He had to back track by publicly assuring his Eritrean audience that the process leading to confederation "will take a very long time, probably generations."[24]

Meanwhile, Meles too was publicly pussyfooting around on the issue of confederation. His approach was declaring that "confederation cannot be the last and the first objective of the Ethiopian and Eritrean peoples" (whatever that means).[25] He was also being badgered as to whether the Eritreans should

46

continue to enjoy various privileges after opting for independence. Resentment about Eritrean involvement in Ethiopia's economy and hints at the need to expel them had evidently been in circulation in non-government circles for a number of years. Even the government owned media was heard querying Meles on the issue of expulsion as referendum day approached. Meles's response was "We categorically reject the idea of expelling Eritreans from Ethiopia, even if the outcome of the referendum is independence."[26] He was destined to execute a *volte-face* on the issue of expulsion only five years later.

While its leaders were putting up this kind of public defence of relations with Eritrea and Eritreans, tension was apparently building up within the TPLF as well as between it and the Eritrean government. There were incidents that indicated this, although the writing on the wall was wasted on those obsessed with either welcoming or resenting the intimacy of TPLF-EPLF relations. The mysterious circumstances under which the TPLF's most renowned commander, Hayelom Araya, was killed by an Eritrean, Jamal Yassin Mohammed, can be mentioned as one such incident. At the time, the Ethiopian army's own newspaper blamed his assassination on an unspecified foreign power.[27] That this actually meant Eritrea can now be surmised from the killer's public execution (the only case of its kind thus far) on the day after the outbreak of hostilities. Concealing the simmering anger and frustration became virtually impossible once the introduction of the Nakfa dashed any hopes of Eritrea ever rejoining Ethiopia. And the outbreak of hostilities exacerbated the apparently rising rancour within TPLF rank and file, as the following section attempts to demonstrate.

Before picking up that topic, we need to mention the concerned parties' divergent portrayal of Ethiopia-Eritrea relations prior to the outbreak of hostilities. The Eritreans perhaps preferred to fit this relation into the conventional inter-state category. It is very likely that they also started convincing themselves that the friendly relations prevailing then involved the whole of Eritrean and Ethiopian society. This would be consistent with the Eritrean authorities' determination to establish Eritrea's image as a distinct nation. Meanwhile, the TPLF appeared bent on blurring the distinction between the Tigrinya speakers of Eritrea and Ethiopia. One way it tried to do this was by emphasising the intra-communal basis of the friendship prevailing until 1998. The fact that contacts with the Eritrean authorities did not even involve the other EPRDF partners (as now admitted by TPLF sources[28]) demonstrates this TPLF signal. This divergent portrayal of parties to peace and friendship, of course, underwent complete a reversal after the outbreak of hostilities. Thereafter, the Eritreans portrayed the conflict as strictly concerning the TPLF, while the latter chose to portray it as involving the whole of Ethiopia. They have stuck to these diametrically opposite opinions ever since.

Intra-TPLF Relations in the 1990s

As the preceding discussion shows, the social basis of Eritrea and Ethiopia relations continued to shrink. The alliance that existed immediately following the Derg's overthrow was perceived as involving only the guerrilla fronts (the EPLF, OLF, and TPLF) and was widely suspected by those who felt excluded. The OLF's expulsion from the alliance in mid-1992 meant that it was reduced to the EPLF and TPLF, further bolstering the sector that suspected and resented Ethiopia-Eritrea relations. Thereafter, the regime in Ethiopia was widely perceived as Eritrea's agent by many members of the first and second camp. The following observation by Negussay Ayele's could perhaps be cited as a common opinion in the first camp. He writes ". . . history has not recorded a case in which a whole regime (TPLF) that rules in one country doing everything possible to benefit another state (Eritrea) at the absolute detriment of the state (Ethiopia) it rules."[29] According to OLF military communiqué No. 2/94, a foreigner was captured while fighting the Oromo Front in the vicinity of Jimma. The "external involvement" evidenced by the "capture of the foreigner" could only be an indirect reference to Eritrea.[30] The Eritrea-Ethiopia dealings of the pre-1998 period did not involve even the TPLF's coalition partners, as has already been mentioned. How these coalition partners took their exclusion is not known for there is no publicly stated opinion. The progressive constriction of responsibility for the pre-1998 Ethiopia-Eritrea relations has now gone one stage further with some members of the TPLF leaders blaming those with Eritrean parentage of being EPLF agents. This can be gleaned from a windfall of information that became public subsequent to a rift emerging in the TPLF leadership.

Eliciting information on EPLF/TPLF relations from internal sources used to be well nigh impossible during the years of their friendship. As K. Tronvoll's interviews with both Front's high ranking personalities demonstrates, this situation started giving way to more openness after the outbreak of hostilities.[31] Getting information on either organisation's internal debates used to be even more unthinkable. We now have a windfall of information on developments within the TPLF due to the public exchange of accusations by its officials after its Central Committee (CC) split almost in half in February 2001. A number of exposés, attributed to prominent TPLF leaders who were then suspended from its CC, are now available at a number of websites. Responses to these opinions, credited to current EPRDF officials, also appear on these websites. Submissions by former TPLF officials now standing trial for corruption and abuse of authority are also posted at these websites.[32] The intention of these writings is naturally skewed more in favour of self-defence and the settling of scores than establishing facts. Regardless, how moods and attitudes within the TPLF were evolving could be discerned from these sources by carefully reading between the lines.

Information now coming to light indicates that relations with Eritrea started being debated as far back as 1995 when Eritrea clashed with Yemen.[33] The year 1995 is also important for other reasons. It was the year the TPLF completed crafting a new constitution to formalise its dominance of Ethiopia. International pressure for upholding the initial promise to democratise Ethiopia also started to wane after this time. On the contrary, Ethiopian leaders started winning accolades as examples of a new brand of leadership in Africa. Internal challenges by other opposition forces to TPLF rule were also falling to an all time low. TPLF leaders hence appeared poised to rule Ethiopia indefinitely and to thereby permanently harvest the benefits of power of success for themselves and for their homeland, Tigray. Evidently wanting to prioritise Tigray's development, some key high ranking TPLF leaders were re-assigned to Tigray from their ministerial or other posts in the central government. Some of these were persons the Eritreans appeared to suspect of harbouring negative intentions regarding Eritrea. During my interaction with them; I could easily observe Eritrean reserve towards such TPLF leaders as Abbay Tsehaye and Siye Abraha.

The TPLF leaders working in the central government and those assigned to Tigray thus started operating in two very different environments. Those operating in the central government and party institutions remained much more aware of other societies' lingering resentment of their power than those dispatched to Tigray. In addition, some of these central functionaries routinely interacted with Western governments and their financial institutions. While the attitude of these perhaps inevitably underwent some modifications, the ideas of those working in Tigray remained more in line with the Marxist-Leninist ideology propounded during of its liberation struggle. Furthermore, it is not inconceivable that the latter started envying Meles's rising stature in the country and in Africa at large, as well as suspecting his cosy relations with Eritrean leaders. Meles's potential contenders perhaps started fearing that his pre-eminence within the Front could start paralleling the TPLF domination of the country, which was taking on an indefinite nature. Whether these developments would have led to internal TPLF conflict or not is not known, but that they surfaced during the war and the negotiations to settle it, is indisputable.

Prominent TPLF leaders now accuse Meles for failing to heed their warnings that Eritrea was preparing for war as far back as late 1996 or early 1997. He reportedly dismissed the warning by asking "is Shabia crazy to commit to such an act?"[34] They list his other pro-Eritrea stands by citing the actions he failed to take. These include failing to curb Eritrean exploitation of Ethiopia's economy, not objecting to the penetration of Ethiopia by Eritrean spies as well as the assassinations of members of Eritrean opposition groups living in Ethiopia.[35] Some go further to accuse Meles of arranging the extension of credits to Eritreans by borrowing from Ethiopian banks to the tune of 2,000 million Birr which allegedly disappeared.[36] Others blame Meles for ceding Zalambessa, Badme, Ayiga and Alitena of Tigray to Eritrea during the liberation struggle, as well as for refusing to claim Assab when Eritrea became independent.[37] These corrosive sentiments evidently remained lurking just under the surface until the Technical Arrangements section of the Algiers 2000 Agreement came up for discussion within the TPLF top leadership. Disagreements regarding the Technical Arrangements played a pivotal role in bringing about the schism of February 2001. The schism is now retroactively being portrayed as pitting patriots and traitors against each other.

Three separate but inter-related documents were drawn up by the Organisation of African Unity (OAU) to settle the Eritrea-Ethiopia war. These were (1) the Framework Agreement, (2) the Modalities for Implementing the Framework Agreement, and (3) Technical Arrangements. The document Technical Arrangements, was presented to the parties on a "take it or leave it" basis. Eritrea, which displayed reluctance by asking for endless clarifications, changed course and accepted the Technical Arrangements after losing Badme in February 1999. Ethiopia then adopted the previous Eritrean practice of delaying acceptance by demanding endless clarifications. Meles was losing a series of debates on the issue during this time, as it has now become public.

Those who opposed the acceptance of the Technical Arrangements were of the opinion that the document clearly failed to demand the restoration of Ethiopia's sovereignty. Although Meles reportedly argued to the contrary, his opponents' stand that the document infringed Ethiopia's sovereignty won majority support in at least three separate internal forums.[38] Things came to a head when an appraisal session got underway after the last round of fighting in the summer of 2000. Meles's opponents appeared determined to put the acceptance of the Technical Arrangements at the top of the agenda and to perhaps unseat him by accusing him of treason. He, on the other hand, wanted to give priority to corruption, probably expecting to take disciplinary measures against some of his opponents. Each side was apparently scrambling to exploit what it identifies as the other's Achilles' heel. In the ensuing debate, Meles succeeded in garnering a slight majority in favour of his stand. At this stage, 12 of the Central Committee's 28 members walked out of the meeting thus paving the way for their suspension.

Meles's opponents subsequently took to publicly accusing him of treason by citing various incidents. He was – they said - opposed to the expulsion of the Eritreans after the outbreak of hostilities and thereby concurred with the Eritrean authorities' designation of the act as ethnic cleansing.[39] They accuse him of succumbing to imperialist pressure thus demonstrating his abandonment of the TPLF's key ideological commitment to anti-imperialism. They went a step further, stating that the various agreements of cooperation with Eritrea were concluded without undergoing the scrutiny of EPRDF leaders.[40] Meles and his TPLF ministers were also accused of personalising power.[41]

His opponents are certain that they were poised to defeat (and to perhaps also unseat him) had another person of Eritrean parentage not come to Meles's rescue. This is Berekhet Simeon of the Amhara National Democratic Movement (ANDM), an Amhara of Eritrean descent. According to the opponents, he played a pivotal role in lining up the ANDM leadership on Meles's side.[43] He too is accused of concurring with the Eritrean authorities' view that the expulsion of the Eritreans was a case of ethnic cleansing.[43] The overall implication of this steadily narrowing of responsibility for Eritrea's asymmetrical involvement in Ethiopia is truly remarkable. In the end, those with Eritrean parentage were made to bear the blame of serving as Eritrea's agents. These, on the other hand, declare that they hated the "Shabia" more than anyone else and did more to bring about its defeat.[44]

Relations Between Isaias and Meles in the 1990s

The organisers of the EPLF and TPLF closely followed the Leninist vanguard party model. Forming and leading a vanguard party was the common aspiration of many other contemporary movements. But none other succeeded in carrying out this aspiration to the extent that the EPLF and TPLF did. Therefore, remembering Rosa Luxemburg's criticism of Lenin's organisational strategy becomes relevant when appraising these Fronts. According to Luxemburg, Lenin's approach would ultimately make the Central Committee the only thinking element in the party with all other groupings serving merely as its executive limbs.[45] This differentiation between the party's brain and limbs was perhaps more advanced in the EPLF than among its contemporary movements, but the TPLF came a close second, as I argue elsewhere.[46] This slight difference has implications for the persons leading the two Fronts, Isaias Afewerki and Meles Zenawi.

The vanguard party system has often gone further to make the Politburo the Central Committee's brain. By the same token, the party strongman, the Secretary General, has ultimately become the Politburo's brain more often than not. When this happens, the leader's personality cult tends to compete with or to even overshadow that of the Front. This tendency perhaps applies more to the EPLF than to the TPLF. This is due to the differing processes that brought the two Fronts into being and the role the two leaders played in shaping them.

Isaias Afewerki played a central role in bringing the EPLF into existence by breaking away from the ELF. He was engaged in this risky exercise at a most fortuitous period. This happened to be the time when educated highlander youth's eagerness to join the Eritrean resistance was at its height. Consequently, the manifesto attributed to him, *Neh'nan Elamaa'nan* (We and Our Objectives), circulated widely among the period's school goers resulting in a windfall of recruits. This steep rise in membership was pivotal in enabling Isaias's faction to survive and to fend off the ELF's attempts to eliminate it. However, it also brought into the struggle people who were eager to challenge Isaias's leadership. The persons harbouring this aspiration, who were veterans of the period's clandestine student movement and thus saw themselves as highly acquainted with Marxist-Leninist ideology, were labelled as the Menka'i. Its leaders were detained and executed some time in 1974.[47] Isaias' stature evidently became unassailable thereafter, as there are no known cases of challenges to his leadership. It is also likely that other potential challengers were persuaded to give priority to the external threat posed by the ELF and the Ethiopian regime. Isaias's prominence was such that many Arab diplomats used to refer to EPLF members as "naas Isiyas" (Isaias's people).

No personality enjoying a similar stature emerged from within the TPLF. In addition, collegial leadership perhaps prevailed more in the TPLF Politburo than in the EPLF. Meles in fact did not rise to the top position even within the Politburo until late into the 1980s. Some irregularity was perhaps involved in his assumption of Chairmanship then as it took place in between TPLF Organisational Congresses. The exact nature of this irregularity, however, remains shrouded in mystery. Regardless, one fact is indisputable. He remained answerable to his Politburo to a greater degree than Isaias was to his own. How this impacted on their interactions as state leaders is not publicly known, but it is possible to arrive at the following suppositions.

Isaias was perhaps much more free to adopt and implement policies, as he was more certain of getting the endorsement of his Front's leadership if this was deemed necessary at all. Meles perhaps needed the prior backing of the Politburo more often than not. Isaias's prerogative could have only been enhanced subsequent to his emergence as state leader. How much Meles's influenced increased within the TPLF Politburo and CC after he became a state leader is not known. However, it is likely that his colleagues watched such a tendency with vigilance. Their fear that his cosy relations with Isaias may lead him to aspire copying the latter's leadership style is not imponderable.

This leads one to wonder if they did not have a stake in spoiling this cosy relationship between the two by triggering the border dispute. Available evidence shows Isaias repeatedly appealed to Meles to avert border incidents leading to a major conflict.[48] Isaias, perhaps because of his own ability to do

52

so, believed that Meles would be able to do so without difficulty. When this did not happen mutual confidence disappeared, resulting in close friendship turning into mutual loathing.

We have already mentioned how the EPLF was seen as the senior partner thus making Eritrea the more influential state in the Horn. This had, of course, implications for how Isaias and Meles were perceived internationally. Isaias continued to be referred to as Meles's "elder brother" as late May 1997. Commentators were then linking Ethiopia's rising regional image with that of Meles as follows: "Ethiopia is once more a force to be reckoned with, as Prime Minister Meles Zenawi emerges from the shadow of his 'elder brother' President Issayas Afewerki of Eritrea."[49] The widely held belief regarding Isaias's seniority easily meshes with the view that Meles takes his cue from the former, lending credence to those who wanted to portray him as an Eritrean agent.

CONCLUSION

Newly independent Eritrea and one of Africa's oldest states, Ethiopia, enjoyed unusually cosy relations from 1991 to mid-1998. During most of this period, the smaller state of Eritrea was widely perceived as the region's most influential power centre. Ethiopia's relegation to a secondary position emanated in part from its leaders' portrayal as Eritrean leaders' little brothers. While many non-Ethiopians welcomed the intimacy of this inter-state cum intra-elite relations, it was widely resented by various sectors of Ethiopia society, who worked to subvert it. Although attributing the outbreak of the war wholly to the manipulation of these forces may appear too far-fetched, it is indisputable that they welcomed it.

We now have the peculiar situation in which both the resumption of war and the restoration of peace and friendship are equally feared. Naturally, the ordinary people of the two countries are tired of war and remain apprehensive of the resumption of full-scale hostilities. There are also those who fear harbour palpable fear lest a new kind of friendship could be concluded behind their backs once again fomenting new concerns that this could negatively impacts on their interests and aspirations. They way in which the Eritrea-Ethiopia conflict emerged and reverberated throughout the region underscores the need to address comprehensively the root causes of both inter-state and intra-state conflicts. The only sustainable way to articulating and instituting a new basis for peace between the two states appears to require a similar process within Eritrea and Ethiopia. Until democracy and self-determination are allowed to flourish within both, it is unlikely that a sustainable basis for peace between the two countries can be established.

Despite the horrendous loss of life and the destruction of property it entailed, there is one positive outcome of the war. Demands for democracy that were being aired from outside the ruling parties have now been taken up from within both of them. As a result, complete unanimity has been achieved on the need to democratise the two countries' political life. There was, of course, a time when members of the ruling parties were certain of enjoying their democratic rights. What they then forgot was Rosa Luxemburg's advice of more than a century ago when she wrote: "Freedom only for the supporters of the government, only for the members of one party – however numerous they may be – is no freedom at all. Freedom is always and exclusively freedom for the one who thinks differently."[50] And in our own life time, Martin Luther King restated the ancient wisdom quoted at the start of this essay when he wrote "Injustice anywhere[51] is a threat to justice everywhere." The leaders of the two countries need to make a fresh start by heeding these words. The rest of us should display enough fortitude and commitment to persuade them to commence on such a course.

ENDNOTES

1. For the most representative of this kind of writing see Addis Berhan, *Eritrea a Problem Child of Ethiopia: Causes, Consequences and Strategic Implications of the Conflict,* (Marran Books, 1998).

2. Ruth Iyob, *Re-Configuring Identities: A Clash of Vision(s) in the Horn of Africa 1991 -1999* (Bern: The Swiss Peace Foundation, 1999).

3. Patrick Gilkes, *Ethiopia – Perspectives of Conflict – 1999* (Bern: The Swiss Peace Foundation, 1999).

4. Richard Trivelli, "Background notes on the Ethiopian-Eritrean war" (a personal communication later on published in Afrika Spektrum, Hamburg, Autumn 1999)

5. Tekeste Negash and Kjetil Tronvoll, *Brothers at War: Making Sense of the Eritrean-Ethiopian War* (Oxford; James Currey, 2000).

6. Leenco Lata, "The Ethiopia-Eritrea War and the Role of the UN and the OAU" in Jane Boulden (ed.), *Conflicts in Africa and the Role of UN and Regional Organizations* (forthcoming).

7. For more on my views regarding the border dispute see Leenco Lata, "The Ethiopia-Eritrea War and the Role of the UN and the OAU."

8. See John Young, "The Tigray and Eritrean Peoples Liberation Fronts: a History of Tensions and Pragmatisms," *Journal of Modern African Studies, 34* (1996) and Leenco Lata, *The Ethiopian State at the Crossroads: Decolonization and Democratization or Disintegration?* (Lawrenceville, NJ: Red Sea Press, 1999), 81 - 117.

9. I hinted to this in the speech I delivered in Asmara on the 30th anniversary of the start of armed struggle, 1 September, 1991.

10. Tekeste Negash and Kjetil Tronvoll, *Brothers at War*, p. 21.

11. Getinet Belay, "A Nation in Transitional Agony: A review of the past two years," *Ethiopian Review* 3 : 7 (July 1993), 17.

12. Listing newspaper and journal articles evidencing this stand is too cumbersome as

they are endless. The TPLF was often described as Even books carrying the same message were written during this time. For example, see Asefa Negash, *The Pillage of Ethiopia by Eritreans and their Tigrean Surrogates* (Los Angeles: Audey Publishing Company, 1996).

13. Abaineh Workie, Wold Zemedkun and Desta Damtew, "Two Years of Transitional Government," *Ethiopian Review*, 3: 7 (July 1993), p. 28.

14. Negussay Ayele, "EPLF/TPLF and Ethiopia-Eritrea Today: Sow the wind; reap the whirlwind," <http://www.ethiopians.com/Views/Ethiopia_Eritrea_today .htm>

15. Ibid. , p. 14.

16. "OLF: Conference on the 'right track'," *Horn of Africa Bulletin 5* (1991).

17. For example, see Leenco Lata, "The Making and Unmaking of Ethiopia's Transitional Charter," in *Oromo Nationalism and the Ethiopian Discourse: The Search for Freedom and Democracy*, ed. Asafa Jalata (Lawrenceville, NJ: Red Sea Press, 1998), pp. 51 - 78.

18. Asefa Chabo, "Fariim Anniliyo" *Raij 2* (Yekatit 1991), pp. 12 – 14 & 30.

19. ibid.

20. The evidence is endless. The following are just samples: (1) The former head of the Confederation of Ethiopian Trade Unions, Dawi Ibrahim, cites TGE pressure to have Eritreans elected to leadership positions as one of the disputes that ultimately led to his departure from the country. "Did foreigners run CETU?" *Ethiopia: Seven Days Update*, 4:9 (19 May 1997), 5; (2) Eritrean privileged access to jobs and investment opportunities at the expense of loyal nationals and even resulting to peasant displacement serve as the topic of numerous commentaries and essays in Urji Newspaper. See Year II, No., Year II, No. 51; Even learned commentators denounce TPLF/EPLF and Tigrean/Eritrean joint exploitation of the rest of Ethiopia. See Oromo Commentary 8:1 (1997), p. 31.

21. Tekeste Negash and Kjetil Tronvoll, *Brothers at War*, p. 12.

22. Richard Trivelli, p. 17.

23. "Isayas Afewerki says confederation with Ethiopia may be possible," *Horn of Africa Bulletin 3* (1993), p. 10.

24. "Isayas Afewerki on democracy, parties, media, and rights," *Horn of Africa Bulletin 4* (1993), p. 7.

25. "Meles Zenawi on relations with Eritrea," *Horn of Africa Bulletin 3* (1993), 10.

26. President and Prime Minister address news conference," *Horn of Africa Bulletin, 1* (1993), p. 8.

27. "Trouble after Araya murder," *Indian Ocean Newsletter 710* (16 March 1996), 3.

28. Tewolde W/Mariam and group, "Ba Lualawinnat Zuriya BaHiWaHat Ma/Komitee Yenabbaraw Liyunnat" <http://www.ethiopianreporter.com/magazine/htm/ R38/r38pol.htm>, p. 15.

29. Negussay Ayele, "EPLF/TPLF and Ethiopia-Eritrea Today: Sow the wind; reap the whirlwind," http://www.ethiopians.com/Views/ Ethiopia_Eritrea_today.htm> , p. 11.

30. Oromo Liberation Front, "OLF Forces step-up the armed struggle in South Western Oromia," *Military Communiqué* No. 2/94 (8 May 1994).

31. Tekeste Negash and Kjetil Tronvoll, *Brothers at War*, pp. 13 - 20.

32. I found <http://www.ethiopianreporter.com > as the most informative website.

33. Tewolde W/Mariam and group, "Ba Lualawinnat Zuriya BaHiWaHat Ma/Komitee Yenabbaraw Liyunnat" <http://www.ethiopianreporter.com/magazine/htm/R38/r38pol.htm>, p. 2.

34. ibid.

35. ibid. p. 12.

36. "Seeye Abraha accuses Prime Minister," <http://www.ethiopianreporter.com/eng_newspaper/Htm/No289/r289new2.htm>

37. "Tamirat accuses Meles of gross abuse of the constitutional system," <http://www.ethiopianreporter.com/eng_newspaper/Htm/No292/r292new1.htm>

38. Tewolde W/Mariam and group, "Ba Lualawinnat Zuriya BaHiWaHat Ma/Komitee Yenabbaraw Liyunnat" <http://www.ethiopianreporter.com/magazine/htm/R38/r38pol.htm>, p. 3 - 9.

39. ibid. p. 4.

40. ibid. p. 13.

41. ibid. p. 15.

42. Tewolde Waldamariam and group, "Yemelesnnaa YeBiADen Politburo Yedibibbiqosh Drama," <http://www.ethiopianreporter.com/magazine/htm/R39/r39pol1.htm>

43. ibid. p. 2.

44. ANDM, "Ato Twolde Yayeh Inkwan Dahinaa Mattu!" http://www.ethiopianreporter.com/magazine/htm/R40/r40pol.htm, p. 10.

45. Rosa Luxemburg, *The Russian Revolution and Leninism or Marxism?* (Westport, CT: Greenwood Press, 1961), p. 85.

46. Leenco Lata, *The Ethiopian State*, p. 90.

47. Ruth Iyob, *The Eritrean struggle for independence: Domination, resistance, nationalism, 1941 – 1993* (Cambridge: Cambridge University Press, 1995), pp. 116 - 117.

48. For a list of these exchanges see Tekeste Negash and Kjetil Tronvoll, *Brothers at War*, pp. 26 - 27.

49. "Ethiopia: Trumpeting the Horn," *Africa Confidential*, 38 (9 May 1997), p. 5.

50. Rosa Luxemburg, *The Russian Revolution*, p. 69.

51. Martin Luther King, Jr, "Letter from a Birmingham Jail," in *A History of Our Time: Readings on Postwar America*, 2nd edition, eds. William H. Chafe and Harvard Sitkoff (Oxford: Oxford University Press), p. 179.

Chapter 4

A VERY PERSONAL WAR:
ERITREA ETHIOPIA 1998-2000
Alexander Last

I arrived in Eritrea's capital in February 1998, a month before my twenty-third birthday, to be the "stringer" (or freelance correspondent) for Reuters News Agency and the BBC. I was to live in the capital Asmara, a compact city with a population of about three hundred thousand. Perched on a mountainous plateau, two thousand metres above sea level, Asmara looked like a modern but pretty Italian town. Built during the days of Italian colonialism, it was famed for its stunning art deco buildings built in the twenties and thirties, for its wide boulevards where Eritreans still did the "passeggiata" in the evening, and for its coffee which was steamed through old-fashioned Italian espresso machines.

Eritrea had a wonderful if slightly dull reputation. The government was born out of the remarkable liberation movement that won independence from Ethiopia after a thirty-year war. The Eritrean Peoples Liberation Front or EPLF had defeated the vastly superior Ethiopian armies, first of Haile Selassie backed by the United States, then of Mengistu backed by the Soviet Union. From the end of the liberation war in 1991, the EPLF had become the new Eritrean government, espousing socialist values, female equality and secular government to maintain the balance in a country split equally between Christians and Muslims. There was a theoretical policy of self-reliance, to avoid becoming yet another African country racked by foreign debt. Corruption was not to be tolerated, and democracy would come in time. In the seven years since the end of the war of independence, there had been rapid development, but there were also some grumblings as to the way the old fighters were running the country. Still, all seemed relatively promising. There had been a dispute with Yemen over some islands in the Red Sea, but that was going through international arbitration. There were problems with Sudan, with whom Eritrea shared its western border. Relations which had once been excellent had deteriorated as the government in Khartoum became supportive of fundamentalist Islam. A secret war was being fought by the Eritreans against Islamic militants who were infiltrating the country from across the Sudanese border.

But most importantly, relations with Ethiopia appeared to be very good. As part of its liberation fight, the EPLF had backed an Ethiopian rebel movement, the TPLF, based to the south of Eritrea in Ethiopia's northern province of Tigray. The TPLF with Eritrean help had eventually taken the Ethiopian capital Addis Ababa just days after the EPLF had secured their own capital Asmara. Old comrades were now in charge of both their countries. Publicly at least, reconciliation and co-operation was the new policy between Ethiopia and newly independent Eritrea. Everything appeared to be going relatively well, but the two governments tended to conduct their business in secret. And beneath the surface, trouble was slowly brewing.

Bada, south-eastern Eritrea, near the Ethiopian border, May 1998.

The scorching black volcanic rocks stretched out across the desert. Sliding, then ploughing through the sand, the car headed towards a dormant volcano near the town of Bada, in Eritrea's Danakil Depression. Clouds of dust swirled around the car, the fine particles of sand coating everything and everyone sweltering inside.

Sweat, mingled with sand, trickled down my temples and collected in the white sheet I wrapped across my face as a shield from the burning wind. There had been dark clouds during the journey down from the port of Massawa. It even rained during a painful camel trek along the coast as the worst storms in recent memory had hit East Africa. Now the sun was unopposed, the temperature outside was in the mid 40s. The volcano would provide a dream-like break from the heat; in its crater was a cool lake bordered by reeds, with little fish. The crater, filled from the Red Sea by underground channels, was accessible across sand dunes which roasted sandaled feet.

Swinging the car over an irrigation channel our driver and guide, Robel, pointed to a high craggy ridge where a soldier stood silhouetted against the blue sky. "See him, he's Ethiopian" said Robel as everyone craned to see. "There's the Eritrean soldier watching him", continued Robel pointing to another ridge. Too hot to think. Eventually I asked the obvious, "What are they doing there?".

"Oh the Ethiopians came here last July", Robel went on, wrestling the steering wheel as the car went over a boulder, " most people have left Bada - when the Ethiopians came, they took it over; now most people live in Boleli nearby". Silence, in the car, followed but Robel sensing the confusion repeated what we all believed. "Don't worry , we are brothers, the governments will sort it out; it's no problem."

But that day was 6th May, 1998. The same day, several hundred kilometres away, on Eritrea's south-western border with Ethiopia, an incident took place near a village called Badme which was to become the spark for war between Eritrea and Ethiopia.

The path to war.

It was never properly explained what happened on that day near Badme. But we pieced together the Eritrean side of the story. Eritrean villagers and their Tigrayan neighbours who lived in Badme had been under the local administration of the Tigray region of Ethiopia since independence. This had been part of the interim quid pro quo between the Eritrean (EPLF) and Tigrayan (TPLF) liberation movements who now ruled the two countries: during the wars against Addis Ababa, the liberation movements would divide control of areas on a practical basis, with the border to be sorted out at some indefinite time after victory. But in Badme in the late 1990s, the Eritrean residents complained to the government in Asmara that they were being harassed by the Tigrayan authorities who were settling more Ethiopians in Badme. One resident of Badme said he had visited the government in Asmara to complain, but was told to be quiet and to go back home. Still the complaints of harassment, confiscation of livestock, burning of crops kept coming. After the Ethiopian army had occupied Bada in the south-east, and with the introduction of the new Eritrean currency, border problems started to be taken more seriously. On May 6th 1998, the Eritrean army unit in the area was asked to respond to these complaints and meet with the Tigrayan militia to resolve the problems. Such meetings were common ways of resolving disputes in border areas.

As the Eritreans walked towards Badme, they passed new stone markers that had been set up by the Ethiopian administration to mark, in their eyes, the boundary between Eritrea and Ethiopia. The Eritrean soldiers were then confronted by the local militia who ordered the soldiers to disarm, saying that they were now on Ethiopian territory. The soldiers refused, the militia opened fire, and several Eritrean soldiers were killed. One managed to escape, and made it back to the Eritrean army post. Senior officers were amongst the soldiers killed, veterans of the liberation struggle. The regular Eritrean army had by that time been whittled down from 90,000 to 35,000. Those who remained in uniform were close-knit. As a General remarked at the time, to die on the battlefield has honour, but they were killed in cold blood. Retaliation was the order of the day.

The story was not made public. Kofi Annan, the UN secretary general, was due in Asmara on the 9th of May. He arrived, met the President, and left. At the joint press conference nothing was said about any problems between

Eritrea and Ethiopia. At that time, skirmishing had been going on for several days between Ethiopian militia and small Eritrean army units. The Eritrean-Ethiopian border commission was meeting at that time in Addis Ababa. The commission had been set up after the Ethiopian army took over Bada in 1997, the place near the swimming-pool volcano. (As it turns out, this relatively insignificant area was just one of several places in dispute, stretching from the far west down to the southern tip of Eritrea near the port of Assab.) The meeting in Addis as usual was making little progress. After receiving a call from Asmara, the Eritrean delegation left Addis and returned home. Early that week, the Eritrean President, Isaias Afewerki, left for Saudi Arabia. Orders had been given.

Asmara

Decorations hung from lamp-posts, and stretched across the wide boulevards. There were strings of coloured bulbs, set in the images of camels, hearts and the number 7 - for the years since the end of the war of independence. Independence Day itself was only a couple of weeks away on the 24th of May, and the capital, Asmara, was gearing up to celebrate. The previous week, tens of thousands of Eritreans had left the cities, called up for the National Development Campaign. The intention, the government said, was to help with agricultural and development projects, while refreshing the military training of the national service reservists. Those who were called up, around forty thousand in total, had completed rounds one to four of Eritrean national service and had been returned to civilian life.

The development campaign was supposed to last a month. Before they left to report for duty, friends discussed when they would be back. Everyone joked that they would be away longer than a month. Few gave any thought to the military aspect of the programme. As far as everyone was concerned, the main thing would be planting trees, and digging terracing on Eritrea's sharp, dry mountains.

On Wednesday, 12 May, Robel arrived back in Asmara. He was a wiry, swashbuckling Eritrean, with a goatee beard, slightly wild hair and big eyes. He was in his mid-twenties, independent, intelligent and funny. He had grown up behind the lines with the ELPF liberation movement, attending the "Revolutionary School" for war orphans and the children of independence fighters. His whole family were in the EPLF, and he himself became a fighter in his late teens. He survived the war, but as in many families, his father and two brothers had been killed. Since then, Robel had managed to be demobilised and had become a guide for tourists around the country – as long as this did not clash with his other adventures. One of his Eritrean friends called him Vasco de Gama, after the wandering explorer.

He said there was some trouble in western Eritrea. He had been driving Belgian bird-watchers in the area - as it turned out, not far from Badme. He said he had seen Eritrean tanks and truck-loads of troops moving south through the area. I assumed it was a problem with Sudan - with whom Eritrea had very strained relations. No, he said, it's a problem with Ethiopia.

I was given a lift by Robel early on Thursday morning, as he embarked on his errands. We decided to visit the office of Solomon Abraha, a famous travel agent and member of the Eritrean independence movement who had lived in exile in Italy. He was a generous, intelligent, urbane man, whose enthusiasm for Eritrea was infectious. We sat and drank sweet tea, as Italian schoolteachers came in and out to book their holiday home or to organise excursions around the country with Robel. It was about eleven o'clock, when Solomon answered a phone call. He spoke in Tigrinya, but he was getting visibly irritated. He put down the phone, and said that Ethiopian Airlines had cancelled their flight to Asmara: "they say it's a problem with the GPS or something". Of all the airline companies and travel agents in Asmara, none seemed to have a single reason for the sudden end of Ethiopian Airlines flights. Some said weather, some said a homing beacon was broken, some blamed satellite problems overhead. At twelve the few journalists who were in town met at the American bar. A Reuters team was in Asmara doing happy stories about independence; together we decided to pass the information onto the Reuters office in Nairobi. Later that day, Ethiopia put out a statement, accusing Eritrea of having invaded its territory. It gave an ultimatum to Eritrea: leave, or force will be used to return Badme to Ethiopian control.

Badme, May 14, 1998

Towards Badme, the ruts left by tank tracks running parallel to the dirt road were the only evidence of the Eritrean mechanised division which had rolled into the small village on the 12th. The Eritrean army had driven the Ethiopian administration and its militia into Ethiopia - militarily effective but very heavy-handed.

Badme itself was surprisingly small, set amongst the dry scrubland of western Eritrea. An administration building stood on a small rise, exercise books and bits of paper lay strewn around outside, amongst hundreds of spent bullet casings. In the books were columns and lists. One book was full of names and numbers, and as it later turned out after translation, it detailed fines and punishments for mostly farmers for various misdemeanours. There were a few military trucks and pick-ups parked in the town, which seemed very quiet. Eritrean farmers, a priest and some elders had gathered in the shade of the tree. They spoke in grateful terms of the Eritrean army which they considered liberators. In turn they related stories, each detailing an injustice

61

that they had endured at the hands of the Ethiopian administration. Most of the Ethiopian population had left. The village was concentrated on one main street, with huts and buildings on either side, some residential, some offering dark sweet tea. Just outside town, beyond the administration building, the flat light-brown Badme plain stretched out towards the shadow of mountains some way in the distance.

Asmara again

There was frantic diplomatic activity. A peace plan was put forward by Rwanda and the United States: it called on Eritrea to withdraw from Badme to be followed by arbitration on the border. It seemed there would be some agreement. The proposal was very similar to the one the Eritrean government had put forward once the dispute became public. One sticking point was the status of the Ethiopian militia who would return to Badme in the event of an Eritrean withdrawal. But then late in May it appeared to unravel. Statements issued by the mediators, whilst in Ethiopia, created an impression in Eritrea that sides had been taken. The Eritrean leader was furious. Conflict seemed almost inevitable but everyone thought it would be over very soon. "It'll be over by Christmas", people said - one of many echoes of previous wars that resurfaced during the conflict. Eritrean veterans were called up, a sense of nationalistic excitement swept through the town. Trucks carrying veterans wound their way up from Massawa, cheered along the route. Of course some were more aware of the reality; parents and wives wept saying good bye to their sons, daughters or husbands who now went off to the army.

But no one blamed the government for the situation. One ex-fighter, on the verge of tears as he talked in his car, kept repeating, almost in whisper, "I loved the peace. We've had only seven years now this." But his anger was focused on the Ethiopians: "why", he asked, "did they want to ruin the brief, joyous years of peace?"

Zalambessa, June 3, 1998

We rose early and walked out of the hotel with its faded facade and shuttered windows onto quiet streets. The only people around were women dressed in long blue jackets and headscarves sweeping the streets with palm fronds, driving up clouds of dust which caught the first light of dawn. Other women in groups of two or three clad in white shawls walked home after church. The Landcruiser drove along the boulevards past the run-down art deco government buildings, along tarmac roads, heading south. The first destination was Senafe, an Eritrean town near the border with Ethiopia, 180 km or so by road south of the capital. Beyond Senafe, on the same road lay the twin border towns of Serha on the Eritrean side, and a bit further down a slight slope, lay Zalambessa. And beyond the border, through more mountains, the road continued to the Ethiopian towns of Adigrat and Tigray's regional capital Mekele.

I had been up to the border before, watching from Serha through binoculars as Ethiopians dug trenches a few hundred metres away on their side of the border. The strange calm days before the fighting started. Trucks rolled up to cart off the grain from the town's silos. The implications were obvious. The Eritrean General in the area went by the nom de guerre of "Wuju" - people said he was a famous soldier during the Liberation war; he had been illiterate, though later I found out he had excelled at mathematics. He was out of uniform when I first saw him, he wore a track-suit and camouflage flip flops. It was he, we were told, who had led the Eritrean forces into Badme. Now he was on Eritrea's southern border. And it was because of his reputation that we had got up that morning. We had heard reports that there had been some shelling in the south. Everyone in Eritrea was trying to guess where the war would start. Wuju's turf was a better bet than most.

A few hours after leaving Asmara we sped over the final ridge of hills and down into the valley where Senafe lay. Fields opened out to the left of the road as it came down from the ridge. A huge rock outcrop stood on the right of the road by the town; on its top a large metal cross had been erected, visible for miles around. Towers of mosques and spires of churches topped the low-built town. Most of the buildings were rectangles, white washed, their iron doors painted turquoise. The new government buildings had just been finished - a new telecommunications block, an administration building. It was there the car stopped. The administrator invited us into his room and we sat on Formica chairs. We told him we intended to go further south to where we heard there had been shelling. "That is no problem. But the war started three hours ago down the road in Zalambessa." Outside, we clambered into the car, and drove south towards the border.

The people in Senafe did not look very worried. The road followed the valley where there stood another single mountain which turned into the shape of rhinoceros horn as the car went round, up a small ridge and onto a plateau. To the left and right of the plateau, canyons plunged away hundreds of metres down. As we looked straight ahead down the road, the mountains of Ethiopia loomed in the distance; we kept driving. People who had not left earlier now carried what they could. A few pots and pans, and white food sacks strapped onto donkeys. We passed Eritrean artillery guns in small hollows off the main road. When one fired it made such a deafening crack that I thought we were being shot at. We soon were. Stupidly we had not thought that a white car would attract attention. It did, and mortars started landing in the field next to the road. Our driver stopped, as a family sprinted across the ploughed field: a mother in a light-green dress and braided hair pulling her two children alongside her. A camouflaged car pulled up, and screamed at our old driver, we turned around and followed him back to the headquarters. They said they were amused as they had watched us acting like idiots. And now we watched and listened in relative safety to the bone-shaking exchanges of artillery, and the roar of rocket launchers, interspersed with the distant crackle of machine guns. I had no idea how the battle was going. Back in Senafe the wounded started to arrive at the hospital, ferried in the back of speeding army

63

pick-ups. They had remarkably calm faces but their eyes looked quite terrified. Only a few would make any noise despite their wounds - arms, legs, heads or abdomens wrapped in white bandages, some leaking blood. Inside the hospital, in darker rooms those lightly wounded slumped against the walls.

The Eritreans won at Zalambessa. Ethiopian forces retreated south, the Eritreans followed. Visiting the town, we passed the old border post; corpses lay in the trenches we had seen being built just a few weeks before. As we learnt throughout the war, the Eritreans looked after their casualties very privately: their deaths, unlike those of their enemies, were not for the media.

A few vehicles were burning. An Ethiopian soldier lay in the middle of the road, ignored by the Eritrean soldiers who walked one way, and the displaced civilians walking the other, hauling their belongings with them. On one side of the town, several buildings had been badly damaged, their walls (such as there were) pockmarked by shrapnel. But much of the town still stood. Pepsi Cola signs decorated the walls of buildings which had been bars - a clear difference from Eritrea where Coca Cola ruled. Now, the Eritreans said, this was rightfully their town.

Asmara, 5 - 6 June, 1998

"Are we safe in Asmara?" asked a slightly anxious volunteer teacher sitting at the American bar on Asmara's main boulevard, at 2 o'clock on a Friday afternoon. The fighting had started just days before. Foreigners were called in to the capital from rural areas ready for an evacuation. "Don't worry, it's safe here". I walked off, happy with myself. Ten minutes later two Ethiopian warplanes roared low over the capital to bomb the airport.

The morning in Asmara had been quiet, there was little activity around the airport which doubled as a base for the airforce whose pilots had graduated a week before. In Asmara, people listened intently on their radios to the news of the war - 180 km by road to the south around the town of Zalambessa. The Eritreans seemed to be doing well; few had thought about air attacks.

The sound of the bombing reverberated around Asmara which stood 2-3 km to the north. As stories would reveal later, people in the high-rise buildings on the way to the airport had seen the Ethiopian jets fly past their windows.

Most of the damage was at the airforce base, where guards and technicians had been caught in the bombing. Some were killed, more were wounded. The number of military personnel who died was not released. Those figures were shrouded in Eritrea's universal black-out on any military casualty figures.

The planes came back, and this time they also hit the civilian terminal and a Zambian airliner sitting in the aircraft park. Outside, before the second raid, a group of civilians waited for the usual bus from the airport under a giant mango tree. Then came the rhythmic boom of anti-aircraft guns, and the sound of jet engines and the deafening crack of explosions. A short time later underneath the giant mango tree, a group of soldiers and police stood around. Most of the road was blocked off. Lumps of rock and earth littered the road. In the middle, the tarmac was stained by bright red fluid and little lumps of pink matter. A man with a piece of cardboard was scraping what was left of human flesh off the road, flicking it into a sack There were no bodies on the road, most had been taken away to hospital, but one man lay under a white sheet in the verge amongst some bushes. When the Ethiopian jets began strafing the civilian airport, they started their firing a little early. It had cut through those waiting for the bus under the mango tree.

Eritrean planes, in retaliation for the bombing of the airport, bombed the Tigrayan town of Mekele four times. Dozens of civilians, mostly children, were killed when Eritrean bombs struck a school building. The horrendous carnage was replayed on the international news. The Eritrean pilots had graduated a week before. They themselves had all grown up at the EPLF "Revolutionary school" behind the lines during the war of liberation. As children they had been bombed, and bombed again. All the pilots said it was a mistake.

The bombing of Asmara airport had a remarkable effect on the population. Instead of cowering inside their homes, people poured onto the streets towards the airport, to see if they could do anything to help. Then came the news that one of the raiding planes had been shot down. In the streets people danced, ululated, celebrating - unconcerned if the Ethiopian planes returned. Others sped out of town using every form of transport available in the hope of picking up a souvenir from the downed MiG.

The Ethiopian airforce bombed the airport again on Saturday but this time the Eritreans did not retaliate. The Ethiopians lost another plane in the raid. It was flown by the Ethiopian pilot Bezabir Petros. He was well known to the Eritreans as he had been shot down before during the war of independence. Then, he was captured by the EPLF. He converted to their cause and spent much of the war campaigning for the liberation movements. After the war he returned to Ethiopia, where he again became a senior figure in the Ethiopian airforce. The new Eritrean and Ethiopian governments had military co- operation agreements, some Eritrean pilots trained in Ethiopia, some Ethiopian trainers lived in Eritrea. They knew each other very well.

When Bezabir made his way unceremoniously to Eritrean soil in 1998, he was rescued by the Eritrean military from angry villagers. He was placed in a car and driven back to Asmara. As he was driven up the avenue, people saw who it was sitting in the back of the car. The news of his capture spread like wild fire, people celebrated. Then came a procession of vehicles which had

65

managed to salvage bits of the plane; one pick-up sped up and down the main avenue, hooting its horn, with a huge aircraft tail fin in the back, along with ecstatic Eritreans waving flags. Bezabir himself was driven into detention, and later spent some time in a military hospital before returning to prison. It is believed that he has since died, but the Eritrean government has refused to confirm or deny the reports.

The effect of the bombing on the foreign community was immediate and quite different. People flocked to the embassies, to sign themselves up for evacuation - an expensive airlift to safety (several western governments charged for the evacuation). The Ethiopian government gave a deadline for the foreigners to leave, after which they said Asmara would be flattened. The expats did leave, some reluctantly, some virtually sprinted for the aircraft. Many of those departing were rather drunk, after quaffing gin and tonic inside embassy grounds while waiting for news of their flight out. Diplomatic officials were either remarkably calm or on the point of breakdown - darting here and there, clutching clip boards, trying to marshall their charges. By the early hours of Sunday morning the evacuation was more or less complete - save for a few Koreans who were left stranded at the airport. The city was quiet, people stayed at home waiting for the bombing. Journalists were camped on the roof of the city's Sunshine Hotel. But no planes came. It would be two years before the Ethiopian planes revisited Asmara.

Many Eritreans were appalled that the foreigners had all gone. It was a sign that the bad times had come again, but there was also real anger and a feeling that they had been let down. One Eritrean businesswoman complained: "you foreigners are happy to drive your Landcruisers and offer help when there is peace, but as soon as there is trouble, when we need help, all of you run away". Those who stayed behind were made to feel especially welcome and privileged to be there. As the World Cup started, people in Asmara relaxed; the fighting was more or less finished for the time being. The city immediately returned to its quiet, laid-back lifestyle, somewhat removed from the war. The two governments, meanwhile, started buying weapons in earnest.

Escalation

The war was not all over by Christmas, as some had predicted. Both Western and Orthodox celebrations had passed. Everyone awaited the next inevitable offensive; bitterness was growing. Just after the fighting subsided in June 1998, the Ethiopian government began a policy of rounding up and deporting those living in Ethiopia who were of Eritrean ethnic origin. The Ethiopian government said it was a security measure. The policy had huge implications, as Eritreans and Ethiopians had lived together and intermarried for years. The policy was denounced as a violation of human rights.

66

The deportation of ethnic Eritreans from Ethiopia was having an impact on Asmara. Many of the first Eritreans to be rounded up, herded onto buses and deported, were the elite. The well educated and wealthy, whose fortunes now depended on how much money they had outside Ethiopia. Many lost everything, and struggled to come to terms with the loss of a lifetime of work. In the countryside, the rural deportees lived in camps or with relatives across the border. They too had lost their homes, their possessions, and crucially their livestock, confiscated before they were sent across the border. The sense of bitterness was very real, in part because no one had imagined that deportation would happen. Eritreans would sometimes mutter that even the former Ethiopian dictator, Mengistu, had never done it. But then again his priorities were different.   Many of those deported did not speak Tigrinya, and many felt more Ethiopian than Eritrean. Many of the young who grew up in the towns and cities of Ethiopia were torn between regret for their lives taken away and a desire not to show that they missed anything in Ethiopia. Addis styles came to Asmara from dresses to dance, the 'Electric Slide' hit the night club dance floors. Since the start of the war, Eritreans would speak of their historic dislike of the Tigrayans of northern Ethiopia. "We never trusted them"… "We helped them and see what they have done to us" were almost standard responses. Then there was the general belief, espoused strongly by the Eritrean deportees, that Ethiopia's majority ethnic groups, the Amhara and Oromo, would remove the minority Tigrayans from power. In all, a rapid transformation from the words of brotherly love repeated about Ethiopia in the months that preceded the war.

Despair and real animosity towards Ethiopia first showed itself publicly following the loss of Badme. In February, the Ethiopians had launched their offensive, on both the western and central fronts. The fighting started a day after the Ethiopian government claimed an Eritrean aircraft had bombed the town of Adigrat - though people contacted in the town were unaware of ever being bombed. (The reality was that on a training flight, an unarmed Eritrean fighter had strayed close to the border and had been damaged but not downed by an Ethiopian anti-aircraft missile.) In Asmara the Ethiopian story could only mean one thing: the Ethiopian offensive was about to start. Across Asmara the dogs howled that night as if they knew what was coming.

For the first two weeks, the Eritreans held on. They claimed they had inflicted heavy losses on Ethiopia. And when Ethiopia claimed territorial success, western journalists were on hand at the front on the Eritrean side to disprove the stories.

On the frontlines the Eritrean army in the west became even more confident and launched its own counter attacks. In the space of twenty-four hours, the situation changed. Ethiopia attacked an under-manned part of the line, and broke through. The Eritrean options were clear, move the entire line back to safer positions, or fight it out with high casualties. The Eritreans pulled back, Badme was left. The effect of the loss of Badme on the population of Asmara was quite devastating. Throughout the city, people sat in groups, heads in hands, talking quietly. It was as if everyone had lost a close friend or relative. Young and old people who had not been called up talked of volunteering. It was the first time since Independence that the Eritrean army had lost. Older veterans tried to explain to the young, and partly to convince themselves, that they had faced defeats or withdrawals in the past but in the end had been victorious. In a strange way, most of the people I talked to that day were worried that the war was over, that this was the way it was to end. The Eritrean government had over-night accepted the peace deal that it had so long balked at signing. As the day wore on, more and more people called to see if we had any information from Ethiopia as to its response to the loss of Badme and Eritrea's acceptance of the peace. Finally Reuters came back and said Ethiopia was not available to comment. In Asmara, people looked around and sensed what it meant. The war would go on. "Fine;" people said, "now we will show them." Then the war could end.

Igremekel, near Tsorona, Central Front, 110 km south of Asmara, March 1999

As I walked across the flat dry land towards the front line, thick black smoke rose into the blue sky. Looking down, the dusty ground sparkled with thousands of sharp lumps of shrapnel, the aftermath of 4 days of intensive shelling. The light blue tail fins of two unexploded Ethiopian bombs stuck out of the ground 50 metres apart. This was Igremekel on the Tsorona front.

At the earthworks, which marked the front-line trench, Eritrean soldiers sat around, smoking cigarettes, chatting happily. Many looked exhausted, the fighting had raged day and night. A few Ethiopian corpses lay behind the earthworks, but that was nothing compared to the sight that awaited me as I walked through a gap in the front line. On my immediate right, in a space of about 10 yards, fifteen Ethiopian soldiers lay dead on and around the earthworks, some were lying in the trench dug into the ground in front of the mounds of earth. Looking along the trench in both directions, the bodies continued. Some were half buried, some had heads missing, some were bloated, killed in the first wave of attacks two days before, some had only died that morning. All had a thin layer of orange dust on the faces, as the wind blew swirling gusts around the trench. How did we know they were Ethiopian? Firstly many wore distinctive Ethiopian uniform; they also wore boots, unlike most Eritrean soldiers. Secondly most were dead on top of the trenches, in positions which suggested they were attacking, and most convincingly, the Eritrean soldiers were very happy to point out any corpses that journalists didn't see. "Look there's one" was a common remark. It's very unlikely that the soldiers would take such pleasure in pointing bodies of their dead friends. The Eritrean dead had already been removed.

I saw at least three hundred Ethiopian dead in two hundred metres, during a brief walk along the trench. At least one every metre. The bodies did not stop after 200 metres, they continued as far as I could see. I just became sick of counting, and time was against us, it was getting late in the afternoon, journalists were anxious to file the story. The army was also getting worried as machine gun and artillery exchanges continued intermittently, the attacks had only stopped 6 hours before. Many more Ethiopian corpses lay in the flat scrub land that was no mans land, which stretched back 3 km to the starting point of the assault.

The horrific thought, which would not leave me, was that these three hundred Ethiopian dead were the ones that had actually made it across the 3 km to this small part of the line while under constant artillery, tank, mortar, machine gun and even rifle fire. The area of the fiercest fighting covered 15 sq. kms, yet I only saw 200 metres. If one extrapolates from what we saw, the Ethiopian casualty figures would easily be in the thousands.

The Ethiopian army was using First World War tactics, with First World War results. Mass slaughter for no ground gained, where human losses did not seem to matter, under the terrible military rationale that since the population of Ethiopia is 60 million, 17 times larger than Eritrea's population, therefore mass attacks must work.

Looking at the carnage, I remembered when I was in Asmara a few weeks before and I met Eritrean soldiers who had been fighting at the Badme front: they would become very depressed talking about the fighting. "It's just slaughter", they would tell me, "we shoot all day, they die, then more come; it's sick."

My mind snapped back to Tsorona. There was too much to take in, bodies to avoid stepping on. No mans land in front of this small section of the line was littered with the burnt remnants of at least twenty Ethiopian tanks, their barrels pointing towards Eritrean positions. Some had been hit just yards from the front line. Two Ethiopian bulldozers lay burning - not what I thought would be used in an attack. Armoured personnel carriers had also been hit, one actually made it on top of the Eritrean trench before being destroyed. There were more; I could see objects in the bush that looked like tanks or APCs, but I did not count them.

The Eritrean soldiers still in position had tissues stuffed up their noses because of the smell of decomposing corpses: "we had no time to bury them", sighed an Eritrean female soldier, stationed on the front, her hair hidden by a khaki bandanna. Fighting had continued for three days and two nights, the bodies piling up around the Eritrean positions, the smell of death getting stronger. The Eritrean commanders said their losses had been very light in comparison. But for those in the front line, the defence had clearly been desperate, even some hand-to-hand fighting. Heavy losses were inescapable.

Days after the trip to the front, when all the media interest died down, with no more TV pictures to show, I still could not get the images out of my mind. Occasionally I could again smell the sickly sweet stench of decaying bodies. The depressing thought was that the scene we had witnessed would be repeated. I thought about the Organisation of African

Unity in Addis Ababa, the sponsors of the peace plan, who had still said nothing about the continued slaughter taking place 600 km north of their headquarters. And I thought about the claims that what we saw was just a publicity stunt, and this only made the thousands of lives lost seem even more pointless. If this war is to end, the public - especially in Ethiopia and Eritrea - must be aware of the reality of this bloody conflict. My personal fear is that for most people, the truth about what happened will be buried by the sand which now covers the bodies of those who died in a futile battle on Eritrea's southern border.

I wrote these words in March 1999, a few days after the battle. It was perhaps the defining moment of the war for me. What we witnessed that day seemed to epitomise so much about the fighting: the large number of casualties, the nature of the battle, the fact that so few people were on hand to report the slaughter, and the general frustration that so little was happening to end the war. That battle was important in its own sake. It came a month after the Eritreans lost the village of Badme, the psychological sore of the conflict. Its aftermath could be read in two ways: the Eritreans had inflicted enough of a defeat that peace was now acceptable - or it was just a foretaste of more to come. The battlefield itself became the Eritrean government's showpiece for visiting journalists. In time, all that remained of the battle were rusting hulks of the Ethiopian tanks and a few human bones or skeletons left in the minefields.

When I went back not long after the battle, the personal effects of the dead soldiers were still there amongst the debris. On all the battlefields during the war, it was this that would move me most, when the number of dead in itself was no longer so shocking. Strewn around were memories of the lives lost. Some items stick out more than others. Photos of a soldier with his friends and family, taken before the battles began, posing with his gun. And a notebook in which one soldier, from Nazareth in Ethiopia, had began to write a diary in English, describing his life in school and work The final sentence was unfinished.

While peace was being negotiated...

After the battle at Igremekel, the fronts returned to relative calm, but the peace negotiations continued with a different slant. Ethiopia swapped roles with Eritrea as the country that had been accepting a truce in principle, yet refusing it in practice. The deportations continued and became almost normal.

In Eritrea, mass mobilisation picked up pace, more rounds of national service were drafted and sent off to the military training camp at Sawa. The sweeps for draft dodgers increased as well. National service applied to men and women between the ages of 18 and 40. Some people were exempt, for example mothers did not serve. But the exemptions for men were few and the government continually tightened the regulations. The effect of mass mobilisation on Eritrea was drastic. The capital was rapidly drained of younger Eritreans. The economy suffered through a diminished workforce and because the people on National Service would only get 150 Nakfa a month pocket money (approximately $15.00). The Nakfa was rapidly depreciating against the dollar, and Eritrea relied almost exclusively on imports. The main income keeping the country afloat came from the loyal Diaspora, in remittances to families and the government. A subculture of how to avoid the draft began to develop and has grown dramatically since the end of the war. It should be said that most people simply went when called, but some really did not want to go. Either they did not want to be in the army, felt they had already been in for long enough, or their families desperately needed them at home to run the business and earn some real money. People became very adept at hiding. There was an informal system of passing information as to when there would be a sweep of military police. The greatest resistance came to the drafting of women. It had always been present amongst some rural Islamic communities in Eritrea, but resistance slowly spread to towns and cities. Concerns were raised especially after stories circulated of sexual harassment, rape, or extra-marital relations and pregnancies out of wedlock. All were considered socially unacceptable in Eritrea's traditional Christian and Islamic communities. The stories were common enough for the government to act, though without making any public statement. Many Eritrean female soldiers were withdrawn from the front after the fighting in 1999 following on complaints from families, but women continued to be drafted for National Service. Part of the problem was that most of the female veterans from the war of independence were no longer in the army because they had become mothers. Key role models had gone.

In between the offensives, the war never seemed far away. Ethiopian aircraft bombed the port of Massawa, destroying a workshop in the port and killing one man who had turned up early for work. The planes bombed the military camp at Sawa and the southern town of Mendefera, where a radar station was located. The small town of Adi Keih was hit one lunchtime, and the local Church was badly damaged. People there said the church had drawn the bombs away from the nearby school. The second Independence Day since the start of the war came and went, with a feeling of false bonhomie. The parties went ahead, the full-scale, Korean-style mass formation dancing took place. But the crowds on the streets were visibly younger than the previous year. So many young men and women were now in the army. Within a month, fighting had restarted, concentrated in western Eritrea. We made our preparations and left for the front.

Elala, Western Front, June 1999

Up the dry slopes, past Ethiopian corpses, turned yellow after lying in the sun since March, we walked to the rough-hewn rock trenches. The hills below extended on all sides. From Hill 1162, the Eritreans had moved forward several kilometres to the last line of hills before the disputed area of Badme. Beyond the ridge, the flat plains of Badme dropped away. Occasionally, the faint whistling of an Eritrean artillery volley could be heard passing overhead, the flash of impact on the ridge beyond marking Ethiopian front line positions. The sound of the explosion would follow seconds later and echo around the hills. It was a quiet day on this section of the front.

Away to the right, however, Eritrean and Ethiopian forces had been fighting since the morning. Artillery from both sides were pounding each other as the infantry scrambled for better positions on high ground. "The fighting has never stopped, it just cooled", explained Colonel Berhane Ogbagober. He said Eritrean forces on all sides of the 50 km-long, u-shaped front line had advanced, some up to six kilometres. The Ethiopians were attempting to retake lost ground, while the Eritreans were trying to make further gains. Many of the hills now being contested had been irrelevant before Eritrean forces were forced to pull back from positions they held on the Ethiopian side of the Badme plains at the end of February. To reach secure ground on Hill 1162, the Eritreans had retreated 17 km. Now hill by hill they were moving forward again.

We had arrived on the front that morning, driving across a ford in the Gash river, as the first rains swept water down from the highlands into the wide rivers of western Eritrea. Soldiers were working in the shallows trying to shore up the ford. They laboured with their combat trousers rolled up, stripped to the waist, or wearing white vests. Further on down the river, herdsmen with cut off trousers and white shawls, accompanied by children and small, angry-looking dogs marshalled oxen across the river. The front was not far. We drove for twenty minutes on winding dirt tracks, flanked by tall date palms with razor sharp fronds. Our Landcruiser pulled up the usual cloud of white dust, which trailed the car - rains had not arrived in the lowlands yet. We conducted our initial tour of the front with Colonel Berhane, a smallish man with a kind round face. He seemed intelligent and honest, thankfully not a politician. He wore a peaked camouflage cap, and a khaki shirt, which strained with his belly. The years of peace had not been too bad.

We arrived back at the camp that evening. It was the headquarters of an artillery battalion on the western front. The camp was spread amongst small hills. A few eucalyptus trees dotted what had been a little village. The residents had long since fled, now living under plastic sheeting in large camps for displaced people which dotted western and central Eritrea.

Few soldiers lived in the small number of huts that still stood. Their homes were the dug-outs cut into the sides of the small hills. Log lintels supported the entrances, outside shell casings and red Coca Cola crates lay around. The soldiers, with thin young faces and cropped hair, were dressed as usual with the mixture of camouflage - the brown "desert storm" and "jungle" green. Several wore T-shirts emblazoned with pictures of Princess Diana, the lyrics to "Candle in the wind" printed on the back. Two Eritrean friends had joined us on the trip. They both grew up abroad and had returned to Eritrea to do national service. Since the war they had been stationed in Asmara, and were desperate to find out what happened to their friends - not seen since they had completed basic training at Sawa.

Also with us was Hagos, an old fighter who worked with the Ministry of Foreign Affairs, and was in charge of liaison with journalists. Yet he was helpful – full of knowledge, humour, and a desire for us to see as much as possible. He had fought at Elala during the liberation war, some twenty years before. Like many of our trips it turned into a bit of a reunion. In Eritrea, military experience bonded young and old. Robel had brought letters and gifts, including cakes, from Asmara. Sweet tea was drunk inside the bunkers lit by kerosene lamps, the walls covered by empty wheatsacks. Conversation switched to who was where, what was happening on different fronts. Finding out who was alive or dead would be done more privately.

Walking in single file through dry riverbeds we made our way to the front line. The crackle of machine guns could be heard. Robel stopped to pick up a piece of shrapnel that littered the parched ground. "If you already have a piece, you won't get hit by another", he explained. I followed his logic, putting a jagged lump of brown metal into my pocket.

Closer to the lines, a few Ethiopian corpses lay unburied, a week old, the smell of decay overwhelming. Others were partly covered by sand. Many rocks were stained by dry blood, the thorny branches of some trees were hung with torn, bloodstained fatigues, the ground littered by contents of knapsacks. In one bush lay an arm, camouflaged, with stiff dark fingers protruding from the cuff. In total, I counted thirty Ethiopian dead during the walk to the line. It was impossible to tell from this whether the claims of over 20,000 casualties made by either side were true. The Eritrean soldiers scoffed at Ethiopian claims about the number of Eritreans killed. "We don't even have that many on the entire front line", said one.

We crawled to the final Eritrean positions. Eritrean soldiers leant into the rocks, makeshift protection from snipers, whose bullets had scratched the rocks white. The front line was new. There had not been time or security to build trenches. The soldiers stared intently at the Ethiopian positions just 50 metres away. They said Eritrean snipers had killed four Ethiopians that morning. The tension was high. Robel, for the first time, seemed worried. The fighting had not reached this section of the line, but just an hour after we left, it did.

We had walked, and crawled, to the front dressed in Eritrean army hats or jackets. They did not want the Ethiopians to know that the front had "guests". We had argued about the issue of proper front-line attire since the start of the war and in the end we accepted the local school of thought: the sight of a journalist in traditional "I am a civilian" colours (bright blue, pink, yellow), though commendable, was certain to draw fire. Unsurprisingly this was not welcome by soldiers on the line, especially as the Ethiopians knew that an officer would accompany any journalists, which made the group an even more tempting target.

As night drew in, the wind picked up and rain clouds approached. Soldiers at a camp

73

in a village behind the lines ran into shelters dug into the hillside, illuminated by the fires for making tea. The rain was expected to stop the fighting but no soldier was confident that it would. As the rain fell, the shelling did subside, until 11 o'clock that night. Then Ethiopian gunners decided to say good night to their Eritrean counterparts, sending volleys of shells over the camp, waking us from a brief sleep. The Eritrean guns answered, then fell silent for a few hours as other parts of the front became the target.

The next morning, the sound of artillery never stopped. A column of Eritrean troops appeared over a hill behind the camp and snaked its way past us towards the front. They walked silently in single file, their eyes ignoring all around them. Kalashnikovs, machine guns or RPGs were slung over their shoulders. A few carried rolled up stretchers, or a long, wrapped bundle, a carefully protected sniper rifle. All wore the coloured twisted Kerchuf, which doubled as a bed sheet and a burial shroud; it was twisted into a kind of rope and dangled from the army belt, or was worn diagonally across the chest.

Further back, behind the lines, soldiers relaxed, ignoring the constant boom of the artillery battle. They ate breakfast and drank tea while listening to reggae, sometimes slowed by the dying batteries in the cassette player. Only the jolting crack of Eritrean guns occasionally broke the strangely peaceful atmosphere. An Eritrean soldier with long dreadlocks spoke as we ate breakfast. He was from Germany, he said, but had been picked up in Asmara and sent for military training. He had dual nationality; no one, he sighed, cared about his German passport. He looked resigned to his fate. As we got up to leave he turned and said smiling, "one love, one heart, peace". Peace, though, still seemed a long way away.

Our final trip to Elala was the following year, just a couple of months before the third round of fighting. We visited a slightly different section of the line. This time there were more journalists, more government control and no Colonel Berhane who was back at his HQ. The Eritrean advances of the previous June had not succeeded in getting back the good positions required for a solid defensive line on the western front. We had learned that the fighting the previous June had resulted in heavy losses for Eritrea. We never knew the number, but clearly being on the offensive always took its toll. No one at the front would talk about such things. Instead, all the talk was about the Ethiopian build-up opposite.

Even though there had not yet been a major offensive, it was clear that the killing on the front had never stopped. Often soldiers in the front would be obliged to crawl out of their trenches on night patrols - through no mans land to the Ethiopian trenches, to raid or just to listen. Any movement would result in a barrage of fire, even from Dushka heavy-calibre machine guns; normally used against aircraft, they can have a devastating effect on a human body.

But there were still some lighter moments. The soldiers with great pride offered us fresh vegetables and salad they had grown behind the lines; part of the Eritrean army's drive for self-sufficiency. A commander talked of being a farmer after the war. A soldier tried to make traditional coffee, but was shooed away by a young woman, one of the few who remained at the front. She was the unit's medic. Apparently medics had a relatively short life expectancy, the third-best target for a sniper after an officer and the radio operator.

During the final phase of the war, we tried to find out what had happened to those at Elala. I was told that the front was under constant air and artillery bombardment, which had been more accurate than anyone had expected. There were casualties but the order had been given for the fronts to be evacuated following the Ethiopian breakthrough to the east, at Enda Amba Simon. I met Colonel Berhane after the war during celebrations to mark the anniversary of the liberation of Massawa in 1990. Robel found that the medic with the coffee had survived. We did not know about the German Eritrean with the dreadlocks.

Away from the war

After the first year of the war, it had dawned on most people that there was little chance of a diplomatic solution - a final military showdown was the only way it would end. But away from the fronts, society had again adapted to make the conflict seem normal. In Asmara, most foods were still available except for the grain teff which was used in the making of the traditional flat bread, injera. (Teff was grown mainly in Ethiopia, and had to be imported by an expensive, circuitous route). The problem was that inflation was considerable, running at roughly thirty percent. Prices continued to rise as Eritrea's currency, the Nakfa, weakened further against the US dollar. Outside the capital, the agricultural outlook was bleak. Poor rains dealt another blow to farmers, already affected by the loss of workers due to the draft. On top of this, at least three hundred thousand Eritreans displaced by the fighting were making do in sprawling tent camps spread throughout the country. The displaced were reliant on hand-outs from the Eritrean government's humanitarian wing (ERREC), the United Nations and the foreign NGOs who had been allowed back into the country. The camps themselves were remarkably organised - divided along the lines of the towns and villages from which the displaced had fled. Schools were set up, run in shifts to accommodate the huge number of children. The displaced were being given food but needed more. There was access to some health facilities, but many living out in the dusty windswept camps had developed illnesses and infections, and were at risk of malaria after the rains. The problem, as far as a cynical international media was concerned, was that though the conditions were bad, they were not bad enough to warrant any special attention. The authorities in Eritrea were organised enough to prevent a humanitarian catastrophe of the kind witnessed in other developing countries. The generosity and dignity of the people in the camps was staggering to an outsider. Despite living with virtually nothing, the old custom of hospitality would be respected - offering visitors coffee or bread. Many used what meagre resources they had to buy basic commodities from nearby towns, and then sell them in the camps. Each camp had its own plastic tent version of a high street.

In the towns of Eritrea, though emptied of civilians by national service, there was also a degree of normality. Football matches continued, as the government exempted first-division players from national service. Cycling races, perhaps Eritreans' favourite sport, also took place. One of the country's leading cyclists, Yonas Zakarias, was removed from his army unit on the Western front by a concerned, cycling-devoted General and sent back to Asmara, so that he could continue to compete.

The music of the war also went through some changes. Already most Eritrean singers, with a few exceptions, would sing songs about sacrifice and the liberation struggle. Of course, the old favourites from the liberation war were replayed on the radio. For the military, Eritrea's top musicians would tour the country playing to soldiers stationed around Eritrea, as they had during the liberation war. Most musicians devoted their songs to supporting the war effort. At the beginning of the war, a former fighter known as Wadi Tokul released a new album, which contained the Tigrinya hits "Sawa", about the national military training centre, and "Teshamo", meaning "come on, let's get on with it". Perhaps the most disturbing song was sung by an Eritrean comedian, the basic refrain of which was translated as "Are You Happy Now?" The video for the song showed the singer dressed in camouflage (which was considered de rigeur), superimposed onto footage of battles, and grisly close-ups of dead or captured Ethiopians. Eritreans remarked, with a smile, that after the loss of Badme, the Ethiopian radio had played the song back to the Eritreans. Not to be outdone, after the Eritrean victory at Igremekel, Asmara again broadcast the song, this time with more up-to-date footage. And thankfully there it appeared to end. During the later stages of the war, though, other songs moved in to replace the original hits, perhaps because these smacked of the slight naiveté and bravado of the early days of the conflict, before reality had set in. Despite the war, Amharic songs, though Ethiopian, were also quite popular. Perhaps because they were just good tunes, or because they would be songs about love and not fighting. No doubt the influx of Eritrean deportees from Addis Ababa had an impact too. But in music, at least, it was difficult to lose the pre-war ties between the two countries.

The final offensive, May/June 2000

A delegation from the UN Security Council led by Richard Holbrooke visited both Addis Ababa and Asmara in a last-ditch attempt to stop the war. It was clear when they left on 10 May 2000 that a new offensive was imminent. On the 12th of May, exactly two years after the Eritrean army first went into Badme, the Ethiopians unleashed their final offensive. They attacked in the west, but at a point no one had expected. Around one hundred thousand infantry, aided by pack animals, gathered in Tigray province just over the border- their presence apparently unknown to Eritrean intelligence.

The Ethiopian army set out across a dry river bed and up steep mountains, where Eritrean defences were virtually non-existent. Calls for reinforcements were ignored, though critics say a small number of well armed and supported troops could have held such a pass, which was steep enough to prevent Ethiopian heavy weapons being brought in with the advance. But even if the Ethiopian troops had made it into Eritrea, they would certainly have been in a precarious position had Ethiopian tanks not been able to break through and link up. The Eritreans thought they could hold the rest of the line and stop the tanks. They could not. Eventually with the line breaking at various junctions the order was given to pull back. Some Eritrean troops retreated north, to block the way to the symbolic regional capital in Western Eritrea, Barentu, while others retreated to the east towards the highlands. The Ethiopian army, facing limited resistance, moved North at a rapid rate and closed in on Barentu. As it turned out, the move to Barentu was a mistake. The bulk of the Eritrean army did not stand and fight on the plains of western Eritrea where, in the face of Ethiopian superiority on the ground and in the air, the Eritrean army would have been decimated. It did though suffer a crisis of identity. Clearly the Eritrean army was not an army of national defence, which would hold ground at all costs. It was being run in part like the old EPLF: giving up land to fight another day. The difficulty soldiers were facing was highlighted by the case of four senior officers, who refused to pull out of the defence of Barentu. They were old liberation fighters who had been through it all, but who as defenders of the new independent Eritrea, would not countenance further withdrawals. The story goes that they sent the rest of their soldiers back as the government had ordered, but they themselves and some of their bodyguards made a last stand on the outskirts of Barentu. I was told that all but one was killed.

In the end, Ethiopia took control of almost a third of the country, but the advance north to Barentu gave the Eritreans time to reorganise the defence of the highlands, where the capital Asmara was located.

The government refused journalists permission to go West or South towards the front. Old travel permits were tried and they worked through

77

some road-blocks but would eventually be questioned, so we would be forced to turn round. In Asmara, new information was flooding in, but for many people, the news mutated under the pressure of rumour and hope. There was often talk that "the Eritreans had counter attacked", "the Ethiopians were cut off and surrounded", "it was all an elaborate plan by the President". The reality took a while to sink in. The news of the fall of Barentu was not anticipated by most of the population. Still people clung to hope; the Eritrean army would not let this happen. The news broadcast by the government was more bizarre - stories about national development, not much about the war. Surely this was enough of a clue. Then one evening five days after the offensive had started, an announcement was made at the very end of the nightly broadcast. Barentu had fallen. It had a catastrophic effect on the people of Asmara, as the reality of what was happening in the West was finally brought home. People had been stocking up on fuel, but now there was a more urgent sense of impending disaster. From Barentu it was not far, east across the plains, to Eritrea's second city, Keren.

The government also missed an opportunity to show the humanitarian cost of the fighting in the West. Without foreign journalists, the bombing of Eritrean villages and towns in the path of the Ethiopian advance went unreported. For four days and nights, Ethiopian aircraft had hit Barentu itself. There were reports of up to sixty civilians killed, many more wounded, in one raid alone. It was impossible at the time to corroborate. The Eritrean army held the town long enough for the civilian population to be evacuated, then it too fell back.

Throughout western Eritrea, hundreds of thousands were on the move. Displaced people living in camps fled North, away from the advancing Ethiopians. Those who had considered themselves safe were inundated with people fleeing the fighting. Then as the boom of artillery came close, they too set out on foot with the few belongings they could carry. Most went East towards Keren, along the flat plains where temperatures were approaching 40 degrees and water was scarce. The civilians were mainly women, children and the elderly; the men were in the army. Some military vehicles stopped to give assistance, but in general transport was very limited. Those who made it to the new makeshift camps around Keren told of scores of people dying by the roadside.

In Asmara there was a growing feeling that the city was under siege. Yet typically the preparations and rehearsals went ahead as planned for the Independence anniversary on the 24th May. The Ethiopians were advancing towards Mendefera in the highlands. Mendefera was only about an hour from the capital and if the Ethiopians made it into the highlands at that point Asmara would surely fall. Hourly, vehicles running through the capital from one front to the other would disgorge the latest news that would spread through the city.

The fall of Barentu had at least psychologically prepared people for the worst. There was some thought given to what would happen if the Ethiopians broke through to Asmara. A return to Nakfa for another long-drawn-out war was an option that was terrifyingly realistic in the minds of many. But an uglier side to the growing paranoia was soon evident. Thousands of Ethiopians had been repatriated during the war, though initially they were not rounded up and stripped of their possessions in the same way as Eritreans had been in Ethiopia. But in some parts of the country, such as western Eritrea, there was popular pressure on the authorities to remove Ethiopians from the area. This was done in various ways: many employers refused to give Ethiopians work, who then became destitute. Many opted simply to return to Ethiopia and were repatriated by the International Committee of the Red Cross. Some were imprisoned as spies. The Eritrean government publicly called for tolerance of Ethiopians and despite tighter regulations on Ethiopian residents, there was still a large number of Ethiopians in Eritrea by the time of the offensive in 2000 - fifty thousand, maybe more. It seemed a considerable number considering that so many Eritreans were away from home in the armed forces. More importantly, a few did work for Ethiopian intelligence. Intercepted transmissions to Ethiopian aircraft would give precise details of troop movements, including the time a convoy left a town. Though this information was not public at the time, there was, in any case, a growing popular fear of an Ethiopian "fifth column" in Eritrea: Ethiopian civilians living amongst the community waiting for the moment when the Ethiopian army came near before striking from within. Ethiopian young men were rounded up and placed in camps around the capital - in some cases for their own protection as Ethiopians became targets for abuse and, on some occasions, physical attack. But these events were relatively rare.

As the Ethiopian advance in the West appeared to halt, attention in Asmara shifted almost entirely towards what was happening on the central front South of the capital. The greatest concern focussed specifically on the situation on the approaches to Mendefera, from the South at Adi Quala, from the West at Mai Duma and Areza, and from the East through the Hazemo plain. The Ethiopians attacked from these three directions. Troops were diverted to the area from other fronts. Most of the convoys moved at night to avoid air attacks.

In the shade of trees outside Mendefera hundreds of soldiers from one convoy lay in the shade of eucalyptus trees. Almost all were sleeping, covered in dust, they had been driven all the way from the western front on a roundabout route to pick up the fight again on the slopes of the highlands. Along the road south from Asmara, Eritrean civilians cooked food and the slightly alcoholic traditional brew of Suwa. The convoys would slow to allow the food and Suwa to be passed up to the soldiers packed into open trucks, festooned with yellow plastic Jerry cans. The women would ululate and clap. The young, exhausted soldiers their heads wrapped in their all-purpose Kerchufs, would manage a smile or a wave. An old, thin man and his plump greying wife, her hair neatly braided stood with other villagers watching. There was a shout from the convoy, "Mama... mama", they both looked up, a soldier balanced on top of crates of supplies waved at the couple. They burst out calling his name, waving maniacally, moving unconsciously towards the departing truck. They kept waving as the truck rolled out along the tarmac road towards the front. "It's the first time I have seen him in two years", the mother explained. They both continued to look South, with tears in their eyes.

The Ethiopian army did not manage to break through on that section of the line, but the situation was clearly desperate.

Former liberation leaders who were involved in a fierce argument with the President over his conduct of the war and their exclusion from it, had travelled to the fronts themselves to see what they could do to help. Petros Solomon, Mesfin Hagos and Ogbe Abraha went to front-line commanders to help devise a defensive line in the South. One of the three, Petros Solomon, was still a minister in the government and had been one of the chief strategists during the war of independence. Mesfin Hagos was one of the top Generals during that war and during the peace had been the Minister of Defence but was then moved to be Governor of the Southern region. Ogbe Abraha had been Chief of Staff in the Eritrean military, but he had fallen foul of the President. These were not minor people. Word of the split within the leadership was starting to become known, mainly amongst Eritrea's key western allies at the Italian and American embassies. As it turned out, the divisions within the leadership had gone back years to pre-war days. Conduct of foreign policy, the internal power of the President, and the time table for elections were all points of friction. But the war was exacerbating the internal debate. There was even talk of a possible coup as the military situation looked to be out of control. But even opponents of the President said this was never seriously considered; unity was still the paramount concern. And so the divisions were never put on public display until after the war was over.

The Assab plain
One of the other senior figures in dispute with the President, the Eritrean foreign minister, Haile Woldensae was trying to get the United States to put pressure on the Ethiopians to stop their offensive. The Ethiopian government had said it would consider stopping if Eritrea withdrew from all areas it

considered were in "dispute". This demand would have the greatest impact on the front line around Eritrea's southern port of Assab. The front was 70 km from the port, and since 1998 had withstood all Ethiopian attempts at breaking through. Now, Eritrean forces were being asked to leave their well prepared and defended trenches, and set up positions again in the open, flat, volcanic plain just 50 kilometres from the port. Since the war began, most people in Eritrea were convinced that what the Ethiopians had wanted all along was the port. Leading a landlocked country of 60 million, politicians in Ethiopia had demanded Assab be captured. But the Ethiopian army in Assab was limited in size - most troops were being used to fight in the western and central fronts. The Eritrean commanders in Assab estimated that there were around 40 to 50 thousand Ethiopian troops facing them. The Eritreans said this was partly due to the Ethiopians having only a limited water supply - critical in the harsh desert terrain where temperatures could reach the high 40s.

The Eritreans complied with the Ethiopian demand and moved back. Their soldiers hastily built a wall out of sandbags and the sharp, black volcanic rocks that lay amongst the sand. It was not long before the Ethiopians attacked. The fighting raged for almost two weeks - mostly at night, as the day was too hot for attacking. Assab was considered to be one of the worst fronts. The fighting had usually been brief, but the weather was so hot that the soldiers' plastic sandals had been known to melt. The land was flat which meant there was virtually no cover from artillery; both sides could see each aspect of the battlefield. And to make matters worse, the volcanic rocks were so sharp they would splinter like shrapnel during an artillery barrage. The situation in Assab was looking quite bad for the Eritreans. In Asmara the word coming out of the President's office, though not official, was that Assab was to be evacuated. In fact, the government's political organisation, the PFDJ, had started evacuating its computers and files. But finally the army commanders on the ground overruled the leadership in Asmara. They refused to evacuate and insisted on holding the line at all costs.

We flew in on a small propeller aircraft buffeted by wind and terrified of crossing paths with Ethiopian fighters. We skimmed over the Red Sea coast, desert bordered by the mottled blue and green of shallow water and coral. We landed on a huge, empty runway. Two defunct Ethiopian fighters stood off to one side, reminders of the days when this had been the last outpost of Mengistu's regime in Eritrea. We were met by army vehicles, this trip had been cleared at the top. From the airport, we raced to the edge of the port of Assab, which seemed quiet, almost deserted. Occasionally you could glimpse, through gaps in buildings, the tall cranes of the port, which had stood idle since the war began. The roads leading from the port were rutted by the heavy tread of tanks, shipped down the coast from Eritrea's other port of Massawa. We skirted the town, and joined the pristine highway, which headed directly towards Ethiopia. It had been the main artery for Ethiopian imports, six hundred trucks a day would roll up and down the road crossing into Ethiopia just 70 km down the road. Now the road was intersected at right angles by the front line, just 40 km from the town. We raced along in the back of an army pick-up - the tyres humming on the black tarmac, which cut like a ribbon through the moonscape of brown sand, dotted with black volcanic rock. We stopped at a stone building by the side of the road, where other military vehicles had parked. There, grouped on one side, squatted about forty Ethiopian prisoners, all covered in dust. One man was clutching a bandage to his face that oozed blood. He wailed, some of the other prisoners told him to be quiet. He was for a while, but gradually his sobbing built up, until again one of his comrades would tell him to hush. He started to speak in quick, sobbed sentences. He said he and his friends had been pinned down under fire and had tried to surrender. But the commanding officer had threatened to kill them if they did. Still, he said they took their chance and stood up to surrender, so his officer threw a grenade, which had blown off his nose.

Back in the pick-ups, we drove further, over a slight crest. The horizon opened, from one edge to the other plumes of smoke rose from the ground as artillery on both sides showered the front line. My own fear grew to extremes, there was nowhere to hide, I felt terrifyingly exposed. It was dusk, the temperature was dropping off slightly. Eritrean tanks and mortars were placed behind protective walls of piled stone and sandbag. Off to one side, six field guns stood in a line, their barrels flashed almost in unison, then - as we drove on - the crack rolled forward a fraction of a second later. The front line was another stone and sandbag wall hastily built up above the ground. They had been ordered to leave their trenches some thirty kilometres further forward, to meet Ethiopia's conditions for a cease fire that was clearly yet to be implemented. I asked the Colonel what he thought of the order to pull back. He said he obeyed his orders, but he spat out the words with disgust. "What can you do?", he said. "We will not let the Ethiopians through". He looked tired, "it's been going like this for over a week", he said, "but now we have things under control". Back in Assab city that night, looking in the direction of the front 40 kms away, the horizon flashed, as if a big electrical storm was hovering over the land.

When the line was held, the decision was made to send more troops to secure Assab. An unmarked airliner, rented by the government, helped ferry hundreds of troops and equipment from the capital to the port in the far south. In the end, Assab was one of the most costly battles for the Eritreans. Of course now the President and his critics blame each other for ordering the evacuation of Assab. Though retaining Assab was of enormous political and national significance, the port remains at a standstill. Ninety percent of its business was with Ethiopia, which has kept up its wartime boycott of Eritrean facilities. And on the battlefield outside of the town, the unclaimed remains of soldiers killed in the fighting are still being collected.

During the fighting in May, Ethiopia succeeded in recapturing the town of Zalambessa on the central front. The town had been reduced to ruins by the Eritrean army and local people were encouraged to strip the buildings to help construct shelters in displacement camps. The Eritrean front line was broken to the East of the town, and the decision was made to pull everyone back. As usual there was the some confusion. Not everyone was informed, and many of the local civilian population were only told at the very last minute. Many elderly simply had to stay put and wait for the Ethiopians, as they pushed on into Eritrea. The Ethiopians marched unopposed into the town of Serha, destroying the customs post from where I had watched the trenches being built two years before. They also took over Senafe and tried to move up to Adi Keih before an Eritrean counter attack forced the army back.

The airport in Asmara was bombed again, on the day the two sides sat down for cease fire talks in Algeria. A building and some fields were set ablaze, though none of the new Eritrean MiGs sitting on the runway were hit. This time the diplomats stayed put. There were fewer foreigners in Asmara, and luckily the bombing coincided with a public holiday in the United States so there was time for a more considered response. By that stage of the war most parts of Eritrea had been bombed at one time or another. Massawa had been hit, in fleeting raids. The new power station near Massawa was also badly damaged. Towns and villages mostly in western Eritrea had been hit, often repeatedly. In the town of Shambiko in western Eritrea, three hundred huts and buildings were destroyed in two days of raids in 1999. The Eritrean airforce had only a few new MiG 29 planes bought at very low, discount prices from Russian factories. Few in the Eritrean leadership considered air power to be a military factor, as it had not effected the outcome of the liberation war. But this war was not the war of liberation, and almost all soldiers I talked to wanted adequate missile defence against the planes and the helicopters which had proved so devastating against the Eritrean lines in the West.

The Aftermath

The cease fire was agreed in the middle of June. Fighting had continued along the Assab front, but the situation there had become more secure for the Eritrean army. In the west, the Eritrean army had launched a belated attack on the Ethiopian forces to retake Barentu. The Ethiopians were already preparing to leave and had looted much of the town. New buildings and hotels were then systematically blown up before the army pulled out. In the far west, along the border with Sudan, the town of Tessene changed hands four times during the course of the war. The Ethiopians finally pulled back on the day of the cease-fire wrecking, burning and looting whatever they could. Interestingly, Ethiopian civilians were also bussed in from across the border in Tigray region to help in the looting, though it was never made clear how one got chosen to take part. There were risks - some Eritrean units were left behind to ambush convoys of looters leaving Tessene.

"We wanted to desert, so we left our units", said three Ethiopian soldiers who sat by a wall in Tessene. "Bullshit", said an old man, " they were drunk; I saw them, they were so drunk they did not hear the call to get into the trucks this morning. They only woke up when you came", he added, addressing an Eritrean officer. They were possibly the last prisoners of the war, and they were captured in Tessene, sleeping off the last great piss-up, and getting left behind. The cease-fire had come into effect, but not before the Ethiopian army with the help of Ethiopian civilians had ransacked much of western Eritrea. The Ethiopians had only left Tessene that morning. Driving into the town, we had been told that it was safe to go. But Eritrean mine-sweeping teams, armed with metal poles, were still at work poking the dirt tracks which were the roads in the town. A member of another de-mining team was being carried away on a stretcher as we pulled up at a hastily set up checkpoint. A tank with a mine clearing flail drove past heading out on the road we had just came down. The town was decimated. By the side of the street bits of furniture, corrugated iron, pots and pans were piled high. There had not been enough space on the departing Ethiopian trucks to take the final loot. But everything else had gone. Houses, hospitals, schools, the church, had all been completely looted, everything conceivable had been taken. The centre of the town had been torched, charred interiors, plastic ceiling fans warped by the heat. About sixty Eritreans, older men, had stayed behind during the occupation desperate to spare their shops from destruction. The rest of the sixty thousand population had fled across the nearby border with Sudan. Those who stayed said they had not been badly treated but would simply stay in their shop with the doors locked. If soldiers came, they would try persuade them not to take everything. Walking through the town was eerie. The doors to all houses, shops and buildings were forced open. It was tempting to peek inside. In the courtyard of several houses, cows, goats and other livestock had been shot. Their bloated carcasses swarmed with flies.

The next morning we drove out of the town towards what was going to be Eritrea's state- of-the-art cotton plantation and factory. The settlement outside the factory, which had been home to veterans of the liberation war, had been torched. The factory itself had been destroyed - used as target practice for rocket-propelled grenades. The empty crates for the RPGs were left strewn around. The cotton inside was burnt, and formed hot ash that was knee-deep. The trail of destruction was not confined to Tessene: throughout the west, a similar price was paid.

The damage had been expected, and the towns regenerated remarkably quickly. But what I only saw later was the destruction of the Martyrs' cemeteries -

those for Eritreans who had died during the independence war. This angered people. In a few towns under occupation, the graves were bull scattering the bones those of who had died during the wars, when Eritreans and Tigrayans had fought together as comrades.

Those who stayed during occupation were mostly women, children and the elderly. Often the local priest would stay to give what protection he could. Some women who were left in the towns under occupation were raped but getting accurate figures is difficult, not least because of social taboos. It did not appear systematic, and many women said they were safe enough if they stayed together.

The Eritrean opposition allied to the Ethiopian army also made appearances in some parts of Eritrea during the occupation. Locals said they had helped with medical supplies, but lost a lot of credibility for not stopping the looting.

On the whole, there was little reaction to the war ending. For most it was simply exhaustion and trying to repair the damage incurred over the two years. The government did not release the names of those who died until June 2003. It said people should celebrate the martyrs' sacrifice but for days Eritreans wept and mourned uncontrollably for those they had lost. The government said that 19,000 had died during the war, still a huge figure for a country the size of Eritrea, in such a short space of time. Some, though, think the real number is higher. Politically, disputes within the leadership became more public. The President was forced to agree to a timetable for elections by the group that had criticised Isaias for his conduct of the war. The newspapers became a forum for a debate on the state of the nation. Every subject was discussed, including allegations of rape and harassment within the Eritrean army, a subject previously untouchable. The United Nations peace keepers started to arrive, disciplined at first, but as time went on many saw them as a corrupting influence in town. Prostitution increased, partly because of the UN and partly because the post-war economy was devastated. The Eritrean army was not demobilised, as the government said the war would not be officially over until the border had been demarcated. Increasingly young people wanted to leave the country, tired of never-ending national service with a salary officially valued at 15 dollars a month. The government further tightened already ferocious restrictions on travel abroad. In the aftermath of the September 11th attacks, while the world was looking the other way, the President moved against his critics. Those who had grouped together against the him in the final phase of the war were imprisoned, the newspapers were banned, independent journalists were arrested. They have been held incommunicado, none have faced trial. The promised elections and laws on political pluralism have been shelved. The President, Isaias Afewerki, said his political opponents were defeatist and had collaborated with Ethiopia. In reality, their unified criticism of him towards the end of the war was, the President felt, a coup-in-waiting. His opponents within the leadership opted for reform of the system, instead of a coup, but in effect the challenge to the President's power was still real. Since the arrest of the leading figures, arrests have continued - the government says there are secret cells of opponents or traitors working inside the country.

Months after the war, flying over the country inside a UN helicopter I looked down and saw the trenches empty. They looked incredible, mile after mile, cutting across the landscape through hills and plains. I thought about the time the soldiers spent digging these engineering feats. I thought of my time spent sitting inside a dugout, musty with the dust, where I felt remarkably safe sipping tea and eating rock-hard bread. I thought back to my first months in Eritrea, the first trip to the little village of Badme, and looking down I saw the scale of the conflict's escalation. It had not been the glorious victory that people thought would again be achieved against all odds. There was some feeling of satisfaction when Eritrea was given Badme by the Boundary Commission, but little rejoicing. The war has changed far more than the border. It has of course affected Eritrea's politics, destroyed the economy and the country is no longer seen as a shining example for the new Africa. But perhaps the war's greatest legacy will not be seen until after demobilisation, when the new generation of Eritreans, whose lives were spent in those trenches, finally come home.

Chapter 5
THE CONFLICT AND ITS AFTERMATH
Martin Plaut

Phase one: May - June 1998

The confrontation between Eritrean troops and Ethiopian forces in Badme on 6th May 1998 led to the outbreak of war. Exactly what transpired in that initial clash is not entirely clear, but the situation was certainly tense even before the first bullet was fired. As the Ethiopian Prime Minister put it later, the incident was like: "Sarajevo, 1914. It was an accident waiting to happen."[1]

Ethiopia says Eritrean troops refused to leave their arms on the outskirts of the town, as they had done many times before. The conflict took place"…when armed Eritrean units entered some localities under the Badme administration. According to the already existing understanding nationals of both countries could freely enter each other's territory unarmed. Thus, members of the Ethiopian police and militia who were on guard in the area brought to the attention of the Eritrean armed units that, according to the agreement of both sides, it was prohibited to cross each other's territory with arms. Hence, they proposed that the Eritreans could only freely enter Ethiopian territory by leaving their arms in their areas or keep them under the custody of the Ethiopian side and collect them later on return to their position. The armed Eritrean group retorted by defying the Ethiopian plea and resorted to violence by opening fire and the ensuing clash claimed lives on both sides." [2]

At first Eritrea gave little in the way of explanation for the confrontation. Officially they said no more than that: "The present crisis in relations between Eritrea and Ethiopia was triggered on May 6, 1998, by an unprovoked attack on Eritrean troops in south-western Eritrea." [3] But as the confrontation grew in intensity, President Isaias Afwerki offered this assessment of the causes of the conflict.

"After struggling side by side for a long period we never thought that border problems would arise in the end, for after 1991 our thoughts for both of us was focused only on our future years. Our mutual relations have always been positive on many domains and border issues were taken lightly as isolated local problems. But over the last year things started to assume larger dimensions especially in the environs of Badme where people were beaten and forced to flee their villages. This resulted in continuous complaints by the people as to the lack of response from the government. On our part we deemed it wise to handle the case carefully and restrained ourselves knowing full well that our people were suffering. Similar problems have also occurred in the Zoba Debubawi Keyih Bahri where certain administrative offices were forced to move. Still we preferred to look at the problem as local border problem and did not want to take it as intra-national issue.

Next, another misunderstanding occurred. Our border administrative post was asked to move further inside and it did. After this incident we decided to find a lasting solution to the problem and formed a joint committee to study the case. Although at first the meeting was decided to be between EPLF and EPRDF it was later agreed to include the government and hence a committee was formed which included the Minister of Defence, Sebhat Ephrem and two other members. Similar action was taken by the Ethiopian government and the dialogue started. But, even then the dialogue did not continue in a very serious way as the members still considered the matter a local one and no serious on-the-spot studies of the case was envisaged.

Finally, as the Ethiopian government decided to handle the case at a national level, the structure of the committee was changed. However, on our part we did not see the motive for changing the structure and we continued as before. Nevertheless, the committee could come up with nothing serious other than fixing appointments for further meetings. As things continued their course without any visible change, a new development took place around Badme during the last two or three months. People started to put up piles of stones here and there for border demarcation and this was accompanied by threats to those who moved around the place with their sheep and goats.

The case was reaching a critical stage and we decided to hold an urgent meeting in order to stop the crisis before it went out of control. About two weeks ago a committee was sent to Ethiopia. But, hardly had the committee set out on its trip, it was reported that an incident occurred where a certain unit posted there opened fire and killed and wounded some of the members of the army. Nevertheless, the committee, which was on its way to Addis, continued its mission with the aim of arriving at an understanding with the authorities in Addis. Unfortunately, things went out of control and led to the amassing of forces and violence on the part of Ethiopia.

This may be stated as a background for the present so-called border crisis." [4]

Unofficially Eritrean diplomats told a similar story. They said that local people told Eritrean military units in the Gash Setit area that the Tigrayan administration had begun marking the border with stones 45 – 50 kilometres inside Eritrean territory. When they went to investigate they met a superior Ethiopian force, which accused them of being inside Ethiopia and instructed them to disarm or be shot. They were surrounded, and in the ensuing gunfire four Ethiopian soldiers were killed, including a senior officer. [5]

While controversy surrounds the build-up to the confrontation what is certain is that on May 6th shots were fired, and some deaths took place. When the Eritrean survivors returned to their base they, reported on what had taken place. The military were outraged. A BBC reporter in Asmara recounted: "As one general told me, banging his fist on the desk in his office: 'To die on the battlefield is one thing, there is honour, but to be killed in cold blood is completely unacceptable. They must be punished.'" [6]

The fighting escalated rapidly. In the next few days Eritrea sent in heavily armed troops including tanks. According to the Ethiopians, the Eritrean forces, of three brigades, one armoured, must have been prepared well in advance of the incident at Badme. There was insufficient time, they argued, for these units to have been mobilised after May 6th, since units of this size require several weeks, even months, of preparation time. Ethiopia said it had only local militia forces in the Badme area, and certainly whatever troops they had were unable to prevent the Eritreans overrunning Badme and the surrounding area. Eritrea's response to the Ethiopian allegation that their action was premeditated was that its forces had been on Sudanese border duty, preventing infiltration by Eritrean Islamist rebels and were deployed from there.

The clashes that took place between May 6th and 12th left the area around Badme badly damaged. Ethiopia claims that the Eritrean action displaced over 24,000 people and destroyed twelve schools, a veterinary clinic, fertilisers and grain stores. After a lull of ten days the fighting grew in intensity with both sides issuing threats of a wider conflict.

Ethiopian foreign minister, Seyoum Mesfin warned that "all out war" was possible unless Eritrea withdrew from the territory it had seized, and declared: "Ethiopia's patience has its limits." [7] An Ethiopian cabinet meeting was called, and issued a statement condemning the Eritrean action and calling for a peaceful resolution of the dispute.

> "Ethiopia demands that the Eritrean Government unconditionally and immediately withdraw from Ethiopian territory and cease its provocative and belligerent activity. In the event that the Eritrean Government and the Popular Front do not desist from this dangerous action and withdraw from Ethiopian territory without any precondition the Ethiopian Government will take all the necessary measures that the situation demands to safeguard the sovereignty and territorial integrity of our country". [8]

The following day the Eritrean cabinet issued its own statement, again calling for a peaceful resolution of the conflict, and for the intervention of a neutral third party to oversee talks on the dispute.

> " 4. Areas under 'dispute' shall be demilitarized temporarily and be free from the presence of armies of both countries. The enforcement of this understanding shall be guaranteed by the Third Party.
>
> 5. If the above proposal for resolving the dispute through the involvement of a Third Party and without further complications is not acceptable, the matter is to be referred to international adjudication." [9]

The position adopted by the two countries remained essentially unchanged throughout the dispute. Ethiopia demanded Eritrea's unconditional withdrawal, since it asserted that Badme was part of its sovereign territory. Eritrea wanted a demilitarisation of the area, and arbitration, since it believed the ownership of Badme was under dispute. Neither position was unreasonable, from their own perspective, but they were, of course, mutually incompatible. Despite months of fruitless diplomacy this stalemate was only finally broken by events on the battlefield. [10]

In the meantime both sides prepared for war. Each reinforced its positions along the border, with reports of up to 200,000 soldiers being deployed. There were patriotic appeals from Addis Ababa to the farmers in Tigray, who were called upon to provide the Ethiopian army with food. In the event the first major round of fighting, which took place between 22nd May and 11th June was brief and bloody, and largely confined to clashes close to the border. [11] Both countries also began a massive purchase of arms and ammunition.

In almost every case, Ethiopian forces were on the defensive and unable to prevent Eritrean troops seizing all the disputed areas - around Badme, at Zalembessa and in Irob, Bada and on the Assab road. They dug in and set up defensive perimeters. Some of the heaviest fighting was in Irob where the local militia put up strong resistance. There were also battles on 31st May around Aigen and Alitiena, some 20 kilometres inside Ethiopia. By 3rd June almost all of Irob was overrun and Alitiena fell to Eritrean forces. The one area where the Eritreans were prevented from taking all their objectives was at Zalembessa. They captured the town but failed in attempts to move further south towards Adigrat to seize strategic hilltops commanding the road. Ethiopian forces managed to hang on but their attempts at a counter-offensive were unsuccessful.

Overall, the Eritrean battle plan at this stage of the conflict, when it held the initiative, was to seize all the areas along the border that were in dispute before Ethiopia could mobilise its forces, and then halt. In retrospect, it appears that Eritrea neither wanted, nor expected, the fighting to continue after early June. Its view was that Ethiopia would not fight, and indeed could not sustain a war for any length of time. At worst, it anticipated that Ethiopia would refer the issue to an international tribunal. This scenario was thrown out by the unexpectedly vigorous Ethiopian response, its declaration that it would fight for its territory and by the emotions released by Eritrea's bombing of Mekele and Adigrat. During the attack on Mekele on 5th June an elementary school was hit and 51 civilians were killed and 132 wounded, arousing enormous anger across Ethiopia.

While the fighting was taking place on the ground, the international community attempted to intervene to end the dispute. On May 15th 1998, just two days after the conflict became public, President Hassan Gouled Aptidon of Djibouti arrived in Addis Ababa offering to mediate to end the hostilities. Two days later the United States Assistant Secretary of State for African Affairs, Susan Rice, flew into the Ethiopian capital, with a team of diplomats, on a mediation mission which she undertook in co-operation with Rwanda. President Aptidon, never in the best of health and well into his eighties, was an important regional actor, even if the state he led is one of the smallest and poorest in the world. The youthful Ms Rice came on behalf of the world's only superpower.[12] That they should both arrive within days of the outbreak of hostilities is an indication of just how seriously both the countries of the region and the wider international community took the outbreak of fighting. From the first there was intensive, ongoing and energetic international diplomatic engagement with the problem.

A formal proposal for a full cease-fire, with an indication of how the conflict might be resolved, was actually worked out remarkably rapidly by the United States and Rwanda, and presented to both countries on May 30th.[13] "The US. - Rwandan recommendations are summarised as follows:

1) Both parties should commit themselves to the following principles: resolving this and any other dispute between them by peaceful means; renouncing force as a means of imposing solutions; agreeing to undertake measures to reduce current tensions; and seeking the final disposition of their common border, on the basis of established colonial treaties and international law applicable to such treaties.

2) To reduce current tensions, and without prejudice to the territorial claims of either party; a small observer mission should be deployed to Badme; Eritrean forces should redeploy from Badme to positions held before May 6, 1998; the previous civilian administration should return; and there should be an investigation into the events of May 6, 1998.

3) To achieve lasting resolution of the underlying border dispute, both parties should agree to the swift and binding delimitation and demarcation of the Eritrea-Ethiopian border. Border delimitation should be determined on the basis of established colonial treaties and international law applicable to such treaties, and the delimitation and demarcation process should be completed by a qualified technical team as soon as possible. The demarcated border should be accepted and adhered to by both parties, and, upon completion of demarcation, the legitimate authorities assume jurisdiction over their respective sovereign territories.

4) Both parties should demilitarise the entire common border as soon as possible."

This text was then taken up and worked on intensively by the Organisation of African Unity, and was tabled on 7th November as the Framework Agreement. [14]

What is remarkable about this draft is that although it was presented to both parties less than a month after the outbreak of hostilities, it contained most of the key elements to be found in the final peace treaty that was signed two and a half years later. These include the idea that an observer mission should be placed along the border, that Eritrea should withdraw from to the areas it held before May 6th, and that the border should be delimited on the basis of colonial treaties and international law.

Ethiopia was broadly satisfied with the US-Rwandan proposals, and declared as much, stating that they are '....in-line in substance with the position of the Ethiopian Government on the crisis.' [15] Eritrea, on the other hand, was not at all happy with the plan. Privately they complained bitterly that the Americans under Susan Rice had attempted to 'bounce' them into accepting the proposals, copies of which were released to the press before Asmara had even had sight of them.[16] Eritrea was not prepared to withdraw from Badme, since this would leave the disputed town in Ethiopian hands. Although point two of the draft peace plan stated plainly that such a withdrawal would be 'without prejudice to the territorial claims of either party' the Eritreans believed that possession was nine-tenths of the law.

Eritrea's concern was probably heightened by its experience during its dispute with Yemen over the Hanish islands in the Red Sea, which erupted in December 1995. After some clashes both countries were persuaded to submit their quarrel to the Permanent Court of Arbitration in the Hague. The initial hearings had taken place in February 1998. By the time war with Ethiopia erupted Eritrea knew they were not going well. In its final arbitration the Court awarded the majority of the islands to Yemen, a decision that Eritrea accepted despite considerable misgivings, since it had promised to be bound by the outcome. In essence Eritrea lost the case because it could be shown that such administration as had been exercised over the islands had come from Yemen. As the Tribunal put it, '...on balance...the weight of the evidence supports Yemen's assertions of the exercise of the functions of state author-ity ...' .[17]

Since Eritrea accepted that the Badme area had been continuously under Ethiopian authority for a considerable period of time, both before and after independence in 1993, this precedent was deeply worrying for Asmara. It is probably for this reason that Eritrea placed such weight on the evidence contained in the Ethiopian treaties with Italy, which defined where the border lay, rather than any more recent events.

The fighting, particularly around the central town of Zalambessa, left thousands of Ethiopians displaced from their homes. By mid June 1998 at least 16,000 men, women and children had fled from the front line. One of them, Shewainesh Meles said "I came here in only what I am wearing. All my clothes and possessions are there. Before this we were like brothers.....Almost half of us were Eritreans...we were living together and eating together. We will not take revenge on them, but our husbands are fighting against them and they have made us displaced." [18]

The conflict was not confined to the ground. On Friday 5th June at around 2 p.m. local time two Ethiopian MIG-23 jet aircraft attacked the airport at Asmara with rocket and cannon fire. An hour later a second wave of two Ethiopian MIGs attacked the airport again. One person was killed on the ground and five others injured, while a Zambian cargo aircraft was lightly damaged.

The Eritrean airforce retaliated, hitting civilian targets in the Tigrean regional capital, Mekele. One Eritrean plane was shot down and its pilot captured. Ethiopia claimed that its raid on Asmara was in response for the bombing of Mekele - a charge vehemently denied by Eritrean Air Force commander, Habtezion Hadgu, who said that Ethiopia had bombed Asmara airport first. But he made it plain that his airforce would replay any attack with interest. "This is tit for tat — one to 100, that's the exchange rate. They hit us, I hit them harder." Eritrean based western diplomats confirmed the commander's version of events, saying the airport attack occurred shortly after 2 p.m. local time (1100 GMT) on Friday and 50 minutes later two Eritrean warplanes took off and headed south. [19]

Whoever launched this air war the civilian deaths in Mekele embarrassed the Eritrean government. President Afwerki insisted that the fatalities were not deliberate. "In a war there are flaws here and there and if an aircraft is bombing, it could miss a target and civilians get killed". Later the president, in a rare public apology, expressed regrets at the deaths, while still insisting that military targets had also been hit. [20] Privately Eritreans blamed the deaths on the inexperience of their pilots. Either way, the air raids and the civilian deaths led to increasing bitterness, as well as the cancellation of commercial flights into Eritrea.

On Saturday 6th June the Ethiopians returned to the air attacking Asmara airport at 9.45 am, causing light damage. One aircraft was shot down and its pilot captured. He subsequently appears to have died in captivity. Eritrea's refusal to comment on his disappearance was bitterly resented in Ethiopia. The raid prompted a flurry of diplomatic activity, and both sides agreed to suspend air raids for 13 hours from 5 p.m. local time to allow the evacuation of foreign nationals, some 2,000 of whom were stranded in Eritrea. American, Italian, German and British planes hurriedly evacuated their nationals during the temporary halt. Asmara was reported to be tense, with Eritreans watching the sky nervously, in case the Ethiopian jets returned. The authorities decided that children should be kept at home until Thursday, as a precaution against further raids.

Considerable diplomatic efforts were by now under way to end the fighting and one intervention now bore fruit. President Clinton, speaking to both President Afwerki and Prime Minister Zenawi from Air Force One, managed to secure an end to the air raids. Eritrea welcomed the "air cease-fire" announced on Sunday 15th June as a first step towards ending the undeclared war, but Ethiopia issued a communiqué warning "We have agreed to an air cease-fire, but if our sovereignty is put under threat we will defend it." [21] Although this agreement only covered combat in the air it took hold on the ground as well.

Phase two: June 1998 – May 1999

From 11th June a cease-fire took hold and there followed several months of uneasy calm. The onset of the rainy season also helped to end the fighting. Apart from some shelling, no further major attacks took place for eight months.

This did not, however, mean that either side had stopped its preparations for war. Ethiopia deployed troops around the town of Adigrat, while the Eritreans strengthened their hold on Zalambessa. Ethiopian Foreign Minister, Seyoum Mesfin said "I cannot rule out an all-out war if Eritrea maintains its present intransigent attitude, but we will not rush to war". [22]

Both sides used this period to continue to purchase arms and ammunition - particularly modern aircraft - and to build up their troop levels. Despite consistently emphasising the need for a peaceful solution to their difficulties, both Ethiopia and Eritrea were clearly prepared to spend, and to spend heavily on armaments after the conflict erupted.[23] Eritrea raised funds from the Eritrean communities overseas, which had been called on to increase their remittances and their donations to the government war effort. In December Asmara started the sale of treasury bonds to raise further finance for the war The result was a dramatic inflow of fund, but even this was not enough. Eritrea resorted to heavy international borrowing, pushing its external debt from 11 million dollars in 1997 to 60.8 million dollars in 2001. [24] Ethiopia also called on its disapora for financial support, as well as drawing on the financial support of wealthy industrialists.

In December 1998 both began to take delivery of significantly improved air capacity.[25] The first of 5 MiG 29s (Fulcrum) arrived in Asmara.[26] For its part Ethiopia acquired 8 Sukhoi 27s (Flanker), together with at least half a dozen Mi24 (helicopter gunships) and M8 (cargo helicopters). The planes were obtained from Russia (Ethiopia) and Ukraine (Eritrea), and according to Russian sources both countries paid for the deals with cash.

Ethiopia signed an upgrading deal for its stocks of MiG 21s (30) and MiG 23s (20) earlier in 1998 with the Israeli Company, Elbit. It also signed a supplementary deal to acquire 10 MiG 21s, already upgraded by Elbit for the Romanian airforce. However, all this was put on ice following Eritrea complaints to Israel.

Eritrea originally had no pilots trained on MiG 29s and Ethiopia none for its Sukhoi 27s, though it did send some to be trained for the upgraded MiG 21s in Romania. The planes which began to arrive in December were accompanied in both cases by a full complement of Russian and Ukrainian pilots and technicians. This was acknowledged by Ethiopian Prime Minister, Meles Zenawi, who told the French news agency: "We have foreign technicians to train our pilots. I assume the Eritreans have foreign technicians." [27]

The two countries also bought extensive quantities of ammunition. Although both inherited huge stocks of ammunition and supplies from the previous regime, a good deal of this had deteriorated beyond use. Ethiopia bought from China and Eastern Europe, while Eritrea purchased supplies from Bulgaria and Romania.

Attempts were made to mediate between the two combatants, but as peace initiatives came and went the situation on the border became increasingly tense. Ethiopia grew restive at the lack of progress towards a negotiated settlement of the dispute and began issuing ominous warnings. In January 1999 the Ethiopian ambassador to Kenya said "We have restrained ourselves so far, but I don't know how long we can restrain ourselves." Then in February Ethiopian Prime Minister, Meles Zenawi warned that fighting could resume. Along the border, he said, there was a "very high level of tension that can get out of hand easily and at any time". Ethiopia closed schools and colleges all along the border, and restricted the movements of foreigners in the area. For its part the Eritrean government declared that it had a number of reports, including some from western intelligence sources, that Ethiopia was planning a three pronged attack between mid-January and mid-February.

The international community also sounded the alarm. On the 26th January the Italian Foreign Under-secretary, Rino Serri warned that the border war could re-ignite at any time. "There is now a high possibility that the war will explode again in a big way". The following day UN Secretary General, Kofi Annan' declared that he was "very, very concerned" about the simmering conflict, and despatched his special representative, Mohammed Sahnoun to the region to try to avert a further conflict. There were strenuous and repeated calls for restraint from the UN, European Union and Organisation of African Unity, but all to no avail.

At dawn on Saturday 6th February 1999 the eight-month lull was abruptly brought to an end. Heavy fighting broke out on the Badme front. Ground forces, backed by artillery were locked in a fierce confrontation, as Ethiopian troops attempted to take Eritrean positions. Both sides accused the other of renewing the conflict. Over the next five days a series of clashes took place around Badme and Tserona. Ethiopian army units, supported by fighter planes and helicopter gunships pounded Eritrean troops positions. No journalists were allowed on the Ethiopian side of the lines, but those with the Eritreans reported soldiers holding their positions and apparently in good spirits.

With the fighting apparently stalemated on the Badme front, attention switched to the area around Bure, close to the Eastern Eritrean port of Assab.

Ethiopia used its airforce to attack Eritrean positions and other targets, including the airport north of Assab. No ground troops were apparently deployed and the damage was light.

On Thursday 10th February a lull in the fighting took place, allowing further diplomatic activity. The UN Security Council called for an immediate cease-fire and strongly urged all states not to sell arms to either country - somewhat belatedly, given the massive re-armament that had taken place in the previous months. But neither belligerent appeared willing to consider an end to hostilities. "The Security Council should point the finger at the culprits," Eritrean presidential spokesman, Yemane Gebremeskel said. "The Ethiopians initiated hostilities when we were both asked to show restraint". Ethiopia's response was equally uncompromising. "This call would be better directed at Eritrea," said Ethiopian government spokeswoman, Salome Tadesse. "We have been invaded and stayed put for nine months. They cannot ask us not to defend our sovereignty".

In late February 1999 there was yet more diplomatic activity. The United States issued a statement saying it deeply regretted Ethiopian use of air power in the conflict - a comment that was rejected by Addis Ababa as "out of synch with reality". The European Union attempted to intervene, with German Deputy Foreign Minister, Ludger Volmer leading a troika ministerial mission to the region. They met the OAU as well as Ethiopian and Eritrean officials. But the Europeans left empty handed, accepting that they had been unable to persuade the parties to renew the cease-fire. The OAU also attempted to send a mediation committee to Asmara comprising the ambassadors of Burkina Faso, Djibouti and Zimbabwe but they too met with no success, never leaving Addis Ababa. First Eritrea objected to the Djibouti emissary's presence on the team, and then fighting re-erupted on the Badme front.

On February 23rd Ethiopian troops, supported by heavy artillery, tanks, helicopter gun-ships and other aircraft, attacked Eritrean trenches along a 60-kilometre section of the Badme front. Western journalists reported a 'seemingly endless river of thousands of troops' being brought to the front from Tserona for "Operation Sunset", as the Ethiopians named the offensive. [28] For three days the only news put out by Asmara and Addis Ababa was that fighting was intense. Then, on the 26th, Eritrea reported that Ethiopia's "human wave" attacks had breached its defences and that its forces it had withdrawn about 20 kilometres to a new front line, leaving the town of Badme in Ethiopian hands.

In fact, Ethiopian forces had concentrated on three particular areas of the front, succeeding in punching holes in the Eritrean line. They then turned right and left to roll up long sections of the defence. Eritrea lost a significant number of troops but managed to withdraw in relatively good order. They failed to hold onto most of the strategic hills on the western side of the Baduma plains, something that was to cost them dearly in their three unsuccessful counter-attacks over the next four months. In this battle, as in the ones over the next few months, the same tactics were employed by both sides - artillery barrages, followed by infantry advances supported by tank units, and in the case of Ethiopian assaults, by helicopter gun-ships.

Until this breakthrough Eritrea had held the military advantage since they were dug into well defended positions. Ethiopia, however, had two crucial assets. It appears to have had access to US satellite information (at least until the US satellite moved to cover Kosovo) providing it with detailed knowledge of Eritrean strength.[29] It also had command of the air, with the Eritrean MiGs proving no match for Ethiopia's Sukhois. This allowed it to pre-empt Eritrean attacks and conceal its own troop movements. In reality this was more of a psychological than a tactical advantage. Ordinary soldiers undertook most of the fighting, and it was their efforts that were decisive in the battles, rather than the dogfights in the skies above them. The shift of focus from Badme (on the Western Front) at the beginning of the month, to Tserona (in the Central Front) and then back to Badme towards the end of February apparently caught Eritrean defences on the wrong-foot with almost all reserves still guarding Tserona. Ethiopia had one other advantage. The Eritrean commanders on the Badme front displayed serious over-confidence and underestimated the strength and determination of the Ethiopian army. There was no defence in depth and only a single trench line for much of the front.

Ethiopia declared that it had won a "total victory", adding that Eritrea had suffered a monumental and humiliating defeat, with thousands of casualties and prisoners. Ethiopians went wild with jubilation, celebrating a victory that came so close to the anniversary of the battle of Adua, 103 years earlier, when their forces trounced an Italian army. Western diplomats confirmed that Eritrean forces had suffered a major reversal.

The day after the breaching of its defences at Badme, February 27th, Eritrean President Isaias Afwerki wrote to the UN Security Council, formally accepting the OAU peace Framework. [30] After informal consultations the Security Council issued a statement welcoming Eritrea's acceptance of the OAU plan and calling for an immediate halt to all hostilities so that the agreement could be implemented without delay.

Eritrea said it was waiting for a response from Addis Ababa, but none was forthcoming. Ethiopia remained sceptical of Eritrean intentions, and refused to accept that Asmara had complied with the OAU proposal by withdrawing from the area around Badme. On the 6th of March, Ethiopia accused the Eritreans of only attempting to buy time to reorganise its forces. "They continue to occupy the Zalambessa-Aiga region, the Bada-Bure region and the Egala region (near Tserona)...the Eritrean government has shown no signs of withdrawing its army from these territories, as it is required to do by the OAU", the statement said, adding that these areas should be liberated.

The next blow fell at Tserona. Eritrea reported a heavy aerial and artillery bombardment by Ethiopia on the 13th of March, with a large-scale ground offensive the following day. This time it was Eritrea that emerged victorious, describing the attack on their well defended positions as having produced an Ethiopian 'slaughter'. Eritrea had responded to its defeat at Badme by rapidly creating defence in depth at Tserona, tripling their trench lines. Ethiopian sources claim the Ethiopian troops broke through two defence lines, but faltered at the third, losing hundreds, if not thousands in an attempt to break the line. The Eritreans took western journalists to the scene of the fighting, and they described a narrow front littered with Ethiopian dead. Journalists saw that up to 20 Ethiopian tanks that had been destroyed in an area the size of a football field. Buoyed up by this success, Eritrea made an unsuccessful attempt at a counter-offensive on the Badme front. Again there was a heavy loss of life.

By early May 1999, the conflict had consolidated along the following lines: Ethiopia had succeeded in re-taking Badme, and Eritrea had failed to dislodge them, despite repeated attacks. Eritrea held the Central Sector, around Zalambessa and Tserona, and neither side had made any real progress in the East. Despite intense diplomatic activity by the United Nations, the Organisation of African Unity, the European Union and a number of individual countries, and organisations, there was no real progress towards a cease-fire. Both sides were locked in intransigent positions. Ethiopia insisted it would not talk to Eritrea until Eritrea withdrew from its territory. Eritrea would not withdraw until the issues that led to the war were resolved through discussion. Neither was prepared to budge.

Phase three: May 1999 – May 2000

The United Nations envoy, Mohammed Sahnoun warned that peace was on a knife-edge once more. He said that the region was living in a situation of "neither war nor peace". A cease-fire was possible if the international community put pressure on both sides, but that if fighting erupted once more the result would be a "catastrophe" for both countries.

In mid-May, Ethiopia again bombed several locations, including the port of Massawa. This was the first attack on the port and warehouses were hit and a watchman killed. On May 22nd 1999 fighting re-commenced on the Western sector with Eritrea making its second attempt to retake Badme. As usual, the two sides produced different accounts of the fighting. Ethiopia said four Eritrean brigades (around 12,000 soldiers) had assaulted Badme, while the Eritrean spokesman, Yemane Gebremeskal told journalists that

Ethiopia had attacked in division strength (between 7,000 and 11,000 men). The main battle appears to have taken place on May 23rd. Eritrean forces lost heavily, failing to take any Ethiopian positions or make any progress towards Badme. An Ethiopian based Western diplomat commented: "The mediators have missed the boat in avoiding further fighting. There was some space for diplomatic activity, but it was bungled. Now we're moving into the third phase of military activity."

Speaking to the United States House of Representatives Sub-Committee on African Affairs, the Assistant Secretary of State for Africa, Susan Rice said that both sides had used the lull in the fighting to improve their military capabilities. "Both Ethiopia and Eritrea used the intervening months to acquire new military stockpiles, including state-of-the-art fighter aircraft and artillery, and to recruit, train and deploy tens of thousands of new soldiers. The United States actively discouraged suppliers to both parties, and the U.N. Security Council urged both governments not to provide weapons to exacerbate the problem".

Between June 10th and 19th minor fighting occurred around Bure, seventy kilometres from the port of Assab, and much more heavily on the western sector. Eritrea launched the attack on Bure as a feint for a much larger offensive on the Mereb front, in what proved to be its last attempt to re-take Badme. It was the largest battle of the war involving at least 50,000 men on both sides. Some thirteen Eritrean divisions were involved in the assault, against at least seven Ethiopian divisions. Eritrean forces captured several strategic points and managed to advance a significant distance towards Badme. They were, however, unable to overcome the handicap of Ethiopian air superiority and the effect of very heavy losses from attacking Ethiopian defensive positions. Finally they failed to make a decisive breakthrough.

As usual, instead of announcing their own losses both sides declared how many of the enemy they had put out of action. Ethiopia said 24,450 Eritreans had been despatched; Eritrea said Ethiopia had lost 21,000 soldiers. All figures should be treated with considerable scepticism; in general, the side attacking fixed defences (as Ethiopia did at Badme in February 1999 and Tserona in March, and Eritrea at Badme in March, May and June) suffered far more heavily. In any event, losses on both sides were heavy. There were claims that casualties on both sides together had reached 70,000 by June, and that there were another 30,000 from the mid-June battles.[31]

During the engagements, Ethiopia bombed Bure and Assab airport. In mid-June, Eritrea claimed to have downed four Migs and an MI35 helicopter gunship which fell 'behind Ethiopian lines'. The Ethiopian spokeswoman's office dismissed these claims, saying they had been made 'to ease the concern and pressure felt by the Eritrean soldiers' because 'the aircraft have caused the Eritrean army human and material losses'. [32]

Ethiopia and Eritrea both organised visits by journalists to their front lines towards the end of June 1999. They reported signs of heavy combat, including hand-to-hand fighting from trenches, at some points no more than 50 metres apart. All the visits were carefully stage-managed and neither side's wider claims could be verified. On June 25th 1999 fighting was renewed on the western front, lasting for four days. The Ethiopian Airforce again attacked Assab airport.

Both sides had thrown their best troops into battle at heavy cost, but had been unable to score a decisive military victory. Another lull in the war followed and on this occasion lasted nearly a year.

During the stalemate, the United States and Algeria, supported by the OAU, UN and the European Union, reinitiated diplomatic efforts. The most difficult work was undertaken by Anthony Lake, representing President Clinton, and Ahmed Ouyahia, representing the Algerian President, Abelaziz Bouteflika, who was the Chairman of the OAU. Between July 1999 and May 2000 they were involved in intense discussions around the trio of texts that form the basis of the OAU plan for peace: the Framework Agreement, the Modalities and the Technical Agreement. [33] The diplomats gradually whittled away the differences between the combatants, but as one issue was resolved, another appeared. Negotiating with Ethiopia and Eritrea was time consuming, complex and endlessly frustrating.

On July 14th 1999 Eritrea announced that it had agreed to the OAU Framework Agreement and the Modalities, "as a mark of goodwill to the OAU". President Isaias presented a letter to this effect to the OAU summit in Algiers. Ethiopia, for its part, said it was studying the Eritrean proposal. The next day Ethiopia declared it did not take Eritrea's acceptance of the Framework document seriously. Foreign Minister Seyoum Mesfin said that Eritrea had placed conditions on the agreement – referring specifically to Eritrea's demand for compensation for Ethiopian deportations. In reply Eritrea accused Ethiopia of stalling.

US Assistant Secretary for African Affairs, Susan Rice gave her support to the Framework document, saying it was the result of long, hard work. On 23rd July Anthony Lake gave this optimistic assessment to the Associated Press: "Each side has now made a decision to try to achieve peace, and those decisions have opened the door that I think each of them has decided to go through."

Exactly what transpired in these meetings is not public knowledge, but the OAU threw its weight behind the peace initiative, sending its own special envoy, the Algerian diplomat, Ahmed Ouyahia to both capitals. The results were positive, and by 27th July President Bill Clinton was able to announce that both Ethiopia and Eritrea had accepted the OAU Framework Agreement and Modalities. He called it a "significant step towards peace". To shore up this progress, experts from the US, UN and OAU met in Algiers to work out the technical details of the Framework Agreement. These were finalised in August, and transmitted to both countries.

On August 8th Eritrea announces its total acceptance of the OAU's plans, pledging its "full co-operation" with their implementation. However, Ethiopia sought 'clarifications' from the OAU regarding the Technical Arrangements. On 22nd August Ahmed Ouyahia arrived in Addis to provide the requested information, which he took on to Asmara three days later. In late August 1999 senior American envoys, led by Susan Rice, sought to shore up the peace initiative by touring the region. On October 29th, Prime Minister Meles Zenawi announced after talks with Ahmed Ouyahia that discussions have been "very constructive" and the "peace process is still going on".

Despite these optimistic remarks Ethiopia was still concerned that Eritrea would be able to use the proposal to "escape from its obligation to leave the Ethiopian territory that it occupied." On 8th December Ethiopia said it was "awaiting a response" from the OAU to its queries regarding the "shortcomings" of the Technical agreement. On the 15th December, Prime Minister Meles complained to an assembly of African diplomats about the concessions being demanded of him: "Ethiopia bent backwards with the US/Rwanda proposals and has bent more with the Framework Agreement. Bending any further would break our back and we are not ready to do that". Later that month the OAU provided Ethiopia with further clarification, which Addis said it would consider.

Prime Minister Meles's essential objective was to portray Ethiopia as the victim of Eritrean aggression that was doing all in its power to find a formula that would put an end to the dispute. In general he found a receptive audience in Washington, but Ethiopia's repeated requests for clarification begin to pall with some sections of the international community. At the start of 2000 the Chairman of the US House of Representatives International Relations Committee, Benjamin Gilman published an article in the Washington Post entitled: "Ethiopia needs a Push Towards Peace". In it he argued that the time had come for the US and the wider international community to condemn Ethiopian intransigence and to urge them not to launch further military strikes. The article left Ethiopia seething, with Foreign Minister Seyoum Mesfin declaring that his country had not rejected the peace plan, but had a problem with the Technical Arrangements, which (in his view) was not consistent with the Framework Agreement and the Modalities.

In February 2000 another round of fighting occurred on the Bure front, but the outcome was again inconclusive. Anthony Lake and Ahmed Ouyhia renewed their shuttle diplomacy, allowing the OAU Secretary General, Ahmed Salim Salim to express optimism at the end of the month about the progress being made. "The mediators will be in the area as long as it takes until the conflict is resolved", he told a press conference.

The combined efforts of the mediators and the pressure of the international community finally resulted in the holding of proximity talks involving both countries in Algiers, starting on 29th April. Announcing this, the OAU chairman Algerian President Abelaziz Bouteflika said the discussions would be held in accordance with the Framework Agreement and the arrangements accepted by both sides and approved by the 35th OAU summit in July 1999.

The talks proved to be fruitless and on the 5th May, after six days of meetings, they collapsed. According to Ethiopia, attempts by the facilitators to get Eritrea to negotiate on substantive matters had failed, and Ethiopia had therefore been unable to find a partner for peace. Eritrea said the talks failed because Ethiopia had refused to sign the Framework Agreement and Modalities. Eritrea had insisted that the outline agreement and the terms of a ceasefire should be signed first. Ethiopia had maintained the position it adopted in July 1999 that such a signing could only take place after the finalisation of the Technical arrangements. Attempts at mediation by President Bouteflika, supported by the United States and the European Union, had been unsuccessful. Neither side was prepared to make the necessary concessions.

With diplomats warning that the failure of the talks could spell the onset of renewed conflict, the UN Security Council despatched a mission to the region, led by senior American diplomat, Richard Holbrook. The mission, which included seven Security Council ambassadors, saw Prime Minister Meles and President Isaias. At the end of their meeting in Asmara on 9th May 2000, Richard Holbrook offered the following assessment of the situation.

"We are very close to a resumption of hostilities. The outbreak of a new round of fighting would immediately constitute the largest war on the continent. Whatever happens now, the UN Security Council is now engaged in support of the OAU to help prevent a tragedy of enormous, perhaps historic proportions. The threat of war has not been removed by our trip, but perhaps we have offered a way, which is the additional involvement of the Security Council, to move forward and resume the talks. The differences between the two sides are real, but they are not enormous. Most of the issues have been resolved. The remaining issues are the sort which nations should and must resolve peacefully. The specifics remain in the hands of the two leaders, in whose hands the fate of millions of people depends. It would be tragic if a senseless and unnecessary war broke out over these differences. They can and should be resolved."[34]

Richard Holbrook's summary of the position came almost exactly two years after the outbreak of the conflict. In that time tens of thousands of soldiers had lost their lives. At least 600,000 people had been displaced from their homes. Each side had deployed around 300,000 troops to the battlefronts. The costs were enormous, yet the most intense efforts by diplomats had failed to achieve peace. The International Institute for Strategic Studies, in its annual report blamed this failure on a misunderstanding of the root causes of war on the part of the mediators, who had seen it as a border conflict. "It has been about regime legitimacy, state sovereignty, nation-building, currencies and access to port facilities." The report concluded that the conflict had dragged on because of the personal pride of the two leaders, Prime Minister Meles and President Isaias.

Phase four: May – December 2000

The war, which had until this point been characterised by short but brutal set piece battles resulting in a huge loss of life, but tiny gains of territory, was about to undergo a transformation.

Prime Minister Meles made clear that his patience with the stalemate and the endless rounds of diplomacy had come to an end. He declared that Ethiopia could not continue to divert its meagre resources from development to war, at a time when the country was facing drought, after three years of poor rainfall. By May 2000 Ethiopia's War Council had concluded that peace would be impossible as long as the Eritrean army remained intact. Its objective for the last few months of the war was to retake all areas occupied by Eritrea, including Zalembessa and Irob, and then destroy as much Eritrean military capacity as possible before international pressure forced a halt to the fighting. Eritrea subsequently claimed that Ethiopia had also intended to take Asmara, overthrow the regime and the capture the port of Assab. All three were considered, but although all were seen as possible, and even desirable, none was built into the strategy. The Ethiopian leadership was fully aware that they would not be internationally acceptable - the idea of regime change was not as unexceptionable in 2000 as it has now become. Ethiopia certainly hoped, however, that Eritreans might respond in the traditional way towards a defeated leader. While Ethiopia was clear it could not be responsible for this, it did create space in western Eritrea where the opposition could have set up an administration, but the Alliance of Eritrean National Forces (now the Eritrean National Alliance) proved unable to take advantage of the offer.

In the early hours of 12th May, after a long build-up, Ethiopia launched an offensive on the Badme front, coupled with a successful flanking manoeuvre across the Merab river to the North of Badme, as well as an offensive against Zalembessa in the central sector. Eritrea appealed to the UN, which unanimously adopted resolution 1297, condemning the renewal of fighting, and demanding the reconvening, without preconditions of the peace talks. It gave 72 hours for this to be implemented, but to no effect. On May 16th, frustrated that none of its appeals were having any effect, the UN proposed resolution 1298, calling for an arms embargo on both countries. This, too, had little effect, and on May 18th the Security Council approved wide-ranging military sanctions for 12 months against Ethiopia and Eritrea. The sanctions were also ineffective since none of the members of the Security Council were willing to enforce the embargo and arms continued to flow into both countries.

Ethiopia rejected the UN's activities and within 48 hours of starting its offensive it had broken the Eritrean defences west of Badme, and the Eritrean army was in full retreat. Ethiopia claimed it had "...completely destroyed the heavily fortified trenches of Eritrea along with eight divisions of the Eritrean army. The Eritrean army is retreating in disarray as the Ethiopian ground forces pursue them and destroy them as they flee". Eritrea denied the claims, saying that after the experience of the past two years of war, claims of quick victories were "mind-boggling". Eritrean presidential spokesman, Yemane Gebremeskel said "if Ethiopia is penetrating deep into Eritrean territory, its forces will be decimated." On May 18th, a reporter travelling in western Eritea saw several trucks full of passengers fleeing east from Barentu towards the town of Keren.[35] On May 21st a French news agency journalist reported having visited over the previous three days a number of towns previously held by Eritrea, including Barentu. He said all were in Ethiopian hands, and that Barentu had fallen without a shot being fired.

The Eritrean retreat from the western front was precipitous. The front collapsed and the troops fell back to Barentu and then retreated to Agordat, abandoning huge amounts of equipment. Army commanders who wanted to try and make a stand at Barentu but were overruled by the president and ordered back to Agordat. The Ethiopian forces, after taking Barentu, left the remnants of Eritrea's army at the western front at Agordat, and turned their attention to the rest of western Eritrea. Within a few days, the Ethiopians had overrun the whole of Gash-Setit and had captured Tessenai. An entire Eritrean battalion retreated into Sudan and surrendered to the Sudanese authorities. The governor of the Sudanese border town of Kassala, Ibfahim Mahoud Hamid, said 25,000 Eritreans had crossed the border, and the influx continued at a rate of 100 – 150 per hour. On the 19th May Eritrea called for emergency air drops to feed more than half a million people displaced by the fighting.

A significant element in the Ethiopian victory was an advance across the Mereb River, with a force using animal transport to cross an unguarded area. They cut the road running north of the border from Barentu to Adi Quala. This outflanked all the Eritrean defences along the western front. It allowed some Ethiopian units to swing left towards Barentu, while others turned right to threaten Adi Quala, no more than 100 kilometres from Asmara on a good tarmac road, though they did not reach Adi Quala, halting well short of the town on May 22nd.

Intense diplomatic attempts were made to halt the fighting. The OAU President, Abelaziz Bouteflika expressed his readiness to hold immediate indirect talks with both sides to end the conflict. The European Union mediator, Rino Serri, visited the region to try to find a way of re-opening negotiations and on 23rd May he announced that Eritrea had agreed to resume negotiations "without preconditions". President Bouteflika arrived in Addis Ababa, and conducted talks with Prime Minister Meles. The United State's said it was "strongly supportive" of his efforts.

None of this was sufficient for Ethiopia, which was determined to destroy as much of the Eritrean army as possible. Ethiopia promptly launched another offensive, in the central sector around the strategic border town of Zalambessa, on May 23. The following day journalists reported that Eritrean fighters near Zalambessa were jubilant as they halted and then reversed the Ethiopian attack. However, their celebrations were short-lived. A day later Ethiopia announced that it had recaptured the town "completely annihilating the Eritrean army that was on the verge of collapsing". Ethiopian radio celebrated what it called a "blitzkrieg" that had "demolished the Eritrean army". Thousands of Ethiopians gathered in Addis Ababa to celebrate in Meskal square. Children bearing the Ethiopian flag of red, gold and green hung onto buses as bands played.

As news of this victory spread to the former residents of Zalambessa some ventured to return to their homes. Five hundred Ethiopian families, who had been living in caves around the town of Adigrat, moved back to the town, where they found that it had been systematically destroyed by Eritrean troops as they had departed. Amete Ghebre, a 52-year-old mother of six, whose husband was away at the front told a reporter: "When we heard Zalambessa had been freed, people began to run there. But when they reached the town, they were shocked. They started to cry, as if somebody had died. An entire town has been turned into a pile of stones".[36]

Eritrea refused to admit that it had lost Zalambessa, merely saying it had withdrawn its forces from this zone of the Central front, which lay 130 kilometres South of Asmara. A government spokesman denied that it was a retreat, insisting that they had merely taken up new defensive positions. A senior Eritrean adviser, Yemane Gegreab said the decision to withdraw had been taken in response to an OAU request to re-deploy to pre-war boundaries. "I fail to see what more we can do" he said, as President Bouteflika arrived in Asmara.

The UN Security Council welcomed the Eritrean withdrawal (or retreat), and called on Ethiopia to do likewise. Ethiopia refused, and the Foreign Ministry issued a statement declaring: "The war can only come to an end when Ethiopia has verified that Eritrea has removed its forces of occupation from all the remaining Ethiopian territory under their control. Even now large chunks of territory in the eastern and north-eastern part of Ethiopia, in Afar Regional State, are still occupied by Eritrea".

On May 26th Algerian President Abelaziz Bouteflika returned to Addis Ababa with an Eritrean agreement to withdraw from all remaining Ethiopian territory. The OAU said Eritrea would remove its troops from Bada and Bure on the eastern end of the border. With this promise the Algerian president finally convinced Ethiopia to attend fresh talks in Algiers on 29th May. But even then the fighting did not end. Ethiopian forces continued to advance, retaking the whole of Irob, and capturing Senafe. It also opened another front, seizing Tserona, and threatened to advance towards Adi Quala once more. Many Eritreans fled towards the town of Dekemhare. More than 250,000 were reported to have left the towns North of the border at Zalembessa. Despite the continued Ethiopian advances, Eritrea maintained its army was still intact and still holding its ground. On May 29th, Ethiopian planes renewed their attack on the airport in Asmara, a final indication of their superiority in the skies.

Talks finally opened in Algiers on 30th May. The meeting was convened by the Organisation of African Unity and attended by Anthony Lake, representing the United States and Rino Serri representing the European Union. Despite vitriolic comments from each side about the other, progress was remarkably swift. It soon became clear that Ethiopia's victories on the battlefield had overcome Eritrean intransigence.

On 1st June Ethiopian Prime Minister Meles Zenawi announced the war was over, although some sporadic fighting continued around Assab for about a week. Finally, on June 18th, both sides formally agreed to end their two year old conflict. A cease-fire came into force, which allowed for United Nations peacekeepers to be deployed between the two sides. They were to take up their positions in a 25 kilometre wide, temporary security zone running inside Eritrea, North of the traditional border between the two countries. Indirect talks continued to flesh out the agreement, focussing on technical issues surrounding the role of the peacekeepers and their mandate.

Both countries maintained large armies along the border, with as many as two hundred thousand troops on each side facing each other in trenches that were as little as 50 meters apart. Despite this, the cease-fire held.

On 14th September 2000 the first fourty six UN military observers arrived in Addis Ababa and Asmara, at the start of the United Nations Mission to Ethiopia and Eritrea (Unmee). In November the Unmee force commander, Major General Patrick Cammaert arrived in Asmara, to begin his assignment. A few days later he was joined in the region by the UN Secretary General's special representative, Joseph Legwaila, who was in political charge of the mission. Finally, on 12th December 2000 the war was formally concluded when Ethiopian Prime Minister, Meles Zenawi and Eritrean President, Isaias Afwerki signed an agreement to formally bring the war to an end. The Algiers agreement allowed for the establishment of a number of independent commission to demarcate the border, examine the financial claims of both sides and investigate the causes of the war. The International Committee of the Red Cross received responsibility for the repatriation of prisoners of war and internees.

After signing the agreement President Afwerki said he hoped that "The chapter of cycles of conflicts and hatred can be closed.......(we can now) forget the past and look into a future of peace and hope for our two brother peoples".[37] Prime Minister Meles was not as optimistic, saying that the peace agreement would not in itself bring about normal relations with Eritrea. That, he warned, would require a change of government. On that depressing note one of Africa's bloodiest and bitterest wars drew to a close. The region could look forward, at best, to the embrace of a cold peace.

The details of the war as outlined above are tentative. Far more detailed work will have to be undertaken, with access to Eritrean and Ethiopian military sources, before we can have a definitive assessment of the conflict. Having said that, it is possible to make some tentative observations.

Firstly, both sides were able to rapidly move from a peacetime deployment of forces onto a wartime footing. This was particularly true for Eritrea, which was able to inflict defeats on its much larger (and more populous neighbour) in the first few weeks of the fighting. Eritrea benefited from its policy of national service, introduced in 1994 and which included a significant amount of military training. It also had the advantage of initiating the conflict with its forces in a far higher state of readiness than those of Ethiopia. Certainly there appears little evidence that Addis Ababa thought that its rather crotchety relations with Asmara would lead to war.

An assessment of the state of the Ethiopian armed forces, drawn from an article published a month before the outbreak of hostilities, pointed out that the government had dismantled the armed forces it inherited when it came to power in 1991 from the government of Mengistu Haile Mariam. It transformed the 250,000 strong armed forces into the Ethiopian National Defence Force of between 60,000 and 70,000 men "dependable and capable of properly executing its constitutional role". [38] The article went on to quote a diplomat based in Addis Ababa as declaring that the country was "…in no position to deal with the spillover effects of regional wars in Sudan, Eritrea and Somalia."

Despite this initial handicap, Ethiopia had little trouble in rapidly mobilising its population to its cause. The threat to Ethiopian sovereignty was, perhaps surprisingly, answered by all ethnic groups, despite the government's policy of allowing ethnic differences to be clearly spelled out and of reforming the country's provincial boundaries to reflect ethnic units. It also freed many former soldiers, especially those with technical skills (like pilots), who had been jailed when the TPLF came to power in 1991.

Eritrea too managed to motivate its people. Yemane Gebreab, senior policy adviser to the Eritrean president, said his country had been able to mobilise nearly 300,000 people, out of a population of 3.5 million. [39] This is remarkable, given that neither side was able to really explain to its people quite why they were at war. At the outbreak of hostilities a Washington Post journalist quoted both leaders as saying that the causes of the war remained something of a mystery. [40] These sentiments should, of course, be taken with a pinch of salt. Neither side lost any time in whipping up popular sentiment and patriotic fervour, but it remains a fact that there has never been a convincing, clear explanation of quite why the war came about, or why it was necessary. It is perhaps a sad commentary on the autocratic hold that many African leaders exercise over their people that none was required, since popular consent plays little role in the policies pursued by the continent's leaders.

The second conclusion was that despite being among the poorest countries in the world, both Ethiopia and Eritrea were able to find the money they needed to fund their war. Some of the sources of finance are now clear. Yemane Gebreab, in the article cited above, stated that his government was able to raise "…something like US $150 million from Eritreans living abroad in defence of the nation….". Ethiopia too mobilised its diaspora, although it is not clear exactly how much was raised. It is also clear just where most of these funds went – into purchasing arms from abroad. Eritrea had the most ground to make up, with its airforce outnumbered 10:1 by the Ethiopians at the start of the conflict. [41] The international community failed to adopt and then enforce an arms embargo against both combatants at any time during the hostilities. The United Nations and its member states must, therefore, bear a measure of responsibility for the war.

Thirdly it is possible to point to the inability of the international community to have make much of an impact on the fighting. Despite investing vast amounts of time and energy the combined efforts of the United States, Europe, the UN and the OAU were unable to have a perceptible impact on the course of the war. Pleas from individual presidents, resolutions of the UN Security Council and shuttle diplomacy were all ignored. This war was settled on the battlefield and since no nation or combination of nations was prepared to intervene directly no amount of diplomatic arm-twisting could change the minds of the combatants. Both leaders were equally stubborn in refusing to make concessions and managed to maintain the support of their political and military leaderships – at least as long as the conflict was active.

Finally, the war has resulted in a frozen peace between the two combatants. A detailed foreign policy document drawn up by Ethiopia described the current government in Eritrea as an "obstacle" to improved relations between the two countries. While dismissing suggestions that hostilities might be renewed, it ruled out any normalisation of ties while President Isaaias and his associates remained in power in Asmara. [42] Eritrea's response was that Ethiopia should stick to administering its own people and territory. Clearly there is little likelihood of a warming of relations across the Mereb River within the foreseeable future.

Aftermath

The Algiers peace Agreement was designed not only to end the war but also to regulate the postwar relationship between Ethiopia and Eritrea. It incorporated a number of earlier undertakings entered into by both sides, including the Agreement on the Cessation of Hostilities, and the Framework Agreement and the Modalities for its Implementation, endorsed by the OAU summit, July 1999.

The Algiers Agreement established or called on four separate organisation to assist Ethiopia and Eritrea to move from war to peace. Each was assigned a specific task, with a separate system of reporting. The fifth – the United Nations peacekeeping mission – had already been envisaged in the Cessation of Hostilities Agreement of 18 June 2000.

1. The International Committee of the Red Cross was called on to ensure the safe repatriation of all prisoners of war.
2. The Organisation of African Unity (which subsequently became the African Union) was asked to establish an investigation into the clash at Badme (or

'the incidents of 6 May 1998' as the treaty puts it) as well as other previous incidents which led to the border conflict.

3. The border itself would be drawn by a Boundary Commission established under the United Nations Cartographer and working out of the Hague. Its findings would be binding on both parties.

4. A Claims Commission would arbitrate on all damages and loss suffered by either government or their nationals. Its findings were also to be binding.

5. The United Nations Mission in Ethiopia and Eritrea (Unmee) established by UN Security Council resolution 1320 of 15 September 2000, in accordance with the Agreement sited above. This authorised the deployment of 4,200 troops along the border to oversee the ceasefire and to assist with the delimitation and demarcation of the border.

The Red Cross and Prisoners of War

In keeping with tradition, the International Committee of the Red Cross said very little about its operations. It visited prisoners of war both during and after the war, but only issued bland press releases from time to time marking the gradual repatriation of prisoners. It even refused the Claims Commission access to its records (see below) In August 2002 the President of the ICRC, Jakob Kellenberger visited Asmara and Addis Ababa and saw the respective leaders. Apart from saying that he welcomed the steps to bring them home and promised to work for the removal of all obstacles to this taking place, nothing more was heard of the mission. [43] But the visit did prove fruitful and in November the Red Cross was able to report that the last of the prisoners of war had returned home: 2,067 Eritreans and 1,067 Ethiopians. In addition the Red Cross had assisted in the repatriation of 5,055 Ethiopian and 1,086 Eritrean civilian internees.[44]

The Organisation of African Union investigation

This was, potentially, the most contentious of all the decisions contained in the Algiers peace treaty, for it was designed to assign blame for the outbreak of the war. In reality it has proved something of a damp squib. No findings of any such investigation have ever been published. The OAU's responsibilities were subsequently taken on by its successor, the African Union. This too has failed to act. In July 2003 the head of the African Union's Peace and Security, Said Djinnit, said the report had not been compiled because its was deemed "not conducive" to the peace process.[45] "Every peace process has its own dynamics", Mr Djinnit argued. "When we started we were faced with more serious difficulties and the issue was not pursued." Off the record African officials indicate that it has in fact been written, but is buried at the bottom of some drawer, never to see the light of day.

The Boundary Commission

The Commission was based at the Permanent Court of Arbitration at the Hague and headed by one of the eminent legal authorities on borders and boundary disputes, Sir Elihu Lauterpacht. The five man commission took evidence from both parties, allowed each side to respond to the other and finally published its binding decision on the border on 13th April 2002. At no time did it visit the region.

The 125-page adjudication, with accompanying maps, was no easy read. It discussed the treaties drawn up between Ethiopia and Italy or 1900, 1902 and 1908. The reasoning behind their adjudication was long and complex, but turned on two specific points: the provisions of the treaties and then whether either party had established by administration a claim so strong that it superseded the provisions contained in the treaties.

The Commission decided that the position of the critical Western portion of the border, which covered the town of Badme, rested on one specific portion of the 1902 treaty (to which Britain was also a party since it related to the frontier between Eritrea and Sudan). Point three of this text indicated that part of the Ethiopia – Eritrea border would be drawn so that "…the Canama tribe belong to Eritrea." From this single phrase the Commission decided that the Eritrean interpretation of the treaty was essentially correct. [46]

The Commission also went on to examine Ethiopia's claim that it had administered the Badme area for such a long time that it had won effective title to the area, even if it had not been awarded it by treaty. Having looked at evidence like the collection of taxes, the establishment of an elementary school and the destruction of incense trees the Commission concluded as follows: "These references represent the bulk of the items adduced by Ethiopia in support of its claim to have exercised administrative authority west of the Eritrean claim line. The Commission does not find in them evidence of administration of the area sufficiently clear in location, substantial in scope or extensive in time to displace the title of Eritrea that had crystallized as of 1935." [47]

That appeared to be clear enough. Certainly the legal team who drew it up thought they had made their decision crystal clear. Unfortunately the Commission did not indicate the location of Badme on the maps that accompanied the decision. Instead they gave the co-ordinates of the line along which the border would run. Exactly why the town was not shown on the maps is open to speculation. There is no doubt that a great deal rested on the location of this little town, since whoever had legitimate title to it could justifiably claim that they had only been defending their own sovereign territory when the initial conflict broke out. Or, to put it another way, whoever had title to

Badme was in the right about going to war. It may be that the jurists in the Hague thought it would be too controversial to rub Ethiopia's nose in this uncomfortable fact. In taking this decision they unwittingly unleashed a controversy that has yet to be resolved.

Both countries had their own legal teams at the Hague when the decision was given. So too were observers from the United Nations and the Organisation of African Unity. According to a senior official all those at the Hague were given very little time to study the lengthy judgement. One of the OAU staff in the Hague had been instructed to communicate with the Secretary General of the OAU, Omara Essy on the decision as soon as possible. So within an hour of it being given to them an email was sent to OAU headquarters outlining the ruling. The first point reads as follows:

"1. Western Sector. Delimitation line follows claim of Eritrea i.e. from common border with Sudan, follows Mereb river down to Setit point 6 and straight to Mai Ambessa, point 9. This confirms the Colonial boundary and Ethiopia retains Badme."[48]

The email concludes with the following assessment.

"The decision appears to be balanced. It is a win-win situation.
- In the Western Sector Ethiopia retained Badme while the rest of the Eritrean claim in the Sector was confirmed.
- In Sector Central Ethiopia retained its claim on Zalambessa, Alitena in Irob and Bada while Eritrea retained Tsorena.
- In Sector East the decision is balanced, the disputed area in Bure/Moussa Ali is shared by an equidistant line between the two check points, one manned by Kenyan Battalion and the other by the Ethiopian Armed Forces."

The contradiction between the statement that the line follows the Eritrea claim and that Ethiopia retains Badme was not explained. Instead, according to an official active in the border dispute, the information was immediately relayed to Ethiopian foreign minister, Seyoum Mesfin. [49]

The result was electric. The Foreign Minister called a press conference to announce the good news. This is from the official transcript of that conference made by the United Nations. [50] "Rarely are press conferences punctuated by applause but at Saturday's press conference given by Minister of Foreign Affairs, Ethiopian journalists punched fists in the air and applauded Seyoum Mesfin as he told them that all the government's territorial demands had been met....Minister Seyoum's demeanor when he finally took the high table was one of wry vindication......After the press conference journalists were in jubilant mood and treated to food and drinks in a party atmosphere. In town people were glued to radio sets and televisions listening to the minister's statement."

On the question of Badme the minister had this to say: "The rule of law has prevailed over the rule of jungle. This decision has rejected any attempt by Eritrea to get reward for its aggression. This decision was fair and legal. Badme and its surroundings which Eritrea invaded and occupied in May 1998 on the basis of its false claims, its now been decided by the Commission that Badme and its surroundings belong to Ethiopia." [51]

Eritrea took the news more coolly, putting out a statement attacking the "flowery and bombastic statements" that were issued by Ethiopia and declaring simply that "it is the Eritrean people have emerged victorious."[52]

When western journalists began to read to the decision it soon became clear that Seyoum Mesfin's interpretation of the text was inaccurate and that whatever other decisions had been taken about the border, Badme had gone to Eritrea. Jubilation in Addis Ababa turned to disbelief and then to anger. [53] However, it soon became clear that academics and the United Nations shared this view. [54]

Whatever outsiders felt about the judgement the reactions of the two parties was rapidly established. Eritrea, although unhappy about aspects of the ruling other than Badme decided it had won a moral victory and asked for its speedy implementation. Ethiopia, on the other hand, was unwilling to accept the outcome and submitted a lengthy Comment on the Commission's decision in January 2003, asking for the ruling to be re-considered. A statement from the Foreign Ministry said, "...the Commission made it known that its decision would be based not on the colonial treaty but the subsequent practice of the parties. It also affirmed in its decision that the boundary co-ordinates are provisional, and that they would only be final and binding after verification on the ground."[55]

The normally rather reticent Commission defended itself robustly against these charges. [56] It pointed out that the decision had been based firmly on the treaties and that it had been given no scope for varying the co-ordinates by the Peace Agreement that ended the war, except for purely technical reasons. Certainly it was precluded from taking into account the human suffering that any of its decisions caused by the terms of the Agreement. The Commission was particularly tart about the question of Badme, saying that the Ethiopian evidence to it had been "inconsistent" about its location and that some of the Ethiopian maps presented to it also had Badme within Eritrea. As a result the Commission found in Eritrea's favour on this point. "This conclusion followed from the inadequacy of Ethiopia's evidence."[57]

While this position may have been entirely consistent, it was not well received in Addis Ababa, which simply dug in its heels. Under intense pressure from his own political party, Prime Minister Meles Zenawi appealed informally to the international community for time and understanding. [58] Asmara continued to insist that demarcation proceed without delay, urging the United Nations to be "more courageous" and expressing its "frustration and impatience."[59] The head of Unmee, Legwaila Joseph Legwaila, was left warning that peace in the region would be endangered, unless both sides started talking to each other. "The status quo, that is non-communcation between the two governments, complicates the situation. When you don't talk to each other, misunderstandings can lead to conflict." Warning of the possibility of stalemate, Mr Legwaila said, "It is not the intention of the UN Security Council to watch and see this become another Cyprus." [60] He went on to point out that without demarcation the peace that Unmee had managed to maintain would be meaningless.

Mr Legwaila's appeals fell on deaf ears. Neither side was prepared to talk to each other. On 9th September 2003 matters took a turn for the worse when Prime Minister Meles wrote to the Secretary General of the United Nations expressing open criticism of the Boundary Commission's work. This was followed by a further letter to the Security Council on 22nd September urging it to salvage the peace process, and declaring that the Boundary Commission was in a "terminal crisis". The three page letter urged the UN body to "sct up an alternative mechanism to demarcate the contested parts of the boundary".[61] "It is unimaginable for the Ethiopian people to accept such a blatant miscarriage of justice," warned the Prime Minister.

The Boundary Commission responded forcefully to this attack on its legitimacy and its chairman, Sir Elihu Lauterpacht, rejected any notion of a terminal crisis. "The Commission does not accept that assessment: there is no 'crisis', terminal or otherwise, which cannot be cured by Ethiopia's compliance with its obligations under the Algiers Agreement, in particular its obligations to treat the Commission's delimitation determination as 'final and binding' (Article 4.15) and 'to cooperate with the Commission, its experts and other staff in all respects during the process of .....demarcation" (Article 4.14).[62] Sir Elihu went on to point out that Ethiopia's proposal to establish an alternative mechanism to demarcate the contested parts of the border was a "...repudiation of its repeated acceptance of the Commission's Decision since it was rendered."

The Claims Commission

While the Boundary Commission has been a relatively high profile operation, with its every decision dissected by both parties in the glare of publicity, the same cannot be said of the Claims Commission. Under the chairmanship of

Professor Hans van Houtte, who had previously undertaken similar work in the Balkans, it has managed to make quiet, if unspectacular progress.

The Commission decided to begin by hearing claims in a number of areas and only then to begin to issue reports on the financial damages to which these give rise.

So far it has only looked at one subject – the treatment of prisoners of war by both countries. Two partial awards (or findings) based on infringements of the Geneva Convention by the other, and on 1st July 2003 the awards were made public, in which claims of mistreatment by both sides were considered, but no monetary awards were made. Other issues still to be investigated include the behaviour of troops towards civilians caught up in the fighting, the siezure of goods and firms of Eritreans living in Ethiopia and vice versa and the siezure of government property in either country.

The reports on the treatment of prisoners of war provides the first comprehensive insight into what befell the approximately 2,600 Eritrean and 1,100 Ethiopians who were taken captive. The reports assessed claims by both countries and their replies to the assertions of the other party. Before considering each case in detail both reports begin with the same paragraph.

> "Based on the extensive evidence adduced during these proceedings, the Commission believes that both Paries had a commitment to the most fundamental principles bearing on prisoners of war. Both Paries conducted organised, official training programs to instruct their troops on procedures to be followed when POW's are taken. In contrast to many other contemporary armed conflicts, both Eritrea and Ethiopia regularly and consistently took POW's. Enemy personnel who were *hors de combat* were moved away from the battlefield to conditions of greater safety. Further, although these cases involve two of the poorest countries in the world, both made significant efforts to provide for the substance and care of the POW's in their custody. There were deficiencies of performance on both sides, sometimes significant, occasionally grave. Nevertheless, the evidence in these cases shows that both Eritrea and Ethiopia endeavoured to observe their fundamental humanitarian obligations to collect and protect enemy soldiers unable to resist on the battlefield. The Awards in these cases, and the difficulties that they identify, must be read against this background."[63]

This even-handed presentation of the evidence that was put before the Commission is somewhat at odds with the details contained in the reports. It is clear from reading this that Eritrea's behaviour towards the prisoners was considerably worse than that of Ethiopia.

116

Ethiopia's treatment was not beyond criticism. Eritrean POW's were frequently hungry and the diet they were given was monotonous and lacked essential vitamins. Some of their water was unfit to drink and they had very uncomfortable conditions to live in. Ethiopian guards occasionally beat their prisoners and subjected them to severe punishments. And taking the shoes of captured Eritreans meant they had to walk for considerable distances over rough terrain on bear feet. But on the whole their treatment was not intolerable.

Eritrea, which had always prided itself on its treatment of POW's during its war of liberation, seems to have forgotten many of its previous standards of behaviour. The Commission found that Eritrea sometimes inflicted brutal beatings and even killed Ethiopian prisoners. This took place both at the front and during evacuation. Eritrea too seized the footwear of their prisoners, forcing them to walk barefoot in rocky terrain. Prisoners were frequently beaten during interrogation – an allegation Eritrea did not even contest. Infringements of detention camp rules and regulations were severely punished with beatings that sometimes resulted in broken bones and unconsciousness. Ethiopians also complained about the quality of the food they were given and the filthy conditions of their camps. The health care was poor and prisoners were forced to work even when they were ill. All in all, it is a sorry catalogue of behaviour that brought shame on an Eritrean leadership that once demanded the highest standards of its fighters.

By the end of 2003 the Claims Commission was continuing its work. Professor van Houtte said both countries were co-operating with the Commission despite the apparent deadlock over the demarcation of the border. "The train continues to travel", he said. [64] In 2004 the Commission would hold hearings into what took place on the battlefields and at the diplomatic and economic claims of each side. Only then would the Commission report on the questions of liability and compensation.

United Nations Mission to Ethiopia and Eritrea, Unmee
The role of Unmee is the subject of the chapter in this book by Ian Martin.

Dead, Displaced and Deported
With the war at an end and international organisations attempting to come to grips with the devastation that had been left behind, it was time to count the cost.

Tens of thousands of soldiers had been killed and wounded. Their exact number will probably never be known. In early 2001 Ethiopian officials began informing families individually of the deaths of their relatives. Each family received a lump sum of six month's salary (of around $300) and a small

117

pension. But there was no announcement of the overall death toll.[65] Eritrea waited until Martyr's Day 2003 - the day in which it commemorates the sacrifice of its fighters during its war of independence - to announce that it had lost 19,000 in the latest conflict. There is no independent verification of this figure and no announcement of the numbers of wounded or disabled on either side.[66] But at least families could now grieve for those they had lost.

In addition to the dead and wounded, over a million Ethiopians and Eritreans were displaced by the fighting. The Ethiopian offensive of May 2000 forced more than a million Eritreans (out of a total population of 3.5 million) to flee as their troops advanced into the western and central regions of the country. [67] Catastrophic as this mass population movement was, it was only temporary. By November 2002 only 58,180 Eritreans were still displaced.[68] Despite this many were unable to work their lands, which were strewn with unexploded ordnance and 1.5 million mines.

Ethiopia too had its share of displaced, although the numbers concerned were considerably lower since Eritrean troops had not penetrated much beyond their mutual border region. Around 315,000 Ethiopians had to leave their homes, mostly in the Tigray region around towns like Zalambessa. A smaller number (approximately 29,000) were displaced in the Afar region. Many returned after the May 2000 offensive and by July 2001 all but 72,000 had been able to go back to their homes. [69]

Death, injury and even the flight of civilians are a tragic, but sadly all too predictable part of most modern conflicts. What was more remarkable about the Ethiopia – Eritrea war was that it was accompanied by the systematic expulsion of the citizens of the opposing country. It would not be possible to call this 'ethnic cleansing' since both countries share a common ethnicity. Nor were all 'foreigners' expelled. Nonetheless, a terrible price was exacted on ordinary people for the 'sins' of governments over whom they had no control.

"In June 1998 Ethiopia set in motion a campaign to round up, strip of all proof of Ethiopian citizenship, and deport Ethiopians of Eritrean origin from the country."[70] Tens of thousands of Ethiopians of Eritrean origin were treated in this way: rounded up, often in the dead of night, stripped of their property and citizenship and bussed across the border. Families were broken up, children separated from their mothers. Travel papers were stamped 'Expelled, never to return.' Many of those who were treated in this way had never been to Eritrea and knew no home other than Ethiopia. In all, about 75,000 people were deported without due process of law.

Eritrea promised at the outbreak of war that Ethiopian residents would not be penalised for the war and at first this was broadly observed.[71] From August 1998 until January 1999 some 21,000 Ethiopians left Eritrea voluntarily.

Many had been working in the port of Assab, which effectively closed down when the fighting got under way, as Ethiopia diverted its trade to neighbouring Djibouti. But as the war grew in intensity the attitude towards Ethiopians living in Eritrea became increasingly hostile. Individuals were beaten up and there were reports of rape after major battles. The Eritrean authorities began to initiate a programme of internment. After the major Ethiopian offensive in May 2000, Ethiopians were forced to register with local authorities in preparation for repatriation and shortly afterwards 7,500 were put across the border. The expulsions continued even after the Algiers peace agreement of December 2000. By March 2003 Unicef estimated that around 60,000 Ethiopians were living in difficult circumstances in Tigray. [72]

The result of two and a half years of fighting can therefore be summarised as follows.

The border between the two countries was left more or less where it had been before the first shot had been fired. By late 2003 it had been decided upon by the Boundary Commission, but still remained unmarked, with none of the 64 concrete pillars in place. At the same time the border was hermetically sealed and all trade across it had ceased. An estimated 100,000 people had lost their lives and many more had been wounded or crippled. At least 75,000 Eritreans had been forced to give up their homes and everything they had built up over generations as they were expelled from Ethiopia. Around 60,000 Ethiopians had gone in the opposite direction, sometimes willingly, but frequently at the point of a sword. The political elites of both countries had been deeply divided, with old friends transformed into bitter adversaries, who were locked up without trial (Eritrea) or disgraced and charged with corruption (Ethiopia). The diaspora of both countries, upon which each had relied, had become disenchanted and divided. The development programmes of two of the poorest countries on earth were put back by a generation, just as a major drought struck. Conflict and weaponry had been spread across neighbouring states. Regional organisations – fragile at the best of times – had been tested to breaking point. The goodwill of the international community towards both countries had been squandered.

All in all, one is forced to concluded that what began as a minor skirmish, over a dusty town that few in either capital had ever heard of, had transformed the prospects of both Ethiopia and Eritrea beyond recognition.

ENDNOTES

1. *The Economist,* 8 May 1999, p. 74.
2   *Ethiopian Foreign Ministry Statement on Ethio-Eritrean Conflict, 12 August 1998.* In Chronology of the Ethio-Eritrean Conflict and Basic Document, Walta Information Centre, 2000, p 161- 162

3. Statement by the Ministry of Foreign Affairs, Asmara, May 23, 1998.
4. *Eritrea Profile*, May 1998.
5. Informal discussion with the author.
6 Alex Last, *Focus on Africa Magazine*, October - December 1998 p. 22.
7. *Al-Sharq al Awsat*, London 3 June 1998.
8. Statement of the Council of Ministers of the Federal Democratic Republic of Ethiopia on the Dispute with Eritrea, 13 May 1998.
9. Statement of the Cabinet of Ministers of the Government of Eritrea on the Dispute with Ethiopia, 14 May 1998.
10. Negash and Tronvoll, *op. cit*, provide details of the United States and Rwandan initiative, together with a valuable account of the unfolding diplomatic efforts to end the war.
11. The conduct of the war is drawn from a number of sources. The semi-official Walta Information Centre produced a very useful document, containing most of the documents pertaining to the conflict and a daily chronology of the fighting. *Chronology of the Ethio-Eritrean Conflict and Basic Documents*. Walta Information Centre, Addis Ababa, 2001. The United Nations also produced a daily chronology. *Chronology of events: 1 May 1999 – 18 June 2000* (unpublished) produced by the United Nations Emergency Unit for Ethiopia. Additional material was provided by informal contacts with Ethiopian and Eritrea officials.
12. For a critique of Ms Rice's performance see 'Irrational Exuberance: The Clinton Administration in Africa'. Peter Rosenblum, *Current History*, May 2002.
13. The United States – Rwandan plan, presented to both parties on 30 - 31 May 1998. Press Statement by James P. Rubin, US Department of State, 3 June 1998. The United States had joined forces with Rwanda since the country was an African third party, and an ally of both belligerents.
14. Organisation of African Unity Proposal for a Framework Agreement for a peaceful settlement of the dispute between Eritrea and Ethiopia.
15. *Ethiopian Foreign Ministry Statement*, 12 August 1998.
16. *The Economist* 8 May 1999, p. 77.
17. *The Eritrea-Yemen Arbitration*, Permanent Court of Arbitration, 9 October 1998, p. 151.
18. *Reuters*, 10 June 2000.
19. *Associated Press*, 9 June.
20. *Reuters*, 15 June.
21. *Reuters*, 15 June.
22. *Associated Press*, 15 June.
23. Journalists reported that neither side was particularly interested in a diplomatic solution. "The Italian Embassy in Asmara volunteered to dig out every map drawn during Italy's occupation of Eritrea from 1890 to 1952, but, according to an Embassy official who asked that his name not be used, neither of the two parties expressed much interest." *Christian Science Monitor*, 22 June 1998.
24. Eritrea: Selected Issues and Statistical Appendix. *International Monetary Fund Country Report, 03/166, June 2003*. Table II-2.

25. Fiona Lortan, The Ethiopia-Eritrea Conflict: a fragile peace. *African Security Review*, Vol 9, No. 4, 2000. p. 2.
26. George Bloch, No compromise for Eritrea and Ethiopia. *Jane's Intelligence Review*, January 2000, P. 43.
27. *AFP* 2 February 1999.
28. The Ethiopian offensive was named 'Operation Sunset' in mocking reference to President Afeworki's statement on Eritrean radio on 10th August 1998. "What the world must know is we will never withdraw from Badme. Withdrawing from Badme is like the sun will never rise again."
29. There were also reports of that Ethiopia had contracted French commercial satellite services.
30. According to the Eritrean government the timing was co-incidental.
31. Ceasefire Under Threat: *Africa Confidential*, Vol. 40, no. 22, 5 November 1999
32. Ethiopian Spokesperson's Office, 16 June 1999.
33. The titles of these documents are "OAU Frame work Agreement for a peaceful settlement of the dispute between Eritrea and Ethiopia". 8 November 1998. "Modalities for the implementation of the OAU Framework Agreement on the settlement of the dispute between Ethiopia and Eritrea." 14 July 1999. "Technical Arrangements for the implementation of the OAU Framework Agreement and its Modalities." August 1999. See Appendices 1, 2, 3.
34. United Nations Emergency Unit for Ethiopia, *Chronology of events: 1 May – 18 June 2000 op cit.*
35. United Nations Emergency Unit for Ethiopia, *Chronology of events: 1 May – 18 June 2000 op cit.*
36. *Los Angeles Times*, 30 May 2000.
37. United Nations Emergency Unit for Ethiopia, *Chronology of events: 1 May – 18 June 2000 op cit.*
38. *Ethiopia Tentatively Calls Defenses "Dependable".* Defence and Foreign Affairs Strategic Policy, 1/4/98.
39. UN newsagency, *Irin*, 17 January 2003.
40. "It's very difficult to easily find an answer". President Isaias Afwerki. "I was surprised, shocked, puzzled." Prime Minister Meles Zenawi. Washington Post, 17 June 1998.
41. Air war between Ethiopia and Eritrea 1998 – 2000. Jonathan Kyzer and Tom Cooper, unpublished paper. ACIG website.
42. Irin 22 July 2003.
43. ICRC press release, 23 August 2002.
44. ICRC press release, 29 November 2002.
45. Irin 11 August, 2003.
46. "Decision regarding delimitation of the border between the state of Eritrea and the Federal Democratic Republic of Ethiopia" *Eritrea-Ethiopia Boundary Commission.* April 2002. Paragraph 5.88, page 83.
47. Ibid. Paragraph 5.95, page 84.
48. Email dated April 13, 2002, in author's possession.
49. Interview with the author.

50. "Transcript of Press Conference (compiled by Unmee public information office) Addis Ababa, 13 April 2002.

51. (sic) ibid.

52. "Statement on the Determination of the Eritrea-Ethiopia Border Commission". Government of Eritrea, Asmara, 13 April 2002.

53. The author was attacked by the Ethiopian Foreign Ministry: "The journalist, Martin Plaut, who wrongly interpreted the decision of the boundary commission, has been a supporter of the EPLF for over two decades, according to sources. Plaut has been also disseminating unfounded news with Alex Last (the BBC Asmara Correspondent. Ed) during the Ethio-Eritrea border conflict" *Ethiopia News Agency*, 18 April 2002.

54. Marc Lancey writing in the New York Times quoted UN officials as saying that Badme appeared to be on the Eritrean side of the borderline. *New York Times,* 16 April 2002. Interview with Martin Pratt, Head of the Boundary Research Unit at Durham University, *Irin*, 16 April 2002.

55. Statement issued by the Ministry of Foreign Affairs of the FDRE Concerning the Ethiopia-Eritrea Boundary Commission's Observations. Undated, but on the Ministry website May 2003, p. 3.

56. Observations. Ethiopia Eritrea Boundary Commission. 21 March 2003.

57. Observations, paragraph 18.

58. The conduct of the war provoked a split in the ruling Tigray People's Liberation Party, with key members arrested on charges of corruption. Details of these political differences, as well as those that occurred within the Eritrean ruling party are beyond the scope of this paper. However, it is important to note that despite the Ethiopian crackdown, senior members of the TPLF remained openly opposed to allowing the Commission to demarcate the border. Dr Solomon Inquai, speaker of the Tigray regional council, said, "They cannot come. We will not let them. Nobody in their right mind will let them demarcate, because everyone is against this." Irin 31 July 2003.

59. *Irin*, 1 August 2003.

60. *Irin*, 31 July 2003.

61. *Irin*, 24 September 2003.

62. Letter from Boundary Commission, 7 October 2003.

63. *Partial Award Prisoners of War, Eritrea's Claim 17*. Ethiopia –Eritrea Claims Commission, p. 2,3. *Partial Award Prisoners of War, Ethiopia's Claim 4*. Ethiopia – Eritrea Claims Commission. p 2,3. 1 July 2003.

64. Phone interview with Professor Houtte, 19 December 2003.

65. *Associated Press,* 30 April 2001.

66. *Irin*, 24 June 2003.

67. *Eritrea Profile*. The Global IDP Project of the Norwegian Refugee Council. (Internet)

68. United Nations, November 2002, *United Nations Consolidated Inter-Agency Appeal 2003,* Eritrea (Internet).

69. *Ethiopia Profile.*The Global IDP Project of the Norwegian Refugee Council. (Internet)

70. *The Horn of Africa War: Mass expulsions and the Nationality Issue (June 1998 – April 2002)*. Human Rights Watch, January 2003. (Internet).

71. Ibid.
72. *Unicef Humanitarian Action: Ethiopia Donor Update.* United Nations Children's Fund (Unicef), 14 March 2003,. (Internet).

Chapter 6

THE ROLE OF THE UNITED STATES IN RESOLVING THE CONFLICT[1]

John Prendergast and Philip Roessler

Expectations of Africa's economic and political emergence at the end of the 20th century were shattered by a chain of conflicts that extended across the continent from Somalia in the northeast to Angola in the southwest. Not least of these was the devastating interstate war between Ethiopia and Eritrea, two countries that many had seen as key players in the hoped-for "African Renaissance."

The brief, but intense, war caused as many as one hundred thousand deaths, displaced one third of Eritrea's population, froze foreign aid and investment, sparked a bilateral arms race and defense spending spree, and drove the two countries' real growth rates to zero. Ironically, two governments that wanted to lead Africa in new directions ended up reinforcing old stereotypes.

Though the war wrought much devastation and undermined international confidence in Africa's rebirth, its resolution provides a model of how U.S. diplomatic involvement can play a key role in ending conflict in Africa. This case therefore has wide ramifications in the debate over how deeply the United States should immerse itself in conflict resolution efforts throughout the continent , if not more broadly. Twice the United States has deployed senior officials to lead a peace process in Africa (Chester Crocker in Namibia and Anthony Lake in this case) and sustained that commitment over an extended period of time, and twice the United States has succeeded. Though not widely recognized as strategically important investments, there is no doubt that these efforts have major repercussions in terms of lives and resources saved.

From Allies to Enemies

Why did the conflict erupt between Ethiopia and Eritrea? What drove two erstwhile friends to wage what was at the time the largest conventional war on earth?

It is important to distinguish between proximate and root causes of this conflagration. The proximate cause was certainly a dispute over their common border. The parties alternately alleged encroachment along the undemarcated border, and the moving of border markings, as evidence of disputes going back years regarding administration of border towns. These border issues simmered on low heat until early May 1998, when frustrations boiled over. A series of military actions culminated in an unprecedented use of force by the Eritrean army, which moved with heavy armor into areas previously administered by Ethiopia. The Ethiopian Parliament met and demanded Eritrea's withdrawal. Eritrea insisted it was only taking back areas that belonged to it, according to its interpretation of colonial treaties. This led directly to a breakdown in relations between the two countries, and hence the war.

But of course the causes of the war run much deeper. Strains in bilateral relations, diverging economic conditions, and popular frustration contributed to the outbreak of the war.

Unresolved Tension in Bilateral Relations

The troubled bilateral relations between the two sides extend back to before Eritrea's independence in 1993. During the civil war against the former Ethiopian dictator Mengistu Haile Mariam in the 1970s and 1980s, the future leaders of Eritrea and Ethiopia, Issaias Afwerki and Meles Zenawi, respectively, were allies on the battlefield, although the relations between the liberation movements they headed were often strained. In the years after the overthrow of Mengistu in 1991, however, the alliance slowly unravelled. Unresolved disputes and tensions continued to fester and were never adequately addressed, though the two leaders kept in close personal contact.

When Eritrea gained its independence, the tensions worsened. The two countries failed to effectively institutionalize bilateral relationships that originated as an opportunistic collaboration between two guerrilla armies but then shifted to relations between two distinct and very different states. Consequently, the relations between both governments were not deeply entrenched but existed merely between personalities in the leadership of both sides. When the crisis erupted, there existed no institutional channel for communication. In the absence of information about the other's true intentions, both leaders felt compelled to adopt aggressive postures.

Conflicting Economic Policies

An additional contributing factor to the tension between the two countries was divergent approaches to state-making after Eritrea's independence. This led to immediate structural and policy differences concerning economic relations between the two states. Ethiopia inherited a huge debt, an enormous population unlinked by roads and commerce, and major internal political divergence. All of which weakened the overall power and economic potential of the state. Eritrea, on the other hand, inherited no debt, a somewhat cohesive and united population, and less daunting infrastructure deficits. Over time, policy differences emerged over trade, currency, port usage, customs, and labor migration.

Scarcity and Populational Demands

A final underlying dimension to the conflict was the conditions on the ground for the people living in the disputed areas. In the key regions of fighting in northern Tigray and southern Eritrea, people live on the knife's edge of survival, and productive land is scarce and irreplaceable; therefore, land is an issue over which peasants are perhaps the most willing to fight and die. Demographic pressure and economic deterioration worsened the living conditions in the region and led to increased demands on the two governments. Northern Tigray is one of most densely populated areas on the Africa continent and thus there was pressure to expand geographically. Furthermore, the local population had elevated expectations for the post-Mengistu era. Despite some economic development, the people remained frustrated. To make matters worse, food insecurity remained a problem because population growth exceeded productivity increases.

Inevitable Conflict?

Despite the underlying tension, could war between the two countries have been prevented? In retrospect, two initiatives on the part of the international community could have reduced the possibility of conflict. First, there could have been pressure immediately after Eritrea's independence to formally demarcate the border. Second, there could have been more effort expended to ensure the institutionalization of the bilateral relationship, rather than relying on the personal relationship of the two leaders to act as the dominant channel between the two countries.

Having said that, there were few visible signs immediately before the outbreak of hostilities that war was imminent. If you surveyed African and Africanist experts—even Ethiopia/Eritrea/Horn experts—throughout the world at the beginning of 1998, no one was predicting conflict between these two states. There were many more logical candidates for potential conflict across the continent.

Furthermore, although the U.S. government and the World Bank were deeply engaged with these two countries at the time, neither Ethiopia or Eritrea indicated any problem on the border that might lead to serious trouble, despite the fact that they had a joint commission of very senior people discussing the issues. Neither government ever contacted any human rights group about the alleged abuses being committed against their citizens by the other government. In short, it was a flatliner. There was no pulse detected by outsiders as to the potential for armed confrontation.

Operating with that limited information, we can see that the war was the result of problems that both parties kept to themselves and thought they could resolve quietly between themselves. And although some form of confrontation may have been inevitable, both parties were very surprised that they could neither contain nor turn it around.

The Role of U.S. Mediation

With the eruption of the war in May 1998, the leaders of both countries looked to the U.S. to play a mediating role. They asked Susan Rice, U.S. assistant secretary of state, and, separately, Paul Kagame, then vice president of Rwanda, to travel to the region to try to defuse tensions. Rice and her American team worked closely with Kagame to craft a formula designed to address the proximate cause of the conflict, the border. Over two years later, that formula would form the basis of an agreement, but at this early juncture only Ethiopia accepted the proposal, while Eritrea wavered and rejected it. Further fighting then hardened attitudes and made agreement more elusive.

Despite the intransigence on the part of Eritrea, Rice sought to rally diplomatic support from other African countries to keep the initiative alive. Soon thereafter, Rice attended the Organization of African Unity (OAU) summit and helped forge a consensus among key African states in support of the basic elements of the formula as the appropriate path to peace.

Later that summer, President Clinton sent a U.S. team to the region to convince the parties to end one of the nastiest elements of the conflict, the air war, which had led to the deaths of a number of civilians and threatened to widen the war beyond the border. With critical support from Pentagon officials, the team brokered an air strike moratorium; also actively involved was President Clinton, who was in frequent contact with the leaders by phone, backing up and sealing diplomatic efforts on the ground. Without an air strike moratorium, the war might have spun out of control, with much more civilian damage and many more deaths, a change in strategic targets to include capitals, and an intensification of other means of fighting the war.

Though the air strike moratorium diffused the potential for a significant widening of the war, the conflict continued. Late in 1998 President Clinton and Secretary Albright named as their special envoy former national security adviser Tony Lake, who immediately launched a series of shuttle visits over the following six months. Lake led a State–NSC–Department of Defense team that worked closely with the OAU to help produce the OAU "Framework Agreement" and "Modalities of Implementation," two documents aimed at producing a set of principles as a basis for resolving the conflict. These documents drew heavily upon the original U.S.-Rwandan proposal. Ethiopia accepted the two documents but Eritrea had serious reservations, so consultations continued, and the United States and OAU continued to press Eritrea for its acceptance.

Another round of fighting in February 1999 deepened mistrust and suspicion between the two sides. The situation was anything but "ripe for resolution." Nevertheless, shuttling missions by Lake as well as continuous engagement by Susan Rice and Gayle Smith, NSC senior director for Africa, forestalled further offensive action for over a year.

In August 1999, Algeria as chair of the OAU hosted a drafting session that included teams from the United States and United Nations, with the objective of producing a set of detailed steps that would provide a roadmap for the two parties to implement the two OAU documents. Negotiations between the United States, OAU, and United Nations were as intense as the follow-up consultations with the parties. These deliberations finally produced the detailed peace implementation plan. Key to the breakthrough was the expertise on security issues provided by the Pentagon, spearheaded by Lt. Col. Mike Bailey. In many conflict resolution efforts, U.S. experience has been brought to bear on ceasefire and peacekeeping arrangements. In this case, Bailey and other U.S. military officials drew from other model ceasefire arrangements globally and adapted proposals to the political and security challenges of Ethiopia and Eritrea.

This time, however, the parties' positions were reversed. Eritrea accepted while Ethiopia expressed reservations. Subsequently, the U.S. team, working closely with Algerian special representative Ahmed Ouyahia and European Union (EU) special envoy Rino Serri, endeavored to gain Ethiopia's agreement. This involved extended visits, shuttling between Asmara and Addis, and proximity talks in Algiers.

This stage of the process lasted nine months, from September 1999 to May 2000. While forestalling further outbreaks in hostilities, the U.S. team worked to address Ethiopian concerns. In April the OAU, U.S., and EU teams met in Algiers with the two partners, but the Eritrean team presented what amounted to conditions for further negotiations, and the process was stymied.

Further inadvertent damage was done when a UN Security Council mission to the Congo veered off to the Horn and threatened punitive measures against Ethiopia if it initiated hostilities, who already had a jittery finger on their trigger. The war resumed a day later. This first and only example of a breakdown in coordinated international action in the Ethiopia-Eritrea process was doubly disappointing in that the U.S. team was on the precipice of presenting a new proposal to the two parties that might have moved the process towards conclusion.

Throughout the process, the mediation focused on the proximate issue of the border, as the parties were unwilling to discuss other issues. But it was the deeper underlying issues referenced earlier that complicated the talks, introduced contradictions at the most perplexing moments, and informed the stances of both parties.

The Turning Point in the War

In May 2000 the war resumed at a ghastly level when Ethiopia launched a massive offensive. The Ethiopians overwhelmed the Eritrean positions at a number of points along the front. The resumption of the fighting prompted the mediators to immediately convene a meeting in Algiers with the two foreign ministers. As the stakes increased, both parties dug in even further, providing more justification for their reputations as tough, uncompromising negotiators.

Round-the-clock negotiations, led by Ouyahia and Lake, were held to bring an end to the fighting. Algerian president Abdelaziz Bouteflika made a trip to the two capitals that helped lay the groundwork for those talks. EU envoy Serri also contributed. Although there were at times disagreements between the external actors, they remained committed to maintaining a united front at all times during the negotiations. This required constant work by the U.S. team in briefing and consulting with multilateral and bilateral officials from around the world.

At this point the mediators and parties made a strategic decision to separate the longer-term issues of determining the border and paying compensation for war damages from the immediate need to establish a permanent cease-fire. The mediating strategy proved fruitful. Intensive negotiations finally produced a document acceptable to both parties in mid-June 2000, and the guns immediately went silent.

In the aftermath of securing the ceasefire, the focus shifted to quickly and competently deploying a peacekeeping mission. A challenging environment pertained at that time, given the problematic missions in the Democratic Republic of Congo and Sierra Leone. The negotiators immediately invited Col. Robert Phillips, chief of planning for the UN Department of Peacekeeping Operations, to Algiers to discuss and plan the peacekeeping mission with the mediators and the parties. The UN contribution in this regard was stellar.

Work also immediately began on building the framework for the more comprehensive agreement involving demarcationof the border, compensation for war damages, and investigation of the origins of the conflict.

These talks followed similar formula—intensive sessions in Algiers during the fall of 2000, shuttling led by Tony Lake between Asmara and Addis, and intensive work from Washington by Susan Rice and Gayle Smith (and their superiors when necessary). The United States took a more prominent role, backed by the new Algerian envoy, Abdelkadir Messahel, and EU envoy Serri.

Despite the lull in fighting, the stakes remained high. If no agreement was forthcoming on demarcating the border, countries may have been reluctant to contribute forces for the peacekeeping mission. Without peacekeepers, the redeployment of Ethiopian forces off Eritrean soil would have been stalled—an issue that certainly could have sparked new tensions.

In this set of negotiations, legal issues replaced security issues as central areas of focus. Rather than Pentagon expertise, which had proved so decisive to the earlier effort, we now turned to State's Legal Office for critical and continuous involvement in the negotiations. Kathleen Wilson and Ron Betthauer became indispensable to U.S. and OAU efforts to mediate the final agreement. This involved countless hours with the legal teams of both parties, which also assumed prominent roles in the push to the finish line.

On December 12, 2000 a peace agreement was finally signed by Eritrean President Issaias and Ethiopian Prime Minister Meles. The peace accord did not address all of the underlying economic and political issues that divided these two countries. Nevertheless, it did address exhaustively: (1) the proximate cause of the fighting—by establishing a commission to delimit and demarcate the border; (2) the reasons for the fighting—by creating an independent commission to investigate all of the causes; and (3) the immediate effects of the fighting, by establishing a commission to address compensation issues.

After the signing of the agreement, the United States made it a priority to support the agreement's implementation and the consolidation of the peace. This included demining, demobilization, peacekeeping training, humanitarian aid, support for resettling the displaced, support to the International Committee of the Red Cross on detainee repatriation, reconstruction aid, the return of the Peace Corps, trade and investment, port issues, International

Monetary Fund/World Bank credits, and debt relief. In addition, the United States made its first troop contribution to an African peacekeeping mission since Somalia, a small yet symbolically important action.

Cognizant of the failure of other peace agreements because international attention shifted too rapidly to other conflicts and issues, key members of the international community sustained support for the implementation of the agreement and ensured the consolidation of peace. This support included resources but also diplomatic engagement that ensured that the parties lived up to their commitments.

Conclusion: Policy Lessons

The mediation effort to end the war between Ethiopia and Eritrea was long and arduous; it took more than two years. What is remarkable is that the U.S. maintained its commitment to end the war throughout. Again, this demonstrates the crucial role the U.S. can play if it provides high level and sustained engagement. The resolution of the Ethiopian-Eritrean war provides valuable lessons for U.S. leadership in helping to end other conflicts in Africa and around the world.

1. *Gravitas.* The naming of Tony Lake as special envoy, and his subsequent full-fledged commitment, was a central factor. Lake's status as a former National Security Adviser plus his personal interest in African issues meant that he was deeply respected in Africa and among allies.

2. *Highest level engagement.* When needed, President Clinton, National Security Adviser Samuel Berger, and Secretary Albright weighed in, as did Undersecretary of State Thomas Pickering. They allowed the team great latitude and provided unswerving support, particularly through phone calls and letters to the leaders of the two countries.

3. *Close partnership between the United States and the OAU.* The joint initiative is perhaps a model for U.S.-Africa cooperation in conflict resolution. The U.S. team closely consulted with the OAU, and undertook coordinated diplomacy first with Kagame and then with the Algerian envoys, and consistently with OAU secretary general Salim Ahmed Salim and his undersecretary, Said Djinnit. No facilitator acted without the knowledge and agreement of the other. This partnership ensured both wider donor solidarity and wider African solidarity centered on one path to peace. There was only one door that Ethiopia and Eritrea could go through to get an agreement.

4. *Intensive, sustained engagement.* Susan Rice and Gayle Smith led and coordinated a monumental effort of constant engagement. The team was in touch with both parties every day, often for hours. The U.S. approachwas a model for State-NSC-Department of Defense cooperation. The case also makes clear the need for sustaining engagement until the very end, which requires a full commitment before launching the effort and the understanding that success rarely comes easily or quickly.

5. *Close coordination with allies and the United Nations.* Early on, the team established a close working partnership with the European Union through its envoy, Serri, with whom they worked closely throughout the negotiations. The team also worked directly with UN secretary general Kofi Annan and his undersecretary, Kieren Prendergast, throughout the entire process. This was done both to take advantage of their diplomatic support and to ensure that the United Nations—as the main would-be implementor of any agreement—was fully on board with our proposals.

6. *Leverage.* The mediators tried to take advantage of various political, economic, and military levers available to put pressure on the parties to reach an agreement:

a. Aid freeze—A combined multilateral and bilateral freeze on key non-humanitarian programs was instituted on both governments by most donors until the peace agreement was signed.

b. Diplomatic isolation—Recognizing both governments sought full integration in the global community, and wanted to participate in global decisions and issues, the UN Security Council and other UN members pigeonholed Ethiopia and Eritrea as countries in conflict. This informal banishment greatly limited their ability to participate normally in global affairs while the conflict was on-going.

c. Pressure from international financial institutions—There was no major lending during the conflict period, and no substantial debt rescheduling.

d. UN Security Council arms embargo (imposed in May 2000)—It probably should have come earlier, but still sent an important signal that these countries could not conduct business as usual.

e. African leaders—The OAU employed other African leaders to weigh in with both parties during key junctures throughout the conflict and negotiations.

f. U.S. Congressional engagement—Critical members of the U.S. Congress expressed moral outrage that was key in underscoring the extent to which the two governments were isolated internationally.

g. U.S. private citizen engagement—The efforts of members of the Returned PeaceCorps Volunteers demonstrated the importance of peace in the Horn for key constituencies in America, particularly those with histories in one or both countries and those interested in investing in the region.

ENDNOTE

1. The following chapter draws in part from John Prendergast, "U.S. Leadership in Resolving African Conflict: The Case of Ethiopia-Eritrea," United States Institute of Peace Special Report, September 7, 2001.

Chapter 7
KEEPING THE PEACE:
THE UNITED NATIONS MISSION IN
ETHIOPIA AND ERITREA
Ian Martin[1]

With the signing of the Agreement on Cessation of Hostilities by the Foreign Ministers of Eritrea and Ethiopia in Algiers on 18 June 2000, the guns fell silent – but they had done so twice before, only for bloody warfare to resume. This time, however, a peacekeeping mission would be deployed to monitor the cessation of hostilities, the redeployment of troops, and the de-militarized temporary security zone to be established between the armies of the two countries until the determination of their common border. The parties went on to sign, on 12 December 2000, a full Peace Agreement providing for the establishment of a neutral boundary commission, mandated to delimit and demarcate this border, whose determination would be final and binding on the parties. The completion of demarcation would allow the exit of the peacekeeping mission.[1]

The demilitarization of the border pending its delimitation and demarcation, together with oversight by what was first called an observer (not a peacekeeping) mission, had been an aspect of all peace proposals, beginning with the earliest recommendations of 1 June 1998 from the Rwanda and U.S. government facilitators during the first round of hostilities. When the Rwanda-U.S. recommendations were replaced by the November 1998 OAU Framework Agreement, the proposed supervising body became "a Group of Military Observers which will be deployed by the OAU with the support

The views expressed in this chapter are solely those of the author and do not represent the official views of the United Nations.

of the United Nations." After the second round of fighting, the July 1999 Modalities for the Implementation of the OAU Framework Agreement still referred to the deployment of military observers by the OAU in cooperation with the UN. But as the OAU worked with the U.S. team and UN representatives to develop detailed arrangements for implementation, the negotiators became convinced that the situation required not just a military observer mission, but a full-scale peacekeeping mission, beyond the capabilities of the OAU. Thus the August 1999 Technical Arrangements for the Implementation of the OAU Framework Agreement and its Modalities proposed that a UN peacekeeping mission would be established under the authority of the Security Council. It would be headed by a Special Representative of the UN Secretary-General, working closely with a representative of the Secretary-General of the OAU, which itself would deploy initial liaison officers/observers.

Ethiopia had accepted three successive sets of proposals: the Rwanda-U.S. recommendations, the Framework Agreement and the Modalities. It took issue, however, with aspects of the Technical Arrangements, maintaining that these introduced ideas and institutions that were not in the Framework Agreement and the Modalities, and were inconsistent with them. One such inconsistency was that the observer mission, which had been proposed to be established by the OAU in collaboration with the UN, was now to be established by the UN, and associated "mission creep" had followed the change from an observer mission to a peacekeeping mission. In subsequent exchanges between Ethiopia and the negotiators, the latter revised their proposed technical arrangements to revert to a group of military observers to be deployed by the OAU with the support of the UN, specifying 300 to 500 observers, and no formed operational units. This proposal was on the table when the third round of fighting began in May 2000.

Eritrea regarded the OAU, with its headquarters in Addis Ababa, as unsympathetic to its independence struggle and biased toward the Ethiopian view of the conflict; it thus favoured a UN leading role over that of the OAU. Ethiopia had conversely preferred the OAU, and it might seem surprising that it became willing to end the third round of hostilities with the acceptance of the very kind of UN peacekeeping mission, with formed units, which it had previously resisted. This is however to be understood in the context of the favourable overall position Ethiopia had at last achieved. With its troops now deep inside Eritrea, it was able to insist that the demilitarized zone should be entirely within Eritrea, not equally on each side of the disputed border as Eritrea proposed. Eritrea would thus be denied a military presence within a 25-kilometre strip of its own undisputed territory.

Representatives of the UN's Department of Peacekeeping Operations were present as the Agreement on Cessation of Hostilities (hereafter "the Agreement") was signed. Thereafter, the two governments sent formal requests to the UN for its involvement, the UN dispatched reconnaissance and liaison teams to the region, and on 31 July 2000 the Security Council established the United Nations Mission in Ethiopia and Eritrea (UNMEE), authorizing an initial 100 military observers.[2] On 9 August, the Secretary-General presented his full proposals for UNMEE, reflecting the findings of the reconnaissance mission.[3] In accordance with these recommendations, when the Security Council fully mandated UNMEE on 15 September, it established its troop strength as up to 4200 troops, including up to 220 military observers.[4] The Secretary-General appointed Legwaila Joseph Legwaila (Botswana) as his Special Representative, Ian Martin (UK) and Cheikh-Tidiane Gaye (Senegal) as Deputy Special Representatives in Asmara and Addis Ababa respectively, and Major-General Patrick Cammaert (Netherlands) as Force Commander.

The two armies remained eye-ball to eye-ball in the positions they held when hostilities had ceased, their trenches often only metres apart. The first military liaison officers began making field visits, and from mid-September were joined by the first military observers. But the separation of the forces and establishment of the demilitarized zone could not take place until formed troops were in place in adequate numbers along the sensitive parts of the 1000-kilometre border. To their credit, for several months both armies maintained the discipline necessary to ensure that their close proximity did not lead to unintended clashes, but early UN deployment was of great importance.

The speed with which UNMEE established itself on the ground was significantly accelerated by the fact that it included the first deployment of the Multi-National Stand-by High Readiness Brigade for UN Operations, or SHIRBRIG. A number of like-minded states had developed SHIRBRIG to create a rapid deployment force available within the framework of the UN stand-by arrangements requested by Secretary-General Boutros Boutros-Ghali. The states included the Netherlands, Canada and Denmark, and these three countries sent SHIRBRIG units to UNMEE, along with staff officers from other member countries. UNMEE Force Commander Cammaert came directly from being Commander of SHIRBRIG, and this deployment sped up the establishment of both an effective Force headquarters and the joint Dutch-Canadian battalion in the central of UNMEE's three sectors. These were followed by the deployment of a Jordanian battalion in the western sector, and a Kenyan battalion in the eastern sector. As a matter of policy, SHIRBRIG deployment is for a period of only six months, and in June 2001 the Dutch-Canadian battalion would be replaced by an Indian battalion. Smaller elements of the UNMEE force came from Bangladesh, India, Italy, and

Slovakia, with later rotations bringing successive contributions from France, Ireland, Uruguay and Finland. On 10 February 2001, the Force Commander was able to inform the parties that he had a credible force deployed to carry out the UNMEE mandate (although the initial presence in the eastern sector was only a reinforced Canadian platoon, pending the deployment of the Kenyan battalion).

While the military deployment went relatively smoothly, UNMEE was meanwhile grappling with its most difficult political challenge: the definition of the Temporary Security Zone. According to the Agreement, this was to be formed by Ethiopia redeploying its troops "from positions taken after 6 February 1999, and which were not under Ethiopian administration before 6 May 1998." This line of 6 May 1998 – the date of the first outbreak of hostilities – would form the southern boundary of the Temporary Security Zone. Eritrean forces would "remain at a distance of 25 km (artillery range) from positions to which the Ethiopians shall redeploy," thus establishing the northern boundary of the Zone.

However, not only was there no agreement between the parties as to what positions had and had not been under Ethiopian administration: that disagreement, at least so far as the disputed western settlement of Badme was concerned, had been the flashpoint for the conflict. The negotiators' earlier proposals had taken this into account, and had included a means of addressing the problem. The Technical Arrangements would have provided for a Neutral Commission, established by the current Chairman of the OAU, to make a determination of what had been the positions prior to 6 May 1998, within three weeks of an agreement. This determination would have been binding on the parties, but would not have prejudiced the final status of the territories concerned. Ethiopia however had insisted that agreement of the parties should be required for the verification findings to become binding. But in the Agreement no mechanism for verification of the pre-6 May 1998 positions was specified, and the initiative was left with Ethiopia "to submit redeployment plans for its troops… to the Peacekeeping Mission."

The priority for the negotiators in June 2000 was to stop the bloodshed. The parties' disagreement over which had been administering disputed areas had been so bitter that attempting to define the 6 May 1998 line might have delayed the cessation of hostilities. The hope was that the issue would become easier to resolve as open hostilities receded - although some among the negotiators correctly predicted that it would only become harder to address, absent the pressure for a ceasefire. In the event, the intractable issue of defining the boundaries of the Temporary Security Zone was bequeathed by the ceasefire negotiators to UNMEE.

UNMEE set about preparing for the establishment of the Temporary Security Zone by inviting both parties to submit redeployment plans, to be discussed in the Military Coordination Commission, chaired by the Force Commander and with military representatives of both governments and of the OAU. Ethiopia submitted a map of its intended redeployment, presented only as a series of positions and not as a continuous line. Eritrea promptly rejected this, denying that Ethiopia had administered these positions prior to 6 May 1998; Eritrea's own map essentially presented its view of the colonial boundary, claiming administration even of places well known to have been under Ethiopian control, such as the town of Zalambessa. In the absence of any agreed mechanism to adjudicate, UNMEE had no alternative but to undertake to submit its own map of the proposed Zone to the parties. Ethiopia maintained that the Agreement gave it the right to determine the redeployment positions it had been required to submit; Eritrea argued that Ethiopia was cheating on the pre-6 May 1998 positions and that UNMEE should take responsibility for defining the line. UNMEE had no first hand knowledge of the situation at a time when it had not been present, and while it rapidly gathered what information it could, it was clear that territorial administration in many border areas had never been clearly defined. Only one area under dispute had been ruled on in the course of the negotiations: in August 1998, the OAU had accepted a report from a Committee of Ambassadors sent to the two countries concluding that Badme town "and its environs" were administered by Ethiopia before 12 May 1998. Eritrea had of course rejected this finding.

In drawing up its own map of the proposed Zone, UNMEE felt unable to depart from the Ethiopian submission, except where it believed it had definite information that Ethiopia had not administered an area where it was proposing to maintain a position. This was the case in the eastern sector, where Ethiopia sought to remain well forward of its 6 May 1998 position; here UNMEE adjusted the map in Eritrea's favour. Eritrea remained deeply unhappy with the UNMEE map, but under great international pressure conveyed its acceptance. At the third meeting of the Military Coordination Commission on 6 February 2001, the parties accepted in general terms the UNMEE proposal. Eritrea however stated that the proposed southern boundary of the Zone did not reflect the line of administration of 6 May. Ethiopia expressed a reservation regarding the need for some adjustments to the line drawn by UNMEE around the positions it had submitted. When these were subsequently conveyed to UNMEE, they were significant, especially in the Irob area of the central sector. After consultations with both parties, UNMEE presented an adjusted, larger-scale map, revised to meet the

Ethiopian insistence. Ethiopia initiated the redeployment of its forces on 12 February and notified UNMEE on 22 February that it was completed.

Eritrea began to rearrange its own forces northwards to establish the 25-kilometre separation, but registered its strong objection to the adjustments UNMEE had made, maintaining that the consultation had been inadequate. In protest, on 1 March it halted the repositioning of its forces, which then remained partly inside and partly outside the proposed Temporary Security Zone. The areas from which Ethiopian troops had been withdrawn experienced a potentially dangerous vacuum of authority, with no civil administration or police, and the possibility that one or other army might be tempted to move back into areas recently vacated. To make matters worse, although UNMEE declared that it had verified that Ethiopia had redeployed according to the map it had accepted, on 15 March it discovered that three companies of Ethiopian troops were present in the Irob area six kilometres north of the southern boundary of the proposed Zone. UNMEE publicly protested the Ethiopian presence, but Ethiopia maintained that it had administered the area before 6 May 1998 and would not withdraw its forces, despite its earlier failure to inform UNMEE accordingly. On examination, Ethiopia's administrative claim had credibility. But by twice failing to make clear to UNMEE the full extent of the areas it claimed to have been administering, yet compelling UNMEE to adjust its map of the Zone, it had undermined UNMEE's ability to convince Eritrea of its objectivity, even though in fine-tuning the southern boundary UNMEE attempted as far as possible to restore Eritrean villages to its administration.

There followed a stand-off between Eritrea and UNMEE, during which UNMEE's repeated reminders that the Zone would be temporary, and without prejudice to the eventual delimitation of the border, fell on deaf ears. Eventually Eritrea announced that it was resuming the rearrangement of its forces, in the interests of enabling the internally displaced people who had fled homes in the Zone during the fighting to return from IDP camps to their homes in time for the planting season. The Eritrean withdrawal to the northern boundary of the Zone was completed on 16 April, and two days later Special Representative Legwaila declared the Temporary Security Zone established. In one respect it failed to conform to the Agreement: where in the Irob area UNMEE had adjusted the southern boundary in favour of Ethiopia, it had not felt it was reasonable to adjust the corresponding section of the northern boundary and ask Eritrea to withdraw its forces further, so this section of the Zone was only half its intended 25-kilometre breadth.

Eritrea refused to concede that the Temporary Security Zone had been formally established, although de facto it respected the boundaries while continuing to reject their legitimacy. Ethiopia too sustained an objection to two aspects of the boundaries, although it had got almost all of what it wanted. Eritrea used its more deeply-felt rejection to limit its cooperation in a number of other respects, and one of these gave Ethiopia further grounds to insist that the Zone was never properly established.

The Agreement provided for the return to the Zone of Eritrean civilian administration, including police and local militia. Both countries had long maintained local militia, formally outside their armed forces although largely absorbed within them in wartime. Eritrea had made the initial advances on the battlefield, so until Ethiopia more than reversed these in the third round of fighting, the negotiations were premised on Eritrean withdrawal from territory administered before the conflict by Ethiopia. Ethiopia had insisted that restoration of civilian administration must include local militia as well as police. The negotiators had agreed, noting in their draft arrangements that this would imply "no change in the traditional functions, lines of authority, equipment and weaponry." With the Ethiopian recovery of all areas it claimed to have administered and capture of substantial Eritrean territory in May 2000, the issue now became the return of Eritrean militia to the Temporary Security Zone. The UN correctly anticipated a tricky issue: the Secretary-General noted in his August 2000 report to the Security Council that "it would be necessary for the implementation of the UNMEE mandate that all relevant information on militia personnel be provided to the mission to enable it to verify that the functions and configuration of the militia do not exceed that which prevailed before the outbreak of the conflict."[5]

Eritrea initially undertook to provide such information, and a negotiation began between its Commission for Coordination with the Peacekeeping Mission and UNMEE to draw up a protocol to enable UNMEE to monitor the functioning of local militia and police within the Zone. But as the armies withdrew, Eritrea began deploying militia and police to the Zone without informing UNMEE of either the numbers in those districts before the conflict, or the numbers it was now deploying. The Protocol Agreement, eventually signed on 16 April, required all militia and police to possess identification and weapons permits, and to wear distinctive uniforms. No heavy weapons (12.5 mm or greater) or live firing exercises were allowed within the Zone. Police-marked armed personnel carriers were allowed, subject to advance notice to UNMEE, and all militia or police grenades, section and crew-served weapons and ammunition were to be stockpiled at locations identified to UNMEE and subject to its inspection. Only the police, not militia, were permitted to establish checkpoints, and movements of 20 or more militia required prior notification to UNMEE, subject only to emergency procedures. Armed persons or weaponry outside these provisions that UNMEE found in the Zone would be held by the peacekeepers and turned over to the local civil authorities.

Ethiopia voiced strong objection to the number of Eritrean militia in the Zone, the types of weapons they were allowed to carry and the fact that they would wear distinctive uniforms, maintaining that it was "totally unacceptable to deploy a uniformed and well-organized force within the Temporary Security Zone under the guise of militia." They thus claimed that the Zone had not been demilitarized. Eritrea responded that "a couple of thousand lightly armed Eritrean police and militias dispersed in more than 400 villages over a total area of 25,000 square kilometres cannot pose a legitimate cause of concern to Ethiopia."[6]

The Eritrean response was disingenuous. UNMEE's military observers estimated that more than 6000 militia and around 3000 police were deployed to the Zone, and there seemed little doubt that these greatly exceeded the numbers before the conflict, even though no estimates were available. Most of the personnel had been in the Eritrean Defence Forces (EDF) prior to their deployment (although this of course applied to virtually the entire eligible population). It became increasingly clear that they operated in practice under an EDF chain of command. Many of the locations to which they were deployed had little to do with law and order requirements or protecting the civilian population: they were deployed in effect as forward elements of the EDF, pushing close to Ethiopian positions along the southern boundary of the Zone.

While this went some way to justify the Ethiopian contention that the Zone had not been fully demilitarized, the numbers and weaponry of the Eritrean militia and police posed no significant military threat to Ethiopia's army at the southern boundary. UNMEE strove, with varying success, to persuade the Eritrean authorities not to deploy police and militia too close to the southern boundary, and made equivalent requests of Ethiopia regarding its army positions. The military observers maintained a strict scrutiny, lodging protests with the Eritrean authorities when the protocol was violated by the establishment of unannounced or unauthorized checkpoints, stockpiles at unannounced locations, possession of unauthorized weapons, absence of identification or weapons permits, and use of EDF vehicles. On one occasion a Kenyan officer at an UNMEE checkpoint refused to allow Eritrean President Afwerki to proceed into the Zone as long as his party included EDF vehicles. Despite the refusal of information on numbers and these breaches of the protocol, cooperation and communication between UNMEE and the police and militia at the field level was relatively good.

A second area in which Eritrea denied UNMEE full cooperation related to its freedom of movement, apparently fully assured by the Agreement, which provided "guarantee of the free movement and access of the Peacekeeping Mission and its supplies as required throughout the territories of the parties." UNMEE told the parties that it required freedom of movement not only within the Temporary Security Zone, but within a 15-kilometre band north and south of its boundaries, in order to monitor – as the Agreement required it to do – Ethiopian and Eritrean forces in their redeployment positions closest to the Zone. Ethiopia accepted this, and its obstructions of the peacekeepers' movements were occasional and subject to apology and correction. Eritrea however insisted that UNMEE's freedom of movement applied only within the Zone: as President Isaias put it, having given up 25 kilometres he was not going to give up another 15 kilometres.

This caused tension and occasionally dangerous stand-offs between the peacekeepers and the EDF. It also undermined UNMEE's ability to be fully convincing in its monitoring of the EDF. In mid-November 2001, Ethiopia alleged that Eritrea was engaging in a military build-up and claimed that UNMEE did not have the capacity to effectively monitor the Temporary Security Zone as a result of Eritrean restrictions on the peacekeepers' movements. UNMEE was confident that, despite these restrictions, it would be able to detect any such build-up, and that nothing out of the ordinary was taking place. The Ethiopian allegations proved to be without foundation, but UNMEE was able to use the international concern they engendered to obtain access to EDF camps and units north of the Zone on the basis of prior notice, although this was not an acceptable substitute for freedom of movement. UNMEE's monitoring showed that although both parties carried out troop rotations, engaged in routine readiness training, and continued to maintain or improve their positions, their postures remained essentially defensive.

By April 2001, the pulling-back of the armies allowed the return of displaced families to their homes in the Temporary Security Zone to commence. A serious impediment was the extent of the threat posed by landmines and by unexploded ordnance. Both parties had used landmines extensively during the conflict, although Ethiopia, which (unlike Eritrea) had signed the Ottawa Convention,[7] publicly denied having done so. The Agreement committed the parties to conduct demining activities as soon as possible, and for the peacekeeping mission, in conjunction with the UN Mine Action Service, to assist with technical advice and coordination. It was crucial for both armies to hand over all their information on the minefields they had laid, but both parties displayed extreme reluctance to allow humanitarian considerations to prevail over their refusal to cooperate with each other through UNMEE. It was only in March 2001 that Eritrea handed over records of some 175,000 anti-personnel mines and 45,000 anti-tank mines, and the Ethiopian prevarication was far worse. Ethiopia maintained that it had no central records of mines laid in the Zone, but under pressure eventually agreed to facilitate collection of information by UNMEE's Mine Action Coordination Centre (MACC) directly from its army engineers. It took until October 2001 for substantial information to be collected, and six months later the MACC was still seeking further specific data. The MACC was however able to work with Eritrean deminers and with international demining and mine awareness NGOs to get a programme of mine action rapidly underway in the Zone, and thus limit the deaths and injuries as the population returned to their villages and fields. While the UNMEE peacekeeping force's demining assets were officially dedicated to ensuring its own safety and mobility, they too made a significant contribution to humanitarian needs. Eritrea's decision to end the operations of three international mine action NGOs when it established the Eritrean Demining Agency in August 2002 resulted in a serious loss of humanitarian mine action capacity in the Zone.

While UN humanitarian agencies and NGOs provided the main support to the Eritrean authorities in meeting the returnees' most urgent needs, UNMEE was able to use its logistical assets to assist them. It first did so in facilitating a series of rapid village assessments in the Temporary Security Zone, carried out jointly by the Eritrean authorities and UN agencies. These found extensive damage to basic infrastructure in most areas, and the need for immediate interventions to provide water, health services and shelter, as well as the procurement of agriculture inputs to farmers. UNMEE was the first peacekeeping mission to have included in its budget a fund for "quick impact projects," and although this provided only $700,000 for a first year for projects not exceeding $15,000 (later supplemented by voluntary contributions from donor governments), it did enable it to respond to urgent needs in its area of operations. The operation of UNMEE CIMIC teams facilitated cooperation in the Zone between the peacekeepers and humanitarian actors. The Security Council mission which visited the two countries in February 2002 noted that collaboration between the humanitarian agencies and their NGO partners with UNMEE was very close and productive, and described as "a model of partnership;" the expression of sincere gratitude the mission received from the local population in the Zone resulted partly from UNMEE's humanitarian efforts.[8]

Eritrea estimated that there were approximately 160,000 internally displaced people in camps when the Temporary Security Zone was established in April 2001, and tens of thousands of others living in host communities. By the end of the year around 180,000 people had been assisted to return to their areas of origin in the Zone, and approximately 57,000 had yet to do so, the Eritrean authorities attributing this to the presence of mines or unexploded ordnance, a sense of insecurity caused by the close proximity of their villages to the southern boundary of the Zone, or the fact that their villages were in areas still under Ethiopian administration. Simultaneously, UNHCR was engaged in the repatriation of Eritrean refugees from Sudan, but the majority were people long-settled there before the 1998-2000 war with Ethiopia, returning to settlements outside the Zone.

A more contentious category of returnees were the prisoners of war held by both parties. Under international humanitarian law the obligation to return prisoners of war commenced with the cessation of hostilities in June 2000, and in the December 2000 Peace Agreement the parties committed themselves to fulfil this "without delay." But after initial releases, which were in practice reciprocal, the repatriations ground to a halt. Ethiopia, which held the larger number of prisoners of war, refused further releases unless Eritrea clarified the fate of one prominent pilot it had captured (for a second time). President Afwerki told diplomatic interlocutors they could inform Ethiopia that the pilot was no longer alive, but Eritrea refused to meet its legal obligation to do so officially through the International Committee of the Red Cross (ICRC) and to return his mortal remains. Both parties remained in breach of their unconditional obligations, until at last the ICRC President and supporting representations secured commitments in August 2002 of the release of all remaining prisoners of war. This resulted in the release of the last 279 Ethiopians by Eritrea that month, and 1130 Eritrean prisoners of war and 95 civilian internees by Ethiopia in November 2002. Since the beginning of the conflict in 1998, 1067 Ethiopian prisoners of war, 5055 Ethiopian civilian internees, 2067 Eritrean prisoners of war and 1086 Eritrean civilian internees had been repatriated under the auspices of the ICRC. The first awards of the Claims Commission established under the Peace Agreement were an indictment of the violations of international law by both parties in their treatment of prisoners of war, but especially damning as regards the treatment of Ethiopian prisoners by Eritrea.[9]

The numbers of prisoners of war are one measure of the impact of the war on Eritrean and Ethiopian families, but they are greatly exceeded by the number of dead and disabled. In June 2001, President Afwerki announced the total of Eritrean dead as 19,000, although notifications were given to families only after two more years of uncertainty. While some doubted that this was the full Eritrean total, it is generally estimated that Ethiopian losses were well in excess of the toll of Eritreans. Beyond this is the huge impact on those of Eritrean origin who were settled in Ethiopia at the outbreak of hostilities, and those of Ethiopian origin settled in Eritrea. As such people were being expelled from both countries in their thousands in 1998 and after, both governments appealed to the UN for intervention against the other. Efforts by the High Commissioner for Human Rights, Mary Robinson, to send human rights monitors to both countries were accepted by Eritrea but refused by Ethiopia. After the ceasefire, however, both President Afwerki and Prime Minister Meles agreed to the inclusion of a small human rights component within UNMEE, to address the human rights issues related to the conflict.

By the time UNMEE's human rights team was operational, civilians were being "repatriated" from each country, with the participation of the ICRC, which required the opportunity to satisfy itself that this was in accordance with the individuals' wishes. One exception, a mass expulsion of some 704 persons, mostly long-term residents of Tigray, from Ethiopia in June 2001, was strongly protested by Secretary-General Annan and UNMEE. This perhaps contributed to the fact that mass expulsion was not repeated. UNMEE obtained the cooperation of both governments in interviewing those repatriated, from which serious human rights concerns emerged regarding their treatment in both countries. These included long-term detention, without due process and often under poor conditions; allegations of ill-treatment; discrimination in access to social services and employment; and harassment by civilians and officials. In many cases, the repatriations resulted in family separations, as families were not able to leave together or, in the case of families of mixed Ethiopian-Eritrean parentage, were not able to remain together in the country concerned. In some cases, repatriated individuals of mixed parentage were left stateless, as the country to which they were repatriated did not grant them its nationality. UNMEE sought, with only a little success, to persuade both governments to ameliorate the treatment of each other's nationals, and especially to allow the reunion of divided families. Against such a background, the decisions to accept repatriation were more induced by circumstances than truly voluntary, and some were "repatriated" from the country in which they had been born to one they had never seen.

The year 2001 saw serious human rights violations associated with internal political developments, first in Ethiopia, and then in Eritrea. In Ethiopia, students and others were killed through use of excessive force against demonstrators, and political leaders, human rights activists, journalists and students were arrested. Eritrea enjoyed a brief period of unprecedented openness marked by calls for the belated introduction of the Constitution and multi-party elections, but this culminated in the arrest of a student leader and mass detention of students, the arrests of political critics from the heart of the ruling party and their incommunicado imprisonment in secret locations, and the closure of the independent press and incarceration of journalists. In both countries the conduct of the war and peace-making by President Afwerki and Prime Minister Meles respectively was subjected to criticism, which before the cessation of hostilities had been bitter but contained within the secret debates of the two ruling parties, and this led to the arrests of former allies. In Eritrea the shutdown of freedom of expression was complete and prolonged.[10] However, UNMEE had no mandate to investigate or pronounce upon these human rights violations, since they were not directly related to the inter-state conflict.

These internal preoccupations, which in Ethiopia saw Prime Minister Meles under constant attack for allegedly being too favourable to Eritrea before and during the conflict, made it even less likely that any international efforts to promote reconciliation between the two countries could be effective. It took many months of patient negotiations, facilitated by Norwegian Church Aid with UNMEE's support, before even the religious leaders of the two countries could meet on their own soil. The greatest victims of their leaders' intransigence were the people of the border areas, in particular nomadic people such as the Afar, who for generations had conducted agricultural, pastoral or commercial activities with little regard for a border. Now they found themselves divided by a militarized frontier, and while the presence of UNMEE's peacekeepers was some assurance of security, those who strayed across a line of which they may have been unaware were the occasional victims of detention and shooting incidents.

The two governments awaited the decision of the Boundary Commission in a mood of undiminished hostility to each other, and only grudging cooperation with UNMEE. Restrictions on freedom of movement and unsatisfactory military liaison was a problem principally with Eritrea, who also refused to meet with Ethiopia in sector or local military coordination commissions which UNMEE urged could defuse border incidents and tensions. UNMEE's efforts to get the parties to cooperate over the recovery of the mortal remains of combatants met with no sense of urgency as the months during which they lay where they fell turned into years. The free broadcast of UNMEE programmes by Eritrean radio started, stopped and started again, but UNMEE was unable to get equivalent access to Ethiopian radio. UNMEE was forced to fly between the two capitals via Djibouti, as the parties would not agree on a direct high-altitude route; by mid-2003 this had imposed an estimated additional cost of $2.5 million on the UN. Governments which had little apparent difficulty in funding their rearmament extracted whatever they could from the mission, the annual cost of which to the international community was over $230 million. Eritrea even required payment for UNMEE's use of the national airport at Asmara. President

Afwerki's insistence that peacekeepers should be subject to mandatory HIV/AIDS testing resulted in Eritrea's refusal to sign a status-of-forces agreement, and Eritrea subjected UNMEE's local staff to national service obligations and carried out arrests in breach of its obligations to the UN.

The decision of the Boundary Commission on 13 April 2002 marked a deterioration in Ethiopia's cooperation with UNMEE, as well as with the Commission itself. Ethiopia took strong exception to UNMEE flying international journalists from Asmara to Badme, the disputed settlement perceived as the symbol of victory or defeat in the boundary decision. Ethiopia's Foreign Minister had immediately claimed that Badme was on Ethiopia's side of the border defined by the Commission, when in fact it fell by a few kilometres to Eritrea. UNMEE's spokesman was recalled, but Ethiopia declared that it had lost confidence in Force Commander Cammaert. It maintained its refusal to meet him or allow him access to Ethiopia; only when he completed his two-year term in October 2002 did meetings of the Military Coordination Commission resume. Immigration formalities at Addis Ababa and security searches were imposed on UNMEE personnel, in violation of the status-of-forces agreement.

On the ground, the ceasefire was never seriously threatened, but cross-border incidents became more serious. The acute drought in both countries intensified the competition for dwindling pastures. Incursions became more frequent, mainly by Ethiopian herdsmen entering the Temporary Security Zone to graze their livestock, sometimes accompanied by armed men. In the first half of 2003 there were a number of shootings, with some fatalities, although UNMEE attributed these to local groups and militia, and saw no evidence of the involvement of the armed forces of either side. Meanwhile the return of Ethiopian nationals with Ethiopian Government support to resettle in a location across the delimitation line determined by the Boundary Commission led the Commission to issue a formal Order in July 2002 requiring Ethiopia to withdraw them; by February 2003 Ethiopia had yet to comply with the Order.

The delimitation decision of the Boundary Commission brought new political, logistical, humanitarian and human rights challenges for UNMEE. First, further patient diplomacy is needed to try to overcome the impediments that the party most unhappy with the Boundary Commission's decision— Ethiopia, as it has transpired—is placing in the way of its implementation. Second, UNMEE is required to assist the Commission as it proceeds to the demarcation stage, including the crucial task of mine clearance related to the sites where pillars are to mark the boundary. Third, in the Peace Agreement, the parties had requested the UN "to facilitate resolution of problems which may arise due to the transfer of territorial control, including the consequences for individuals residing in previously disputed territory." There are significant settlements that regarded themselves as Ethiopian on the Eritrean side of the border, and vice versa. UNMEE has identified a range of human rights issues involved in the transfer of territorial control: nationality/citizenship rights; protection from statelessness; property rights; family rights/avoidance of family separation; protection of children's rights; immigration and residency rights; avoidance of forced migration and population movements; right of return of previously displaced persons; resettlement/reintegration possibilities; and cultural rights and traditions of communities in border areas. [11] Addressing these issues would be a challenging responsibility even if the two governments cooperated with the UN and with each other; it will be far more difficult if the two political leaderships continue to sacrifice the interests of ordinary citizens to their own intransigence.

ENDNOTES

1. The *Agreement on Cessation of Hostilities between the Government of the Federal Democratic Republic of Ethiopia and the Government of the State of Eritrea* was circulated to the Security Council as S/2000/601, 19 June 2000. The [Peace] *Agreement between the Government of the State of Eritrea and the Government of the Federal Democratic Republic of Ethiopia* was circulated to the Security Council as S/2000/1183, 13 December 2000.

2. *Security Council Resolution 1312(2000)*, 31 July 2000.

3. *Report of the Secretary-General*, S/2000/785, 9 August 2000.

4. *Security Council Resolution 1320 (2000)*, 15 September 2000.

5. *Report of the Secretary-General*, S/2000/785, 9 August 2000, para. 31.

6. See letters from the two Ministers of Foreign Affairs, S/2001/448, 7 May 2001 (Ethiopia), and S/2001/477, 14 May 2001(Eritrea).

7. The *Ottawa Convention on the Prohibition of the Use, Stockpiling, Production and Transfer of Anti-personnel Mines and on Their Destruction*. Eritrea signed the Ottawa Convention after the war, on 27 August 2001.

8. *Report of the Security Council mission to Ethiopia and Eritrea 21-25 February 2002*, S/2002/205, 27 February 2002, paras. 31, 36, 37.

9. Eritrea-Ethiopia Claims Commission, *Partial Award – Prisoners of War – Eritrea's Claim 17* and *Partial Award – Prisoners of War – Ethiopia's Claim 4*, both 1 July 2003, on-line at http://www.pca-cpa.org/ENGLISH/RPC/#Eritrea-Ethiopia Claims Commission.

10. See Amnesty International, *Amnesty International report 1992*, p. 96-97 (Eritrea) and p. 98-99 (Ethiopia), and *Eritrea: Arbitrary detention of government critics and journalists*, September 2002, AI Index: AFR 64/008/2002, on-line at http://web.amnesty.org/library/Index/ENGAFR640082002.

11. *Report of the Secretary-General*, S/2003/665, 23 June 2003, para. 25.

Chapter 8
REGIONAL IMPLICATIONS OF
THE ERITREA-ETHIOPIA WAR
Lionel Cliffe

The War led to horrendous immediate and medium term suffering caused by the battles and troop movements that occurred. It also had a longer term effect on the relations between Eritrea and Ethiopia because of the sanctions taken by the governments against each other and the mutual hatred generated, factors which are still making it difficult three years after the end of hostilities to return to the co-operation that mostly characterised the period from 1991-97. The war also had both an immediate and long-term impact on the two countries' relations with neighbouring countries and on the internal situation in some of them. These have in turn changed a whole array of political and economic forces throughout a region where conflicts have always cross-infected each other.

For the last 40 years the region can be accurately characterised as having had an 'insecurity regime'. The most obvious symptom can be seen in the fact that all countries have been marked by internal violent conflict. Moreover, in almost all cases this has involved violent challenges to the state, as well as conflicts at other levels. A further characteristic has been that the open conflicts have extended across state borders: clashes over resources like livestock and water have crossed frontiers; ethnic groups involved in conflict are found on both sides of the old colonial boundaries; these and other armed groups have found sanctuary across state lines, often with their ethnic kin. But even more destabilising—and particular to this region of Africa (West Africa is the only one comparable)—has been the fact that rebel groups have been encouraged, even sustained and sometimes been fostered by neighbouring governments. This has in turn generated 'tit-for-tat' support for the neighbouring countries' rebels in a pattern of 'mutual intervention' (see Cliffe, 1999). Occasionally this has taken the form of the actual intervention of state armed forces in other territories. In two major cases these forays blossomed into all-out inter-state war – making the Horn the only region in Africa to experience such wars. The first of these was that between Somalia and Ethiopia in the late 1970s. The most recent was the war between Eritrea and Ethiopia in the late 1990s. Given these various levels of conflict over a long period it is thus appropriate to use a phrase like insecurity regime to bring out the endemic and systemic character of all these conflicts.

This systemic pattern leads to any one conflict between states or across borders fuelling and amplifying others, and to conflicts at local, national and inter-state levels interacting with each other. The recent Eritrea-Ethiopia war certainly had these consequences: it reshaped relations of the belligerents with neighbours; it shifted alliances between states inside the region and beyond, including the operation of the regional body, Inter Government Agency for Development (IGAD); it impacted on other, internal conflicts – amplifying them or promoting greater destabilisation in some cases, redefining cleavages or even, perversely, dampening conflicts in others. Overall though, the war ratcheted up the level of destabilisation of the region as a whole.

Controversy surrounds all discussions about the 'causes' of all these conflicts – although most analyses concentrate on one case or one country. There has been similar argument and disagreement about the causes of the inter-state wars, especially that between Eritrea and Ethiopia. But seldom has explanation been attempted at the regional level to analyse the interactions. Nor will a formula to explain causes be offered here, beyond stating that most conflicts emerge from the still unfinished business in the region of state formation and the definition of borders, which in turn take place against a background of contestation over resources, especially oil, water (the Nile in particular) and land. Up to 1990 the great powers' imperatives of Cold War confrontation were one crucial ingredient. In the present day, international forces of a different sort still come into play: the geo-strategic imperatives of the world's super-power, now in relation to the 'war on terrorism', on the one hand, and on the other, economic interests, such as the oil companies, and those associated with the often illegal, cross-border trade in such things as arms, natural resources, drugs and food. Related to the former, but with its own dynamic and 'logic', if that is the right word, is another factor: the rabid Christian fundamentalist lobby so powerful an influence on the Bush Administration, which has had its own agenda of a crusade against Islam in the region – generally a massively destabilising influence in this multi-faith region.

Although this was a war fought between the state armies of Eritrea and

Ethiopia (as distinct from the usual pattern of auxiliary combatants and civilian casualties elsewhere), there has been a wide range of military and political impacts across borders throughout the region. First, each of the belligerent governments has sought to exploit political and even armed resistance to central authority inside the rival state. This exploitation of divisions has inevitably spilled over borders, and together with the fact of war, has had a second impact: interventions or changed stances by the two enemies towards neighbouring states. Most directly, Ethiopian forces have made incursions into Somalia and Kenya; Eritrea has provided support, perhaps even weaponry, to movements in Djibouti and Somalia. On the other hand both countries have reduced their support to the opposition confronting the regime in Khartoum, and generally courted Sudan. Their tactical efforts to avoid having to fight on two fronts have in fact had a transforming impact on Sudan's international standing and potentially in resolving its internal conflicts, in a manner that some might consider desirable, but others would not. The net result of the multitude of such knock-on effects on other countries has had a fourth consequence: the intensification of the tensions within the region as a whole. The pattern of 'mutual interference' has been reinforced and in some respects reconfigured. The fragile bilateral and multilateral arrangements and institutions for regional security and peace making, most notably IGAD, have been further undermined. These several dimensions have a fifth implication: if the peace between the two countries is to be sustainable it will require the resolution of a number of cross-border and even internal issues in neighbouring states, and it will also ideally depend on an adequate regional structure for security being put in place, and policies which will reverse mutual fuelling of internal conflict. Each of these five dimensions – intervention in each other's conflicts, intervention in neighbours' conflicts, the effect on Sudan's domestic and external politics, the effect on regional structures, and the prospects of a sustainable, regional zone of peace – will be explored below.

Exacerbating Belligerents' Internal Conflicts

It is a natural element of war strategy to stoke up internal opposition to one's enemy and if possible to force redeployment of forces away from the front lines to deal with internal conflict. Both sides in this war employed those tactics, and indeed, both claimed in their propaganda that the opposite regime was in such a weak position in terms of legitimacy that the war would quickly generate internal forces for its overthrow. In the event, the strength of the incumbent regimes and their popular support, with some exceptions that will be considered below, were strengthened, in the short term at least. Such completely erroneous miscalculations on both sides that some imminent internal up-rising would be sparked off, contributed to the lack of meaningful dialogue during the first months of the war. For such mistaken analyses the intelligence agencies that made them deserve to have been sacked! Nevertheless efforts to promote up-risings were made.

Eritrea has not thus far been exposed to serious internal disruption nor does the regime face any significant internal challenge. However, some rump organisations surviving from the rival Eritrean Liberation Front (ELF) have had a presence in Khartoum – and among Eritrean refugees still resident in eastern Sudan – and also in Addis Ababa. In the recent past the Khartoum military regime provided some backing for them and a more recently formed movement, Eritrea Jihad. But since 1998 the Ethiopian government has taken over as their main sponsor. A new umbrella body, the Eritrean National Alliance, was formed linking these mainly islamicist (and historically fiercely anti-Ethiopian) entities with some Eritrean politicians close to the TPLF who had relocated in Addis Ababa. It was even proclaimed in some Ethiopian propaganda as a government-in-exile. But such support had little political or security impact.

Somewhat more unsettling for the Eritrean government was Ethiopia's espousing of the cause of the Afar people, found in the southern coastal panhandle leading to the port of Assab, which was a strategic target for Ethiopia. But this was a complex issue, as the Afar people spread into Ethiopia itself and into Djibouti, so the cause of greater Afar unity can also backfire on Ethiopia. It is but one element in the regional complexities explored below with particular reference to Djibouti.

As the war drew to a close, however, more authentic voices from within the country, speaking from a perspective of solidarity during the war, began to urge a wider public debate, starting with a post-mortem on how the war was allowed to get out of hand. This internal opposition to the leadership, including its single-minded pursuit of military means of dealing with the war, became public in 2001, when 15 senior party leaders, all veterans of the liberation struggle issued a statement calling for internal dialogue rather than rule by fiat. Eleven of them were detained, without due process, as were journalists, student leaders and other critics – marking a retreat into one-man repressive rule. This political process has been documented in the media and the shunning of a constitution that had been approved is well-documented in the account by Bereket Habte Selassie (2003), who presided over the constitution-making. An insightful analysis of how the war generated these leadership divisions is offered in the introduction to a forthcoming volume (Connell, forthcoming). Eventually in 2002, the internal opposition forces that escaped or were already abroad coalesced in to the Eritrean People's Liberation Front – Democratic Party (EPLF-DP) – its name indicating its ideological and institutional origins in the ruling party. In short, the state leadership has paid a heavy price in losing some of the most committed ex-fighters, popular support, the young generation choosing exile, much of the remittances from the diaspora so crucial to the state revenues and the balance of payments. Any internal political threat is being nipped in the bud, external incidents are not yet significant, so the regime is not decisively weakened. But the die has been cast: henceforth it can only rule by repression.

Ethiopia with its great diversity of populations, its size and its history of regionalism offered a much greater target for immediate destabilisation. The Eritrean government targeted two areas where there was already some low-intensity conflict and opposition to the central authorities. There had in fact been national movements mobilised against the Derg in these two areas, among the Oromo people, the largest single 'nationality' (as ethnic groups are officially referred to in Ethiopia), and the Somalis (or rather the predominant clan among them, the Ogadeni). The two movements, the Oromo Liberation Front (OLF) and the Ogaden National Liberal Front (ONLF), had been part of the loose alliance of forces represented in the Transitional Government after 1991, but had both fallen out with the TPLF-dominated central authorities and gone into direct opposition to the state, resorting to armed resistance on occasions. At the same time both movements from their inception had close ties with the EPLF, which the Eritrean government sought to exploit. Both the OLF and the ONLF condemned the war against Eritrea, whereas other Ethiopian opposition groups called for a cease-fire in these local conflicts while the war was on. There did seem to be an escalation of the continuing conflicts with central authorities in the two areas which did force the dispersal of the Ethiopian forces. An example of the complex events set in motion are reports in mid-1999 that referred to a 'mysterious ship' that docked at Merca on the southern Somalia coast with Oromo personnel on board. Among the Oromo there were also initiatives to unite various groups: an OLF meeting in 1999 in Stockholm, no less, urged links with a smaller group more directly sponsored by the Eritrean regime. In 2000 Asmara was the actual venue for another conference to unite six bodies into the 'United Liberation Forces of Oromo', at which plans to root bases in Bale in the south of Oromo Region and in Hararghe in the east were put forward.

Clashes in the south east of the region in 1999 had repercussions across the border with Kenya as Ethiopian armed forces employed hot pursuit, to the point where Kenya protested 'invasions' in August. The regional dynamics of this particular conflict also had ramifications in Somalia; the Aideed faction, which had been supporters of the OLF switched its support under Ethiopian pressure in August 1999 and actually closed the OLF office in Mogadishu. These events heralded the later turn around in 2000 when Ethiopia became backers of the coalition forces, including Aideed, which opposed the transitional government (see discussion of Somalia below).

Immediately after the war the inner circles of the ruling party split after some leaders of the TPLF attacked Meles's leadership on a broad front, including the conduct of the war. This faction stood for a harder line against Eritrea, in the war and after. It was ousted by internal manoeuvring, but its views have been widely echoed since the announcement of the findings of the International Border Commission. The Government initially welcomed an outcome which they claimed gave them all that had fought for. But opposition in Ethiopia mounted after opponents within the ruling party and outside finally read the small print and studied the maps in detail and realised that the symbolic town of Badme would be in Eritrea. The already geographically and ethnically limited political base of the regime has narrowed further, and the regime while remaining in control is isolated and forced into greater authoritarianism.

Eritrea and Ethiopian Involvement in Neighbouring Countries
Somalia
Both countries have opportunistically taken sides among the divided clan factions and warlords still battling it out for control of southern Somalia. A Reuters report of June 1999 concluded that they were both "pouring soldiers, weapons and ammunition into Somalia". Eritrea had earlier denied such reports, for what that was worth. Ethiopia even sent military columns into the country in 1999 and 2000, and even conducted hot-pursuit operations into Oromo-speaking and Somali areas of Kenya. It has also taken a position opposing the new alliance of forces that formed the transitional national government (TNG) in 2000, and it moved to back the alternative alliance of warlords, the Somalia Restoration and Reconciliation Council (SRRC). Eritrea meanwhile had first thrown its influence behind the faction of Aideed, later to become a central element in SRRC, but then switched its backing to the TNG when Ethiopia turned to back SRRC. Somali commentators spoke to me in early 2003 of Eritrea and Ethiopia still fighting a proxy war in Somalia. A UN Panel (UN 2003) set up to look into the operation of the prohibition on arms supplies and the effectiveness of sanctions on those who broke the embargo reported in March 2003 that both countries were still involved in weapons supply. Even if some of these charges are exaggerated and couched in hyperbole, the perceptions of mistrust have undoubtedly spread outwards from the war. Ethiopia's impact on Somalia was always going to be more significant; apart from being much bigger, Eritrea has no common border with any part of Somalia, whereas Ethiopia has one that is porous, that divides Somalis on both sides and that has been marked by conflict for decades.

Ethiopia was thus doing more than export the conflict; it had an imperative to get involved inside Somalia proper as a way of containing internal conflicts emanating from its own Region V, the Somali region. Even though Eritrea's position was limited to a spoiling operation, stirring up Region V, it made sense for them to engage in initiatives in Somalia that would tactically support that aim and embarrass or make things difficult for Ethiopia.

The backing the two countries have given to different factions within Somalia has limited the positive role either could play in the IGAD sponsored initatives to get a settled peace in Somalia. In particular, Ethiopia with its backing of SRRC was seen as a far from neutral member of IGAD's Technical Committee made up of bordering states. Indeed the head of the TNG delegation to the talks in March 2003 accused Ethiopia of massing troops along the border and demanded it be dropped from the Technical Committee. To some extent Ethiopia's partisan position was balanced by the backing of one of the other members, Djibouti, for the TNG and the talks have proceeded to the point of agreement.

The distinct territory of Somaliland, that created a settled peace, chose an all-inclusive government and declared itself independent before 1998, was affected in different ways when the war broke out. Like the rest of Somalia it only had common borders with Ethiopia, which was already using its port, Berbera, as a trade route by then. With Ethiopia's boycotting of Eritrea's ports, this alternative route became more useful for Ethiopia. It has been a party to getting aid for the reconstruction and further development of Berbera and its road links. Ethiopia also provided economic opportunities and revenues for the port and the government, whose only collectible tax are import duties. Despite these closer ties and some economic dependence, the Somaliland government sought to maintain a neutral stance toward both countries. Many members of the government had close personal links with EPLF personnel from the 1980s and tried to use these to urge peace. Eritrea also relied on Berbera as an air link to the Middle East, Africa and beyond, and was allowed to use this life-line.

Djibouti

This small port enclave has borders with both of the combatants. Moreover, on both sides of the borders are found Afar people, who are the sizeable minority among Djibouti's two communities. Within the territory, long-standing tensions between political groups representing them and those representing the Issa, who are Somali, have periodically broken out into civil war over the last 40 years. This tension first delayed Independence until 1977, following which the Afar felt marginalized despite balancing mechanisms installed by the departing French (who nevertheless have continued to keep a garrison there). Elite elements among the Afar formed the Front pour la Restauration de l'Unité et de la Démocratie (FRUD), which seized control of some northern regions in 1991. This bout of fighting continued, with a cease-fire during 1992 until 1993, itself made feasible by events in Ethiopia and Somalia, with the fall of the Dergue regime and that of Siad Barre. The regime was able to gain the upper-hand with the help of improved security relations with the new Ethiopian regime, but did put a constitution in place and hold elections (though excluding FRUD), and eventually made a peace and reconciliation agreement with FRUD at the end of 1994. But one faction of FRUD, under Ahmed Dini continued some form of armed resistance until more comprehensive agreements in 2000 and 2001.

These precarious steps toward internal peace and reconciliation were potentially put under threat by the forces unleashed by the Eritrean-Ethiopian War. For all three countries their Afar minorities pose problems and there are movements among them opposed to the existing regimes. In the circumstances of the War, the two combatants were, as we have seen, prone to foster further disruption on the part of Afar opponents in the enemy country. Without any intent to do so, such support for opposition ran the risk of fuelling the internal tensions within Djibouti. But Eritrea was tempted to pursue such an intent as it increasingly saw Djibouti moving away from its proclaimed neutrality in the War toward a close alliance with Ethiopia. This perception was not unreal; relations between Djibouti and its larger neighbour did become closer. Much of this was due to Ethiopia's reliance on the port of Djibouti – always an important entrepot, it assumed a near monopoly role once Ethiopia refused to trade through the Eritrean ports. Specific plans were hurriedly put in place to improve the road and rail links to Addis Ababa, to upgrade port facilities and transport systems. Ethiopia naturally sought to assert some security over such links, proposing joint commissions and then some sort of union. Eritrea sought to resist or undermine all these arrangements: officially by breaking off diplomatic relations purportedly because of Djibouti staging arms imports into Ethiopia, and unofficially by stirring up trouble.

On Djibouti's part, Ethiopia's near total reliance on the port provided a boost to traders and transporters, to port authorities and to the economy as a whole. Trade in fact doubled in a year after the start of the war and Ethiopia's decision (still in place) to boycott the ports of Massawa and Assab in Eritrea, which had carried the greater part of Ethiopia's trade. It also gave the Djibouti regime some political weight vis-à-vis Ethiopia. In late 1998 and 1999 the idea that Djibouti had floated earlier of some union or confederation began to be taken seriously by Ethiopia, and got a further boost when President Guelleh, who had been born in Ethiopia and spoke Amharic, succeeded his uncle in Djibouti in April 1999. But arguably the government was to become somewhat overwhelmed by the eagerness of Ethiopia's overtures and the tightness of its 'friendly' embrace. The counters that this tiny republic had were on the one hand the French garrison (although its permanence was at least be questioned by France), and on the other the counterweight of their other large neighbour, Somalia – but that would only come into play if unity and peace was restored. These probably were the motives that led the Djibouti government to take the initiative, and spend its own resources, on a new peace process for Somalia, hosting a large gathering at Arta in 2000. On the economic side they struggled to get Ethiopia to pay increased port tariffs, and only overcame Ethiopian resistance after the port management was made over to the Dubai Port Authority.

Very soon after the war started Eritrea accused Djibouti of taking sides and of handling arms for Ethiopia. As tensions mounted during 1998, diplomatic relations were severed by Eritrea in November. It is not coincidence that very soon thereafter FRUD rebels mounted attacks in the north of Djibouti near the border with Eritrea, and the Djibouti government made counter-accusations that Eritrea was providing refuges for the rebel attacks. There were also some terrorist incidents in the south in 1999, one of which halted the Djibouti-Addis Ababa railway for three days in August. By the end of 1999 both countries had realised the dangers of escalation and made an agreement to safeguard border security; diplomatic relations were restored in early 2000 and at the same moment the Djibouti government signed a peace agreement with the rebel faction of FRUD.

Impact on Sudan's Internal Conflicts, Prospects for Peace & International and Regional Status

As indicated, Eritrea inherited an unusually united people at the end of the liberation war. At the same time, there is recognition of the need to avoid and pre-empt the one basis for political cleavage: divisions that could be based on the social-cultural differences between highlanders, who are largely agriculturalist, Tigrinya-speaking and Coptic Christian, and lowlanders, agro-pastoralists with several different languages who are adherents of Islam (see Cliffe, 1989 for an early discussion of the potential danger of this kind of 'ethnic' division). Some material basis for this has emerged on a small scale in the western lowlands, with disputes over land as a result of incoming returnees and commercial farmers. A clandestine political movement, Eritrean Jihad, seeking to operate from that region and using bases in Sudan has tried to stir up such discontents, and has also been responsible for some minor security incidents. The Jihad emerged in the 1990s with a more explicit rhetoric of islamicised politics, partly from rump elements of the former ELF still active in Sudan.

Relations of Eritrea's ruling group with Sudan governments of course date back to the 1970s and 1980s. By and large, successive regimes provided offices for EPLF and ELF, sanctuary for refugees and at certain times some passive support. It was also the conduit for humanitarian assistance across the border into liberated areas of Eritrea—and Tigray. But such support was not consistent. With liberation in 1991 and the overthrow of the Derg regime in Addis Ababa, the two new governments worked closely with the Khartoum regime. Declarations of mutual co-operation and non-interference in each other's internal affairs were made, and some steps were made to curb each other's internal oppositions resident in the neighbouring country.

This period of détente came to an end in early 1994 when Eritrean troops detected and destroyed a small column of Jihad cadres infiltrating across the border from Sudan into western Eritrea—many of whom were Eritreans. Over the next year relationships worsened with Eritrea accusing Sudan of fuelling the Jihad, and allowing proselytisation among refugees, while Sudan's relations with Ethiopia and Uganda simultaneously worsened. Eventually the Eritrean government retaliated by ending diplomatic relations, handing over the Embassy in Asmara to the exile opposition coalition, the National Democratic Alliance, which brought together the Sudan People's Liberation Army (SPLA) with a range of democratic political movements from the north of Sudan. Eritrea supplied them with weaponry and provided training, developing a force based on the Beja people of the Red Sea province of Sudan, as well as providing logistical support for SPLA. In some of these political and military initiatives Eritrea made common cause with Uganda and Ethiopia. From 1995-98 relations between these three countries grew stronger—although they still continued to participate in the committee set up under the regional body, IGAD, to try and resolve conflicts within Sudan.

The Eritrean government believed that certain sections of the Khartoum regime had a long-term agenda to destabilise neighbouring countries as part of a strategy for putting Islamicist regimes in power. As a consequence, President Isayas Afeworki declared in 1997 that Eritrea's opposition to the Sudan government was not merely tactical but a matter of 'principle'. However, their attitude toward Khartoum changed dramatically, and pragmatically, with the onset of the Ethiopian war; diplomatic relations with Sudan were restored and flights resumed. Almost immediately, the two governments signed a memorandum of understanding after a meeting in Doha in November 1998, and had further meetings in April 1999 in Libya. Diplomatic relations were finally resumed in early in 2000, and President Issayas visited Khartoum in October. Military assistance to the opposition coalition, the National Democratic Alliance (NDA) and its main armed forces, the SPLA, was scaled down by Eritrea—and ended by Ethiopia. A Joint Security Committee met for the first time in August 1999; but a similar meeting in early 2000 was postponed citing disagreements over border security and opposition groups. The main road from Eritrea to the eastern city of Kassala was officially reopened, however.

But Eritrea's relations with Sudan seem to have been marked by continued ambiguity. It did not remove the NDA from the Sudan embassy building in Asmara even after the Doha agreement. It continued to allow access to the key positional front in Sudan's Red Sea Province with its potential to threaten Khartoum's electricity supply and the road to Port Sudan. In January 1999 it accused Sudan of bias toward Ethiopia. At that same time Khartoum was the venue for a gathering of Eritrean opposition groups. Tensions between the two countries mounted in late 1999 and early 2000 with NDA/SPLA's attacks across the border and Sudan army hot-pursuit close to it. Eritrea allowed Sudan monitors into Asmara to confirm their forces were not themselves engaged in such incursions, claiming NDA/SPLA were based inside eastern Sudan. But relations remained sour. There was an attack and brief occupation of Kassala in late 2000. Although Eritrea denied involvement or prior knowledge, they certainly allowed SLA troops to withdraw into Eritrea after the attack on the eastern Sudan border town. And the Sudan has subsequently deployed troops along the border. Eritrea did allow a NDA conference in Massawa as late as September 2000. It has nevertheless been putting pressure on NDA to make concessions in the IGAD-sponsored peace talks on Sudan.

In the mid-1990s Eritrea's suspicions of an islamicist plot had been shared by Ethiopia, which had its own further cause to support the Sudan opposition after attempts to assassinate President Mubarak of Egypt on Ethiopian soil were attributed to Sudan-based elements. Ethiopia never went as far as Eritrea in ending diplomatic links with Sudan completely. But its reversal of its stances was if anything even swifter and less ambiguous. Full diplomatic links were delayed as Ethiopia continued to press for the hand-over of those linked with the Mubarak assassination attempt, but ministerial meetings were held in late 1998 and Ethiopian Airlines reopened flights to Khartoum. In early 1999 trade talks were held. But the major rapprochement was seen in 2000: a joint border committee was set up in March; soon thereafter the main road from Kassala to the northern highland Ethiopian city of Gondar was reopened and a protocol was signed in March to begin up-grading roads. What no doubt added to Ethiopia's security considerations of avoiding exposure on two fronts and isolating Eritrea was the crucial strategic significance of **oil**. Sudan began pumping crude in mid-1999 and Ethiopia held talks about importing directly from Sudan in September 2000. By 2002 the imports were meeting a substantial part of Ethiopia's needs – and making reliance on the port and refinery in Assab or even the reliance on Djibouti less significant.

Despite the IGAD talks reaching close to agreement as this is written, whether there will be internal peace, an end to exporting conflict between neighbours and a secular state is still an open issue. Certainly an interventionist islamicist state, if it were to persist, would be objectively a greater threat to either Ethiopia and/or Eritrea than they are to each other. But pragmatic, strategic calculations that started with the war have solidified and evolved, especially in the case of Ethiopia, with the emergence of a significant Ethiopia-Sudan axis. This brings the two largest countries of the IGAD region together and, with an alliance with Yemen, has resulted in a coalition of Eritrea's 'enemies'. In the last two years this Sanaa Alliance, as it has been termed, seems to have acted in concert to curtail Eritrea's economic and political options.

Regional Patterns & International Pressures

The international forces that came into play over the war itself and in efforts to settle it are dealt with elsewhere in this volume. The impact of the war on the wider region was played out through interaction with these broader influences. In particular, the US war on terrorism has involved a focus on the Horn. The most significant consequences were to be observed in Sudan, where the two countries' efforts to rebuild bridges with the Sudan regime have reduced Sudan's pariah status in the region and internationally. The Sudan had already been characterised by the US as a 'state supporting terrorism'. It was targeted for a bombing raid on what was asserted to be a facility belonging to Osama bin Laden in 1998. The Christian right wing constituency in the US has been engaged in a holy crusade against the efforts of the Sudan's Islamicist military regime against the rebellion in the south of the country, supplying food and bibles and lobbying for a tough US line against the regime. In the event, as we shall see, a process of accommodation with the Sudan has occurred, calculations about accessibility of Sudan's oil emerging as more decisive than the influential Christian fundamentalist lobby.

In 1999, European countries and the EU itself began openly to urge 'normal' relations with Khartoum. Even the US eased sanctions in early 1999. Although Sudan did figure on a list of possible areas for intervention just after 9/11, this was not pursued. Instead the US became heavily involved in efforts to resolve Sudan's major civil war. It sent Senator Danforth on mediation missions, and played a leading role in the IGAD Partners Forum, and in 2002 appointed a special envoy to the peace talks. It also set up its own civilian monitoring group to investigate any violations of agreements to end violent targeting of humanitarian relief. Internal political moves to dampen the

Islamicist rhetoric and promote dialogue, also contributed to the improvement in Sudan's international standing. Sudan also showed its good will by sharing intelligence it had on Osama bin Laden and al-Qaeda with US.

Somalia was also targeted as a prospective candidate for US intervention in late 2001, early 2002. It was said that movements in that country like Al-Ittihad had links with the al-Qaeda network. Investigators were sent out by the US to establish these connections. The chances of anything specific turning up when some small gang of so obviously American intelligence dudes showed up in some town like Baidoa or Johar were always ludicrously small. In fact, as Hussein (1998) points out the shadowy Al-Ittihad apart, Islamicist influences can be found as one element across the board in almost all of the many Somali movements and factions, and are not pre-dominant in any of them. Another US initiative has been more sustained with the stationing of a fleet (using Djibouti as its servicing base) along the Red Sea coast of Somalia, although its chances of detecting any 'terrorist' landings are not likely to be too much higher. But it may well play a role in disrupting more localised trade in weapons and drugs. Meanwhile, the TNG has sought to counter the image of an Islamicist influence and to gainsay Ethiopia propaganda by offering itself as an ally in the US war on terrorism. Like in Sudan, a possibly effective peace-making process has got under way, and is seen even in Washington as the option to be backed. Meanwhile these initiatives against terrorist infiltration in Somalia and the wider strategies to do with the war in Iraq have lead to Djibouti hosting US troops, and German, alongside the French garrison.

Even if areas in the Horn are not immediately targeted as sites for direct intervention, other actors in the region have been scrambling to position themselves in a stance where they might take advantage of the situation since 9/11 and of the US war on terrorism. The Ethiopian government has sought to argue that Al-Qaeda influence is pervasive in Somalia, at least in the Transitional National Government (TNG), to get sympathy in the West for its backing the alternative coalition of warlords. It has also sought to present itself to the West as a more reasonable and reliable ally than its recent enemy, Eritrea. That country's government has on the other hand made a vigorous and blatant PR exercise to sell itself as the ideal partner in other dimensions of the war on terrorism, especially an invasion of Iraq. It claims its Red Sea port and its airport are within easy flying distance of Baghdad, and are thus an alternative base to a reluctant Saudi Arabia, that it has terrain that is similar to that found in Iraq and Afghanistan that is suitable for training. Some commentators in the US have even bought this bill of goods, including the image of Eritrea as 'democratic'. That misconception is precisely what the embattled leadership is seeking: getting the international heat off as it becomes more internally repressive. In the event they have not been notably successful as recent US statements have declined any military collaboration and condemned the repression. One result of these competitive manoeuvres by Eritrea and Ethiopia to catch the eye of the US was that when US unveiled its grand coalition against terrorism, just prior to the invasion of Iraq, they were two of the only four African countries that were listed.

The consequences of the jockeying to take advantage of the war on terrorism have done little to reverse the insecurity regime of the region. Getting into the good books of the US has been a smokescreen and an excuse for increased internal repression, especially in Eritrea and to some extent in Ethiopia and Sudan. These efforts and the general international climate stemming from the priority given to the war on terrorism have fed into the patterns of on-going conflict, intensifying some and redefining cleavages in others. The emphasis has been on short-term tactical improvement in a country's or a movement's international position rather than any long-term vision of peace. The context has done little to reduce tensions between the two combatants in the Eritrea-Ethiopia war, or to broaden popular support in the post-war political crises that have emerged in each country. The hand of arguably the most repressive regime in the region, in Sudan, has been strengthened by these manoeuvrings (and by the Eritrea-Ethiopia war), although this may have been accompanied with some steps toward internal peace.

The context and the manoeuvrings have also served to reinforce the islamicisation of existing conflicts, as different movements and regimes have been dubbed as supportive of terrorism by their opponents. Such trends make the long-term peace and even survival of the multi-faith states in the region more problematic.

The Effect of the War on IGAD

The virtually unanticipated outbreak of the war, the escalation of a theoretically containable border clash into a major confrontation of armies, the long drawn out peace negotiations – these all showed the limitations of IGAD as a conflict prevention and resolution body. When successful mediation came it was from the Organisation for African Unity. Even the protracted period of continued antagonism without any steps to restore 'normal' relations tends to confirm this. None of the other member states, nor any IGAD mechanism, has taken any public initiative to generate dialogue between the two countries.

IGAD's inability to act was not surprising. Any international or regional organisation is a product of its member states and their limitations. In this case the long history of hostility and mutual intervention, interspersed with only occasional periods of détente, provided a context in which resolution of conflict by bilateral diplomacy was virtually unknown. Clearly too inter-state fighting between two core members immobilised the organisation. IGAD had begun to set up a Politics and Security Division as part of a revitalisation process from the mid-1990s. It could claim some small success in at least agreeing to tackle internal conflicts that were destabilising of the wider region, as in its Sudan initiative. But IGAD was unprepared for open antagonism between member states. The Secretariat was also a frail instrument to tackle such conflicts. The Division had not found a head for two years after it existed on paper. At the time of the war, the Division's head was only part-time and its staff was a mere handful of professionals with inevitably little experience. Antagonisms emerged between the Divison's head, an Ethiopian who made public statements about the war in his other capacity, and the Eritrean who was Executive Director of IGAD as a whole – although this was more a symptom of the problem rather than a cause of the limited role. Some of the lessons of the war are being taken on board by IGAD as it seeks to strengthen its capacity, to facilitate joint border commissions, to put early warning systems in place.

But the harm done to the organisation ran much deeper than its inability to take decisive action – it may well be that in such potential wars a larger body like the African Union or the UN, that does not have a direct interest in the conflict, is a more appropriate body for mediating. The war damaged the de facto alliances that had been at the heart of IGAD's revitalisation. It had in fact been the new regimes in Eritrea and Ethiopia acting in common cause and forming something of an axis with Uganda that had provided the dynamic for a change. They articulated the view that conflict was as much the cause of famine as 'drought', and that term was dropped from the organisation's title and the new peace and security agenda was taken on. They were almost acting together in relation to Sudan; it was their initiative that got IGAD to address this 'internal' issue and kept a focus on it. Of course, they all had their own grievances and conflicts with Sudan: as we have seen, Eritrea and Ethiopia felt Sudan was backing internal, Islamicist oppositions in their countries and after the breakdown of the brief détente with Sudan in 1994 began to give succour to opponents of the Khartoum regime; Uganda's most serious internal conflict in the north was, they thought, fuelled by the Lord's Resistance Army using bases in Sudan, and Uganda in turn backed the SPLA. From Khartoum's perspective the three countries' concern was not seen as disinterested, but it kept Sudan at the fore-front of IGAD's agenda even when little progress was being made. The support of Sudanese opposition forces was indeed a lever – it implied the promise of containing those rebel forces in return for improved relations between states and a commitment to resolve internal disputes politically. So despite Ethiopia and Eritrea putting constraints on SPLA/NDA for opportunistic reasons during their war, there has been some progress in the IGAD-led agreement to end the civil war in Sudan. But in the short and medium term the total break-down of relations between Eritrea and Ethiopia (simultaneously with Uganda's turning its attention away from the Horn to the Great Lakes – and seeking some resolution of its antagonism with Sudan for similar reasons) meant that the crucial axis that had driven a new IGAD was lost. Just as the prospects of a 'new leadership' in Africa, so much identified with the heads of the three countries, was trampled in the dust.

Conclusions: An Alternative Vision for the Future

The period of 'détente' between Sudan, Eritrea and Ethiopia, also involving Uganda, during 1991-94, when they each foreswore interference in each other's politics, can be seen with hindsight as an exception to a much longer history in the region, one of **mutual intervention**. The only other such interruption in the general pattern was when the Ethiopia and Somalia regimes stopped supporting each other's rebels in 1988, but too late to turn back the tide before they were both overwhelmed. That pattern, whereby they interfere in neighbouring countries to support unrest on a 'tit-for-tat' basis and thus deal with their own internal oppositions essentially by externalising the problem and its solution is continually being reshaped and also reinforced. But this complex set of interactions makes it difficult to resolve completely either internal conflicts or tensions between states, whether by military elimination of opponents or by negotiation. One set of divisions impinges on the other. The war between Ethiopia and Eritrea has merely redefined some of these complex regional interactions and realigned some of the temporary alliances. But those regional dynamics also add to the complexity of sustaining the peace that they signed in 2000. Equally, this pattern does point to the potential importance of regional mechanisms for conflict resolution in this part of Africa. However, the regional organisation for the Horn, IGAD, with its relatively new Peace and Security Department and agenda, played little role in the resolution of the war and has been weakened by it – hopefully not permanently. It was thus left to the continent-wide body, the Organisation of African Unity (OAU) to play the main role in negotiations, and it was under its auspices that the Algiers agreement was signed.

But this context can also be seen as offering an **opportunity** to confront the inherited systemic insecurity. The previous periods of détente offers some lessons: that there is nothing determined and irreversible in the mutual insecurity regime, nor is there anything necessarily of a political or religious ideological nature about the antagonisms – even though these may present an additional complication. Similarly the détente between Sudan and each of the two belligerents in the war, whatever the tactical reasons behind it, can provide a

building block to reverse the regional pattern – but only if there is détente between Ethiopia and Eritrea. Otherwise one likely outcome would be a region revolving around a strong Ethiopia-Sudan axis that seeks to 'contain' Eritrea. The other countries have an interest in promoting the broader formula for détente not the narrower one, and in helping to normalise relations between the belligerents – in the interests of regional peace and security. Another ingredient in an alternative future is the need to develop mechanisms apart from inter-state initiatives such as joint border commissions, mediation talks and monitoring of cease-fires. Some kind of civil society dialogue across the region is vital. There are some initiatives: local community organisations have taken the lead in setting up and involving governments in cross-border mechanisms; inter-faith dialogues between Ethiopian and Eritrean, between Sudan and Uganda to deal with cross-border conflicts. This latter is particularly important so as to generate tolerance between Islam and Christianity, in countries which have citizens of believers of both major religions (except Somalia and Djibouti). An understanding of the broader regional forces operating outside each other's country is needed. This can hopefully generate another crucial ingredient: the development of a long term vision of an alternative peace regime. The future does not have to repeat the past. It does not have to be one of death, famine and destruction. It is customary to add: 'all that is needed is the political will'. As true as that may be, and certainly the solution has to be a resort to political means rather than arms, one must think beyond that. An alternative political will does not emerge from out of the sky. It has to be worked for – by political mobilisation, from below as well as above, across borders, by a wider political understanding of issues and of other actors' point of view and circumstances, by long-term vision, and by painstaking commitment to tiresome negotiations.
September 2003

REFERENCES

Abbay, Alemseged, (1997), 'The Trans-Mareb Past in the Present', *Journal of Modern African Studies*, 35.2: 321-334.

Bruchhaus, E. & Amanuel Mehreteab, (2000), '"Leaving the Warm House": the Impact of Demobilisation in Eritrea', in Kingsma.

Cliffe, L., (1989), 'Forging a Nation: the Eritrean Experience', *Third World Quarterly*, 11.4, October: 131-147.

Cliffe, L. (1998), 'The Regional Dimensions of Conflicts: The Horn of Africa & Southern Africa Compared', *Occasional Paper No. 5 on Environment & Development in an Age of Transition*, (Centre for Development Studies, University of Leeds).

Cliffe, L., (1999), 'Regional Dimensions of Conflict in the Horn of Africa', *Third World Quarterly*, 20.1: 89-111.

Cliffe, L. & R. Luckham, (2000), 'What Happens to the State in Conflict?: Political Analysis as a Tool for Planning Humanitarian Assistance', *Disasters*, 24.4.

Connell, D., (1993), *Against all Odds: A Chronicle of the Eritrean Revolution*, (Red Sea Press, Lawrenceville, N. J.).

Connell, D.,(forthcoming), *Collected Articles on the Eritrean Revolution: Vol.2 Building a New Nation*, (Red Sea Press, Trenton).

Doornbos, M. *et al.*, eds., *Beyond Conflict in the Horn of Africa: the Prospects for Peace, Recovery and Development in Ethiopia, Somalia, Eritrea & Sudan*, (J. Currey, Oxford).

Doornbos, M. & Alemseged Tesfai, (1998), *Post-Conflict Eritrea: Prospects for Reconstruction and Development*, (Red Sea Press, Lawrenceville, NJ).

Gilkes, P. & M. Plaut, (1999), *War in the Horn: The Conflict between Eritrea and Ethiopia*, Royal Institute of International Affairs, Discussion Paper 82, (London).

Green, R. & Ismael Ahmed, (1999), 'Rehabilitation, Sustainable Peace and Development: Towards Reconceptualisation', *Third World Quarterly*, 20.1: 189-206.

Heinrich, W., (1999), 'End of the "African Renaissance"?', *New Routes: A Journal of Peace Research & Action,* (Uppsala), 4.4:23-28.

Kaldor, M. (1999), *New & Old Wars: Organised Violence in a Globalised Era*, (Polity Press, Cambridge).

Kingsma, K., ed., (2000), *Demobilisation in sub-Saharan Africa: the Development and Security Impacts*, (Macmillan, London).

Kibreab, Gaim, (1996), *Ready & Willing ... but Still Waiting*, (Life & Peace Institute, Uppsala).

Makki, Fuad, (1996), 'Nationalism, State Formation & the Public Sphere: Eritrea, 1991-96', *Review of African Political Economy*, 23. 70.

Rock, J., 'Relief & Rehabilitation in Eritrea: Lessons & issues', *Third World Quarterly*, 20.1: 129-42.

Sorenson, J., (1991), 'Discourses on Eritrean Nationalism & Identity', *Journal of Modern African Studies*, 29.2.

UN (UN Panel of Experts), *Report on Weapons Supply contrary to Sanctions (pursuant to Security Council Resolution 1425)*, S/2003/223, 25 March.

White, P. & L. Cliffe, (2000a), 'War & Famine in Ethiopia & Eritrea', *Review of African Political Economy*, 27.84. June.

White, P. & L. Cliffe, (2000b), 'Conflict, Relief & Development: Aid Responses to the Current Food Crisis in the Horn of Africa', *COPE Working Papers*, No. 38, (Centre for Development Studies, University of Leeds).

Young, J., (1996), 'The Tigray and Eritrean Liberation Fronts: A History of Tension and Pragmatism', *Journal of Modern African Studies*, 34.1.

Chapter 9

POSITIVE NEUTRALITY: DJIBOUTI
Anonymous

The war between Ethiopia and Eritrea came as a shock to the tiny Red Sea state of Djibouti. Although many had speculated on the tensions between its neighbours, none were prepared for the conflict when it arrived. The eruption of fighting was a threat to the cornerstone of the government of Djibouti's foreign policy – the concept of positive regional neutrality. Djibouti has gone to great lengths to put this across, arguing that "good neighborliness and non-interference" are the cardinal points of stability and security in the Horn of Africa. Positive neutrality in Djibouti's view required the authorities to spare no effort in the promotion of regional peace.

This was illustrated as early as 1986, at the first summit meeting of the Inter-governmental Authority on Development (IGAD). The organisation has its headquarters in Djibouti, and brings together Djibouti, Eritrea, Ethiopia, Kenya, Somalia, Sudan and Uganda. Although it is nominally a developmental body, which grew out of attempts to limit the impact on drought and locust infestations on the region, it has taken on a number of directly political roles. The first IGAD summit was the occasion for burying a dispute that had festered for nearly a decade. The war between Ethiopia and Somalia in 1977 had been one of the bitterest conflicts in the Horn in the last quarter of the twentieth century. It was only after much behind the scenes diplomacy that the President of Djibouti, Hassan Gouled Aptidon, was able to persuade the Ethiopian ruler, Mengistu Haile Mariam, and the late Somali head of state, Mohamed Syad Barre, to use the IGAD summit as an opportunity for the two men to shake hands and to put past differences behind them.

It is not difficult to see why preventing regional conflict is so important to Djibouti. On the one hand it tends to serve as a safe haven to which refugees can flee. This happened during the 1977 war between Ethiopia and Somalia over the Ogaden. Thousands of refugees from Eastern Ethiopia poured in Djibouti, which had only just won its independence and was ill-prepared for the influx. On the other hand Djibouti is critically reliant upon its port facilities for revenue and employment. Any regional conflict is likely to threaten the flows of trade. The Arab-Israeli war in 1967, which had led to the closure of the Suez canal, is still fresh in the mind of many Djiboutians who saw the devastating impact this had on their standards of living.

It was therefore with considerable apprehension that the people of Djibouti greeted the news that war had broken out in May 1998. Although many ordinary people were fearful of what the future might hold, they were not entirely surprised by the turn of events. Months before the conflict erupted, the simmering tension between Ethiopia and Eritrea was the talk of the town in Djibouti. Local observers and ordinary citizens would speculate about the reasons behind Eritrea's decision to create its own currency—the nakfa—as opposed to relying on the Ethiopian currency—the birr. Despite the increasing tension between the countries, many in Djibout believed that Eritrea and Ethiopia would eventually find a negotiated solution to their differences. Many thought that Eritrea, as youngest Red Sea state, had every right to assert itself as a nation while maintaining good relationships with Ethiopia. Observers pointed out that Djibouti, the smallest in the Horn, had managed to assert its independence (after more than a century of colonial experience) while keeping its ties with France, the former colonial master. Indeed, independence had not prevented Paris from maintaining its largest African military base in Djibouti, with more than 2,000 troops.

It was therefore entirely consistent that when the Ethio-Eritrean conflict broke out President Hassan Gouled Aptidon should intervene to try to end the hostilities. He declared that the war between Djibouti's neighbours was "adding to the instability and political strife" already affecting the Horn of Africa following the collapse of Somalia in 1991, and the downfall of the regime of Colonel Mengistu Haile Mariam in Ethiopia. These two events had resulted in over 20,000 Somali and Ethiopian nationals seeking sanctuary in Djibouti as refugees. "We cannot afford to shoulder another conflict in the region", declared the president before embarking on shuttle diplomacy between Addis Abeba and Asmara in his capacity as chairman of IGAD.

The initiative was destined to fail. President Gouled's efforts were, from the first, overshadowed by another joint American and Rwandan mediation effort, which drew much greater publicity and media attention. It was also fatally undermined by Eritrean suspicions that were aroused by the switching of all Ethiopian foreign trade from the Eritrean port of Assab to Djibouti. Eritrea remained unconvinced by repeated assurances from President Gouled that his port facilities would not be used for the trans-shipment of military materials. Throughout the conflict, the Eritrean government refused to accept Djibouti's argument that its port was a regional facility open to all users.

Djibouti – Ethiopia's natural outlet to the sea

Traditionally the Eritrean port of Assab was regarded as one of Ethiopia's natural gateways to the outside world. It was considered a strategic asset by the Ethiopian regime of Colonel Mengistu Haile Mariam, handling around 90 % of Ethiopia's import and export traffic. Neighbouring Djibouti had to be content with roughly 10% of the transit traffic, despite having modern equipment. A major shift in the share of the Ethiopian traffic was something that Djibouti did not realistically anticipate. Years of aggressive marketing to woo Ethiopia port users had produced very few results. This had much to do with events that almost coincided with the birth of Djibouti in 1977. The Ethiopian war with Somalia had convinced the authorities in Addis Ababa that Djibouti was not sufficiently secure an outlet to the sea. The route to the Djibouti corridor went via regions of Ethiopia inhabited by Somalis, Oromo and Afars - three ethnic group that maintain a volatile and unpredictable relationship with the authorities of Addis Ababa. Ethiopia felt more comfortable and familiar with the port of Assab.

The war with Eritrea swept aside these preconceptions and induced the Ethiopian authorities to make a dramatic switch to the port of Djibouti. Soon an average of 200 trucks a day were making the journey between Djibouti and Addis Ababa. Petroleum products, strategically vital for the Ethiopian army, constituted a sizeable proportion of this diverted traffic. The Eritreans were, quite predictably, unhappy that their enemy's war machine was being fuelled by the shipment of oil brought in via Djibouti. Their worst fear was that Djibouti had agreed to allow Ethiopia to import military hardware and weaponry by the same route. Djibouti repeatedly denied any military involvement in the Ethio-Eritrean conflict. Instead they reminded the world that the port of Djibouti had been free to all users since its establishment by the French at the end of the 19th century. It was precisely as a link between Ethiopia (then known as Abyssinia) and the outside world, that the port of Djibouti was developed. This was the main line of argument of the country's new President Ismail Omar after his election in April 1999 following the retirement of President Gouled, Djibouti's first head of state. " We picked up from where the French colonial legacy had left off, because this is in our interest" Djiboutians never tire of arguing. They point out that the port and its extension – the eighty one kilometer long railway linking Djibouti to Addis-Abeba - was a living testimony to Djibouti's role as "the natural sea outlet to Ethiopia. The French built the railway in 1897 at almost the same time as the port, but despite being among the oldest African railways it is sadly neglected. Under-funded and in a state of decay, it now carries only a tiny fraction of the freight carried by road.

Relations with Eritrea

Despite having little success with its initial efforts, Djibouti maintained its diplomatic activity. It was chosen, along with Zimbabwe and Burkina-Faso, to lead the Organisation of African Unity's attempts to end the conflict. In November 1998, President Hassan Gouled Aptidon and the leaders of Zimbabwe and Burkina-Faso held a special summit on the Ethio-Eritrean conflict, in the Burkinabe capital Ouagadougou, Burkina-Faso. The meeting was presided over by the then current chairman of the OAU, the Burkinabe leader Blaise Compaore. But the mini-summit failed to make any real headway after Eritrean President Isayas Afwerki made scathing remarks against President Hassan Gouled Aptidon. The Eritrean head of state accused his Djiboutian counterpart of siding with Ethiopia in its war efforts. Eritrean resentment against Djibouti for allowing Ethiopia to use its port was behind this extraordinary outburst on the African diplomatic scene. President Hassan Gouled took it as a personal affront to his pride and dignity. He also saw it as a breach of African tradition, with its emphasis on respect for elders.

Although he was clearly furious, President Gouled made no official remark on the events at Ouagadougou, leaving that to others. The government of Asmara refused further discussions with the OAU mediation panel as long as Djibouti was among its members. The OAU therefore set up another team consisting of senior officials from its headquarters in Addis Abeba. It was this delegation, led by OAU secretary-general Salim Ahmed Salim that continued talks with the Eritrean government. Djibouti had been edged out of the diplomatic process.

Back in Djibouti, President Afwerki's accusations triggered a political uproar. The government controlled media hit back, saying that Eritrea's accusations were baseless. They went on to point out that Eritrea had already been at loggerheads with neighbouring Sudan, Yemen, Djibouti and most recently with Ethiopia – suggesting that Asmara was belligerent towards its neighbours. Stung by the allegations made by his Eritrean counterpart, and reacting to the hostility towards Eritrea at home, the notoriously prickly President Gouled decided to break off diplomatic relations with Asmara in November 1998, within weeks of the failure of the Ouagadougou summit.

Eritrea's hand in the internal politics of Djibouti

One year after its diplomatic break-up with Asmara, Djibouti raised the alarm over what it described as a deteriorating situation on its border with Eritrea.

In November 1999, President Ismail Omar Guelleh accused Eritrea of supporting the radical-wing of a former Djiboutian insurgency movement known as the Front for the Restoration of Unity and Democracy (FRUD).

This rebel group took up arms against the central authorities of Djibouti almost ten years earlier in the period between September and November 1991. The uprising was almost exclusively led by the Afars, an ethnic community inhabiting the northern and south-western regions of the country as well as parts of Ethiopia and Eritrea. The rebellion was aimed at toppling the government, which is dominated by the Issas, a northern branch of the Somali tribes living in the Horn of Africa. Both the Afars and the Issas are nomadic people who have been engaged in territorial disputes since time immemorial. In Djibouti, the ethnic divide resulted in a struggle for political power. In 1991 FRUD launched an all-out war against the government, because of what the rebels described as the under-representation of Afar interests in Djibouti society. They said that Afars had lost out in key political and senior administrative positions ever since Djiboutian independence in 1977.

In 1993 the civil war devastated Afar-inhabited regions. In the summer of that year government troops flushed the rebels out of key positions in the north of the country. Ali Mohamed Daoud, a senior rebel official and Ougoureh Kifleh, the group's chief military commander, signed a peace agreement with the government on 26 December 1994. But not everyone within the political and military command of the FRUD accepted the setback as a defeat. The civil war turned into a low-intensity conflict, as the radical wing of FRUD, led by former Prime Minister Ahmed Dini Ahmed, who decided to carry on the struggle. Relations between Djibouti and Eritrea worsened and eventually resulted in a diplomatic break in 1998. Afar rebels intensified their operations along the border with Eritrea. This prompted President Ismail Omar Guelleh to accuse the government in Asmara of supporting the Ahmed Dini's wing of the of the FRUD. President Ismail Omar Guelleh went as far as saying that the two countries were on the brink of war.

This was not the first time relations between Djibouti and Eritrea had gone sour, although the two states had been cordial enough at first. President Gouled had been among African dignitaries who attended the festivities in Asmara in 1993 marking the independence of Eritrea. But the warmth was not to last. At the end of April 1996 the Djiboutian authorities accused Eritrea of shelling a border post at Ras Doumeira, on the northernmost tip of Djibouti. President Gouled went to the scene of the alleged incident in a symbolic manifestation of his determination to maintain his country's territorial integrity. At this critical time Eritrean Foreign Minister Petros Solomon arrived in Djibouti on a diplomatic mission. It is believed that he showed President

Gouled an Eritrean map incorporating a stretch of present-day Djibouti ranging from Ras Doumeira to Moulhoule in the far North of the country. Petros Solomon reportedly claimed this area for Eritrea, based on a border agreement apparently signed between France and Mussolini's Italy in the 1930's. Eritrea subsequently denied that these claims had ever been made, saying they were accusations designed to damage relations between the two countries. Asmara also denied Djibouti's claim concerning the reported border incident.

By 1998 relations were so poor that Eritrea and Djibouti were on the brink of war. There was no way that France, with its military presence, could remain indifferent to the fate of its former colony, although it had refused to take sides in the previous civil war. A military conflict between Djibouti and Asmara was an altogether different matter. Any external military threat to Djibouti's territorial integrity would activate the country's defense agreement with France. It was against this backdrop that France sent its army chief of staff, General Jean-Pierre Kelch, to Djibouti. On the ground, France strengthened its capability. It brought in three additional radar networks to cover the Red Sea area. It also beefed up its monitoring of Djibouti's airspace. France deployed an airborne surveillance aircraft known as "Breguet-Atlantique" and a number of frigates fitted with missiles, to patrol the Red Sea corridor off the coasts of Djibouti and Eritrea. This was enough to deter Eritrean Mig jets based at Assab, just fifty kilometers from Djibouti's border. By rattling its sabre, France had prevented war from breaking out between the Red Sea neighbours. On the contrary, regional diplomacy was to bring about a rapprochement and then a normalisation of the Djibouti-Asmara relations.

Mending fences

Djibouti and Eritrea are both members of a little known African regional grouping known as the Community of Sahelo-Saharan countries or CEN-SAD, led by Libya's Muammar Kadhafi. In February 2000, it emerged that the Libyan leader had been mediating between Djibouti and Eritrea when Colonel Kadhafi appeared at a CEN-SAD summit in the Chadian capital, N'Djamena, flanked by Djibouti's President Ismail Omar Guelleh and his Eritrean counterpart Isayas Afwerki. After this meeting, the Presidents expressed their gratitude to Libya for helping the two parties mend fences. In February 2001 President Ismail Omar Guelleh went to Asmara to consolidate the normalisation process between the two countries. This was followed by a visit to Djibouti by Eritrean Foreign Minister Ali Said Abdallah, in January 2002. His visit revitalised a peace and cooperation treaty the two countries had signed in December 1993. Both Djibouti and Asmara are now keen to say that their relations are improving. The two sides say that trade, transport, education, health and immigration are the key areas they want to rejuvenate, to strengthen and renew their ties. It also appears that President Ismail Omar Guelleh's visit to Asmara has given rise to shared views on how to tackle the Somali crisis. The two capitals put great emphasis on the idea of a unified Somali state, pointing out that the current fragmentation of Somalia could have a ripple effect on the region. Asmara supports the Somali Transitional Government (TNG) that emerged from the Djibouti conference held in the summer of 2000. This stand has irritated Ethiopia intensely since Addis Ababa argues that the TNG has done nothing to fight or curb attacks allegedly carried out by Somalia-based Islamist organisations that are believed to be operating in the predominantly Somali-speaking Ethiopian region of Ogaden.

Reconstruction

Djibouti and Eritrea are keen to maintain that their misunderstanding is now a thing of the past. Many in Djibouti believe that the end of the row with Eritrea made it easier for the country's leaders to tackle unresolved issues that led to the signing, in May 2001, of a peace agreement between the Djibouti government and the FRUD wing led by Ahmed Dini Ahmed. The peace deal marked the end of years of armed conflict, which had caused tens of thousands of civilians to flee their homes. Most of these displaced people sought refuge in Djibouti-town. Thousands of Djiboutians also took refuge in neighbouring Ethiopia. Djibouti's army and paramilitary forces have grown from 3,000 before the civil war to around 18,000. Djibouti is now faced with rebuilding its war-torn districts, and integrating the former fighters on both sides into the social, economic and political fabric of the country.

The war against Terror

Since 2002, Djibouti has been sheltering an American led anti terror force in the Horn of Africa. This force, which is chiefly made up of hundreds of US special forces and about 1000 members of the German navy, has been tasked with hunting down such terrorist organisations as Ousama Ben Laden's Al Qaeda in East Africa and the Arabian peninsula, including Yemen. This endeavour has put Djibouti on the political and strategic map of a region that most observers fear to be a possible haven for terrorists. To the Djibouti government, the arrival of the coalition against terror is an opportunity to demonstrate that it is a reliable ally of the West. It is also another opportunity for the Djibouti government to ask for more assistance from Western countries. In late July 2003, the Bush administration opened a USAID office in Djibouti with the pledge to provide assistance in the fields of health and education.

The increased US presence in Djibouti is being perceived with some degree of apprehension among the country's traditionally conservative

Muslims. Ahmed Dini Ahmed, the country's main opposition leader and a devout Muslim said that the fight against terror in the region might create resentment among fellow Muslims and backfire in Djibouti. Ahmed Dini said that the war against terrorism should not be implemented at the expense of the pressing needs and concern of the people of Djibouti. Despite such misgivings, the arrival of US forces in Djibouti and their subsequent quartering at Camp Lemonier (a former French Legionnaires' barracks in the southern outskirts of Djibouti-town) is seen as a god-given opportunity for work in a country where more than half of the young active adults are out of a job. The arrival of the US soldiers and their Western allies has provided a range of manual and semi-skilled jobs for a great number of Djiboutians. The job opportunities have even lured some Djiboutian exiles back to a country they left years ago.

Chapter 10

TWISTING ETHIO-ERITREAN ECONOMIC TIES: MISPERCEPTIONS OF WAR AND THE MISPLACED PRIORITIES OF PEACE, 1997-2002

David Styan

Section 1: Introduction and argument

This chapter examines the failure of actors and analysts to appreciate the linkages between economic issues and the political and military aspects of conflict. It argues that the low priority given to economic ties was critical in generating misperceptions of bilateral relations before and during 1998-2000. More importantly, it highlights that *none* of the contentious bi-lateral economic issues which sparked distrust in the years *prior* to 1998 have been resolved by the ensuing war. Rather war has increased the scope for future economic tension. In the light of this, the text then argues that this absence of discussion over *future* economic ties in the post-war settlement now runs a serious risk of repeating the earlier failure; of not taking the economic foundations of Ethio-Eritrean ties seriously. This is dangerous and short-sighted and is likely to undermine the sustainability of a longer-term settlement.

The UN plan provides comfort to the current, beleaguered political leaderships in Addis and Asmara as it privileges short-term political and military issues over discussion of longer-term substantive issues of restoring bi-lateral trade, migration and investment. While the military and technical aspects of settlement clearly *are* essential pre-requisites to peace, they should not be seen as an end in themselves. They are merely a means to the end of re-establishing

David Styan, School of Politics, Birkbeck College, November 2002 (amended June 2003)

substantive economic ties, on which the future prosperity, stability and health of around ten millions people in northern Ethiopia and Eritrea rests. The text is structured around the following four propositions:

i)   *It is wrong to see economic policy as the sole or primary trigger of hostilities in May 1998. Yet while not the cause of war, debates over economic policy were the single greatest source of misunderstanding between two governments between 1993-97.* Retrospectively, what is striking is that at the time neither leadership perceived that failures to resolve economic differences seriously threatened to destabilise bilateral ties. Equally, since the conflict, aspects of economic normalisation have been singularly lacking from political discourse in either country.

ii) Such misunderstandings were the *inevitable outcome of the low priority given to economic matters*, which were overshadowed by the primacy of political and military prerogatives of the leaderships of the two states. This low priority reflected two facts; firstly that in 1991 they had together successfully defeated the Ethiopian government, a foe with vastly superior economic resources. Given the primacy of military and political factors in 1991, economics appeared a secondary factor to the leaderships during the 1990s when both controlled the resources of state-based economies.

iii) Contrary to most liberal analysis, it is easily forgotten that *war brings specific short-term advantages to governments.* In the short term, going to war in 1998 greatly strengthened the – essentially *dirigiste* – economic policies pursued by both the TPLF and EPLF/PFJD. In Ethiopia the sharp rise in government defence spending both boosted economic activity, and greatly strengthened de-facto control of ruling party over key sectors of economy. Yet, while highly significant in the short term, such "benefits" are illusory in that they are both inherently unsustainable, and have unpredictable domestic political consequences. The economic burden of sustaining the colossal costs of war across a third financial year may have been decisive in the timing of Ethiopia's final May 2000 assault.[1] More importantly, the channelling of such vastly increased military spending through a political apparatus, comprising a very limited number of trusted decision makers, had greatly exacerbated personal and policy divisions, generating intensely bitter rivalry *within* the ruling TPLF. Thus in Ethiopia, the ostensible victor of the war itself, such divisions culminated in the decisive split within ruling party in March 2001, an event of more significance than the war itself in the broader history of the TPLF. This fact bedevils current attempts to analyse the war; the most decisive long term impact of what was unambiguously an *international*, inter-state war is ultimately on the *domestic* politics of each country. In the Ethiopian case the war can be viewed simultaneously the catalyst and product of internal divisions which existed well before 1997-98.[2] The pressures of mobilising and maintaining a war economy were even starker for the vanquished Eritrean leadership. Here defeat accelerated the haemorrhaging of domestic political legitimacy. This in turn threatened to strip the Eritrean economy and its leadership of their prime source of external finance and foreign exchange, remittances from diaspora (see section 3.2). The war also deprived Eritrea of its largest export market and a key source of agricultural imports. This latter fact has grave implications for the future direction of Eritrean economic policy, and is explored briefly in section three below.

iv) Finally and most crucially, the text argues that *restoring and enhancing bi-lateral economic ties is a critically neglected component of the settlement process*. In failing to give priority to the resumption of economic ties of trade, investment and migration UNMEE and associated diplomatic and donor interventions risk sewing the seeds of future conflict. This long-term risk is exacerbated by the immediate danger that substantive discussion of reparations will delay or derail the progress made to date. The current curtailing of the possibilities of trade and migration is encouraging autarchic and thus economically myopic development strategies on either side of the Mareb. This runs the risk of undermining both the sustainability of the current settlement, and the long-term economic prosperity of peoples of the region.

Section 2: The misperception and neglect of economic factors in the genesis of war

Prior to 1997/98, information on the state of bi-lateral economic negotiations between Addis and Asmara was scarce and little analysed. Neither administration was keen to discuss economic issues publicly, and the Tigrayan-dominated EPRDF in Addis was acutely averse to publicising its negotiations and relations with the EPLF. At the time this was presumed to be due to rampant criticism of its alleged favouritism towards both Tigray and Eritrea, by non-EPRDF private businesses, politicians and the (virulently anti-EPRDF) Amharic-language private press in Addis. However, in retrospect it is clear that sensitivities were as much due to acute divisions *within* senior TPLF ranks, both in Mekelle and Addis, over what stance to take vis-à-vis ties with their erstwhile Eritrean allies.

Since the war, the role of economic factors and misunderstandings between Addis and Asmara, notably surrounding the introduction and implications of Eritrea's new currency, the Nakfa, in 1997 have become better understood. The significance of economic friction in the collapse of cooperation and communication in the months leading up to May 1998 are narrated in two existing English texts which sketch the contours of debates and divisions.[3] These demonstrate that economic policies were the most significant arena of disagreement *between* the two governments at the time, although the politically more significant contours of dissent on currency and trade *within* senior echelons of the TPLF and EPLF respectively remain obscure.[4] The problems surrounding the botched 1993 agreement to harmonise economic ties in what was *de-facto* a single currency area have also subsequently been narrated in greater detail than was made public in either country at the time.[5]

Ethiopian and Eritrean governments signed what was intended to be a comprehensive cooperation agreement in September 1993, four months after Eritrea's *de-juré* independence. Although annual joint-ministerial commissions and technical committees were formed to oversee implementation, and in May 1995 Ethiopia even announced that a Free Trade Area was already in place, in practice the two countries were far from trading freely. Despite three subsequent meetings of a joint-committee on economic issues, by mid-1996 an impasse had been reached on economic harmonisation. However, it should be stressed (given it is so easily forgotten in the wake of the 1998 rupture) that notwithstanding disagreements, extensive economic exchange was occurring between 1991-97; daily flights between Addis and Asmara ferried people and goods, with a considerable volume of cross-border trade being conducted by air and land.

In essence between 1991-97 economic disagreement centred on three contentious and interlinked issues: currency; trade and investment; and what I'll term the "identity of economic actors".

i) **Currency**. Following independence in May 1993, Eritrea continued to use the Ethiopian birr as its legal tender, while stating that it would eventually create its own national currency. The two countries therefore formed a de-facto single currency area. Between 1993-97 while monetary policy was set unilaterally by Addis (Eritrea thus following the progressive devaluation of the Birr during the mid-1990s), Asmara benefited from Ethiopia's relative monetary stability and ensured control over its own remittance flows by offering a slight premium on rates in Addis. Logically the single currency should have facilitated trade and enhanced prospects for economic integration. Indeed the apparently comprehensive agreement signed in Asmara in September 1993 provided a framework for bi-lateral cooperation between the two states. This contained protocols on economic cooperation, trade and policy harmonisation. It aimed to harmonise monetary and foreign exchange policies, and trade-related aspects of fiscal policy were also to be brought into line. Provisions were also made to ensure equal and reciprocal access to investment opportunities for national of each other's countries. However, despite apparent commitment to integration, by the time Eritrea announced that it would be introducing its own currency, the Nakfa, in late 1997, substantial mistrust had accumulated over bi-lateral economic ties. This distrust rendered dialogue and agreement over the modalities of the introduction of the Nakfa (and its necessary counterpart, the withdrawal of Ethiopian Birr from circulation in Eritrea) impossible.

ii) **Trade and Investment**. The inability to resolve currency matters amicably simultaneously reflected and exacerbated deeper tensions over trade and investment. Firstly Eritrea had a relatively large trade surplus with Ethiopia, generating resentment; secondly the Ethiopian government was hostile to Eritreans buying products within Ethiopia, most notably coffee, which were destined for export. Such transactions deprived Ethiopia of foreign exchange to the benefit of Eritrea. The true scale of such trade has never been established, despite being the subject of considerable polemics within Ethiopia since May 1998. Thirdly and finally, Eritrean citizens were eager to reinvest funds within the far larger Ethiopian economy. Such investment was hardly new. Complex patterns of private capital flows existed for much of the 20th century, although these had been stymied in the 1970s and 80s by state socialism and war. Yet in the post 1991 economic context (characterised by a formal fraternity between regimes which served to mask acute economic rivalry between rival Tigrinya-speaking investors) these capital flows sparked incendiary debates over the status and identity of each others' nationals and companies as investors in each other's economies.

iii) **The identity of economic actors.** This final question of "the identity of economic actors" was, and remains, far more complex and contentious than it might at first appear to outsiders for two reasons. *Firstly* the problems inherent in distinguishing in legal terms between resident and non-resident Eritreans in Ethiopia. This distinction is further clouded by the fact that many, indeed the majority, of individuals with parental and family links to Eritrea had *not* opted for Eritrean nationality by participating in the referendum in 1993, and thus remained full Ethiopian citizens.

Secondly, had such legal distinctions concerned only *private* economic actors, whose activities respective governments were seeking to license and regulate, the problems of identity and regulation would have been complex enough. However, individual private economic actors were not the crux of the matter. Throughout the 1990s both the Eritrean and Ethiopian ruling parties had invested heavily in companies which, while ostensibly "private" in a legal sense (in that they were not state owned enterprises), were in fact owned wholly by the parties themselves, albeit often via proxy individuals. These "para-party" companies were a continuation of practices established prior to 1991 during the liberation struggle. In the Ethiopian case, the trend was most pronounced in Tigray itself, where many of the TPLF's holdings were grouped under the Endowment Fund for the Rehabilitation of Tigray (EFFORT). Clearly it is reasonable to suppose that a fear that Eritrean nationals desiring to invest in Ethiopia's transportation and financial sectors, would in fact be acting as proxies for, or be beholden to, the Eritrean government, was uppermost in the minds of Tigrayan policy makers. Clearly such concerns were heightened via fears that such investment would be in direct competition with TPLF owned companies within Tigray itself. Such suspicions lay at the root of the sharp gulf between the official policy and rhetoric of bi-lateral economic cooperation and harmonisation, and de-facto protectionism of nascent industries in Tigray. Finally a third, markedly less important issue should be noted. Both of the above factors were entangled in a broader policy issue crucial to Ethiopia's overall, ongoing economic reform programme; the degree to which economic liberalisation in general should be widened to include foreign investors.[6]

Even this short summary of contentious economic issues prior to 1998 demonstrates how festering problems around trade and investment served to undermine apparently good bi-lateral political ties. However in retrospect it is also important to stress the degree to which respective leaderships, most particularly Meles Zenawi and Issaias Afeworki themselves, seemed to systematically underplay the importance of economic ties. This perception that economics really wasn't an insurmountable problem is apparent in the critical direct communications, which have been published since the conflict.[7]

Section 3: The economic costs of war
No attempt has been made to evaluate the overall economic burden of the 1998-2000 war, the actual and opportunity costs of which will continue to be borne by Ethiopian and Eritreans for many years to come. The foregoing section suggested that Ethiopian and Eritrean leaders were complacent and

negligent prior to 1998 in ignoring the threat to bilateral ties posed by failure to resolve currency, trade and investment disputes. However, the economic benefits and losses at stake in the 1993-98 economic wrangles were totally dwarfed by the colossal costs of both the war itself and its economic aftermath. This section aims only to provide a brief outline of the costs of the actual conflict, indicating some factors for consideration, and sources of information. Its primary purpose is to stress the scale of both the actual and opportunity costs of the conflict. In particular it highlights the impact on Eritrean trade patterns and livelihoods, and stresses that a failure to promptly and progressively restore trade links between Eritrea and Ethiopia will exacerbate to hardship generated by the war itself.

Evaluating the relative impact of the war on each economy is greatly complicated by inequalities in both the magnitude of the two states and the availability of economic information on each. The vastly differing sizes of the two economies mean that the fighting had a proportionally far greater impact upon Eritrea's far smaller population and economy. In addition, for the past decade, Ethiopia has been undergoing an externally supported and monitored economic reform programme. Thus for Ethiopia, the publicly available data generated for and by the reforms makes some basic estimations and comparisons of the economic cost and impact of war possible. Very little such data existed, even prior to the war for Eritrea, making such evaluations far more problematic.

3.1 Calculating costs for Ethiopians

Ethiopia's public expenditure review, conducted by the World Bank with Ethiopian government officials in 1999 provides an overview of the costs of the first year of fighting. The World Bank estimated the costs of war in three separate categories[8]:

i)   Firstly the burden of massively increased defence spending. By the mid-1990s defence spending in Ethiopia was averaging Birr800m. The 1997/98 budget planned for Birr850m expenditure on the armed forces. War in the last two months of that fiscal year meant actual spending leapt to Birr2.1bn. In the year to July 1999 (FY1998/99) military expenditure totalled Birr4.2bn, 5 times the pre-war planning total, representing almost half the government's total current expenditure. Given the nature of the final year of fighting (1999/2000) it is reasonable to assume military expenditure was *at least* of a similar magnitude to that of 1998/99.[9] The Bank estimated this *increased* burden of defence spending at around 3.8% of total GDP.

ii)   In 1999 the World Bank estimated the secondary costs of war at between Birr1.1 and Birr1.4bn. These incorporated the costs of falling investment, loss of tourist revenues, a lower rate of overall growth than forecast, and the cost (put at between Birr550-950m) of emergency assistance to around 350,000 people displaced by the war. In addition, increased transport costs from Djibouti are estimated at Birr180m a year. Coupled with the burden of military expenditure, the Bank put the overall cost at 2.5-3.5% of overall GDP.

iii) On top of this, around Birr1.5bn of external economic assistance, much of it from the World Bank itself, was suspended by the war. This, according to Bank figures, represented the equivalent of a further 3% slice off GDP. However, while the suspension of such funds did clearly adversely dent economic growth and planning for the duration of the war, much of this assistance has simply been rescheduled for disbursement since the peace agreement of December 2000. As such, it cannot be strictly viewed as a net overall loss or cost due to the war.

Put in the most general terms, this way of assessing the costs of war suggests that at around 7% of GDP, the total immediate financial impact of war over two years was around Birr8,000m, or $1bn.[10]

Clearly such guesstimates are highly approximative, but are the only data which analysts have to draw upon. Using the same data but different methods, a tentative independent Ethiopian study of the economic impact of the war upon the Ethiopian economy was prepared by the nascent Ethiopian Economic Policy and Research Institute (EEPRI) in August 2001. This drew on the World Bank's Public Expenditure Review to conclude that the overall costs of war were $2.9bn,[11] detailing direct destruction of property (including the estimate of $133m of goods seized in Assab) as well as more comprehensive secondary effects via the multiplier effects of the loss of tourism, the impact that the hike in military expenditure had on both government borrowing and the overall balance of payments, as well as the longer-term investment implications. The latter include the impact of switching government expenditure from economically and socially productive uses – on health, education and direct productive capacity – to military purposes.

In addition the EEPRI report highlights that the re-orientation of government expenditure and its impact on the economy exacerbates one of the more worrying long-term trends, the collapse of domestic savings in Ethiopia. This leads the 2002 EEPRI report to highlight the essential paradox, that on the one hand government expenditure was a spur to short-term growth —while not leading to sustained production, government military expenditure nevertheless contributes to GDP—yet had severely undermined already weak long-term growth trends, by undermining savings and investment rates.[12]

3.2 Eritrea: short term devastation & long term trade uncertainty

No such comparable aggregate estimate of the immediate financial costs of the war can be made for Eritrea. An IMF Staff Country Report was compiled in April 2000, but only the Statistical Annex has been made public.[13] In absolute terms, Eritrea's military expenditure is likely to have been lower than Ethiopia's. The patchy data available suggests it had slightly fewer troops mobilised. As opposed to Ethiopia, where troops were mobilised via both conventional calls to patriotism as well as salary incentives, most Eritrean troops were conscripts recruited via national service obligations and received only nominal pay. Eritrean supply lines were also shorter, making fuel and transport costs far lower. However, this pales into insignificance when compared with the costs as a proportion of Eritrea's far smaller economy, and the fact that the defeat of May-June 2000 wrought far higher cost in material destruction of both military and civilian property. Eritrea's overall GDP was estimated at Nakfa5.8bn in 1999 (c$725m), just under one tenth the size of Ethiopia's; Eritrea's population was a little over 3m, as opposed to Ethiopia's 65m.

The scale of the devastation and disruption renders conventional macro-economic calculations meaningless. In the wake of the war, in mid-2000 the UN estimated that a million people had been displaced by fighting, while an additional 600,000 were affected by drought. The bulk of those displaced were from agriculturally productive border regions. The mining of such regions along the border, the flight of peasant cultivators, the destruction of infrastructure and dispersal of livestock hugely disrupted agricultural production in 2000/01, a situation further aggravated by poor climatic conditions. Consequently, in 2002 UN and local agencies were providing food assistance to 800,000 people, a quarter of the population.

As for Ethiopia, the war also prompted a suspension of external development assistance to Eritrea. However, of far, far greater short *and* long-term significance was the effect the war had upon remittances from Eritreans in the diaspora, Eritrea's primary source of foreign exchange. While in Ethiopia the government was able to finance soaring defence expenditure in 1998-2000 by drawing on domestic resources of taxation[14] and internal borrowing from domestic banks, Eritrea's ability to do the same was constrained by its far smaller economy and reserves. While official statistics are inevitably exceedingly patchy, it is clear that remittances are one of Eritrea's core sources of finance. Indeed in the Eritrean case "remittances" in effect form a key part of the taxation and foreign exchange systems. While the term remittances in general connotes the voluntary repatriation of a portion of income home, in the Eritrean case, initially the EPLF, then the Eritrean state effectively levied a contribution, usually a set portion of monthly income, on its supporters and citizens abroad.[15]

An IMF staff report published in June 2003 starkly highlighted the centrality of remittances to the Eritrean economy: "The importance of the diaspora for the public finance and foreign exchange is demonstrated by the fact that the level of bonds issued to the diaspora reached 3.1% of GDP in 1999 and grants amounted to 3.2% of GDP in 2000. On the external account, private transfers from the Diaspora are the largest single source of foreign currency inflows into the country, with the ratio of these transfers to GDP averaging 37 per cent over the last ten years".[16]

Such dependency on remittances clearly poses acute problems for future growth. Firstly demands for "voluntary" contributions from members of the disapora abroad were ratcheted up by the Eritrean representatives in 1998 in response to the war. Initially, many expatriate Eritreans did respond, however, it seems that over the duration of the war, and more acutely since its end, contributions declined. Since the end of the war, with the implosion of the Eritrean government and the crisis of legitimacy surrounding the increasingly authoritarian president, and the collapse in the value of the Nakfa, such remittances have further declined.

Of even more significance for the core concerns of this article are the ways in which the war effected a drastic change in Eritrea's pattern of foreign trade. For Ethiopia trade with Eritrea was of minor significance overall. Clearly trade with Eritrea was of greater importance for neighbouring Tigray, although remittances from Tigrayans working in Eritrea were almost certainly financially more significant. Data is lacking on all aspects of cross-border trade, migration and remittances and is clearly an area requiring further research.

However, for the Eritrean economy, trade with Ethiopia was of major importance. It represented two thirds of all export earnings in 1997. With exports representing around 10% of overall national income in 1997, and Eritrea pursuing an avowedly export-orientated trade policy, the loss of the Ethiopian market therefore appears of crucial long-term significance. The nature and magnitude of its importance can be roughly gauged with reference to the tables below.

Tables

1.1   Eritrea: Composition of overall Imports, and imports from Ethiopia

Millions of birr/nakfa [1]

	1995	1998
Food	427	460
Of which Ethiopia	91 (21%)	19 (4%)
Manufactures & Machinery [2]	1811	1267
Of which Ethiopia	182 (10%)	5 (0.4%)
Total Imports	2536	2693
Of which Ethiopia	146 (6%)	25 (1%) [3]

1.2   Eritrea: Composition of Exports, and exports to Ethiopia

Millions of of birr/nakfa [1]

	1995	1998
Food	141	58
Of which Ethiopia	57 (40%)	3 (5%)
Manufactures & Machinery [2]	197	45
Of which Ethiopia	150 (76%)	18 (40%) [3]
Total Exports	529	197
Of which Ethiopia	354 (67%)	52 (27%) [3]

2. Eritrea; Overall direction of exports, origins of imports; & trade with Ethiopia 1994-1998 millions of Nakfa/Birr [1]

	1994	1995	1996	1997	1998
Total Exports	397	529	520	375	197
Exports to Ethiopia	208	354	342	238	52
As % of overall exports	52%	67%	66%	63%	27%
Total Imports	1993	2536	3063	3062	2693
Imports from Ethiopia	91	147	262	275	25
As % of overall imports	5	6	9	9	1

Sources: derived from: IMF, Eritrea Statistical Appendix, IMF Staff Country Report No 00/55, April 2000, tables 29, 30, 31 & 32; which gives full 1994-98 figures; these in turn compiled from Eritrean Customs sources

Notes:

[1] In original, millions birr 1994-97, 1998 figures in million nakfa. Given that throughout 1998 birr and nakfa were both trading at slightly over 7 to the dollar, the figures here remain directly comparable.

[2] In original, Manufactured goods; machinery and transport; and miscellaneous manufactures are disaggregated.

[3] These figures imply that some trade with Ethiopia did continue in the first quarter of 1998, despite the sharp deterioration of economic relations.

Thus in 1995 while just 6% of overall imports, worth Birr146m, came from Ethiopia, a full two thirds of Eritrea's exports (67%, worth Birr354m) went to Ethiopia, the bulk of which was manufactured goods, notably textiles, footware and beverages. Thus not only was Eritrea's export sector critically dependent on Ethiopia, but the large trade surplus with Ethiopia represented a key part of Eritrea's balance of payments profile. This was doubly important given the emphasis put on an export-orientated, industrial growth strategy for the economy as a whole.

This is significant in that industry accounts for a far larger share of GDP in Eritrea than agriculture; around 27% in the late 1990s (as opposed to 16% for agriculture) according to IMF figures. Given that the war, temporarily at least, removed industry's primary market, this has very significant implications for economic stability and the potential for future recovery and growth. There were credible expectations that Eritrea's industrial base, integrated to its natural markets in northern Ethiopia and eastern Sudan, would provide a foundation of post-1991 Eritrean economy.

Although imports from Ethiopia represented only a small fraction of overall imports, their significance was far greater in the agricultural sector, where produce from Ethiopia represented a fifth of food imports, notably the staple highland grain, *teff*. Clearly the loss of access to such produce not only imposes a significant cost on the economy but also further dislocates the already exceedingly fragile agricultural markets.

An additional dimension to the economic impact of the war on Eritrea is evidently the loss of port traffic transiting to and from Ethiopia via Assab and Massawa. Loss of port fees has had a major impact on Eritrea's government revenue. The IMF estimates that port fees—primarily paid by Ethiopian companies for the use Assab—fell from 22% of total government revenue prior to 1998, to just 5% during and since the war. To this initial revenue loss needs to be added the multiplier effect of the loss of associated economic activity and employment in both Assab and Massawa.

Section 4: The bi-lateral economic questions of 1991 still need answering

Section two highlighted the fact that the failure to resolve serious disagreements over bi-lateral economic questions critically undermined relations between Asmara and Addis in the four years to 1997. Significant mistrust and misperceptions surrounding economic ties were nevertheless concealed, firstly by the reluctance of either government to allow domestic public debate on the direction of economic policy, and secondly by the belief that bilateral *political* ties were what mattered, and that these could and would be resolved amicably and privately between leaders. The naivety and falsehood of this belief was shattered disastrously in May 1998.

If, as is argued here, understanding this failure to resolve economic disagreements is central to understanding the background to war, it follows that anyone concerned with the long-term future of bi-lateral ties, or indeed the more pressing short-term question of whether the settlement currently pursued by the parties and UNMEE is sustainable, is therefore now faced with two questions. Firstly, has the war itself, or the terms of the fragile and partial settlement since December 2000, provided answers to the outstanding economic questions of pre-1998? Secondly, has the war created any *additional* economic obstacles to peaceful bi-lateral relations.

As seen in section two, the unanswered questions which poisoned relations prior to 1998 revolved around four interlinked issues: *firstly* bi-lateral currency arrangements, *secondly* the regulation of foreign trade, *thirdly* the reciprocity of investment by each others nationals and *fourthly* the legal and economic identity and status of such nationals. Analysing and disentangling these issues is evidently greatly complicated by the fact that in practice this fourth issue underpins all others in that it determines the nature and status of economic actors engaging in trade, investment, migration and remittances across the Mereb.

War has convincingly answered only the first question, concerning currency, on which there was already agreement in principle prior to 1998. Answers to the others have simply been dropped from domestic agendas, apparently postponed indefinitely. Indeed the fact they are not on the public agendas of the policy makers in Asmara, Addis or Mekelle – or of the UN and other foreign legations who have invested in the settlement – is not accidental. For the foreseeable future it suits the short-term agendas of all actors to currently assume that Eritrea and Tigray will effectively remain sealed, autonomous territories with little or no economic interaction.[17] This despite the fact that it contradicts not just all historical precedents in the region, but also basic economic logic *and* will work against both the long term welfare of Eritreans and Tigrayans and also the viability of the settlement as currently presented.

Taking each outstanding question in turn. On the first currency issue there was no doubt or dissent, either between or within respective governments, that Eritrea would introduce its own national currency. Disagreement centred only on the modalities of its introduction and the nature of the link and exchange rate between Nakfa and Birr. Despite the lack of agreement and consequent climate of distrust, it should be stressed that the introduction of the Nakfa and simultaneous withdrawal and sterilisation of Birr circulating in Eritrea occurred relatively smoothly in late 1997. Since then, each country has run its own foreign exchange and monetary policy independently. A point of contention during 1997, was that Eritrea sought a fixed 1:1 Birr:Nakfa parity, presumably on the basis that Ethiopian underwriting of the Nakfa would both partly provide the kind of monetary stability enjoyed 1991-97, and facilitate economic interaction with Ethiopia, still by far the largest trade partner. Ethiopia rejected this, albeit via the "dialogue of the deaf" which characterised the bitter bi-lateral climate of 1997. Yet in the absence of agreement, what happened in reality was that both currencies traded at very similar rates to the US dollar throughout 1998 and 1999, despite the pressures of war. In Eritrea, defeat and turmoil since 2000 prompted a depreciation of the Nakfa.[18] Yet even in the absence of war, a 1:1 tie was not likely to have been sustainable; very different fundamental economic forces shape foreign trade and financial flows in both countries. However, the key point now is that the currency question is resolved; if and when financial flows are restored between Ethiopia and Eritrea, the two separate currencies will trade at the prevailing, externally determined dollar rate, as between any two normal, independent neighbouring trading partners.

On the questions of trade and investment, the war has simply meant a suspension of all exchange. Both governments maintain a de-facto embargo on any economic ties. Cross border trade is non-existent, with even smuggling severely curtailed.[20] There is currently no discussion of how and when trade is to be re-established, or what trade regime is desirable. This contrasts with the situation of 1993-1997, when, while there were serious differences in approaches, there was at least dialogue and agreement on what issues required resolving. Negotiation secured agreement on the desirability of trade, the principles and objectives underpinning policy, the parameters of trade regulation, tariffs, investment flows etc. This was true for both bi-lateral trade, as well as the more significant volumes of Ethiopian transit-trade via the port of Assab. (In the furore and recriminations since 1998, it is easy to forget that Assab functioned fairly smoothly until the war, to the mutual benefit of both countries.) Therefore not only has the pre-1998 trade question not been answered, but the partial and imperfect trade regime of 1993-97 has been replaced by entirely protectionist, autarchic trade policies. Producers in both Eritrea and Ethiopia are producing and trading, both internally and internationally completely insulated from each other.

This situation has significant implications for both current (1998-2002) economic developments and future patterns of trade and production in the region. These implications are beyond the scope of this text, but the impact is felt particularly in Tigray and other northern Ethiopian provinces most involved in economic exchange with Eritrea. There has been relatively rapid physical development, directed by the state and ruling party, in large part via "private" companies under its control, (including the establishment of a growing number of industries, most notably by EFFORT) in Mekelle and other parts of Tigray since the mid-1990s. This has occurred in an economic environment where neighbouring Eritrea, either as a source of imported substitute goods, or a market for export production, effectively does not exist. Tariff barriers, quotas of other forms of protectionism are not necessary in the context of a border which is sealed by war. Major new infrastructure projects, most recently the hydro-electric plan to dam the Tekesse river, appear to the have been planned in isolation from the wider regional economy. In the absence of indications to the contrary, one has to assume that the current policy markers in Tigray prefer this autarchic development, without links to Eritrea. Indeed whereas policy prior to 1998 was ambiguous, with a clear gap between official rhetorical commitment to integration and free trade and a de-facto protectionism, the current position is clear; no trade. This raises a series of key policy questions, prominent among which is whether the current situation is either sustainable or desirable in the long-run? For Eritrea, historically, demand for Eritrean manufactures in Ethiopia provided economies of scale for Eritrean producers, and Eritrea reciprocally providing a market for Ethiopian agricultural produce. Will the significant investment in manufacturing in Tigray in the past decade (notably in engineering, construction materials and pharmaceuticals) alter this pattern? Could such nascent industries compete with revived Eritrean industries in the absence of tariff protection? With the border and Eritrean ports closed to Tigrayan merchants and investors, imported inputs—not least fuel—currently arrive via long and costly supply routes from Addis Ababa, Djibouti and Port Sudan. In the future, will the cost savings made by importing manufacturing inputs to Tigray via Massawa allow production to be competitive vis-à-vis new finished imported manufactures which could also enter Northern Ethiopia through Eritrean ports? Clearly the answer to such questions will rest on the appropriate levels of tariffs which will require complex and arduous negotiation. Similarly, the resumption and regulation of labour migration across the Mereb will also require careful thought and cooperation.

In addition to the devastation and disruption occasioned by fighting (and its side effects such as the mining of agriculturally productive border regions), the free functioning of the region's extremely precarious agricultural markets, both for produce and for seasonal agricultural labour, have been further compartmentalised. This exacerbates the dependency of rural populations on both sides of the border on foreign food assistance. It seems clear that even in the absence of a comprehensive trade agreement, the resumption of trade in agricultural produce in particular, in addition to flows of food aid across the border, is an urgent requirement, one in which foreign agencies have a key role.[20] If an incremental approach to reopening trade negotiations is adopted, this may be a place to start.

As with the trade issue, the answers to questions three and four, concerning investment ties, and the legal status of each others citizens (thus the very people who will be investing and trading), have not simply been postponed by war, but have been greatly complicated by it. As noted in section two, the fragmentary evidence available suggests that the question of the status and scope of investments by Eritrean citizens in Ethiopia prior to 1997 was the most complex, controversial and least publicised element of the Ethio-Eritrean economic dossier. It seems probable that this issue not only greatly exacerbated the suspicions of Ethiopia's economic decision markers over Eritrean intentions but also that it further accentuated grave disagreement *between* leading TPLF members over what their attitude to Issaias and the Eritrean leadership should be.[21] Such problems may also have been heightened by uncertainties surrounding the liberalisation of the Ethiopia's overall financial architecture.[22]

Notwithstanding this, evaluating to what degree such investment actually existed, or what potential there was (or in future may be...) for it to occur is complicated by two factors. Firstly – a key uncertainty running through the whole of this analysis – is that the scale of party-owned investments in either economy remains largely unknown. Nevertheless, within Ethiopia by 1998 the broad contours of policy had emerged which envisaged that the components of the EPRDF each would replicate the "para-party" model of development, with companies close the ruling party taking key state contracts. This is most clearly demonstrated in the public works (particularly road construction) and distributive service sectors. However, despite evident alarm among senior TPLF members in the debates of 1997-98, there is no evidence that EPLF had, via proxy individuals, come to control economic assets that threatened the TPLF's own para-party holdings.[23]

The second complicating factor is that the expulsions abruptly redefined what it meant to be "Ethiopian" and "Eritrean". Such is the confusion surrounding the motivations which provoked the decision to begin expelling Ethiopians of Eritrean origin from Ethiopia from May 1998 onward, that it is likely that clarity over the extent of concerns about EPLF influence over the economy will never be forthcoming. Up until 1998 the issue of investor identity, despite certain ambiguities, was relatively clear, at least in relation to the situation of chaos since. Several weeks into the war, such relative clarity was wrecked by Ethiopia's decision to start expelling its own, full *Ethiopian* citizens who happened to have historic and family links to Eritrea. The impact and rationale, or rather lack of it, behind the expulsions from Ethiopia is— mercifully—beyond the scope of this article. However, what is crucial to our central task of disentangling economic issues is to appreciate how these expulsions have fundamentally altered the nature of our fourth question; the need to clarify the legal and economic status of each other's citizens before cross-border trade and investment can re-start.

In economic terms, the expulsions from Ethiopia, hit three distinct categories of Ethiopians:

1. Firstly Ethiopian business owners with family ties to Eritrea who had effectively become entitled to de-facto Eritrean nationality by dint of their participation in the 1993 referendum on Eritrean independence. These people found themselves effectively trapped by the ambiguity in Ethiopian nationality law which forbade dual nationality.
2. Secondly Ethiopian nationals, who while not being Eritrean citizens, were expelled anyhow because of family ties to Eritrea.

3.   A third category is mostly overlooked by existing analyses. However, it is probably both the largest group, and is likely to have the most significant impact on the Ethiopian economy. These are Ethiopian entrepreneurs, employees and their dependents who while of Eritrean origin, had neither taken Eritrean nationality, nor were actually targeted or threatened with expulsion. Nevertheless, in the climate of bitterness, apprehension and arbitrariness both over their citizenship and property rights, chose to leave Ethiopia anyhow, preferring "voluntary" exit, rather than a precarious future threatened with expropriation and expulsion to Eritrea, a place where most had neither capital, nor substantive ties, and in many cases not even any linguistic affinity.[24] While some migrated directly to OECD states, in the chaos of mid-1998, many fled to Kenya, Djibouti, Uganda and South Africa.

The identity issue has thus been radically, and violently reconfigured, by the war. For Eritrean policy makers, the issue remains clearcut. Eritrea legally recognises dual citizenship. On the Ethiopian side things remain exceedingly unclear. In late 2001 there were several indications that Meles Zenawi viewed the expulsions as a grave error, reinforcing the impression that the policy was the result of acrimonious debates within the TPLF in May 1998. Once again, the issue remains yoked to the broader questions of both the recognition of dual-nationality within Ethiopian law, and the role of diaspora investors. In January 2001 a further reform of Ethiopia's Investment Code provided new incentives for Ethiopians resident abroad to invest in the country, the foreign minister publicly supporting the principle of dual-nationality. However, Eritreans were explicitly excluded from the provisions.

So far this section has examined how war reconfigured the four bi-lateral economic issues of importance in the period 1991-2002. We also need to consider whether war had created *additional* economic obstacles to peaceful future economic cooperation. There is one, potentially deeply worrying economic issue which is embedded in the terms of the peace settlement. This is the provision for reparations and compensation arising from war damage. The fact that reparations and compensation are part of the peace settlement, but that negotiations over them have barely begun two years after the settlement,[25] prompts three observations.

Firstly, while it is understandable that such provisions appeared integral to peace in 2000, to date they have not figured in substantive negotiations on the political settlement.

Secondly, given what might best be described as begrudging and tetchy adherence to the settlement by the parties to date, the risk of the existing progress and long-term stability of settlement being undermined by wrangles

194

over retrospectively apportioning costs of the war is a real danger. Given the rhetoric and emotion surrounding the issue, apportioning blame and extracting compensation claims will be highly divisive, and could be used by either party to derail substantive progress.

Thirdly, and crucially for the core concerns of this article, disagreement over reparations and compensation may well overshadow and ultimately derail real negotiations over the future rules governing trade, investment and migration, i.e. precisely those factors that in a practical sense must bind the two territories together and on which lasting peace must rest. The need to provide durable answers to the questions of trade, investment and national identity, with the primary objective of fostering trade and investment, are far, far more important that short-term wrangles over the cost of war and damages will serve to derail momentum to a sustainable settlement. This fourth, new economic question thrown up by the war is therefore potentially very dangerous. This is not because it requires answering, but because it is a distraction from the more fundamental economic issues. Resolving it will requires visionary leaders whose concern is the long term economic future, rather than short-term settling of scores and financial gain.

Section 5: Conclusion; the need for a longer-term economic vision.

What agendas and suggested actions stem from the foregoing sections? Firstly there needs to be far greater awareness among both domestic and foreign actors that economic issues must be placed on both medium and long-term agendas both within and between the two countries. Such issues need to be an integral part of the settlement process.

The two years following the signing of the cease-fire in December 2000 have been characterised by short-term strategies; local leaderships are immobilised by immediate survival struggles, while the UN's vision is circumscribed both by its six-month rolling mandate and its limited leverage over the parties.

Both local and international actors will no doubt argue that consideration of longer-term bi-lateral economic ties is premature, that political and military issues are paramount; and that a demilitarised, demarcated border is necessary. To re-state the point made earlier, this is myopic; *all* the technical military issues which have pre-occupied the parties and UNMEE to date, while indeed being necessary pre-conditions to progress, nevertheless need to be viewed firmly *not* an end in themselves, but as the means to an end. The economic nature and shape of that end needs to be discussed now.

Debate needs to focus on a series of medium and long-term questions. In the medium-term, defined as 2003-05 (years 3-5 of the UN settlement plan), once the border demarcation is achieved, do the two governments propose to restore some form of freedom of movement across the border? Do they envisage establishing visa requirements, or will they revert back to allowing movement on internal identity papers? Will such movements be initially for personal travel only (such as family reunions), or will remittances and small scale trade be also allowed? Will they take place initially just across selected land crossings, or will direct flights also resume? Will Eritrean ports re-open to Ethiopian transhipments? Will cross-border food aid deliveries form a part of the progressive opening-up of the border?

The longer-term agenda, beyond 2005, has to provide substantive answers to the questions explored in section four. The text sought to demonstrate that these questions, on the nature of trade and investment ties, rest on at least three deeper policy issues. These need wider public discussion and debate if they are to form the foundations of mutually agreed, sustainable policies. It is also obvious that debate and the formulation of even tentative answers to such issues will require far more background research and data on cross border exchange than is currently available.

- Firstly, for those on the Ethiopian and Tigrayan side of the border, how will the re-establishment of trade with Eritrea fit with ongoing plans for the economic development of Tigray? More specifically, is the industrial and infrastructure development of the late 1990s sustainable in the absence of tariffs or other forms of protectionism from Eritrean competition?
- Secondly, will Eritrean post-2000 strategies for development policy still be premised on export-orientated growth? If so, is post-settlement Ethiopia still envisaged as its key market? If not, what is the alternative?
- Thirdly what will be the respective roles of state- and party-owned companies vis-à-vis private sector actors in re-kindling bi-lateral economic ties?
- Fourthly and finally, what about even longer-term infrastructure development? Reciprocal use of Ethiopian highlands' hydro-electric power generation and Eritrea's Ports being just the most obvious points of departure for such explorations of mutually beneficial ties.

These and related questions need airing, not just among Ethiopians and Eritreans on either side of the border, but also among the diasporas (whose remittances will necessarily form part of the future economic equation) and among foreign diplomats and UN strategists.

Indeed whereas the leverage of external, "international" actors and their agendas were almost wholly irrelevant to the conduct of the war, in the post-war settlement foreigners have several forms of leverage both as economic donors and the architects and managers of the UN implemented settlement. As such, foreign involvement presents both a problem and an opportunity. This text has argued that as currently configured the foreign presence - and outsiders' silence over future economic ties – is a problem. In appearing to support the belief that a long-term settlement can rest purely on political and military arrangements UNMEE and foreign economic donors to Ethiopia, fail to appreciate the need to prioritise economic normalisation. In doing so they appear to endorse the short-term, autarchic economic strategies currently being pursued, particularly in Tigray.

However, with foresight, foreign involvement could become an opportunity for obliging local actors to consider longer term issues. Indeed given the short term political fixations of both governments, and the fact that economic resources will necessarily have to come from outside, foreigners have a legitimate role to play in the discussion and formulation of the economic settlement. Both in framing the debate and posing serious questions about future ties, and seeking commitment from parties to finding long-term economic solutions while discussing and negotiating immediate, short-term military and political matters related to the border and its demarcation.

Given both the levels of bi-lateral distrust still prevalent in 2002, and the fraught domestic struggles in both countries (bi-lateral ties appear inextricably bound up with the splintering of the TPLF executive and the implosion of Eritrean authoritarianism) many will see both the analysis pursued in this text, and the agendas presented above as both absurdly utopian and far too premature.

Yet the purpose of this article is to argue precisely that *the sooner such issues move into the public domain and onto policy agendas, the more likelihood that in decades to come, sustainable bi-lateral ties can be consolidated.* For this the mistrust and secrecy surrounding economic policy which characterised bilateral relations prior to 1997 needs to be dissipated.

Few paid heed to bi-lateral economic issues prior to 1991; voices in the public domain raising such issues were entirely marginal.[26] For much of the nineties, including during the critical months of 1997, it was left to leaders to discuss such matters in private. As seen in section one, domestic leaders, their publics and external analysts consistently underestimated the importance of economic issues. They naively believed both in the primacy of political and military relations and the ability of personal ties between the erstwhile allies to resolve problems. The debacle of 1998 and its horrific aftermath should be an adequate reminder that the economic foundations of bi-lateral ties now need deeper thought and action.

ENDNOTES

1. Economist Intelligence Unit, *Ethiopia Country Report*, September 2000, p.9.
2. Meles alluded to the deeper rivalries that pre-dated the war in an interview with the *Financial Times*; "Ethiopia, World Report", 24.09.02.
3. Gilkes P. Plaut M. (1999) *War in the Horn; the conflict between Ethiopia and Eritrea*, London, Royal Institute for International Affairs, pp 13-15 & 47-52. Tronvoll K. and Tekeste Negash (2000) *Brothers at war; making sense of the Ethio-Eritrean war*, Oxford, James Currey, ch.5 "Economic Relations", esp. pp. 32-34.
4. As a result of the splintering of both Tigrayan and Eritrean fronts since the war, key actors in the bi-lateral economic debates of 1993-96 are now in jail or exile. Although currently silenced, the accounts of individuals such as Eritrea's longstanding finance minister Haile Wolde Tinsai, and EFFORT's head Seye Abraha, are likely to eventually provide a clearer picture of economic contours of argument fateful twelve months led to conflict.
5. See Tronvoll & Negash, who in appendices 1 & 2 provide extracts from the agreements of 1993 and January 1997, on which the subsequent paragraphs partially draw.
6. Two observations are pertinent here: firstly Ethiopia's investment code went through a succession of, progressively more liberal, revisions in the 1990s. In the early months of 1998 prior to war the Ethiopian government and the country's largest "foreign" investor, Sheikh Mohamed Alamoudi had staged a major charm offensive to attract foreign investment, although evidently war in May 1998 entirely negated such efforts. Secondly, in early 2002 a further amendment opened investment to Ethiopians resident abroad holding foreign passports; pointedly, Eritrean nationals were explicitly excluded from its provisions.
7. Key letters between Issaias Afeworki and Meles Zenawi dated between 10-25 August 1997 were published first by *Huwyet* and in April 2002 English translations were placed on the *Awate.com* website Edited translations of the same letters, omitting much of the economic material, form Appendix 3 in Tronvoll & Negash. While the catalyst for the August 97 letters were the armed clashes in Bada and Adi Mung, it is clear that:
   a) both sides were nevertheless pre-occupied with the implications of the introduction of the Nakfa,
   b) attempts to mediate, including by Meles' lead economic advisor, had failed, but that nevertheless
   c) both seemed confident that the current trade issues would not fundamentally undermine ties.

Future historians might also profitably ponder the role of external economic agencies in the gestation of the crisis. Their influence on both governments was less than elsewhere in Africa in the late 1990s. Yet while negligible in Eritrea, Ethiopia was under an IMF/world Bank sponsored ESAF. In the August 97 letters above both Meles and Issaias saw a role for the Bank in currency and trade negotiations. While relations with the IMF were rocky, Ethiopia had become a star pupil of Bank by early 1998. The fact remains that external analysts and advisors failed to underscore the severity of trade and currency crisis.

8. World Bank, *Ethiopia Public Expenditure Review; Volume 1*, Washington DC, 30.11.99. Report No.20283-ET. Available via www.worldbank.org. Ethiopia's fiscal year (FY) runs July-July and thus the report covers the budgetary impact of the first year of war; 1998-99.

9. These figures include significant arms purchases expenditure on military hardware, notably advanced MIG-29 fighter planes. The EEPRI report puts military expenditure for 1999/2000 at Birr6.84bn: EEPRI, 2002, pp 46-48.

10. According the National Bank of Ethiopia, GDP at market prices was Birr56bn and Birr60bn respectively for the 98/98 & 99/2000 fiscal years.

11. Report by Abebe Teferi/EEPRI. Although the report circulated in restricted circles in Addis, coverage of its findings by the BBC World Service ("War devastated Ethiopian Economy", 07.08.02) heightened its profile, prompting government rebuttal of some of its findings. A summary of sections of the report are contained in Befekadu Degefe et al (2002) "Second annual report on the Ethiopian Economy", The Ethiopian Economics Association/EEPRI, Addis Ababa, Box I.1, pp. 42-48.

12. Befekadu Degefe et al (2002) "Second annual report on the Ethiopian Economy", The Ethiopian Economics Asociation/EEPRI, Addis Ababa.

13. IMF, *Eritrea Statistical Appendix*, IMF Staff Country Report No 00/55, April 2000. Available via www.imf.org.

14. This included a "patriotic contribution" on employees. While nominally "voluntary", this was in effect a new tax and was compulsory for all state employees.

15. The IMF estimate Net Factor Payments at 50% of private remittances in Eritrea's National Accounts, suggesting that private remittances totalled Nakfa2500m in 1997. Interestingly IMF data shows that these fell sharply, to Nakfa1820m in 1998 the first year of war, only slightly increasing, to Nakfa1960m in 1999. This despite official pressure on diaspora communities to contribute to the war effort. Statistics on remittances are inherently problematic. Evidently Eritrean figures should also reflect the abrupt termination of remittances to Eritrea from Ethiopia, although given these were in Eritrea's own currency, seem unlikely that counted in pre-1998 accounts.

16. IMF "Eritrea; selected issues", June 2003, para 45, p. 24.

17. Of course it could be reasonably objected that, while true, the reason for this is precisely because of the precarious nature of power in both capitals since the war; crisis management dictates that the foreseeable is not very far, and logic very short term indeed.

18. In mid-2002 USD1 was worth 8.5 Birr and 14 Nakfa.

19. Imported *teff* available in Asmara in 2002 is reported brought via Yemen or Djibouti, selling at 3-4 times its cost in Ethiopia.

20. Evidently controversy over food supplies forms part of the deeper history and

distrust in TPLF relations, the rupture of 1985-6 threatening food supplies to TPLF controlled areas of Tigray. Battle lines of 1980s necessitated both cross-border food supplies into Eritrea and Tigray from both Massawa and Assab.

21. To date the strategic thinking behind the ad-hoc expulsions policy, or who proposed and supported it within the TPLF executive, has not been made public. There is circumstantial evidence to suggest that Meles was in a minority in *opposing* such a move. Following the 2001 split and purges within the TPLF executive, Meles is reported to have told cadres that he viewed the expulsions as a mistake. In September 2002 Meles was more explicit in stating that he viewed the war as just one incident in clarifying divisions *within* the TPLF, 24.09.02, *Financial Times*, London.

22. Ethiopia, under IMF pressure had begun cautiously liberalising its banking system. Ethiopian policy makers at the time were in dispute with the IMF over the timing of financial sector liberalisation. While these disagreements, which continued in a modified manner to date, were unrelated to Eritrea, given the controversy over Horn International (see below), and that the same individuals were dealing with both dossiers at the same point in time, it seems likely there was some overlap of issues

23. Horn Bank International, which had just been registered as what would have been the sixth private, indigenous bank in Ethiopia, was abruptly closed in early 1998, apparently because of allegations that it was owned by Eritrean capital close the EPLP.

24. Three points need noting here: firstly the degree of coercion, blackmail of, and direct theft from those expelled remains unclear. As so often in such war situations, in the chaos surrounding the expulsions, denunciation by neighbours, settling of personal or petty economic scores and rivalries may in part explain the apparent arbitrariness of the expulsions. Secondly not all expulsees' properties were sold at knock-down prices or expropriated. Some property was left in trust and continues to be managed on their behalf, reportedly in some cases by prominent Tigrayans. Thirdly, one of the more perverse by-products of war has been the resurgence of Amharic as a lingua-franca in Asmara, many of the younger people expelled from Ethiopia not speaking the Tigrinya of their parents or grandparents.

25. In May 2003 the Claim Commission issued a note outlining progress to date; 40 claims having been filed overall. Details via www.pca-cpa.org.

26. Amare Tekle (ed), *Eritrea and Ethiopia; from conflict to cooperation*, New Jersey, Red Sea Press, 1994. Published in 1994, this collection brought together reflections first aired in 1989.

Chapter 11
SOVEREIGNTY AND STARVATION:
THE FOOD SECURITY DIMENSIONS OF THE
ERITREA-ETHIOPIA WAR
Philip White

INTRODUCTION

Some two months before the major Ethiopian offensive of May 2000, the world's media woke up to the threat of famine looming in the Horn of Africa. The United Nations had warned that up to 16 million people in the region faced starvation due to drought, half of these in Ethiopia, the rest in neighbouring areas of Somalia, Kenya and Uganda. Food reserves in Ethiopia had been depleted and relief commodities were in short supply. Television images of starving children in the southern and western Ethiopian lowlands prompted comparisons with the famine of the mid-1980s and questions as to why such a situation had been allowed to develop once again.

During the major Ethiopian famine of the mid-'80s, centred in the north of the country, neither the belated international media coverage nor contemporary aid agency reports paid much attention to the war then being waged by Ethiopia's *Derg* regime against the respective Eritrean and Tigrayan rebel fronts, the EPLF and TPLF. The links between conflict and famine, including the use of food as a strategic weapon of war, went largely unnoticed or were discretely ignored at the time. In 2000 things were different. This time, the international media aired a substantial amount of public debate on the nature of war-famine links in the Horn. But the Ethiopian government, and many of the aid agencies, were keen to point out that the 'epicentre' of the food crisis was hundreds of miles away from the fighting and completely unaffected by it. Under these circumstances the debate was for the most part confined to different views about the opportunity cost of the war, and to an argument about how donors should respond.

As events in this final phase of the war unfolded, its immediate humanitarian costs in terms of military and civilian casualties, mass displacements and deportations were starkly evident if only approximately quantified. Agencies responded with relief for the war-displaced in Eritrea and across the border in eastern Sudan, as well as for 'drought victims' in both Eritrea and Ethiopia and in neighbouring Somalia and northern Kenya. After the June 2000 ceasefire, and once substantial relief had begun to flow into drought-affected regions during the second half of that year, the crisis appeared to recede and a major famine was deemed to have been averted. This chapter explores the food security implications of the war, but in doing so looks beyond the headlines of starvation and relief operations that dominated the international media in April 2000 to take a broader and longer-term view of trends and developments in food security and livelihoods in the two countries in the period leading up to and during the war. It aims to show that war and food insecurity were in fact linked, directly and indirectly and on a number of levels, in more ways than was generally acknowledged. These linkages included but were not confined to diversion of government resources into the war effort. Not only did the 1998-2000 war have significant impacts on food security in both countries, but in some ways it was itself influenced by food security considerations. Moreover, while drought may trigger successive episodes of food crisis which attract the headlines, there is a substantial degree of continuity in factors causing food insecurity in Ethiopia and Eritrea over the last few decades, and these impacts are still in evidence and further reinforced by the ongoing failure to resolve this and other conflicts in which the two states are involved as the latest food crisis unfolds.

One of the ways in which the war affected food security was via its impact on donor attitudes. It is argued here that the tragically slow donor response to the impending food crisis of 1999/2000 was at least partly a reflection of aid givers' disapproval of the war being waged by these two countries at a time of food crisis, and that this occurred despite the policy announced by major donors of cutting development aid to the two warring governments while maintaining support for humanitarian assistance. Moreover, even if adhered to, this donor policy of 'principled conditionality' is logically problematic in that much of what is characterised as development aid addresses longer-term factors responsible for food insecurity and famines.

Two hungry States

The 1998-2000 Eritrea-Ethiopia war was fought between two of the poorest and most food insecure countries in the world, as well as the most conflict-ridden. Ethiopia ranks 169 out of 175 countries in the UN's human development index, Eritrea not much higher at 155 (UNDP, 2003:240). Both are food deficit and famine-prone countries, with amongst the highest rates of chronic undernourishment found anywhere: 44 percent of the population in Ethiopia and a staggering 58 percent in Eritrea according to the Food and Agriculture Organisation (FAO) (2002). In 2001 as much as 82 % of the population were agriculture-dependent in Ethiopia, 77 % in Eritrea (FAOSTAT 2003). Per capita cereal production has been falling since 1973-74 despite some recovery during the 1990s, with an annual national cereal deficit averaging some 700,000 tonnes (9% of total production) over the last 15 years. In Ethiopia, humanitarian assistance is required each year for an average of around 5 million food insecure people or 10% of the population (FDRE 2001). Given the importance of agriculture for food security in both countries, it is significant that while African developing countries as a group registered a slightly positive annual growth in per capita agricultural production index during the 1990s, Ethiopia's was -0.64 percent. During the 1970s and 1980s (with Eritrea included) it was -0.84 and an alarming -1.98 percent respectively. (FAO/WFP 2001)

The Horn of Africa has a long history of drought and drought-related famine. Ethiopia has seen at least ten major drought/famine episodes in the last four decades, the famines of 1973/74 and 1984/85 being among the worst in Africa's history. The attempt coercively to engineer a socialist transformation of agriculture during the Derg period (1974-91) through land reform, rural cooperatives, state farms, villagisation and resettlement schemes fell short of its objectives and left a legacy of failed rural institutions with which subsequent federal and regional governments have had to grapple. While the Derg's land reform measures represented a significant advance on what went before, the usufructory basis of tenure which has persisted largely unchanged until now provides little land security for smallholders.

During the interwar period 1991-1998 both countries experienced improvements in food security which can at least partly be seen as a 'peace dividend'. In Ethiopia grain production was boosted by a concerted campaign to promote wider use of 'green revolution' packages, and broadly kept pace with population growth with fertiliser use rising by some 64 percent. The World Bank has claimed that these gains were part of a general reduction in poverty during this period which can be credited to liberalising reforms, including those which resulted in increased agricultural producer prices (Dercon,

2002). There were even expectations that the country would soon become a surplus food producer in normal years. The years 1996 and to a lesser extent 1998 saw bumper cereal harvests allowing the build-up of cereal reserves, though in 1994, 1995 and 1997 harvests were poor.

However others question the evidence on which the assertion of a general reduction in poverty during the 1990s is based, and point to studies such as the 'household food economy' assessments of Save the Children UK in Wollo which suggest that "a subgroup of virtually assetless rural Ethiopians is emerging who are effectively destitute." (Devereux, 2000:8). According to Save the Children (SCF, 2000) people in Wollo were more vulnerable to food shortages at the end of the 1990s than they had been at the time of the famine. Significant sections of the population remained, and still remain, prone to food insecurity and malnutrition. Even in years of relatively good harvests, over 40 %—some 26 million people—were unable to meet their basic nutritional requirements from their own crop production and depended on other food sources (FAO, 1998). For some communities recovery of livestock and farming equipment after the 1984/85 famine was still incomplete in the mid-1990s (Heyer & Campell 1999).

In Eritrea, which also includes adjoining, drought-prone highlands and pastoral lowlands and a similar climatic regime, a parallel situation prevailed. During 1991-1998 the country rarely produced more than half its food requirements and had a structural dependence on food imports from commercial and donor sources. Until 1998 a significant portion of food imports came from formal and informal cross-border trade with Ethiopia. Successive food crises have been generally characterised as being most immediately precipitated by drought, with rural overpopulation, land degradation and underinvestment in agriculture as underlying causes. Those familiar with food security issues in the Horn provide a rather more nuanced analysis of vulnerability to drought as a function of several interrelated factors:

- Overwhelmingly rural populations (86 percent of Ethiopia's 63 million) whose livelihoods are heavily but not exclusively dependant on agriculture and pastoralism.

- In the highlands which normally receive adequate rainfall for arable agriculture, landholdings are too small to provide subsistence under prevailing farming systems, and access to new land is physically and legally constrained. In lowland areas, on the other hand, which are more marginal for crop production due to lower rainfall and where livelihoods depend more on pastoralism, livestock diseases and periodic drought are major constraints.

- Population growth rates of around 3% per annum result in further reduction in landholdings, increasing landlessness, reduction in fallow periods and expansion of cultivation onto hillsides and grazing land, leading to land degradation and interrupting mobility in pastoralist systems.

- Intensification of smallholder agriculture through adoption of yield-enhancing technologies including irrigation has not occurred to any great extent, and is constrained by unfavourable input-output price ratios as well as poor infrastructure. The gains in productivity during the early 1990s, occurring as they did without concomitant development of domestic and external marketing systems, ultimately depressed grain prices to levels at which commercial production became uneconomic. At the same time the slump in world prices of Arabica coffee, which during the mid-nineties provided 60% or more of Ethiopia's export revenue (Resal, 2000:12) and is hugely important both as a source of agricultural wage labour on commercial farms and as a smallholder cash crop, meant that prices paid to Ethiopian growers fell from well over 100 US cents per pound in the mid-90s to under 40 in 2001. (ICO, 2003)

- Marked inter- and intra-seasonal rainfall variability both for the *kiremt* rains on which the main *meher* agricultural season (May-Oct) depends, and for the minor *belg* season (Feb-Apr). Changing weather patterns have led to shorter and weaker *belg* rains, yet these are important for:

  1. short-term *belg* crops which account for 5-10% of overall cereal production but much more in some areas (e.g. Wello, Shewa, Bale in Ethiopia)

  2. even more so for timely sowing of higher yielding longer-term crops (maize and sorghum) in these and other highland areas;

  3. maintaining grazing resources and water supplies in both highland and lowland pastoral areas.

- In both countries livestock are of prime importance - indeed Ethiopia's national herd is the biggest in Africa. Cultivation remains dependent on ox-drawn implements, yet scarcity of fodder resources has led to a shortage of livestock, resulting in lack of draft power, manure and saleable assets, and inability to breed up herds. The viability of pastoral and agropastoral livelihoods has been steadily declining due to a combination of long-term reductions in rainfall, encroachment onto grazing land and physical barriers to mobility, and an adverse policy environment favouring sedentarisation, all making recovery of herds between drought years more difficult. While humanitarian efforts in successive crises have largely focussed on the 88% of people who live in the highland areas, less attention has been given to the more thinly populated lowland areas of eastern and southern Ethiopia, eastern and western Eritrea and bordering areas of Somalia/Somaliland and northern Kenya where agropastoral and pastoral livelihoods predominate. Recent estimates put herd losses in many areas varying in extent between 20 percent and 90 percent.

- The vast majority of rural households are dependent on multiple sources of livelihood including non-agricultural income, but access to markets is constrained by poorly developed infrastructure, poor health status, and illiteracy. Livelihoods lack resilience: they are increasingly vulnerable to periodic shocks including drought, malaria epidemics, disruption of food trade, displacement of people and variations in food prices, as well as to the longer-term impacts of HIV/AIDS and endemic malaria and tuberculosis. Dependence on food purchases has increased as poor harvests oblige households to sell basic assets or compete for income-earning opportunities in order to buy the food they need. Vulnerability has increased amongst households, but also within households, for example as household dissolution leaves women without oxen and they are forced take up long distance trading activities to make ends meet.

Alongside these explanations several analysts have examined the role of conflict in the decline of food security and livelihoods in these two countries during the period of Eritrea's liberation struggle (Bondestam et al, 1988; Cliffe et al, 1991; Cliffe, 1994; Duffield & Prendergast, 1994; Rock et al, 1997). These studies highlighted a complex web of interactions between drought, food security and direct and indirect effects of several conflicts over many years. Effects included conscription, displacement, loss of access to arable land and pastures and consequent changes in farming systems and herding strategies, disruption of trade and access to markets and relief supplies, diversion of resources into war effort, and problems associated with demobilisation and reintegration. Many of these impacts ended with the advent of peace in 1991, but many re-emerged in various forms with the 1998-2000 conflict. Some were longer term impacts which persisted throughout the intervening period but received little attention during the interwar years, despite several smaller conflicts which flared up or were ongoing.

Together these factors resulted in a situation where, despite post-war rehabilitation efforts in both countries after 1991, large numbers of rural households in Ethiopia and Eritrea were left at the threshold of survival with little capacity or breathing space for recovery before the arrival of the next shock. Multiple threats to livelihoods and food security, nutrition and health go beyond periodic drought-induced production shortfalls and are facets of a progressive impoverishment in which conflict, including the 1998-2000 war, is one important factor.

Food security developments during the war
The situation at the start of the war
The two countries embarked on hostilities in the wake of what was for Ethiopia a significant reversal of the steady upward trend in food production since 1991. Grain output, which had reached a record level in 1996, fell dramatically in 1997 following widespread failure of the *belg* rains, erratic rains during the *meher* season affecting main crops, a 20% fall in fertiliser use in key agricultural areas due to subsidy removal and a squeeze on credit. Livestock in all areas were weakened by the *belg* failure, and those in the lowland agropastoral zones of Ethiopia, already suffering from drought in late 1996, were further hit by long mid-1997 dry spells which resulted in a fall in livestock prices of as much as two-thirds as pastoralists off-loaded stock. The government had appealed for assistance for nearly a million pastoralists in early 1997, but by August that year estimates of numbers in need had increased to 3.4 million. Donor response had been slow, ration sizes had been reduced in many areas and there had been concern that the level of the emergency food security reserve (EFSR), set up in 1992 to bridge the lead-time required for food aid delivery – on average 5 months – was down to 65,000 tons compared with a target level of just over 300,000 tons.

Eritrea's national food security was in an even more parlous state. Agricultural conditions in both 1996 and 1997 had been poor, grain production being 29% below the previous 5-year average in 1996, and at about the same level in 1997 (FAO/GIEWS 1997). The introduction in January 1996 of a directive that all food aid must be monetised rather than distributed directly had brought food-for-work projects to an abrupt end and led to an overall fall in the volume of food aid, thus increasing reliance on commercial food imports including the normal substantial cross-border inflows from Ethiopia. However with the introduction of the *nakfa* in November 1997 and Ethiopia's response insisting on a Letter of Credit system with trade in hard currency, food imports from Ethiopia were also threatened. Although Ethiopia later announced an exemption from the Letter of Credit conditions for cross-border trade valued at under EB2000, it moved to regulate such trade through licensing and border posts. Eritrea's rejection of these terms was followed by a suspension of bilateral trade, though official and unofficial cross-border movements of grain and other commodities continued at a reduced level until the closure of the border when hostilities began in May 1998 and Ethiopia boycotted the Eritrean ports. Substantial cross border grain price differentials resulted, affecting consumers on the Eritrean side and producers in Ethiopia, especially in Tigray. Uncertainty surrounding the status of the *nakfa* also affected remittances by large numbers of Tigrayan workers in Eritrea. These developments had a substantial adverse effect on food security in both Eritrea and Tigray even before the fighting started.

Impacts in 1998

The most immediate and severe impacts of the war on already food insecure communities resulted from displacement of population from the zones of conflict. The Eritrean advances into Ethiopian-administered territory on the Badme plains and in and around Zalambessa during the first phase of the war in May-June 1998 meant that the displaced were mostly Ethiopian, and most of these gravitated towards the towns of Adigrat, Adwa, Axum, Enda Sellasie and Mekele. While a minority were from Zalambessa and other towns, and a few thousand were Ethiopian port workers and their families in Assab, most of the displaced were from rural farming households. Some could take their belongings with them, others had to leave everything including animals and farm tools. Occurring during or just after the main planting season, these displacements meant crops were left untended and unharvested and the displaced were totally dependent on help from others. Also affected were at least as many households on either side who accommodated the displaced, despite being themselves close to the margins of survival.

Initial humanitarian responses on each side of the border came respectively from the Relief Society of Tigray (REST) and the Eritrean Relief and Rehabilitation Commission (ERREC) and, on both sides, from Red Cross brigades with ICRC support. As early as 15 June the Ethiopian Government's Disaster Prevention and Preparedness Commission (DPPC) launched an international appeal, entitled "Assistance Requirements for Population Displaced by the Eritrean Government's Act of Aggression", for food, shelter materials, household utensils, clothing, medicines and medical equipment for 150,000 people so far displaced. The appeal gave a 'planning figure' of 300,000 people who would be likely to need assistance because of the displacements over the coming six months. Later the same month the UN Country Team in Ethiopia conducted their own assessments in Tigray and Afar regions broadly verifying DPPC findings, but noting that needs assessment was complicated by the fact that the displaced were often being accommodated within communities rather than camps – indeed this was in line with the REST policy of as far as possible avoiding the establishment of camps which were strongly associated with the horrors of 1985. Another issue was the difficulty in these areas of distinguishing between needs due to drought and needs due to the conflict – the two were closely intertwined and overlapping, and at the time as many as 4.3 million people in Ethiopia had been identified as in need of relief assistance due to crop failure.

The flow of displaced people on the Ethiopian side continued during the second half of 1998, swelled by sporadic artillery exchanges and by the decision to evacuate people from areas thought to be most exposed. By the end of the year the Tigrayan authorities estimated the number of displaced people needing assistance at 315,000 excluding 40,000 Ethiopians who had returned from Eritrea, and conceded that some may have to be accommodated in camps. An estimated 24,000 people had already been displaced in Afar region, making close to 400,000 in all. (UNEUE Jan'99)

On the Eritrean side, a September 1998 UN Consolidated Inter-agency Flash Appeal set out emergency needs for 275,000 people affected by the conflict, including 100,000 displaced from the border zone and 17,000 'Eritreans' expelled from Ethiopia. Along with food and non-food relief the items requested included shelter materials to house people in camps, and agricultural inputs and implements so that those beneficiaries who had been given land in their new locations could replant crops. Looking at the likely future course of the conflict, the appeal assumed a 'no peace, no war' scenario in which the several months of uneasy calm which had followed the May-June hostilities would persist throughout 1999 and that although those displaced would be unable to return and deportation of Eritreans in Ethiopia would continue, there would at least be no further waves of mass displacement from the border zone to contend with. This was, as it turned out, sadly over-optimistic.

For Ethiopia, closure of the border and its boycott of the Eritrean ports of Massawa and Assab meant that its maritime trade had now, at least in the short-term, all to be channelled through the port of Djibouti. Hitherto, Djibouti had handled only about 10% of Ethiopian transit trade, was equipped for container rather than bulk cargo, and had inadequate road and rail links to Addis Ababa and other Ethiopian centres. This posed problems for the importation of much-needed food assistance as well as oil and fertiliser. Ethiopia set aside an immediate US$3 million to help Djibouti expand its port capacity, and set about improving the road and rail links. WFP contracted locally a fleet of trucks to handle food aid imports, securing a government assurance that these would not be diverted to military uses. Another headache for the Ethiopian government was the almost 200,000 tons of Ethiopian goods held at Massawa and Assab when the border closed, including about 70,000 tons of WFP and USAID emergency food aid (UNEUE, June 1998). For Eritrea, the border closure meant not only the immediate loss of its substantial revenue from port handling operations and levies and its Ethiopian market for manufactured products (see Styan in this volume) but the closing down of a vital supply of food imports.

Then, as 1998 drew to a close, food security prospects appeared to improve dramatically. In Ethiopia, the FAO/WFP-supported pre-harvest crop and food assessment exercise at the end of the year (FAO/WFP, 1998) noted that the *belg* rains had once again been very poor and the *meher* season began late, but that crop conditions had thereafter been good, and high prices and the new National Extension Package Programme had encouraged use of improved inputs unlike the previous year. The grain production forecast of 12 million tons was only slightly below the record 1996 level, and the estimated overall surplus of 540,000 tons would allow not only stocks to be replenished but even grain to be exported to Kenya and Somalia (though not to Eritrea because of the closed border, or to Sudan which also had a food surplus). This optimistic outlook was however tempered by the mission's observation that 1.9 million people would still require 182,000 tons of food assistance in 1999 due to localised 'unusual' factors such as flooding, drought or malaria outbreak. Significantly, the report made clear that this assessment excluded Internally Displaced People (IDPs) from the Eritrean border zone who by that time had been estimated by the DPPC at 400,000, as well as the needs of the 40% of Ethiopian farm households considered to be chronically food insecure. It also excluded pastoralist populations, mainly in Somali and Afar regions, whose needs were deemed to be beyond the scope of the mission, though the situation of pastoralists was recognised as problematic due to an extended period of poor rainfall, prices depressed by the Saudi ban on livestock imports from the Horn over fears of Rift Valley Fever and by the blocking of herd movements into Eritrea because of the war, and consequent failure to recover from losses in 1997. These latter observations were reinforced by a warning in the January 1999 UNEUE situation report of an 'emerging crisis in the Somali region' due to these factors but also because of an influx of similarly affected pastoralists from across the Somaliland and Somalia borders. Rates of malnutrition had already climbed to alarming levels in the region and a DPPC appeal in December 1998 had included 220,000 people there in their national estimate of 2.2 million who would need 283,000 tons of food assistance in 1999. Donors largely ignored these caveats, however, and in early 1999 believed the food situation in Ethiopia to be generally good and gave little attention to the pastoralist areas (Hammond & Maxwell 2002). Eritrea also benefited from a better-than-average main cropping season in 1998, with estimated grain production of 460,000 tons, over three times that of the previous year, expected to meet 90% of 1999 national needs excluding stock build-up (FAO, 1999) – this despite the displacement of the farming population in the border zone. However, the winter rains on which the coastal

Northern and Southern Red Sea Regions depend failed in 1998/99, and here too pastoralists had been pushed further into decline.

Impacts in 1999

The optimism that had accompanied the early food supply forecasts for 1999 soon began to evaporate. In February and March 1999, as hostilities erupted once again near Badme, Tsorona and Bure, Ethiopia launching its 'Operation Sunset' counter-offensive to push through Eritrea's Badme front and in mid-March its suicidal yet unsuccessful assault on Eritrean positions south of Tsorona, the humanitarian situation deteriorated further. The consequences for civilians were difficult to ascertain as journalists and aid workers were excluded from the war zone, yet it was clear that further waves of displacement were occurring which included the secondary movement to more southerly locations of those on the Ethiopian side who had already flocked into Adigrat. Meanwhile ERREC reported in February that the Ethiopian recapture of Badme had generated a further 100,000 Eritrean IDPs. Authorities in the Sudanese town of Kassala to the west of the disputed border began to report flows of refugees crossing into Sudan from both Eritrea and Ethiopia. At the same time there were worrying reports of increasing numbers of landmine casualties amongst those who had returned during lulls in fighting to inspect their homes and crops or retrieve livestock and other possessions. An Ethiopian government report on demining operations highlighted the large areas of farming land put out of action due to mines in the border zone. (UNEUE May-99)

Thus despite the good cropping season ERREC was obliged to appeal in April 1999 for food and other humanitarian assistance for 550,000 war-affected people including 100,000 IDPs and 60,000 Eritreans deported from Ethiopia, pointing out that its appeal to donors for the previous year had only been one-third funded. The weak donor response had been in part a result of the government's decision in 1997-98 to expel international NGOs through which much aid had been channelled. Hoping for a better response, the government had partially reversed this decision by inviting Oxfam International and Save the Children to return to Eritrea to assess the situation jointly with ERREC as a basis for this appeal, and to provide humanitarian assistance.

During the remainder of 1999 the Ethiopian DPPC made a series of updates to its December 1998 appeal. The previous main harvest had turned out to be rather less outstanding than earlier predicted due to heavy rains and hail just before the harvest. Moreover the 1999 *belg* rains had almost completely failed, especially in North and South Wollo and in East and West Haraghe. Heavy loss of livestock in these highland areas led to late planting of the main *meher* crop. Evidence of a deteriorating nutritional situation in many parts of the country mounted during the year. In the lowland pastoral areas of the south and east the main March-May rains were the worst in several years. The number of people estimated to be in need of assistance rose to 3.3 million in April, 4.6 million in May, 5.4 million in July and peaked at 7 million in October. Of these, the number *directly* attributed to 'man-made causes' (i.e. the war) remained in the 360,000 - 400,000 range. Although May and June had seen further heavy fighting in the western sector and around Bure, as well as bombing by the Ethiopian airforce, this did not add significantly to the displacement of civilians on the Ethiopian side. A further appeal was made in November to cover the needs of 5.8m people during the first quarter of 2000 pending the findings of the 1999 assessment exercise, reflecting expectations of a lower *meher* harvest and limited carryover stocks.

Donor responses to these Ethiopian appeals were slow in coming. The December 1998 appeal for 283,000 tons of food assistance yielded just one pledge from the EU of 30,000 tons. Subsequent appeals and reports of a deteriorating food situation in several parts of the country did result in further pledges, but deliveries lagged significantly behind requirements. Relief rations had to be significantly diluted, with families in some cases receiving as little as 12.5 kgs of cereals per month. By the end of 1999, 405,000 of the revised request of 461,000 tons for June-December 1999 had been pledged and 352,000 tons 'delivered'. Significantly, however, the bulk of the latter—294,000 tons—was borrowed from the Ethiopian Food Security Reserve (EFSR) against confirmed pledges, which had not yet actually been delivered. While the EFSR had helped to avert a major disaster in 1999, its depletion and slow rate of subsequent replenishment was to prove a major factor in the crisis that followed.

In Ethiopia, the 764,000 tons relief needs assessment for 2000 made by the FAO/WFP mission in January of that year was the highest in 8 years, and represented the needs of 7.8 million people for an average of about 6 months at the standard monthly ration of 15 kg. It followed a 1999 *meher* season in which the failure of the *belg* rains, the loss of livestock, the war-induced displacement of population in Tigray and Afar regions and a late start to the rains had reduced planted area by some 4 % from the previous year's level. Average per hectare yields had also been reduced, partly because food stress had forced people to switch to short-cycle but lower yielding crops. The overall *meher* harvest forecast was down 6 percent from the previous year's level, but in the normally deficit areas of the north, east and south the drop was much greater – 12% down in SNNPR and 35 % down in war-affected Tigray. This assessment, while attempting to account for both 'current' and 'chronic' vulnerability, once again excluded the needs of the war-displaced, which the government had put at 47,000 tons for 349,000 people. The areas with highest proportion of the population requiring relief were identified as Somali Region and especially Gode and Fik (over 75%), Borena, Konso and South Omo in southern Oromiya and SNNPR, Gambella in the west, Central, East and South Tigray, North and South Wello, Wag Hemra and South Gonder in the north.

As in Ethiopia, 1999 grain production in Eritrea suffered from drought and delayed sowing, and was put at 160,000 tons, barely a third of the previous year's level. Spring rains had failed, the main rains in agricultural areas had started late and the drought in coastal areas had continued, affecting both crops and pasture, as had the disruption due to population displacement in the war zone. By the end of the year some 600,000 people affected by the war were in a very precarious food situation and facing unseasonably high food prices. These included 266,000 IDPs of which almost half were accommodated in camps, and 67,000 deportees from Ethiopia of which 28,000 were rural, over half of these again in camps. It also included 77,000 people in communities in Gash-Barka and Debub that were hosting IDPs, in which half of households were women-headed. Of the US$31 million requested for emergency relief in January 1999, less than half had been pledged – for food this proportion was better at 70%, but for non-food assistance (around half of the total) only a fifth of needs had been covered. Moreover the food pledges were late and almost exclusively as cereals with very little pulses or vegetable oil. For 2000, the UN Country Team Appeal of January 2000 was for US$ 43 million, targeted at 584,000 people of whom most – 372,000 – were war-affected IDPs and their hosts in Gash Barka and Debub. The remainder were drought-hit farmers in Northern Red Sea and Anseba Regions. As in 1998, the appeal considered a range of future scenarios, opting for one which assumed a continued stalemate in the conflict, but with a contingency plan to assist up to 70,000 people should hostilities resume. (UNCT Eritrea, Jan-00)

The food crisis of 2000
It was not until late March 2000 that the prospect of famine in the Horn began to receive international media attention. An increasing number of surveys in different parts of Ethiopia were confirming what humanitarian agencies in the country already knew. True famine conditions had already emerged in some areas, in particular in Somali Region where prevalence of malnutrition in Gode, for example, had already been measured at between 32 and 55 percent in surveys between December 1999 and March 2000. As estimates of numbers of people in need of emergency relief climbed to 10.2 million and relief requirements to 1.3 million tons by the middle of 2000, the donor

response finally began to gather pace. Yet as we have seen the food crisis was in fact almost a year old by this time. Indeed, it was in June 1999 that the World Food Programme had warned of "a potentially major humanitarian crisis" in Ethiopia. Given the low level of food reserves available for relief efforts in mid-1999, the failure to build them up significantly over the following November-January period when the main harvests become available, and the lead time required to turn pledges into deliveries, one might have expected alarm bells to be sounding loud and clear in donor headquarters around the world long before 1999 drew to a close. Yet the sluggish donor reaction to the mounting food crisis continued well into early 2000. This played a significant part in the allowing the crisis to deepen and is a factor we return to in the next section.

The relief effort in Ethiopia in early 2000 was also hampered by constraints to the food assistance pipeline. The port of Djibouti could not match Assab and Massawa in capacity for food imports. Efforts were made to bring the Somaliland port of Berbera into play, though its capacity was far more limited still. Haulage constraints affected movement of relief supplies from both ports, Berbera especially, as well as their distribution within Ethiopia. In April/ May the unloading of a shipment of 16,000 tons of EU-supplied food at Djibouti took more than 20 days to complete due to a lack of trucks. Above all, as already noted, the EFSR was depleted by donor borrowings in 1999 which had not been repaid. As Hammond and Maxwell (2002:273-274) observe:

> throughout the worst of the crisis, the EFSR was owed a total of nearly 300,000MT of food — over 80 per cent of its total reserve capacity — which was the main factor crippling its capacity to bridge the gap in the pipeline.

The relief operation did accelerate after mid-2000 and this enabled the situation to be brought under control in the latter part of the year. During the first quarter, however, only around a third of food assistance requirements were met. When the momentum of food distribution did pick up, the maximum ration had to be reduced to 12.5 rather than 15 kg/person/month, and in practice the average ration was only 8.6 kg/person/month. In some needy areas only supplementary rations of 4.5 kg per *family* per month were available. (FAO/WFP, 2001) Moreover, throughout the year the pledges and deliveries of non-food assistance, including that for agriculture and livestock, were seriously inadequate and this represented a significant missed opportunity to assist recovery from the crisis.

Reliable measures of excess human mortality attributable to the 2000 food crisis are not available. Although the verdict of the major agencies involved was that this was a 'famine averted', there is disagreement on this. One study, based on a household survey in Gode Zone, suggested that the total in Somali Region – the worst hit part of Ethiopia – may have been as many as 100,000. (Salama *et al*, 2001). Longer-term impacts on livelihoods were also severe – in Somali region and parts of Oromiya losses of cattle were put at up to 80 percent just for the year to May 2000 (Sandford and Habtu, 2000).

During the first four months of 2000 the food security situation in Eritrea was overshadowed by the crisis in Ethiopia and received relatively little attention. The appeal of January 2000 met with no response at all until March that year, when 12,000 out of 63,000 tons of food needs were pledged. By 1 July only 39% of the appeal had been funded. Yet the events of the following May meant that needs had to be drastically revised. First, a Red Cross assessment in Anseba region provided evidence that the food situation in the drought-hit north was worse than had been thought, with widespread resort to 'famine foods' and perhaps 300,000 people in the region needing relief rather than the 100,000 stated in the appeal (IRIN, 15-May-03). These revised drought-related needs were included in a new UN Horn of Africa drought appeal in June 2000.

Eclipsing this, however, were the impacts of Ethiopia's full-scale offensive between 12 May and 18 June 2000. The immediate humanitarian impacts of the offensive were massive and far exceeded the worst-case scenario of the January appeal. ERREC reported in June that the number of people displaced by the war had trebled to over 1.1 million, many of whom were on the move and searching for safe havens. A further 94,000 had fled across the Sudan border, adding to the 160,000 Eritrean refugees already in camps in the Sudan. Consequences for food security were also profound. The two regions primarily affected by the fighting, Debub and Gash-Barka, are responsible for 80% of Eritrea's agricultural production. The offensive took place just before the main planting season for food crops, so that an entire season's production was effectively lost. Infrastructure for provision of government services, including those to agriculture and livestock, had been wiped out. Herds and other assets needed to pursue livelihoods had been abandoned and destroyed or appropriated by the invading forces. A revised UN Country Team Appeal was issued in July 2000 covering the remainder of the year. The US$43m worth of relief requirements for the whole year in the January appeal was now raised to US$87m for the remaining half-year. A two-stage aid response was planned for Eritrea, the first focusing on life-saving interventions for the war-affected, the second on return of the displaced and community-led reconstruction and rehabilitation programmes. The relief operation faced severe difficulties imposed by the poor state of Massawa port facilities, lack of haulage capacity and the remoteness of needy populations. As it turned out, the dramatic events of May and June 2000 led to a good donor response as far as the food assistance component of the revised appeal was concerned – this was 96% funded. Yet the non-food components, also vitally important for survival and even food security, and comprising over half of the total, were only 41 % covered. The difference was even more marked for the June drought appeal, where donor coverage for food and non-food assistance was 100% and 20% respectively. (UN Country Assistance Programme Eritrea, 2001)

Upon the signing of the Cessation of Hostilities Agreement in June 2000, the displaced began to return home, and by the end of the year the majority of IDPs were back in their home communities. However many of these found their homes destroyed, their possessions looted, and their land mined. Those who still had their livestock found that preferred dry season grazing areas in the border region were now inaccessible. In February 2001, the first ever UN Consolidated Appeal for Eritrea estimated that there were almost 2 million people in need of assistance, two-thirds of whom were categorised as 'war-affected'. The Appeal highlighted the need for adequate donor funding for non-food as well as food assistance if the longer term challenge of restoring livelihoods to pre-war levels was to be effectively addressed.

Multiple linkages between the border war and food security
Food security factors in the war
During the famine of the mid-1980s, food security considerations became factored into the war strategies of the *Derg* in a number of ways that are now well known, though were not given much attention at the time. For example, international agencies were coopted into a famine relief effort in the worst hit areas of Wollo and Tigray which effectively corralled the hungry into feeding centres from which they could be forcibly resettled, ostensibly to provide them with more productive land but also as a means of depopulating rebel-held areas. Another less well-known instance of use of food as a weapon during this period involved the EPLF and TPLF and is part of the souring of their mutual relations that forms the background to the border war. As Gilkes and Plaut (1999:9) note, the EPLF responded to a TPLF move to support other Eritrean movements by cutting off its food supply route from the Sudan through Eritrea at the height of the famine, necessitating the TPLF to mobilise 100,000 peasants to construct an alternative road bypassing Eritrea and engendering lasting bitterness against the EPLF.

While the border war was not characterised by such blatant manipulation of food for war aims, it is worth noting that Ethiopian Prime Minister Meles Zenawi justified the May 2000 offensive in terms of the need for a 'quick end to the war because his drought-stricken country cannot afford another year living in a state of conflict.' (BBC Online News, *Casualties mount in Horn*, 15-May-00), though the impending election must have been part of the rationale as well.

Immediate war impact in conflict zones

The direct, immediate humanitarian and food security impacts of the war in the conflict zones are starkly evident from the above. Over a million people were displaced from relatively high potential agricultural regions and, for varying timespans, lost their homesteads, livestock and other assets, their access to arable and grazing land, their access to labour, input and produce markets, their livelihoods. The capacity of both governments and of international humanitarian agencies to respond to these impacts was constrained by security conditions in the war zones and by logistical constraints arising from closure of the border and Ethiopia's loss of access to Eritrean ports. For people in conflict zones, therefore, the war affected food 'entitlements' of all kinds: ability either to produce food, or to acquire it though trade, through selling their labour or through transfers.

Wider connections: the media, donors and resource diversion

Yet a wider range of links between the war and the food security situation in the two countries can usefully be examined. The major food security story of the period was the emergence of famine conditions in 1999/2000 in southeast Ethiopia, far away from the conflict. But it is argued here that the war was nevertheless undoubtedly a significant factor in this crisis, in a number of ways. It also had longer-term repercussions for food security in both countries. We have seen how donors were reluctant to pledge the required assistance in 1999 and early 2000 despite the warning signals of nutritional deprivation and inadequate emergency reserves, and it is instructive to assess this and other aspects of aid policy towards the two countries during this period in the context of the media debates of the time. As noted earlier the coincidence of the 1999/2000 food crisis and the border war did not escape public attention. During the decade and a half since the mid-80s famine, when western responses were largely triggered by Buerk and Amin's fortuitous TV report from Korem in October 1984 when the crisis was almost two years old, much had changed in terms of public access to information on events in the developing world. The timeliness, amount and sophistication of media attention generated and the level of public awareness which had resulted from it owed much to improved systems of information collection and dissemination, including the growth of the internet and the fact that all major media actors and charities now had websites with up-to-date reports and analysis, but also to the proliferation of disaster appeals and its effects on the public learning curve. At the same time 'complex political emergencies' had come to the fore in international humanitarian discourse and war-famine links were much more widely recognised. Yet the influence of the media on donor policies had not dwindled – arguably just the opposite.

Western public opinion on the crisis ranged between two extremes. One held that Ethiopia and Eritrea had no right to expect western taxpayers/charity-givers to dip into their pockets to bail these countries out of famine when they were squandering what resources they had on a pointless war over a few square miles of barren land, and was outraged by Ethiopian criticism of donors in early April 2000 for their slow reaction to the crisis. The other, exemplified perhaps most vociferously by Sir Bob Geldof, focused exclusively on the humanitarian imperative, pointing out that nothing could be done about the war, but that the children who were starving and dying could not be held responsible for the decision of the two governments to wage war and should not be punished for it, and that nothing should stand in the way of an immediate and massive humanitarian response. Between these two extremes were a number of positions which proposed some linkage between aid and progress in peace talks.

The Ethiopian and Eritrean propaganda machines also made extensive use of the internet, conducting a sophisticated 'cyber-war' – much of it in English and perhaps aimed partly at a western audience including those responsible for aid and foreign policy decisions. The Ethiopian side portrayed the war and the food crisis in the south and east as completely independent. This perspective was supported by some of the international agencies involved in emergency operations in these areas, who were concerned about the aid pipeline and wanted to assuage any donor fears about legitimising Ethiopian war aims. It was echoed by the BBC correspondent in Addis Ababa, Peter Biles who suggested that:

> The reality ... is that the conflict on Ethiopia's northern border is having almost no effect whatsoever on food distribution in the drought-stricken regions of the country.
> (BBC News Online, 24 May 2000)

Ethiopian Prime Minister Meles Zenawi added his own view:

> "We do not believe protecting one's sovereignty is a luxury for the rich ... You do as much as you can to save lives and at the same time protect your sovereignty."
> (BBC Africa Media Watch, 14-Apr-00)

The Eritrean news agency Visafric voiced the opposite view:

> "[The Ethiopian foreign minister] seems to have forgotten that the primary responsibility for caring for his people lies first and foremost with his own government. But judging by his statement ... one would say that he and his cohorts always expected Western governments to feed their hungry while they went on an arms shopping spree." (Ibid.)

In the event, a number of western governments as well as the World Bank and International Monetary Fund espoused a policy of 'principled conditionality': stepping up aid for relief to cope with the humanitarian crisis, while cutting development and financial aid to signal their disapproval to the two warring states. British development aid to Ethiopia was halved, and to Eritrea was put on hold. Clare Short, International Development Secretary, justified this by saying:

> "I do not believe that anyone in the UK believes we should be providing long-term assistance to a country which is increasing its spending on arms, year on year." (Ibid.)

Yet it appears that this neat separation between humanitarian and development aid was not observed in practice, and that the diplomatic/political aims of donors spilled over into the humanitarian sphere and got in the way of a timely relief response, at least until March/April 2000 when the media story on the famine broke. From that point pledges and deliveries of food aid accelerated, more so once the ceasefire agreement was signed. But even then the response to non-food emergency needs – which received less media attention – was poor. Further, the embargo on non-emergency aid itself made little sense to the extent that aid was aimed at longer-term improvements in food security, for example through measures to boost the resilience of livelihoods to periodic shocks such as drought, to improve the timeliness, coverage and accuracy of early warning systems or to establish more effective preparedness measures. In this respect the dividing line between relief and development aid suffers from the same arbitrariness as that between food emergencies and underlying downward trends in food security.

This diversion of aid resources away from tackling food insecurity, then, compounded the effects of the diversion of public expenditure into the war effort that preoccupied the international media. In fact, as Styan's chapter points out, estimated immediate costs to the Ethiopian exchequer range between 7 and 20% of Gross Domestic Product (GDP), and must constitute a much higher percentage on the Eritrean side with its far smaller economy. It is a fair point that this level of public expenditure, if devoted to humanitarian assistance and longer term food security, could have had substantial positive impacts.

There were other ways in which resources were diverted. Haulage constraints affecting food shipments from Red Sea ports have already been mentioned. In May 2000 the Ethiopian Government introduced a national coordination mechanism involving transport coordination cells in the regions controlled by the Road Transport Authority. Hauliers and requests for transport were obliged to work exclusively through these bodies, and pay officially sanctioned tariffs. (UNCT Ethiopia, May-00) Added to a 10% surtax on imported goods imposed by Ethiopia between December 1999 and December 2000, this caused concern amongst aid agencies who feared that the Government was seeking to tax emergency aid to fund its war with Eritrea. Once shipments gathered pace, there was a severe shortage of trucks for the distribution of relief supplies in Ethiopia, especially modern multi-axle drive ones that could handle wet-season roads in remote areas, and logic would suggest that this situation could have been more easily addressed were it not for the massive transport demands of the military build-up and subsequent invasion to the north.

Finally, the scale of conscription and displacement in these two countries added up to a massive diversion of personnel, especially in Eritrea with its much smaller population. The men and women (the latter mostly on the Eritrean side) of the opposing forces were largely drawn from sections of the population which provided the greatest contribution to food production, though the economic loss to households from which they were conscripted was mitigated to some extent by remittances of military pay. Education was sacrificed. Perhaps most critically key middle-level officials that provide the link between central authorities and rural communities had to be remobilised.

The war and the longer-term crisis of livelihoods in Somali Region[1]

The conscription drive had particular consequences in the famine-affected Somali Region of Ethiopia which need to be seen in the context of a longer-term and ongoing crisis of livelihoods and survival experienced by people in pastoral and agropastoral areas in the Horn of Africa, resulting from decades of massively damaging conflicts – some still unresolved or simmering – interspersed with serious drought. The chapter by Cliffe in this volume documents how the border war followed the pattern of other conflicts in the Horn: essentially internal in origin, but spilling over to neighbouring countries, through refugees and support for insurgencies by neighbouring states—often in a mutually reinforcing manner.

Ordinarily, as the January 2000 FAO/WFP assessment (FAO/WFP 2000) recognised, it takes years for herds to reach pre-crisis levels. The poor usually have to dispose of all the natural increase even in good years to repay debts, buy essentials, re-equip themselves with tools and meet social obligations. The prolonged and mutually reinforcing effects of drought and war have often eroded the additional survival mechanisms: grain stores, access to emergency grazing, 'borrowing' beasts from kin. And precisely these avenues for survival are made more difficult by continuing conflict: Somali people who traditionally moved back and forth across the borders of Kenya, Somalia and Ethiopia with herds to seek alternative pasture are severely inhibited in such movement. Their ability to recover herds and livelihoods has been further limited as very little of the provision of aid for rehabilitation has met their special needs. Agriculturalists were given replacement seed, tools, even plough oxen but seldom have there been restocking programmes for herders or even continued food aid to avoid the need for continual sell-off of the natural increase. All these problems have been further compounded by governments which lack any informed understanding of the development needs of such people. All too often the slogan is simply 'sedentarise the nomads'—a perspective that prompts the dangerous view that famines are a blessing in disguise in the long run!

The Somali Region of Ethiopia has been caught up in various conflicts that have disrupted people's lives and livelihoods for more than a generation. In the late 1970s they were involved in the war between the Ethiopian and Somalia states and over a million fled as refugees into Somalia as well as into Kenya and Djibouti. There they were caught up in Somalia's increasingly divisive internal politics in the 1980s and forced to flee back when civil war broke out, along with other refugees from that internal conflict. Their return without any support programme, plus the extra refugee population, put great stress on available land and other resources. These pressures amplified the effect of fighting initiated by a movement that had grown up in the area, the Ogaden National Liberation Front (ONLF), that became one of the several regional movements seeking to overthrow the military rule of the *Derg* in Ethiopia. All these conflicts and those continuing today have interrupted the movement of people and herds back and forth across the political border in search of grazing. The displacements also led to great loss of livestock.

The *Derg* conducted counter-insurgency measures which involved destroying animals and crops, withholding food relief, interrupting herd movements and markets, and also used divide-and-rule measures which restricted movement between the three administrative areas which were created. The further constraints on herd mobility seriously limited people's ability to counter the results of the severe drought of 1991. Further influx of refugees from Somalia in the early 1990s caused local over-grazing, which was harder to control as the incomers were outside the mechanisms of the Ogaden clans that provided the management of water and land access and resolved conflicts.

Since the overthrow of the *Derg*, the ONLF had occupied an uneasy place in the new political dispensation in Ethiopia and low intensity conflict has persisted. Many Somalis were ambivalent, to say the least, toward their regional government, and the administration of the regional assembly and its revenue base had not been effective - specifically affecting relief food delivery. All these pressures and disruptions had had direct impacts and coming on top of each other had allowed very little of that time herds need for recovery and few opportunities for people to rehabilitate or diversify their livelihoods. There had also been a cumulative effect that had undermined the livelihood systems and the 'coping mechanisms' on which people in such a harsh and arid environment rely for their survival. In some of these areas people plant crops, and even though harvests are notoriously unreliable and livestock are the basic insurance, every few years there might be a bumper harvest —the surplus from which can be a further survival mechanism—but only if properly stored for some years. However, the underground storage systems had also become victims of disruption, flight and social dislocation. Another alternative source of livelihood, the collection and trade in gums and resins such as myrrh and frankincense, had also been disrupted, partly by heavy-handed control imposed by the previous government. As a result of physical and social breakdown wells had not been maintained or, if they had, had fallen into private hands so that those most in need were often denied access to them. Earlier famine victims who were resettled on irrigated plots around the severely affected area of Gode had also suffered periodic disruption, their

222

water channels not always maintained—though they did get good crops in 1995 to 1998 before falling foul of the 1999 drought.

Against this background, the border war had two main impacts in Somali Region. First, the ONLF reported that 'voluntary' patriotic exactions had been made every two months or so linked to the government's conscription drive. These extra taxes had often been in kind—one beast exacted from every household, just at the time the herds were being decimated by drought. The alternative was for poor families to yield up a young man to the military. So the youth pre-emptively fled to towns, to Somaliland or Somalia to escape conscription in a war they often did not see in 'patriotic' terms. This further decimated the available labour for herding in this drought season with its extra demands. How far these claims were true and how great any impact in turning drought into famine are subjects that should be explored – but independent observers were normally barred from entering the region.

Secondly, these pressures were compounded in that region by the fuelling of local conflict by Eritrea as part of a proxy war against Ethiopia. Similar patterns emerged elsewhere in Ethiopia, where Eritrea began to support the Oromo Liberation Front (OLF), and elsewhere in the Horn as Cliffe's chapter describes. This intensification of fighting precisely throughout the drought-affected areas of the Horn further restricted the traditional coping strategies of people seeking to ensure the survival of their herds by searching for pasture further afield.

The legacy of mistrust and its food security consequences

The war's legacy of mistrust, with the two governments failing even to begin to normalise bilateral relations since the December 2000 Peace Agreement, has had – and continues to have – distinctly adverse food security consequences for both Ethiopia and Eritrea.

As David Styan details in this volume, the economic cost to Ethiopia of its ongoing boycott of the Eritrean ports and diversion of maritime trade via Djibouti, Berbera and Mombasa is considerable, and brings with it opportunity costs in terms of support for food security. These include the effects of widening further the gap between import and export parity prices for cereals and the consequent increase in price instability faced by both producers and consumers. By the same token Eritrea's loss of port commission for transit of Ethiopian imports and exports has deprived its government of significant revenues which could have been used to combat the effects of drought.

The post-war programme of rearmament pursued by both countries has also constrained resources available for government food security programmes. In February 2003, the OLF added its voice to those denouncing the Ethiopian government's rearmament programme at a time when millions were suffering hunger, in particular the purchase of 100 ground-to-air missiles on top of aircraft and radar equipment recently acquired at a cost exceeding US$600m, and conscription of youths across the country for training as a military reserve. Critics have attributed the 2003 Ethiopian food crisis in part to government preoccupation with Eritrea, as well as to its coercive and poorly planned resettlement programmes. Eritrea's public finances and external debt, which deteriorated substantially during the war years when defence spending reached 20% of GDP, have yet to recover (IMF 2003b).

With continued closure of the border with Ethiopia, Eritrea in addition to losing its main export market (almost two-thirds of all exports in 1997 went to Ethiopia, mainly in crude materials and manufactured goods) has lost a significant source of imported grain and livestock (Ethiopia provided one-third of these imports in 1997) with direct consequences for food security in terms both of prices and required lead-time for food imports.

For those displaced from the border zone, the loss of land and of livelihoods has yet to be made good and they, along with communities that accommodate them, are amongst the most food insecure groups in Eritrea. Pastoralist livelihoods, which in these semi-arid grasslands depend on the unrestricted freedom to move herds in search of better pastures as well as livestock and food markets, have been particularly hard hit by the loss of cross-border mobility.

Both countries have lost the trust and support of donors at a time when their support to food security is sorely needed. Donor assistance to Eritrea has been limited to humanitarian assistance and backing for the demobilisation programme on account of "political governance issues related to the imprisonment of dissidents and journalists and delays in the implementation of key constitutional provisions." (IMF 2003a). The loss of trust of the Eritrean diaspora, remittances from which are as Styan's chapter points out of even greater significance, contributes to this constraint to the Eritrean government's capacity to take action to improve food security. Ethiopia's intransigence with respect to implementing the Delimitation Decision of the Eritrea-Ethiopia Boundary Commission has also affected the stance of donors, who are using aid conditionality to apply what leverage they can to bring about Ethiopian compliance, again with direct and indirect food security consequences. The costs of United Nations Mission to Ethiopia and Eritrea (Unmee) must also be considered in this light: over half a billion dollars to date is "money which might be better spent fighting a four-year drought afflicting both countries" (Michela Wrong, Financial Times 12-Jun-03).

CONCLUSIONS

Three years later, the Horn of Africa is once again in the grips of potential famine. At the time of writing more than 13 million people in Ethiopia and over a million in Eritrea are in need of emergency food aid, and the outlook for the next few years is not much better. Once again comparisons have been drawn with 1984/85, this time with a warning by Ethiopian Prime Minister Meles Zenawi that 2003 could be as bad or worse. The trigger factor is again serious drought, but as Lautze *et al* (2003) have pointed out this is as much a crisis of livelihoods and of health care as a food crisis. Though all food crises are different there are some strong continuities between the 1999/2000 crisis and the present one – in both cases it is the populations in remote areas most marginal to government services and agency assistance who have tended to suffer most, and both crises have involved breakdowns in systems and strategies whereby people normally eke out a livelihood. It is increasingly being recognised that along with other food crises suffered in these two countries in recent decades, these can most usefully be seen not as isolated episodes of food entitlement failure, but as an interconnected series of crisis points in a longer term trend of increasing livelihood and health vulnerability for sizeable populations who live at the margins. Liberal and hopefully timely doses of food and other emergency aid can successfully treat the periodic crises, but reversing the secular decline in people's resilience to shocks requires measures that are more imaginative, holistic and participatory and based on better analysis of complex livelihood processes and their regional and international dimensions.

Interconnected conflicts have long been a key element in the nexus of cause and effect determining livelihood outcomes in the Horn, including positive outcomes for some. The 1998-2000 border war has produced little in the way of identifiable positive outcomes apart from those enjoyed by the arms traders, but its adverse influence on livelihoods continues to be felt in many ways which are not easily separated out from each other and from other factors, whether political – including strategies of mutual disruption/ destabilization across the region – demographic or environmental.

Aid donors can draw a number of lessons from this experience: the need for rapid response alongside a wider and longer-term perspective, more support to regional organisations, more thought to an ethical framework within which aid provision is circumscribed by conditionalities or not.

REFERENCES

Bondestam, Lars, Lionel Cliffe and Philip White (1988), *Eritrea Food and Agricultural Production Assessment Study*, Final Report for Emergency Relief Desk, Centre for Development Studies, University of Leeds.

Cliffe, L. (1994), 'The Impact of War on Food Security in Eritrea: Prospects for Recovery', in J. Macrae & A. Zwi, eds., *War & Hunger: Rethinking International Responses to Complex Emergencies*, Zed, London.

Cliffe, L. *et al* (1991) *Eritrea 1991: A Needs Assessment Study*, Final Report for Emergency Relief Desk, Centre for Development Studies, University of Leeds.

Dercon, Stefan (2002), 'The Impact of Economic Reforms on Rural Households in Ethiopia, a study from 1989 to 1995', *Poverty Dynamics In Africa Series*, World Bank, Washington, D.C., April.

Devereux, Stephen (2000), *Destitution in Ethiopia's Northeast Highlands (Amhara Region)*, Conceptual Paper, Consultancy for Save the Children (UK), Addis Ababa.

Duffield,M. and J. Prendergast (1994), *Without Troops & Tanks: Humanitarian Intervention in Ethiopia and Eritrea*, Red Sea Press.

FAO (2002), *The State of Food Insecurity in the World 2002*, FAO, Rome.

FAO/GIEWS (1997), *Food Supply Situation and Crop Prospects in Sub-Saharan Africa*, Global Information and Early Warning System on Food and Agriculture, FAO, Rome, February.

FAO/GIEWS (1999), *Food Supply Situation and Crop Prospects in Sub-Saharan Africa*, Global Information and Early Warning System on Food and Agriculture, FAO, Rome, April.

FAO/WFP (1998), *Special Report, FAO/WFP Crop and Food Supply Assessment Mission to Ethiopia*, Global Information and Early Warning System on Food and Agriculture, FAO and World Food Programme, Rome, 21 December.

FAO/WFP (1998), *Special Report: FAO/WFP Crop and Food Supply Assessment Mission to Ethiopia*, Global Information and Early Warning System on Food and Agriculture, FAO and World Food Programme, Rome, 21 December.

FAO/WFP (2000), *Special Report: FAO/WFP Crop and Food Supply Assessment Mission to Ethiopia*, Global Information and Early Warning System on Food and Agriculture, FAO and World Food Programme, Rome, 26 January.

FAO/WFP (2001), *Special Report: FAO/WFP Crop and Food Supply Assessment Mission to Ethiopia*, Global Information and Early Warning System on Food and Agriculture, FAO and World Food Programme, Rome, 9 January.

FAOSTAT (2003), FAOSTAT online datbase, http://apps.fao.org/default.htm (accessed 15-Aug-03), FAO, Rome.

FDRE (2001), *Food Security Strategy: An Update*, Federal Democratic Republic of Ethiopia, Addis Ababa, August.

Gilkes and Plaut (1999), *The War in the Horn – The Conflict between Eritrea and Ethiopia*, Discussion Paper 82, Royal Institute for International Affairs, London.

Hammond, L. and Dan Maxwell (2002), 'The Ethiopian Crisis of 1999–2000: Lessons Learned, Questions Unanswered', *Disasters*, 26(3): 262–279.

Heyer & Campell (1999), *The Effects of Famine on Capital Assets in South West Ethiopia, 1984-1993*, Report to DFID-ESCOR by J. Heyer and I. Campbell, University of Oxford.

ICO (2003), 'Indicator Prices - Monthly and Annual Averages', International Coffee Organization, London (http://www.ico.org/).

IMF (2003a), *Eritrea: Staff Report for the 2003 Article IV Consultation*, International Monetary Fund Report No. 03/165, June.

IMF (2003b), *Eritrea:Selected Issues and Statistical Appendix*, International Monetary Fund Report No. 03/166, July.

IRIN (15-May-03), *Ethiopia-Eritrea: IRIN News Briefs, 15 May*, UN OCHA Integrated Regional Information Network for Central and Eastern Africa.

Lautze *et al* (2003), *Risk and Vulnerability in Ethiopia: learning from the past, responding to the present, preparing for the future*, (Sue Lautze, Yacob Aklilu, Angela Raven-Roberts, Helen Young, Girma Kebede, Jennifer Leaning), Report for USAID, June.

Resal (2000), *Continuous deterioration of the food security situation*, European Food Security Network (Resal) – Ethiopia, Quarterly Report, January 2000.

Rock, J., Cliffe, L., and White, P. (1997), *Household Food Security After War and Drought in Eritrea*, Centre for Development Studies Working Paper, University of Leeds.

Salama, P. *et al* (2001) 'Malnutrition, Measles, Mortality and the Humanitarian Response during a Famine in Ethiopia', *Journal of the American Medical Association* 286(5): 563–71, cited in Hammond and Maxwell (2002).

Sandford, S. and Y. Habtu (2000) *The Pastoral Assessment Team: Emergency Response Interventions in Pastoralist Ethiopia*, DFID-Ethiopia, Addis Ababa, cited in Hammond and Maxwell (2002).

SCF (2000), *Ethiopia Emergency Bulletin 1: Ethiopia Food crisis*, Save the Children Fund, 27 March 2000, (ReliefWeb).

UN CAP Eritrea (2001), *UN Consolidated Inter-Agency Appeals For Eritrea – January-December 2001*, Office For The Coordination Of Humanitarian Affairs, New York & Geneva.

UNCT Eritrea (Jan-00), *UNCT Appeal: Humanitarian Assistance to Eritrea, January 2000*, UN Country Team in Eritrea, 28 Jan 2000 (ReliefWeb).

UNCT Ethiopia (May-00), *Ethiopia Humanitarian Update: 12 May 2000*, UN Country Team in Eritrea (ReliefWeb).

UNDP (2003), *Human Development Report 2003*, United Nations Development Programme, New York, Oxford University Press.

UNEUE (Jan-99), *Situation Report For Ethiopia: December 1998 & January 1999*, UN Emergencies Unit for Ethiopia, Addis Ababa, January 1999.

UNEUE (Jun-98), *Monthly Situation Report For Ethiopia: June 1998*, UN Emergencies Unit for Ethiopia, Addis Ababa.

UNEUE (May-99), *Situation Report For Ethiopia: May 1999*, UN Emergencies Unit for Ethiopia, Addis Ababa.

White, Philip and Lionel Cliffe (2000), *Conflict, Relief and Development: aid responses to the current food crisis in the Horn of Africa*, COPE Working Paper No. 38, Centre for Development Studies, University of Leeds.

ENDNOTE
1. This section is based on White and Cliffe (2000).

Chapter 12
VIOLENCE AND IDENTITY ALONG THE ERITREAN-ETHIOPIAN BORDER
Patrick Gilkes

INTRODUCTION

Two years of fighting, a hundred thousand dead, a peace agreement and a Boundary Commission have all failed to settle the problems of the border between Eritrea and Ethiopia, or, more pertinently, deal with the relationships of the peoples who straddle this border: Kunama, Tigrean, Saho and Afar. The Boundary Commission, set up under the Algiers Peace Agreement of December 2000, finally issued its Decisions on Delimitation in April 2002. These were based on the December Peace Agreement (Article 4) "The Parties Agree that a neutral Boundary Commission composed of five members shall be established with a mandate to delimit and demarcate the colonial treaty border based on pertinent colonial treaties (1900, 1902 and 1908) and applicable international law. The Commission shall not have the power to make decisions ex aequo et bono." [1]

Surprisingly, the April Decisions did not specify the position of Badme/ Badume, whose seizure by Eritrea had led to the war, but subsequent clarification made it clear that it was to be found on the Eritrean side of the border. Ethiopia, despite protesting its acceptance of the Border Commission's Decisions, raised a series of objections to the way the Commission had gone about its work before finally making in clear in September 2003 that it would not accept the results on Badme or on Irob. A number of other areas remained in dispute by both sides, though Eritrea to avoid jeopardising the award of Badme made no public protest over the loss of other areas to which it had laid claim.

The Boundary Commission had based its findings to a major extent on the first element in its remit, and almost entirely ignored the latter part, producing a solution fraught with uncertainties and offering little possibility of any solutions to the problems posed by the border.[2] Ethiopia's intransigence, coupled with Eritrea's refusal to open any dialogue before demarcation, meant that the result far from providing a solution to the conflict actually reinforced the central problem of the border – the trauma of thousands of people displaced by the fighting and after three years still unable to return to their own lands. Indeed, the Decisions not only ensure that tens of thousands will probably never be able to return to the land they regard as their own; they also make quite certain the border will remain in a state of permanent instability, and almost guarantee further conflict.

The people most affected by this are those already largely ignored by virtually all the commentary on the border crisis, the local populations actually living or previously living along the border. Irrespective of the accuracy of the Decisions or their acceptance by one government or the other, the effects on local people will remain long-lasting and serious. It is already clear that the Decisions will increase the antipathy that has grown out of the conflict and out of the policies of both governments over the last decade. By no means all of the allegations of misbehaviour by Eritrean or Ethiopian troops, or of the treatment of civilians on both sides, were exaggerated, and the effects of the deportations of Eritreans from Ethiopia in 1998/99, and of Ethiopians from Eritrea in 2000/01, widely criticised by human rights bodies, will be permanent. The Boundary Commission Decisions, in fact, will do nothing at all to improve relations within those previously single and united communities torn apart by the war, even those from the same ethnic group. They will merely reinforce all the worse aspects of the propaganda that filled the air waves during the war and which has continued unbroken since December 2000.[3]

The history of the communities along the border is important, and should be an obvious and central factor in any attempt to produce a settled border. The border itself, wherever it ran after the creation of the Italian colony of Eritrea, originally divided ethnic communities all along the border, Kunama, Tigreans, Saho and Afars. Between them these people covered the whole length of the border between the Italian colony of Eritrea and the Empire of Ethiopia, apart from the boundary along the Setit river in the west.

Eritrea was an Italian construct of the late 19th century, but it was built up from two distinct elements. One was the Christian highland area of the Tigreans which had for centuries been an integral part of the various Abyssinian/Ethiopian empires to the south. In the 19th century the Tigrean princes, like those of the Amhara and Oromo further south, vied for control of the shadow emperors in Gondar, and subsequently fought among themselves for the crown. The area north of the Mareb River, the Kebessa, was as much a part of this as the area south of the Mareb, now the Tigrai Regional State (Killil) of Ethiopia.

The second element was the non-Tigrean peoples: Afars, Saho and Kunama. Afars lived along the Red Sea coast south of Massawa and inland to the Bada oasis and to the foothills of the escarpment. The Saho lived on the escarpment and in Irob where the majority were Christian, Catholics or Ethiopian Orthodox. The Catholics were converted by French not Italian missionaries. Historically Irob was administered from the south, from Adigrat and should be considered with the Tigrinya speakers of Tigrai rather than the Saho pastoralists living in the lowlands or on the escarpment. The Kunama live in the south western lowlands of Eritrea, between the Merab/Gash and the Takazze/Setit rivers. They were used by the Italians as part of the expansion of their colonialist ambitions into western Eritrea. The 1902 treaty between Italy and Ethiopia specifically mentions that the boundary when delimited should allow for the Kunama to be within Eritrea. In 2002, the Boundary Commission subsequently identified this as one of the major criteria of the boundary prior to 1935. In fact, after 1902, the Italians used the movements of the Kunama as a basis for advancing their control steadily, pushing the border forward a few kilometres on an almost annual basis. It was exactly the same technique employed along the Ethiopian border with Italian Somaliland which precipitated the invasion and conquest of Ethiopia by Italy in 1935 after the incident at Wal Wal.

Boundaries

The history of the boundaries of "Eritrea" goes far to provide an explanation for the problems that arose in the course of the 1990s. The colonial boundary was agreed in the series of treaties in 1900, 1902 and 1908 between Italy and the Emperor Menilek, though Italy persisted in probing the borders almost from inception. It was a policy aimed ultimately to take revenge for the defeat of Adua in 1896, and the policy climaxed with invasion in 1935. Italy then set up its East African Empire under which it once more unified the historic Tigrai province of Ethiopia which had been sundered at the beginning of the century by the Italian creation of Eritrea. The Italian empire lasted no more than five years. In 1941, the Italian armies surrendered to British and Commonwealth forces and to those of Ethiopia. Haile Selassie was restored as emperor in May. Ethiopia's largely un-delimited pre-war boundaries with Eritrea were restored by the Anglo-Ethiopian Agreement of January 31, 1942. In practice, however, Britain retained a major role in Ethiopia as well as in Eritrea and Italian Somaliland, both administered directly as captured enemy territory. Ethiopia was seen as a vital link in the defence of Egypt and the Middle East against Italy and Germany. With the Mediterranean virtually closed off, the British were determined to keep control over communication links through Ethiopia and Eritrea for the safety of Egypt and Sudan. They saw the Horn of Africa as an element in the wider war.

The British were less than sympathetic to Ethiopian claims to Eritrea and to the Unionist feelings that appeared in Eritrea with the creation of the Mahiber Fekri Hagar in 1942, supporting the unification of Eritrea and Ethiopia. The British military administration was more prepared to support the idea of a greater Tigrai, to include an Eritrea united with the Tigrai province of Ethiopia and independent of Addis Ababa, something which might make it easy to attach the western Muslim lowlands of Eritrea, indeed all the areas west of Keren, to Sudan. In fact, although British support for this was never more than a passing idea born of wartime conditions, it certainly appealed to a number of leading Eritrean Tigreans, and appalled Emperor Haile Selassie. He certainly wanted Eritrea but nothing would have convinced him to place all Tigreans into a single province. He would have seen it as much too dangerous. For much of the pre-war period he had played off leading Tigrean princes against each other. After the war, Ras Seyoum Mengesha, descendant of the last Tigrean emperor, Yohannes IV, was eventually made governor of Tigrai. He was succeeded by his son, Ras Mengesha Seyoum, who married a grand-daughter of the Emperor. To have had either of them as ruler of an enlarged Tigrai province, however, would have been highly dangerous. Nor would it have been welcomed by other equally ambitious and well-connected governors like Ras Asrate Kassa, governor of Eritrea in the 1960s.

Greater Tigrai might not have been politically acceptable in the 1940s or subsequently, but the concept had considerable significance in Eritrea, looking back to the ethnic and political reality at the end of the previous century. The border had been drawn in the first decades of the century. A lot of people could remember Tigrai before Eritrea had been created; its brief re-appearance between 1936 and 1941 was an almost unnecessary reminder. The Italian-Ethiopian colonial border was in theory restored after 1941 but only slowly came into effect as the British continued to insist on a direct role in keeping communications moving through Ethiopia into Eritrea while the war lasted. Even after the Second World War ended, the British never delimited their sphere of authority, except with reference to Italian activity. In some areas where no river boundary existed, this could mean advancing until Ethiopian officials were met.

From 1952, the boundary was one between the Federation of Ethiopia and Eritrea, and then from 1962 it became an Ethiopian provincial boundary, and meaningless in any political sense for those living along it. For the Kunama, the Tigreans, Saho and Afar, the boundary did not exist. All it defined was relationship the centre to which one paid taxes or took court cases, to Asmara or to Makelle. This could and did vary during the post Federation period, depending upon the political standing of the provincial governor and his activity. Ras Mengesha Seyoum who succeeded his father as governor of all Tigrai, was an energetic governor, spending a good deal of his time building new roads to open up remoter areas of his governorate including one down into the Danakil desert, to Bada, and another to the north west to the Badume plains, and to Sheraro to provide a link to Barentu. A side-effect of this was the creation of a number of new settlements, including the village of Badme, as centres for Tigrai agricultural development some under the auspices of the Ras Mengesha's Tigrai Development Association, others organised by private individuals authorised by the provincial government or local administration. The majority of settlers came from elsewhere in Tigrai, but there was no objection to farmers from the Kebessa, the Tigrinya speaking area of Eritrea, moving into the "open" lands of north-western Tigrai.[4] The Kunama, if considered at all, were not thought to have a claim. The governors of both Eritrea and Tigrai had identical and dismissive views of the Kunama, a view largely shared by the Tigrinya speaking populations.

The issue of specific administration in the Baduma plain area and this area of north-west Tigrai was, however, complicated by the rise of the Eritrean Liberation Front in the 1960s, and the appearance of the Eritrean Peoples Liberation Front (EPLF) in the early 1970s and the Tigrai Peoples Liberation Front (TPLF) in 1975. The Baduma plain was remote from the centres of the provincial governments of both Eritrea and Tigrai and was valued as a centre for guerrilla operations. The area around provided both staging points for operations and as a base area. Indeed it was in north-west Shire, in which Badme lies, that the Tigrai Peoples Liberation Front first started their operations. Subsequently, both the TPLF and the EPLF felt they had claims to the region.[5]

However, the central point for the populations living along the border was that for the lifetime of most of the inhabitants on either side there has been no constraint or hindrance to movement across the border at any time. There has indeed only been a border in any theoretical or semi-formal sense since 1993. For the previous thirty years the only difference was who provided the administration – the regional governor in Asmara or Makelle, or one of the guerrilla units. The same peoples lived on both sides of the border for almost its entire length, and, significantly, the push for independence in Eritrea was slowest to take root in these border areas.

The war of independence in Eritrea started in the north-western lowlands among the Beni Amer, and serious ELF activity was largely confined there for the first decade. Even after the creation of the EPLF with a much greater appeal to Christian highlanders large sections of the border areas remained reluctant to support either movement. In 1976/77, the guerrilla forces of the ELF and the EPLF overran all of Eritrea with the exception of five towns, Asmara, Massawa, Assab, Barentu and Adi Caieh. The explanation for the first two of these is clear: Asmara, the capital, was the major centre of Ethiopian military power and was kept supplied by air; the main port of Massawa survived major EPLF attacks with the help of Russian naval bombardments and incompetent assaults. The continued Ethiopian control of the other three towns, however, can be explained by a rather different factor – support from local populations, Afars in and around Assab, Kunama at Barentu, and Saho around Adi Caieh. Without local support none of these three towns could have survived the sieges they were subjected to in 1976/77. Certainly, disputes between the guerrilla units contributed to the Eritrean failure both at Barentu and Adi Caieh where EPLF and ELF were both present, but the Ethiopian garrisons benefited significantly from supplies of food and of information about the activities of the EPLF and ELF, as well as military support from among Kunama and Afars.

The Kunama

Originally one major factor explaining Kunama reluctance to join in the independence struggle and their continuing involvement with the Ethiopian administration was resentment at the way they had been treated in the past by the Beni Amer people among whom the ELF originated. A Nilotic agro-pastoral people they were despised by both the nomadic Muslim Beni Amer to the north and west, and by the Christian Tigrean agriculturalists to the east and south. They were regarded as a reservoir of cattle and slaves, to be raided at will. This continued, if on a smaller scale, during the colonial period and under the British administration. The man credited with sparking off the Eritrean independence struggle, Hamid Idris Awate, with his attack on a police post in September 1961, shortly before the end of the Federation, is seen rather differently by the Kunama. A well-known bandit in the 1940s and 1950s, the Kunama had suffered frequently from his raiding, and indeed from what Kunama remember as his "murderous violence". The Kunama scepticism towards Idris Awate's past was only reinforced by the ELF's approach towards the Kunama throughout the 1960s. It behaved exactly as the Beni Amer had done, seizing food and cattle as well as kidnapping young men, though by the 1960s this was to use them as fighters rather than slaves.

When the EPLF was created, the Kunama could perceive little difference. Historically, they had suffered as much from the Tigrean highlanders as from the Beni Amer (Idris Awate for example was compared with the great Tigrean general Ras Alula whose raids, from his headquarters in Hamasien, had decimated the Kunama in the later 19th century before the Italians took over Eritrea). Originally, at least, the EPLF took the same approach towards the Kunama, treating them as those from the highland Christian provinces, the Kebessa, had always done, carrying out forcible recruitment and seizure of supplies.

The effects of these policies became apparent during the siege of Barentu in 1976/77, where the Ethiopian garrison received active military support from the Kunama. Hundreds fought alongside the garrison and were recruited into the Ethiopian army. They played a major role in the town's survival on at least one occasion, recapturing Getachew Hill, a strategic hill overlooking the town. Its loss threatened the airstrip, a vital lifeline for the garrison. Kunama forces with their local knowledge of paths and concealed routes up the hill played the major role in retaking the hill without which the garrison could not have survived. [6]

When the EPLF became aware of the strength of Kunama support for the Ethiopian administration during the joint EPLF/ELF siege of Barentu, it did respond. For the first time it began to implement the Front's policies in Kunama area, inaugurating its social, educational and political programmes. It had some success, and recruited a number of Kunama into the EPLF. The ELF, similarly, attempted to launch its social programmes in Gash-Setit region. The problem in both cases was that neither organisation was prepared to take into account the cultural beliefs of the Kunama and their social attitudes. According to the Kumana, neither the ELF nor the EPLF cadres were seriously prepared to argue their case; in the last resort, both organisations were equally ready to react with violence to disputes or disagreements. Nor was it long before the practice of forcible recruitment was restarted.

The Kunama as a whole continued to suffer at the hands of the EPLF after the expulsion of the ELF from Eritrea in their civil war in 1981/82. Barentu was unexpectedly captured from the Ethiopian forces in mid 1984. As Kunama women and children fled the town they were shot down by advancing EPLF fighters. As the EPLF were being driven out of the town by an Ethiopian counter-attack a few weeks later, they shot over 30 influential detainees, mostly Kunama, who had been arrested on their arrival.[7] The EPLF also continued their policy of seizing Kunama youngsters, male and female, particularly after the Ethiopian army retreated to Asmara, abandoning western Eritrea after defeat at Af Abet in 1988. Several thousand Kunama accompanied the retreating Ethiopians to Asmara.

Unsurprisingly, the majority of the Kunama remained unconvinced by the efforts of the liberation front to recruit them. In total, some 6,000 Kunama served in the Ethiopian army during the 1970s and 1980s. Many would have welcomed the concept of an autonomous Kunama polity, something to which the Ethiopian government gave serious consideration in the later 1980s. The Ethiopian aim would have been to split Eritrea up into separate, ethnically based, elements. One step towards this was the 1987 creation of the Assab Autonomous Region, for the Afars along the Red Sea coast. Its relative success encouraged the idea of repeating the process elsewhere in Eritrea though no progress was made in this direction.

Inevitably, when Mengistu's regime collapsed in 1991, and the EPLF took over in Asmara, the EPLF was suspicions of the Kunama, and the Kunama were concerned by the EPLF. They were right to be worried. A significant number of Kunama were immediately detained for alleged involvement in human rights abuses under the Ethiopian administration of Eritrea. At least 50 were still held a decade later, uncharged, untried. Hundreds, possibly thousands of Kunama ex-soldiers were held for at least two years; some were detained for longer, and it is possible some may still be held. The Eritrean government has always refused to answer any questions about those it detained in 1991. Others were among those deported in 1991/1992 when a total of about 150,000 soldiers and civilians were abruptly pushed across the border after Eritrea achieved de facto independence.[8] Included among these deportees were Eritrean women who had married Ethiopian civil servants based in Asmara prior to 1991, and their children. Some were Kunama, though a majority of Kunama who married people from elsewhere in Ethiopia, and their children, appear to have remained in Eritrea despite the suspicion and allegations of treachery made against these "collaborators" in the years after the achievement of independence.

Kunama problems with the government in Asmara were not confined to the issue of Kunama support for, or "collaboration" with Ethiopia. Within a matter of months the new government needed land on which to settle demobilised fighters from the war of liberation, and returning refugees from Sudan. The EPLF, which became the Peoples Front for Democracy and Justice (PFDJ) in 1994, also needed land to settle growing numbers of Tigreans from the Kebessa and from the urban areas, particularly Asmara, to satisfy the increasing shortage of land in the new state. In government eyes, the Kunama's agro-pastoral lands, in Gash and Setit provinces, was significantly under-utilised. During the 1990s, Ali Gidir in western Gash became the centre of large-scale agricultural development projects, and thousands of highlanders moved into Barentu and other Kunama towns and villages, over 30,000 into the area of Barentu alone. The Kunama governor of Gash-Setit region, Germano Nati, later to be one of those arrested after the G15 criticism of president Issayas, was "frozen" and transferred from his governorship in 1996 after his objections to the seizures of land from the Kunama had led him into dispute with senior military officers. Following the pattern established by the previous Ethiopian regime, he was sent off to Assab. His replacement, Mustafa Nur-Hussein, has been described as by the Kunama as "our main enemy".

Barentu became a show place of development with streets of new houses and town administration buildings, but it had little to do with the Kunama. The Kunama were forced out of the central areas and confined to the peripheral sections of the town. When the Ethiopian army took the town in May/June 2000, the Eritrean authorities subsequently accused the Ethiopians of wanton and extensive destruction of the town (see below).

There was much truth in this, but the areas destroyed were almost entirely the newer parts of the town owned and inhabited by recent Tigreans settlers, the "….. infrastructure developed there [was] to satisfy only the highland Eritrean urban recently moved to and settled in Barentu…". The Kunama houses around the edge of the town were largely left untouched. It has been suggested that the destruction was deliberately intended to parallel that caused in Badme by the Eritrean troops when they had seized it in May 1998, destroying government buildings, the school, houses, even a church. Other Kunama towns, Haicotta, Shambuko, Tecumbia, also suffered serious damage from the Ethiopian advance. Again it was most often the houses of highland settlers which were most affected.

The immediate Eritrean government response to defeat in 2000 was to explain it away by treachery. Responsibility was first laid at the door of the Kunama, either for failing to resist properly or alternatively for allegedly showing the Ethiopian army secret unguarded crossing points on the Mareb river.[9] Later defeat was blamed on the dissident members of the PFDJ central committee who had had the temerity to question the president's actions.[10] This did not lift the cloud of the suspicion over the Kunama. When Ethiopian troops pulled back from Eritrea after June 2000, several thousand Kunama went with them. The Kunama still in Eritrea, the vast majority, remain politically marginalised, their lands continuing to be seized by the government for highland settlement and returning refugees; arrests and disappearances continue unabated. According to a letter sent to Amnesty International by a Kunama group in November 2000, immediately after the war ended some 600 men, women and children were taken by truck into the Sahel area of Eritrea. Six months later people had no clue to their whereabouts. They have still not returned to their homes. The letter also claims another 80 had "recently" been arrested from four villages and taken to the "far desert areas of Assab". Others were being detained in Barentu as part of "a pre-planned [government] policy of deportation and displacement…in order to give the members of its own Eritrean Tigrean folk group an ample opportunity to settle in the evacuated rich and fertile Kunama territory…".[11]

Irob

Irob, lying to the east of Zalambesa, appears much smaller on the map than the area around Badme, but it has a larger population on its steep-sided mountains and in the valleys. The three main lineages in Irob (Adgabe Ari, Buknayto Ari and Hasaballa) are Saho speakers and used to have close relationships with the Saho in Eritrea. A majority of the population practised mixed agriculture with some livestock and bee-keeping, but many households were also involved in small-scale trade and migration for seasonal work. Prior to 1991 much of this was in Eritrea, but after Eritrean independence both became harder. Even prior to the conflict there had been a number of trade disputes around the border post established outside Zalambesa by the Eritrean administration, and since 1998 it has, of course, been impossible to take goods into Eritrea or to look for work there. Few think either are likely to resume.

> "..I have a sister married to an Eritrean in Monoixioto village...I have not been able to cross into Eritrea [from Tigray] and visit with my sister and her family. Sadder still, though, is the fact that her eldest son has been conscripted into the Eritrean army to fight against his own people, including his own grandmother, uncles, cousins, nieces, and many other relatives as well, just in the name of nationalism and border claims..."[12]

When Eritrean troops tried to push through this area at the end of May 1998 to take Alitiena and outflank the Ethiopian defences on the road to Adigrat south of Zalambesa, they ran into fierce resistance from the local militia.[13] It was this that apparently sparked off the destruction that followed the Eritrean capture of the area, and the flight of a majority of the inhabitants further south. The livestock they had to abandon was slaughtered by the Eritrean troops and even the beehives destroyed. Irrigation systems were deliberately broken, and extensively polluted with military debris, including mines. Houses were knocked down and churches desecrated. The Catholic priests in Irob were forced out of their churches, and several disappeared: "...the churches have been desecrated and used to store weapons and ammunition, or as sleeping quarters for the troops. The priests [who did reach Adigrat] have heard that the structures not being used by the troops have been mined..."[14] The Ad-hoc committee of Zalambesa-Irob Region claimed later that "...the mines that were maliciously planted with intent to kill and destroy are taking steady toll on the lives of our people and their livestock on a daily basis. After all, it is no secret that they were systematically planted including in out homes and backyards...".[15]

An Irob response to the Decisions of the Boundary Commission in April 2002 claimed that not enough attention had been paid to the activities of the invaders: "Killing of civilians, imprisonment, harassment, rape of women, desecration and looting of churches, eviction of residents from their homes, destruction of houses, health centres and schools were daily activities of the Eritrean troops. Peasants were expelled without being allowed to take their property...the people who were thrown out from their homes were elders, disabled, women and children who were left behind when people left the area to escape the war...the invader Eritrean government took more than 100 innocent civilians and no news is heard yet. More than 300 innocent civilians also dead...". [16] The article refers to handing over the Irob, a minority group in Ethiopia, as a crime against humanity, claiming that "...changing the identity and citizenship and dividing the Ethnic group into two or more diversified area by force is eradicating them..." . Two months earlier, an Eritrean Irob Association had surfaced claiming Irob had always been part of Eritrea, that it had never been administered by Ethiopia and indeed had fought strongly against this in the past. It insisted that the Irob, part of the Saho, were located inside Eritrea and were surrounded by many Eritrean villages "with whom we have historical ties in terms of trade and marital relationships...".[17]

In August 2003, the Catholic Bishop of Adigrat, in whose diocese all of Irob falls, wrote an open letter to the UN Secretary General, briefly outlining the damage suffered in his diocese and questioning the Demarcation Decisions: "Within my jurisdiction alone over 300,000 were displaced: their homes destroyed; their cattle ran wild; their lands remained uncultivated; schools, clinics and churches looted, either severely damaged or totally destroyed. Zalambesa, for instance, was systematically bulldozed...and in Zalambesa alone the Catholic Church lost 8 institutions." The Bishop then went on to outline the effects of the proposed demarcation in parts of diocese: "...To have access to Zalambesa from the east, the region surrounding Alitiena, the people would be obliged to cross the border four or even five times. Without making a very long detour on foot there is no alternative market where they might sell produce or buy commodities....they would be deprived of vital services and for which alternatives simply do not exist. ..Parishes belonging to this ecclesiastical jurisdiction, the Eparchy of Adigrat, which were founded from here over 100 years ago and whose national status has never been questioned or doubted, would be sliced off....not once has either members of the Commission or their delegates taken the slightest trouble or shown the slightest interest in consulting those who would be so adversely affected...".[18]

Afar

East of Irob and the Saho lies the Danakil desert and the Afars. Most of the Afar region is desert or semi-desert, and the Afar themselves largely nomadic pastoralists, though there is some agriculture along the Awash river in the southern Danakil, in the Bada oasis in the north. Rainfall distribution is minimal though there are small rains in March/April, and the longer rains in July and August. Both are erratic, and have been poor for the last two years. The whole area is now affected by a shortage of water resources affecting Afars, Issa Somalis and Oromo pastoralists and agro-pastoralists. Afars have recently been suffering from several other factors including conflict with Issa Somalis encroaching on Afar lands. The Issa have been steadily moving westwards and are attempting to take control of the main Awash/Logiya road, and gain permanent access to the Awash river. Afars are also running into problems along the escarpment to the west. Traditionally, Afar move onto the escarpment during the dry season while the Oromo on the escarpment come down into the lowlands during the wet season. With recent increases in agricultural development, and drought, it is becoming harder for the Afar to use these areas. Even without drought conditions, Afars in the Awash valley are facing problems from the increased extraction of water from the river for irrigation of cotton plantations.[19]

These difficulties have been compounded by the restrictions imposed by the closed border between Ethiopia and Eritrea. Afars are past-masters at avoiding and ignoring borders but the actual conflict and then the post-war situation along the border has meant that it has been difficult if not impossible to get to grazing areas, and any cross-border animal trading has been largely impossible because of the soldiers and the Transitional Security Zone keeping the two sides apart. Two hundred Afar families live in one camp near Assab, forced to flee when their village was destroyed in the fighting: "...Before the war, [we] lived in a village close to Debai Sima, which is now in Ethiopia. We traded cloth and household items, and we had some goats and camels. When the war broke out, our animals died because we could no longer take them to the grazing lands...Now trading is impossible, because of the closed border....we have to walk for at least six hours to collect firewood...".[20]

One specific area along the border, long predating Badme as a problem, was Bada. This is an extensive plain in the northern Danakil desert where the delta of the seasonal Ragalu river flowing from the escarpment to the west fans out into the plain. The water flow allows for irrigated agriculture and is one of the few fertile areas in Afar lands. The main stream in Bada is given the name of Wadi Kabuia or Wadi Ragalu and during the Italian period and subsequently this was taken as the boundary. Of the four Afar villages in this area two are on each side of the Wadi, Adi Murug and Eri Millea on the south (Ethiopian) side and Bollali and Laen Bada on the north (Eritrean) side. In 1963, the then Governor of Tigray region, Ras Mengesha Seyoum, built a road through to Adi Murug and provided a school and a clinic. This division of control over the oasis largely held during the 1980s when the EPLF and the TPLF were operating in the area with the EPLF administering the northern part and the TPLF the southern. Land was not an issue between the Afar clans in the area but water was. In the 1980s, the TPLF apparently brokered a deal which allowed some 75% of the water to be taken to the northern half, with 25% going to Adi Murug and Eri Millea.

Afars again took over control of Bada during the later 1980s, after the establishment of the Assab Autonomous Administration by the Derg. This was designed to try and appeal to Afar nationalism and it was seen by many Afars as a preliminary step towards Afar autonomy, something that was not on offer from the EPLF. The Derg's aim was less to support any idea of Afar nationalism than to boost resistance to the EPLF among the Afar. Part of the process was the establishment of an Afar militia, the Ugugumo, to fight the EPLF. It had a number of successes and continued to fight even after the fall of the Derg. When the EPLF tried to move into Bada in July and August 1991, Ugugumo resisted fiercely. They were driven out after some heavy fighting, but they then claim to have defeated Eritrean attempts to move into the hills at Aligarab and subsequently to have forced the Eritrean troops out of Bada with considerable losses. [21] It was no more than a temporary success, but Ugugumo continued to launch attacks on Eritrean forces when they tried to reoccupy Bada from time to time, as well as on any Ethiopian military bases established in the area.[22]

There was further substantial fighting in 1996/7 when the TPLF launched a major effort to wipe out the guerrilla bases of the Afar Revolutionary Democratic United Front (ARDUF) in the Afar Depression. ARDUF was forced to abandon most of its bases and retreat into the hills towards the Eritrean border. It subsequently managed to reorganise and fighting continued the next year, the year of the "Bada" incident between Ethiopia and Eritrea. According to Eritrea, Ethiopian troops pursuing ARDUF moved into Bada and, on discovering an Eritrean administration in Adi Murug which they regarded as Ethiopian, promptly dismantled it. ARDUF has a slightly different interpretation of events as it claims Ethiopia and Eritrea were colluding in the operations against it. It was forced out of Bada and most of its other bases in the area by Ethiopian forces. [23] ARDUF, incidentally, confirms Ethiopia's claim to Adi Murug and the southern half of Bada. This may in part explain Eritrea's seizure of Irob and Alitiena in May/June 1998. It is strategically impossible to hold onto Bada unless Alitiena and the escarpment above Bada, from which the Ragalu river descends, are also held.

241

Ethiopia's success in 2000 has not brought conflict in the area to an end. The Ethiopian government has launched several offensives against remaining ARDUF bases around Bada, and in the escarpment between Adigrat and Berhale. Despite ARDUF's aim of bringing the Afars of Eritrea and Ethiopia under a single administration within Ethiopia which might have been expected to appeal to the Ethiopian government, and its opposition to the Eritrean regime, the Ethiopian administration made little serious effort to come to terms with ARDUF during the war with Eritrea. It has made more effort since, persuading ARDUF's foreign affairs spokesman to defect in mid 2002.[24] A significant element of ARDUF, however, have yet to accept the deal and some fighting was reported in late 2003. It is far from certain that they have sufficient trust in the EPRDF or be prepared to participate in Afar Regional State politics under the present government. [25] The recent conflict in southern Afar area, where the Issa Somalis have been encroaching on traditional Afar lands, has led to allegations that the Ethiopian government has been allowing Issa expansion to satisfy the government in Djibouti where the President, Ismail Omar Guellah, is an Issa.

The Afar live in some of the harshest terrain in the world and the conflict has come close to tipping the balance between success or failure in survival. In times of severe shortage of water, as in 2002-2003 as well as earlier, the conflict, and its aftermath, has had a particularly serious effect on the availability of water resources, with difficulties over maintaining and regulating wells and bore holes. It has prevented the repair of water pumps; it has stopped water tankering; it has affected the condition of livestock and prevented their sale; it has minimised the possibility of buying water from private birkads. It has increased the pressure on available water supplies, even on the Awash River where both the Afar and the Somali Issa moving in from the south want unrestricted access, and where increasing agricultural activity and irrigation have been having a noticeable effect. Fighting, and subsequent military patrolling of the borders, has meant significant changes in livestock grazing availability and increased pastoral mobility, or, in other words, it has become much harder to find acceptable grazing. Another consequence is over-grazing of the accessible areas.

The destruction of border towns and the impact on border communities

Almost all the towns along the border areas are seriously damaged in the war, some during the fighting but much of the destruction came after they had been captured. In some cases it appears the damage was deliberately carried out as an act of spite and revenge on both sides.

Om Hajer was captured by Ethiopia troops in May 2000 as they advanced north to Tessenai, and it was left in ruins, but not apparently by the troops. "Shops were gutted. Doors and window-frames had been ripped from their cement fastenings. Metal roofs were missing. A mosque sat defaced with trash and human faeces. A church has remained cluttered with bits of clothing and broken straw baskets, evidently used to store personal belongings looted from nearby homes. The town suffered no fighting between Ethiopian and Eritrean soldiers, but Ethiopian civilians looted and burned it after the contending armies moved northward...".[26]

North of Om Hajer, at Ali Ghidir, the largest irrigated agricultural site in Eritrea and the centre of the main settlement area for demobilised guerrilla fighters of the independence war, the farm equipment was destroyed and holes blown in the cement storage sheds. Bridges and telecommunications facilities were wrecked and most buildings looted. Tessenai, the main town in western Eritrea, was worst effected, changing hands four times in two months in 2002. Tessenai administrator, Mohammed Said Montai, claims the damage came from both Ethiopian troops and civilians they brought along to loot: "Schools and offices were destroyed, desks were burned, roofs were taken. Everything they could carry they took. What was not easy to take, they burned. They also moved goods from house to house, wherever they slept, so people come back and find things in their homes that they never saw before – broken furniture, carts, clothes." [27]

It is not entirely clear when this destruction happened. In mid June, a month after Tessenai was captured by the Ethiopian forces, it apparently showed little sign of battle "...aside from the occasional pall of smoke rising from one of the thatch and wattle huts on the outskirts. Other buildings in the centre remained intact, and bore no mark of shelling or machine-gun fire. No civilians were visible in the town...".[28] Ethiopian troops then withdrew from the city, but briefly returned when it was reoccupied by Eritrean forces. Ethiopian troops then withdrew from the city but briefly returned when it was reoccupied by Eritrean troops a couple of weeks later

Barentu was another town that suffered extensively in the fighting in May 2000. "...As the Ethiopian forces marched into Barentu, they brought with them trucks and Ethiopian civilians. The troops then directed their civilians as they systematically looted most everything of value from the entire town— desks, tables, chairs, beds, tea kettles, grain, seeds, farm tools, oil, shoes, clothing, photographs. Almost everything that could be carried out was loaded onto trucks and shipped back over into Ethiopia. Right behind them came a second wave armed with dynamite, landmines, heavy artillery, tanks and fuel. Government and local administrative offices, the bank, the open air market, hotels, businesses, and private homes were set on fire, dynamited and destroyed…Barentu was left a guted, heavily damaged shell of its former self – its administrative and economic capacity annihilated with one fell swoop..".[29]

Similar allegations were made against Ethiopian troops after the occupation of Senafe after they had recaptured Zalambesa and advanced north up the road towards Decamere in May/June 2000. Under the ceasefire agreement of June 2000, Ethiopian troops remained in occupation of Senafe until the arrival of UNMEE forces. According to refugees arriving at the Alba refugee camp in August the troops stripped the villages around Senafe of anything movable: "They took the tin roofs of the houses. All the money and the gold, they just took it away. They even took our clothes, they left us in our underwear. They took the scarfs of the Muslim girls […] in Mai-Gundi where roofs and doorframes were removed only the stones of the walls are left. If they could have, they would have taken the stones too." Other refugees quoted stories of rape and pillage on Senafe itself: "The Ethiopians took everything. We buried our trinkets or hid them in the toilets. But one night, they found one of the hiding places in someone's house. After that, they dug up everything in all the houses and broke all the toilets…. The young people who were the main victims, ran away to hide in the mountains…Every day, the young people were arrested, interrogated and beaten to try and make them admit they were spies."[30]

Badme is little more than a village, with a primary school, two small hotels and several bars, and a clinic. Virtually destroyed in the fighting in 1998/1999, it has now been largely rebuilt. Its population is no more than 5000, and they normally depend largely on farming; sorghum and sesame are supplemented by cattle and goats. Now they also play host to substantial numbers of troops. Badme is in the Badume plain and was founded about 50 years ago as Tigrean farmers from further east in the Tigrean *awraja* (province) of Shire began to move onto the plain, previously grazing areas for the Kunama. It is black cotton soil and fertile when irrigated. They were joined in the 1960s and 1970s by a number of Tigrean farmers from Serai, one of the *awrajas* of the province of Eritrea, and before 1998, the Eritrean element of the population had reached about 1,000; they left when the Eritrean army was driven out of Badme in February 1999. The present population, who moved back into the village after June 1999 after the second Eritrean failure to retake the town, as might be expected regard themselves as Ethiopian. "…I simply don't understand why there is confusion. We are Ethiopians and we have been in Badme for generations', said 47-year-old farmer, Haile Gebre… We were occupied by Eritreans for almost a year and we don't want them back….I want things to go back to the way they were before the war, but they have to accept that Badme is Ethiopian'…".

On the Ethiopian side, the most substantial destruction came in Zalambesa, a thriving border town before relations between Eritrea and Ethiopia deteriorated. Badly damaged in the fighting in 1998 when captured by Eritrea, it was destroyed when they left. Everything that could be taken was taken by the retreating Eritrean troops who then blew up or tore down most of the buildings. "…The flourishing town of 16,000 was turned into an ancient ruin and haunted city. No standing building, no wooden work, no metal work, no ceilings were left. …the EPLF mined and booby trapped the ruined houses. Many old residents, who came to visit their ruined abode, were maimed and killed by the evil schemes…".[31] The Ad Hoc Committee claimed this destruction demonstrated a "depth of vindictive hatred" arising from the success of the population of Zalambesa in preventing Eritrean efforts to move coffee and other products across the border into Eritrea. Zalambesa also took a lead in boycotting Eritrean goods, shoes and beer, and in refusing to accept the use of the Eritrean "Nakfa".

Unlike Badme, repairs to Zalambesa have been slow. Two years later the former inhabitants were still complaining that the government had made no progress in rebuilding the town nor had it provided sufficient assistance for them. The population remain in camps or in some cases were apparently staying in caves. "…at the moment [we] have to travel to Adigrat to get health service…students attending ninth grade go to school in Adigrat while those below that are receiving schooling in different places in the countryside…women are facing great difficulties at the time of giving birth and some women have delivered two to three babies in caves".[32] There was also concern over rumours that the town was going to be relocated away from its original centre because of the way the Boundary Commission had virtually isolated the town in a thin sliver of land, cutting it off from virtually all of its surrounding resources of food and water. Critics of the government described the town as "dead or lost", "a useless piece of enclave surrounded by hostile territory." Tserona has been similarly isolated from its surrounding resources on the Eritrean side.

Even where houses and facilities have been found intact, there is an ever present threat of mines which both sides appear to have used with reckless abandon. Mines, indeed, are common to all the areas of fighting, particularly along the Badme front, and around Tserona and Zalambasa. These areas and large sections of the Temporary Security Zone are now reckoned to be one of the most heavily mined areas of the world. Latest estimates are that there are some 1.5 million mines in Eritrea and at least 300,000 pieces of unexploded ordnance; and at least another 2.0 million mines in Ethiopia.[33] It has so far proved impossible to mark and fence all the minefields even though the Mine Action Coordination Centre of the United Nations Mission to Eritrea and

Ethiopia (UNMEE) has been constantly active. Neither side has been as helpful as they might in detailing the placement of mines, and new fields are being discovered regularly, usually when a fatal incident occurs or some livestock are killed. It is not just mines. There is an enormous amount of unexploded ammunition, shells and grenades lying around, and these are not necessarily to be found in minefields. Nineteen people were killed during the first ten months of 2003 alone.

In fact, the threat of mines and unexploded ammunition means that thousands, tens of thousands of people are still unable to return to their villages along the border area. One of the results of this is that villages just outside the danger zones have often doubled in size. Many of the people displaced by the fighting went into camps. Some remain there but in many cases people have been resettled in villages nearby, putting severe pressure on already scarce water and fuel resources. Both governments and NGOs have done much to improve the situation since the end of the fighting, but the situation will remain critical until people can return to their homes without constraint, and that still looks a long way away.

Before the war, in the period 1991-1997, towns and villages on or close to the border like Zalambesa, Adigrat, Rama, Sheraro, Humera, Badme in Ethiopia, or Senafe, Decamere, Mandefera, Tekombia, and Om Hajer in Eritrea all benefited substantially from the building up of peaceful relations after the long decades of guerrilla struggle and the removal of the troops from the towns and villages. Despite the abrupt expulsion of some 150,000 Ethiopians from Eritrea in 1991/1992, including many civilians and even their Eritrean wives, thousands of seasonal migrant workers from Ethiopia's Tigrai region were soon able to find jobs in Eritrea again; Eritreans similarly took up work in the agricultural estates near Humera. Ethiopia exported cereals, sugar, coffee and spices to, and often through, Eritrea, though allegations soon surfaced claiming that Eritrea had achieved status as a coffee exporting nation in this way. This was greatly resented in Ethiopia, and did much to sour relations at the main border crossings. Eritrea in turn exported goods and services to Ethiopia, and Massawa began to achieve its obvious position as the port for northern Ethiopia. Humera benefited twice over from this, gaining labour from Eritrea and exporting its cash crop production of sesame, cotton and sorghum, through Massawa.

In 1997/98, all this collapsed. Humera, unable to use Massawa, essentially lost its markets. The cost of transport from Humera to other areas of Ethiopia meant it could not compete with the more central surplus producing areas of Gojjam and Arsi. Sudan offered little alternative as the war spilled over along the Sudan border. Ethiopian troops operated up the border inside Sudan; Eritrean forces crossed the border on more than one occasion to attack

246

Eritrean opposition bases and Sudan opposition fighters were given free use of Eritrea to attack Sudanese positions inside Sudan. Economic conditions turned bleak all along both sides of the border with all official transit trade and border crossings stopped. Since 1998 they have remained non-existent with the border closed and the 25 kilometre wide Temporary Security Zone (TSZ) established on the Eritrean side of the border. Since 2000, this, and the threat of minefields as well as the legacy of ill-feeling, has provided a barrier across which economic movement has been impossible.

Both governments have attempted to avoid the creation of camps for those displaced by the fighting. They had only limited success as the existing communities pressed into use were rapidly overwhelmed by the numbers involved, and the facilities of local villages and their capacity to provide food, water and shelter, were rapidly swamped. By April 1999, the Tigrai administration calculated it had over 315,000 Internally Displaced Persons (IDPs) from the districts bordering Eritrea. These were rapidly outstripped by the numbers of IDPs in Eritrea, reaching to over 600,000 after the Ethiopian advances of May and June 2000. In fact, the return of most IDPs proved remarkably swift; a substantial majority were back in their original areas by the end of 2001, though still suffering from significant problems from the destruction of houses and the presence of mines which inhibited much agricultural activity. Agriculture was also affected by the failure of the governments to provide sufficient input of seeds.

However, considerable numbers do remain in camps. They include IDPs who cannot return to their homes because of the mines, in some cases planted in and around houses apparently in deliberate attempts to render communities unusable, or failures to rebuild houses or other facilities, or in some cases the continued presence of troops. Others who stay in the camps may be traders or people providing services to the military. The prevalence of HIV/AIDS in both the Eritrean and Ethiopian armies is far higher than in the general population, and there is a presumption that the border communities are likely to show a marked increase as well.

Another factor is the significant number of deportees from Ethiopia to Eritrea, the majority in 1998/99, and from Eritrea to Ethiopia, the majority after 2000. Many of those deported to Eritrea were distributed into urban areas and existing communities unless they had families, but thousands ended up in camps as well. In many cases because people had lived for so many years in Ethiopia, and their children often spoke no Tigrinya, integration was difficult. Land, schools and other facilities were, inevitably, in short supply. It required an enormous effort for the government to deal with the 70-75,000 deportees. Ethiopia faced a similar problem with the 95,000 or so Ethiopians returned to Ethiopia from Eritrea. The majority (about 75,000) were from

Tigray families and ended up in Tigray urban areas, in many cases relocating themselves after the government placed them in rural communities. Adigrat, with a pre-war population of 50,000, found its population nearly doubled, to about 90,000. As in Eritrea the numbers put a massive strain on local facilities and, not surprisingly, the packages provided for returnees/deportees proved to be inadequate.

Related to this have been the strains of providing for demobilised soldiers and for the families of those killed in action. Both governments tended to avoid the latter problem by simply not telling families for some time. Eritrea only announced the names of those killed in mid 2003, and even then there was widespread speculation that the government had manipulated the figure. According to President Issayas 19,000 died in the war, but most other estimates suggest a much higher figure with the most plausible indicating 36,000 dead[34]. Ethiopia has still not announced a figure but its former Chief of Staff during the war has been quoted as saying the numbers of dead are at least 40,000. Reportedly, the present Chief of Staff has quoted a figure of 60,000 dead; again the higher figure appears more likely. Whatever the exact figures, the effects have been felt nationally, but in both cases the numbers have had a proportionally greater effect on the Tigrean populations along both sides of the border who were the most involved. Indeed, other groups in both Ethiopia and Eritrea essentially regarded the conflict essentially as a Tigrean civil war. Although four different ethnic groups were involved in the conflict and remain caught up in its consequences, the war itself centred on Tigrean areas. In some respects, it seemed to look back to the 19th century feudal struggles between the rulers of Adua, Agame, Hamasien, Akele Guzai, Tembien, Avergelle and other districts.

As of 2003, demobilisation has been confined to Ethiopia which cut its forces back by 160,000 in 2001-2002 with the aid of a World Bank demobilisation programme. By mid 2003, with the Ethiopian army standing at about 150,000 troops, Eritrea had demobilised virtually none of its troops. It has even continued with national service conscription, and its forces must now stand at nearly 400,000. The effects of removing so many able-bodied people from the productive sectors of the economy and, particularly, from agriculture, intensified an already serious food situation following several poor harvests. Two thirds of the Eritrean population were in need of food assistance in 2002/2003. Not all of this can be blamed on the war or the continued cold war between Eritrea and Ethiopia, but it has certainly seriously exacerbated the situation in both countries. The point is emphasised by the continuing political problems of both President Issayas and Prime Minister Meles.

One final point of instability along the border, with wider repercussions in both Eritrea and Ethiopia, might be mentioned. This is the activity of opposition movements along and across the frontiers. Both countries use opposition movements as surrogates in their continued struggle. The anti-Eritrean government movements in the Eritrean National Alliance are mostly based in both Ethiopia and Sudan; various anti-EPRDF groups, including the Oromo Liberation Front, and the Ethiopian Peoples Patriotic Front, are based in Asmara. Both sides encourage regular infiltration across the border and there have been a number of landmines laid in Eritrea, most outside the TSZ, and in Ethiopia.

CONCLUSION

A recent statement on the Internet claimed the Boundary Commission had "...carelessly and mercilessly exposed a tiny ethnic minority [the Irob] living between the countries of Eritrea and Ethiopia to the danger of disintegration and possible ethnic cleansing...", and added that the Irob were now being divided between "two bitter enemy countries....two bitterly hostile nationalities ...".[35] Exaggerated as this may indeed be, it makes a point that has been constantly repeated by people along both sides of the border in recent months. The two governments are locked into a spiral of conflict that has already gone far to poison relationships all along the border, and it emphasises the divisions and splits already forced on border communities in the name of nationalism by the war itself and by the constant stream of propaganda from both governments.

Any comprehensive peace agreement needs political will; any successful restoration of relations will need the rebuilding of assets for the war-affected populations. There is little indication of the former, and the cross-border reconciliation needed for the later appears equally distant. Ideologues from both sides continue to indulge in virulent propaganda encouraging divisions among the cross-border populations. Indeed, they have arguably spent considerable efforts over the last few years actively encouraging hatred between the people on each side of the border. The destruction of property, including desecration of churches, in Irob, Zalambesa and Badme, by Eritrean forces was clearly deliberate; Ethiopian troops responded in kind in Barentu, Tessenai and Senafe. The war, and the related expulsions by both sides, have defined, or redefined the meaning of Eritrea and Ethiopia that did not exist before 1998. Prior to the war, the border communities could, and did, largely see themselves as neither Eritrean nor Ethiopian but as one or the other almost at will. There was little problem adjusting nationality at need. This is no longer possible and the effects will be lasting.

At one level, Eritrea's aim appears to have been a deliberate political and ideological effort to divide these populations as a means of defining the identity of Eritrea, to subsume those elements of the trans-border communities in Eritrea within a single and centralised Eritrean state. It was a central part of President Issayas' policy of a "dialogue of conflict" to define Eritrea. It contrasted sharply with the more devolved, though still strongly controlled, ethnically-based federation of Ethiopia which President Issayas has made clear he regards as an ideological threat to Eritrea. Intentionally or not, the Boundary Commission effectively supported the Eritrean approach, emphasising national political claims at the expense of existing local cultural cross-border or trans-national links.

Ultimately, no permanent peace along the Eritrean-Ethiopian border is possible at the expense of the needs of the local populations, of the Kunama, the Afar, the Saho and the Tigreans, or without their agreement. It is clear that those divided by the Boundary Commission or misplaced, as many claim to be, will not accept the ruling. This is as true of Ethiopians in Badme and Irob as of Eritreans around Tserona. The effect of the Boundary Commission's Decisions has been to raise a whole series of new problems along the border and offer no alternatives. Neither government is prepared to take the necessary steps to allow local people to provide alternative solutions. Between them and the Boundary Commission a solvable crisis shows every sign of turning into a permanent instability.

SELECT BIBLIOGRAPHY:

Abbink, J. "Creating Borders: exploring the impact of the Ethio-Eritrean war on the local population", *Africa* (Roma) LVI, no. 4, 2001.

Alemseged Abbay. "'Not with them, not without them': the staggering of Eritrea to nationhood", *Africa* (Roma) LVI, no.4, 2001. "The Trans-Mareb Past in the Present", *The Journal of Modern African Studies*, 35 (2), 1997.

Alexander Naty. "Memories of the Kunama of Eritrea towards Italian Colonialism". *Africa* (Roma) LVI, No. 4, 2001.

Gilkes, P. and Plaut, M. *War in the Horn: the Conflict between Eritrea and Ethiopia.* Royal Institute of International Affairs, Discussion Paper no. 82, London. 1999

Gilkes, P. "Propaganda war – media coverage and comment on the Ethio-Eritrean conflict 1998-2000", in *Ethiopian Studies at the End of the Second Millenium,* Proceedings of the XIV International Conference of Ethiopian Studies, November 2000, ed. Baye Yimam et al. Addis Ababa, 2002.

Joireman, S. F. "The Minefield of Land Reform: Comments on the Eritrean Land Proclamation". *African Affairs,* 95, 1996.

Tekeste Negash. *Italian Colonialism in Eritrea 1882-1941: Policies, Praxis and Impact.* University of Uppsala, 1987 Eritrea and Ethiopia: The Federal Experience. Uppsala, The Nordic Africa Institute, 1997.

Tekeste Negash and Tronvoll, K. *Brothers at War: Making sense of the Eritrean-Ethiopian War,* James Currey, Oxford, 2000.

Tronvoll, K. "The Process of Nation-building in Post-War Eritrea: Created from Below or Directed from Above". *The Journal of Modern African Studies* 36 (3), 1998.

Tronvoll, K. "Borders of Violence – boundaries of identity: Demarcating the Eritrean Nation State". *Ethnic and Racial Studies*. No. 22 (6), 1999 Walta Information Centre. Despatches from the Electronic Front, Addis Ababa, 2000.

Useful Web Sites include:
Eritrea – http://www.awate.com
http://www.asmarino.com
http://www.dehai.org
http://www.shaebia.org
http://www.meskerem.net
http://www.eritrea1.org
Ethiopia http://www.waltainfo.com
http://www.EthiopiaReporter.com
http://www.dekialula.com
http://www.addistribune.com
http://www.tigrai.org

ENDNOTES

1. As quoted in Professor Sir Elihu Lauterpacht et al.: *Eritrea-Ethiopia Boundary Commission Decision Regarding Delimitation of the Border between the State of Eritrea and the Federal Democratic Republic of Ethiopia.* The Hague 13.4.02. This document repays careful reading, particularly Chapters 4 and 5 relating to the Central Sector (Zalambesa, Tserona and Irob), and the Western Sector (Badme).
2. C. Clapham in an impressively argued paper has even gone so far as to describe the political implications of the BC's boundary line as "disastrous", adding that the Decisions go "a long way towards destroying Eritrea's future as a viable independent state." C. Clapham. "Notes on the Ethio-Eritrean Boundary Demarcation", October 2003. Posted on http://www.dehai.org/dehai-news 6.11.03
3. See: "Propaganda war – media coverage and comment on the Ethio-Eritrean conflict 1998-2000", P.S. Gilkes in *Ethiopian Studies at the End of the Second Millenium, Proceedings of the XIV International Conference of Ethiopian Studies*, November 2000, ed. Baye Yimam et al. Addis Ababa, 2002.
4. Kebessa (the Tigrinya for highlands) is the Orthodox Christian Tigrinya speaking area of Eritrea, made up of the historic regions of Akele Guzai, Hamasien and Serai. It was sometimes referred to by Tigreans south of the Mareb River as Trans-Mareb.
5. See Tekeste Negash and Kjetil Tronvoll. *Brothers at War – Making Sense of the Eritrean-Ethiopian War*, James Currey, Oxford 2000.
6. Ethiopian commander at Barentu, June 1979.
7. The EPLF deny this, but the evidence from Kunama sources is compelling.
8. David Chazan. "Thousands Deported from Eritrea". *AFP* 5.7.1991. See also *The Independent* 25.7 1991; Jane Perlez. "New Civilian Refugees", Makele. *New York Times*. 15.7.1991

9. "Ethiopia/Eritrea – Force Majeure", *Africa Confidential*, Vol.41 no. 11, 26.5.00; see also http://www.eritrean-kunama.de for extensive detail of Kunama concerns.

10. "Eritrea Crackdown", *Africa Confidential*, Vol 42 no 19, 28.10.01 Mark Turner: "Isolation Threat to Eritrea after Envoy Expelled". *Financial Times*, 1.10.01 See also comment on http://www.asmarino .com; http://www.shaebia .com etc.

11 Representatives of the Kunama Peoples at Home and Abroad: "Letter to Amnesty International", November 2000. http://www.ndh.net/home/kunama.

12. Rev. Tesfamariam Baraki. "A Statement on Behalf of Irobland", March 2002. http://wwww.ethiopiafirst,com

13. "Yesenbet TaTakiwitch", *Addis Zemen*, Tahsas 23, 1991

14. Dr. Ann Waters-Bayer. "Another Letter from Tigray", 1.6.99 http://soc.culture.ethiopia.moderated].

15. Ad-Hoc Committee of Zalambes-Irob," Open Letter to Mr. Kofi Annan", 10.4.01 http://www.ethiopiafirst.com.

16. The Entire Irob People. "The Ethio-Eritrea Boundary Commission's Decision Regarding the Irob Land and People". 15.5.02,. http://www.waltainfo.com.

17. "Letter from the Eritrean Erob Association", EEA, 11.3.00. http://www.Asmarino.com

18. *Abune* Tesfasellasie Medhin,. "Open Letter to Kofi Annan", 26.8.03, http://www.ethiomedia.com .

19. Francois Piguet. "Afar Region: A Deeper Crisis Looms", UNEUE, Addis Ababa. October 2002.

20. ICRC News 03/109. 17.9.03 http://www.icrc.org.

21. Military Communique 5.5.1992; Interview with Mohamooda Gaas, April 1993

22. An Afar political opposition to the new Ethiopian government also appeared in Djibouti after 1991 - the Afar Revolutionary Democratic Union (ARDU). This co-operated closely with Ugugumo for several years before formally uniting with it in the Afar Revolutionary Democratic United Front (ARDUF) in 1995.

23. ARDUF Military Communique 24.8.96.

24. "Europe's Afar Rebel Chief Defects to Meles Camp", by a Deki-Alula reporter. 24.6.02. http://www.tisjd.net.

25. Afar clan politics are too complex to be detailed here, but the present Afar Regional Government includes elements from six political parties.

26. US Committee for Refugees: "Getting Home is only Half the Challenge – Refugee reintegration in war-ravaged Eritrea". August 2001

27. US Committee for Refugees op.cit.

28. Anthony Morland . "The Scars of Battle in Western Eritrea", Tessenai, *AFP*. 16.6.00.

29. Jeffery L. Shannon. "Barentu – Hope Amid the Ruins". Eritrean Development Foundation, Asmara 13.7.00.

30. Aymeric Vincenot: "Eritrean Refugees tell Tales of Horror", Alba Refugee Camp, Eritrea, 23.8.00. *AFP*

31. Ad Hoc Committee of the Zalambesa-Irob Community "Zalambesa: A Contextual

Background Note of the Gulo-Makeda and Irob Area." 19.2.01 http://www.mediaethiopia.com

32. "Aggrieved Voices of Inhabitants of Zalambesa". *The Reporter*, July 2002 http://www.ethiopianreporter.com.

33. *Addis Tribune*, 21.11.03

34. This is a figure provided by several former senior government officials.

35. Rev. Abba Tesfamariam Baraki. "The EEBC's Crime of Injustice, the Complicity of the UN and the Betrayal of the International Community against the Irob minority in Ethiopia", 14.10.03– Http://www.Aiga1992.org.

APPENDICES

APPENDIX 1: PROPOSALS FOR A FRAMEWORK AGREEMENT FOR A PEACEFUL SETTLEMENT OF THE DISPUTE BETWEEN ERITREA AND ETHIOPIA 19 NOVEMBER 1998

We, the Heads of State and Government, mandated by the 34th Ordinary Session of the Assembly of Heads of State and Government of the Organization of African Unity, held in Ouagadougou, Burkina Faso, from 8 to 10 June 1998, to contribute towards the search for a peaceful and lasting solution to the unfortunate conflict which erupted between the brotherly countries, the State of Eritrea and the Federal Democratic Republic of Ethiopia;

Deeply affected by the outbreak of the conflict between the two countries that are united by historic links of brotherhood and a common culture;

Saddened by this conflict which occurred at a time when the Federal Democratic Republic of Ethiopia and the State of Eritrea had launched a new era of relations built on a partnership and a common vision and ideals as regards the future of their peoples, the region and the whole continent;

Noting, however, that differences had emerged between the two countries relating particularly to their common border, differences which the two countries endeavored to resolve peacefully;

Deploring the fact that, notwithstanding those efforts, an open conflict broke out between the two brotherly countries, with which our 34th summit was seized;

Paying tribute to the commendable efforts made by friendly countries aimed at finding a peaceful solution to the conflict;

Conscious of the fact that resorting to the use of force results in loss of human lives, the destruction of property and socio-economic infrastructures as well as creating a division between the peoples, all the things which the two brotherly countries and our continent cannot afford at a time when all efforts must be channeled towards the promotion of peace and development which we greatly owe to our peoples;

Encouraged by the commitment made by the two Parties to the OAU High-Level Delegation to settle the conflict peacefully and by their positive response to its appeal to continue to observe the moratorium on air strikes and to maintain the present situation of non-hostilities;

Having considered and endorsed the Report and Recommendations of the Committee of Ambassadors, as submitted by the Ministerial Committee to the parties on 1 August 1998 in Ouagadougou, Burkina Faso;

Having listened to the two Parties and made an in-depth analysis of their respective positions, taking into account their legitimate concerns and after having thought deeply about the ways and means likely to contribute to the peaceful settlement of the crisis in a ffair and objective manner;

MAKE on behalf of Africa, its peoples and leaders, a solemn and brotherly appeal to the Leaders of the State of Eritrea and the Federal Democratic Republic of Ethiopia to do everything in their power to opt for a peaceful settlement of the dispute and find a just and lasting solution to the conflict;

SUBMIT, hereunder, for the consideration of the two Parties, the elements of a Framework Agreement based on the following principles:

-resolution of the present crisis and any other dispute between them through peaceful and legal means in accordance with the principles enshrined in the Charter of the Organization of African Unity;

-rejection of the use of force as a means of imposing solutions to disputes;

-respect for the borders existing at independence as stated in Resolution AHG/Res. 16(1) adopted by the OAU Summit in Cairo in 1964 and, in this regard, determine them on the basis of pertinent colonial Treaties and applicable international law, making use, to that end, of technical means to demarcate the borders and, in the case of controversy, resort to the appropriate mechanism of arbitration.

We recommend that:

1. The two Parties commit themselves to an immediate cessation of hostilities;

2. In order to defuse tension and build confidence, the two Parties commit themselves to put an immediate end to any action and any form of expression likely to perpetrate or exacerbate the climate of hostility and tension between them thereby jeopardizing the efforts aimed at finding a peaceful solution to the conflict;

3. In order to create conditions conducive to a comprehensive and lasting settlement of the conflict through the delimitation and demarcation of the border, the armed forces presently in Badme Town and its environs, should be redeployed to the positions they held before 6 May 1998 as a mark of goodwill and consideration for our continental Organization, it being understood that this redeployment will not prejudge the final status of the area concerned, which will be determined at the end of the delimitation and demarcation of the border and, if need be, through an appropriate mechanism of arbitration;

4. This redeployment be supervised by a Group of Military Observers which will be deployed by the OAU with the support of the United Nations. The Group of Military Observers will also assist the reinstated Civilian Administration in the maintenance of law and order during the interim period;

5.a) The redeployment be subsequently extended to all other contested areas along the common border within the framework of demilitarization of the entire common border and as a measure for defusing the tension and facilitating the delimitation and demarcation process. In effect, the demilitarization which will begin with the Mereb Setit segment, will then extend to the Bada area and the border as a whole;

b)   The demilitarization process be supervised by the Group of Military Observers;

6.a) The two Parties commit themselves to make use of the services of experts of the UN Cartographic Unit, in collaboration with the OAU and other experts agreed upon by the two Parties, to carry out the delimitation and demarcation of the border between the two countries within a time-frame of 6 months which could be extended on the recommendation of the cartographic experts;

b)   Once the entire border has been delimited and demarcated, the legitimate authority will immediately exercise full and sovereign jurisdiction over the territory which will have been recognized as belonging to them;

7.   In order to determine the origins of the conflict, an investigation be carried out on the incidents of 6 May 1998 and on any other incident prior to that date which could have contributed to a misunderstanding between the two Parties regarding their common border, including the incidents of July - August 1997.

8.a) At the humanitarian level, the two Parties commit themselves to put an end to measures directed against the civilian population and refrain from any action which can cause further hardship and suffering to each other's nationals;

b)   The two Parties also commit themselves to addressing the negative socio-economic impact of the crisis on the civilian population, particularly, those persons who had been deported;

c)   In order to contribute to the establishment of a climate of confidence, the OAU, in collaboration with the United Nations, deploy a team of Human Rights Monitors in both countries;

9.a) In order to determine the modalities for the implementation of the Framework Agreement, a Follow-up Committee of the two Parties be established under the auspices of the OAU High-Level Delegation with the active participation and assistance of the United Nations;

b)   The committee begin its work as soon as the Framework Agreement is signed;

10. The OAU and the UN working closely with the international community, particularly, the European Union, endeavor to mobilize resources for the resettlement of displaced persons and the demobilization of troops currently deployed along the common border of both countries;

11. The Organization of African Unity, in close cooperation with the United Nations, will be the guarantor for the scrupulous implementation of all the provisions of the Framework Agreement, in the shortest possible time. On the decision of the OAU Delegation of leaders that met in Ouagadougou, the above peace plan was later submitted to the OAU central body for conflict resolution.

APPENDIX 2: MODALITIES FOR THE IMPLEMENTATION OF THE OAU FRAMEWORK AGREEMENT ON THE SETTLEMENT OF THE DISPUTE BETWEEN ETHIOPIA AND ERITREA

Submitted to both parties on Monday 12 July 1999 and reported to the 35th OAU Heads of State and Government Summit in Algiers on Wednesday, 14 July 1999

The two Parties reaffirm their commitment to the principle of the non-use of force to settle disputes.

The two Parties reaffirm their acceptance of the Framework Agreement and commit themselves to implement it in good faith.

There shall be a return to positions held prior to 6 May 1998.

On the basis of these principles, the two Parties agree on the following modalities for the implementation of the Framework Agreement:

1. The Eritrean Government commits itself to redeploy its forces outside the territories they occupied after 6 May 1998.

2. The Ethiopian Government commits itself to redeploy, thereafter, its forces from positions take after 6 February 1999 and which were not under Ethiopian administration before May 6, 1998.

3. The two Parties agree to put an end to all military activities and all forms of expression likely to sustain and exacerbate the climate of hostility and thus compromise the implementation of the Framework Agreement.

4. The redeployment of troops shall commence immediately after the cessation of hostilities. This redeployment shall not, in any way, prejudice the final status of the territories concerned, it being understood that this status will be determined at the end of the border delimitation and demarcation.

5. The modalities for the re-establishment of the civilian Administration and population in the concerned territories shall be worked out after the cessation of hostilities.

6. The two Parties accept the deployment of Military Observers by the OAU in cooperation with the United Nations. The Group of Military Observers will supervise the redeployment of troops as stipulated in the present modalities and carry out all other duties that are entrusted to it, in conformity with the relevant provisions of the Framework Agreement.

7. The two Parties commit themselves to sign a formal Ceasefire Agreement which provides for the detailed modalities for the implementation of the Framework Agreement.

APPENDIX 3: TECHNICAL ARRANGEMENTS FOR THE IMPLEMENTATION OF THE OAU FRAMEWORK AGREEMENT AND ITS MODALITIES AUGUST 1999

- Recalling that the Government of the State of Eritrea and the Government of the Federal Democratic Republic of Ethiopia, hereinafter referred to as the Parties, have accepted the OAU Framework Agreement and the Modalities for its implementation;

- Underlining that the OAU Framework Agreement and the Modalities have been endorsed by the 35th Ordinary Session of the Assembly of Heads of State and Government, held in Algiers, Algeria, from 12 to 14 July, 1999, as well as strongly supported by the United Nations Security Council and accepted as they are by the Parties;

- Having carefully examined the views submitted by the Parties;

- Recalling the acceptance by the Parties that any interpretation of the OAU Framework Agreement and the Modalities is the sole responsibility of the OAU and its Current Chairman;

- Noting that the present Technical Arrangements have been elaborated on the basis of the letter and spirit of the principles contained in the OAU Framework Agreement and the Modalities, in particular the respect for the borders existing at independence, as stated in Resolution AHG/Res. 16(I) adopted by the OAU Summit in Cairo in 1964, the resolution of disputes through peaceful and legal means, in accordance with the principles enshrined in the Charters of the Organisation of African Unity and the United Nations, and the non use of force to settle disputes;

- Further recalling that the present Technical Arrangements are the result of collective work of the OAU, the United Nations, the United States and other interested partners;

- Stressing that the ultimate goal of the process is to find a peaceful and lasting solution to the conflict:

1- The Parties agree on the principles and other provisions contained in the Framework Agreement and the Modalities and accept the Technical Arrangements (which includes its four Annexes) as binding. In that regard, the Parties agree to use the Framework Agreement, the Modalities and the Technical Arrangements as the sole basis for resolving the dispute.

The Parties will initiate separate requests to the Secretaries General of the United Nations and the OAU as necessary for assistance to implement the Framework Agreement, the Modalities and the Technical Arrangements.

2- In order to facilitate the process of implementing the Framework Agreement, the Modalities and the Technical Arrangements, including the work of the Commission which will be charged with determining the redeployment positions (referred to as the Neutral Commission in paragra 3) and the establishment of a peacekeeping mission, the Parties agree to put an end to all military activities and all forms of expression likely to sustain and exacerbate the climate of hostility.

In particular, the Parties agree to the following:

a-cessation of all armed air and land attacks;

b-cessation of any other action that may impede the implementation of the Framework Agreement, the Modalities and the Technical Arrangements;

c-guarantee the free movement of the peacekeeping mission and its supplies as required through and between the territories of the Parties,

d-respect and protection of the members of the peacekeeping mission, its

installations and equipment;

e-respect for international humanitarian law.

3- In order to facilitate the process of redeployment of Eritrean forces as referred to in paragraph 1 of the Modalities and, thereafter, of Ethiopian forces as referred to in paragraph 2 of the Modalities, and to facilitate the full implementation of paragraph 5 of those Modalities, with a view to returning to positions held prior to 6 May 1998, a Neutral Commission shall be established by the Current Chairman of the OAU, in consultation with the Secretaries General of the United Nations and the OAU. Utilizing whatever information it deems relevant and in consultation with the Parties, the Neutral Commission will determine what those positions were.

The Parties agree to cooperate fully with the Neutral Commission.

The Neutral Commission will endeavour to complete its work and submit its report to the Current Chairman of the OAU in three weeks.

The determination of the Neutral Commission is binding on the Parties.

The determination of the Neutral Commission shall not prejudice the final status of the territories concerned, it being understood that this status will be determined at the end of the delimitation and demarcation process.

4- In order to monitor and assist with the implementation of the Framework Agreement, the Modalities and the Technical Arrangements, and verify compliance with the implementation of the Technical Arrangements, it is understood that a peacekeeping mission will be established under the authority of the United Nations

Security Council and led by a Special Representative of the UN Secretary - General. The Special epresentative of the UN Secretary - General will liaise and work closely with the representative of the OAU Secretary-General. The deployment of the UN peacekeeping mission will be preceded by the deployment by the OAU, with the support of the United Nations, of liaison officers/observers. These liaison officers/observers will subsequently become members of the UN peacekeeping mission. The Parties will be consulted, as appropriate, throughout the establishment process.

5- In line with article 9 (a) of the Framework Agreement and in order to facilitate the implementation of the Framework Agreement, Modalities and Technical Arrangements, a Follow-up Commission (for political aspects) and a Military Co-ordination Commission (for military aspects) will be established by and under the authority of the Special Representative of the UN Secretary General. The Parties will each appoint a senior representative to the Follow-up Commission. The Special Representative of the UN Secretary General will appoint a UN senior representative as Chairman. Decisions will be made by the Chairman of the Follow-up Commission in consultation with the Parties.

The Parties will each appoint a senior military representative to the Military Co-ordination Commission. The Special Representative of the UN Secretary - General will appoint a UN senior military representative as Chairman. Decisions will be made by the Chairman of the Military Co-ordination Commission in consultation with the Parties.

In fulfilling their mandate, the Follow-up Commission and the Military Co-ordination Commission will co-ordinate and resolve issues pertaining to the implementation of the Framework Agreement, Modalities and Technical Arrangements.

6- Upon the signing of the Framework Agreement, the Modalities and the Technical Arrangements, both Parties will conduct demining activities with a view to creating the conditions necessary for the redeployment of the peacekeeping mission, the return of civilian administration and the return of population as well as the delimitation and demarcation of their common border (see Annex I).

The Peacekeeping mission, in conjunction with the United Nations Mine Action Service, will assist the Parties' demining efforts by providing technical advice and co-ordination.

The Parties shall, as necessary, seek additional demining assistance from the peacekeeping mission.

7- The Parties will submit detailed redeployment plans to the peacekeeping mission within 5 days of receipt of the determination of the Neutral Commission (see paragraph 3 above and Annex II).

8- The process of redeployment and restoration of civilian administration will then begin, it being understood that this process shall not prejudice the final status of the territories concerned, which will be determined at the end of the delimitation and demarcation process.

Following approval of the redeployment plans of the Parties by the peacekeeping mission, the sequence will be as follows:

a-Eritrea re-deploys its troops within 2 weeks. This redeployment is verified by the peacekeeping mission;

b-upon verification of Eritrean redeployment by peacekeeping mission, the peacekeeping mission observes and assists the restoration by Ethiopia of the civilian administration, including police and local militia, within 7 days, to enable the restored civilian administration to prepare for the return of the population;

c-as soon as paragraphs 8a and 8b above are completed, Ethiopia re-deploys its troops within 2 weeks. This redeployment is verified by the peacekeeping mission;

d-upon verification of Ethiopian redeployment by the peacekeeping mission, the peacekeeping mission observes and assists the restoration by Eritrea of the civilian administration, including police and local militia, within 7 days, to enable the restored civilian administration to prepare for the return of the population.

9- In order to enhance the security of local populations in and returning to areas where civilian administration is restored:

a-the parties commit themselves to:

a.1 full co-operation with the peacekeeping mission;

a.2 close co-operation between the restored civilian administrations and the international civilian component of the peacekeeping mission, which will observe compliance by the restored civilian administrations:

a.2.1-with prohibitions on displacement and deportation of civilian populations;

a.2.2-with facilitation of human rights monitoring;

a.2.3-with prohibitions of display of weapons by militia in populated areas where civilian administration is restored;

b-the peacekeeping mission will:

b.1-observe and assist if requested and as appropriate, police in areas where civilian administration is restored;

b.2-establish, as necessary local liaison and grievance resolution mechanism, ensuring access by the local population to those mechanisms.

10- In order to determine the origins of the conflict, an investigation will be carried out of the incidents of 6 May 1998 and of any other incident prior to that date which could have contributed to a misunderstanding between the Parties regarding their common border, including the incidents of July/August 1997.

The investigation will be carried out by an independent, impartial body appointed in accordance with appended (Annex IV) time-line by the Current Chairman of the OAU, in consultation with the Secretaries General of the United Nations and the OAU.

The independent body will endeavour to submit its report to the Current Chairman of the OAU within 3 to 6 months.

The Parties agree to cooperate fully with the independent body and accept its determination.

11- The Parties agree that the delimitation work on the ground will commence segment by segment, beginning with areas of redeployment, moving to other contested areas and, finally, to the remaining common border.

Upon the acceptance by the parties of the delimitation of each segment, the binding demarcation of that segment will be carried out. Such signed acceptance shall be given to the UN Cartographic Unit within one week, unless arbitration is requested by either Party (see paragraph 13 below).

The delimitation and demarcation process will be done on the basis of pertinent colonial treaties and applicable international law.

12- The Parties agree to demilitarise in those areas as may be required by the peacekeeping mission in order to defuse tension and facilitate the delimitation and demarcation process (see Annex III).

13- Delimitation and demarcation will be conducted by the UN Cartographic Unit, supported by other Experts the Unit may employ.

In line with article 6(a) of the Framework Agreement, delimitation/demarcation will be carried out expeditiously and completed within 6 months, unless extended by the Special Representative of the UN Secretary - General at the request of Cartographic Experts.

Should the need arise for arbitration over delimitation, a Boundary Commission shall be established by the United Nations Secretary - General in consultation with the OAU Current Chairman. The Commission shall decide such issues as expeditiously as possible and on the basis of pertinent colonial treaties and applicable international law.

The Parties agree to accept the outcome of the arbitration as binding.

14- Consistent with paragraph 8(a), 8(b) and 10 of the Framework Agreement, the Parties commit themselves to addressing all humanitarian concerns, resulting from the conflict, particularly the issues of those persons who have been deported or displaced, as well as the socio-economic consequences of the dispute.

For their part, and in accordance with the pertinent provisions of the Framework Agreement, the OAU and the United Nations, working closely with the International Community, will endeavour to mobilise resources to assist in addressing such concerns.

The Parties agree to refer any specific claim on such issues to an appropriate mechanism of arbitration for binding resolution, should efforts at negotiated settlement or mediation not succeed.

If the Parties are unable to agree on the appropriate mechanism of arbitration within a period of three months starting from the signing, the UN Secretary - General, in consultation with the OAU Secretary - General, will determine the appropriate mechanism of arbitration.

15- As the demarcation process is completed in each segment, the legitimate authority will assume full and sovereign jurisdiction over that part of territory which will have been recognised as being within its boundary.

16- The Parties agree to sign and implement in good faith the OAU Framework Agreement for the settlement of the dispute, the Modalities for the Implementation of the Framework Agreement and the Technical Arrangements for the Implementation of the Framework Agreement and its Modalities (including its Annexes listed below*).

17- The OAU and the United Nations will be the guarantors for the scrupulous implementation of all the provisions of the OAU Framework Agreement, the Modalities for the Implementation of the Framework Agreement and the Technical Arrangements for the Implementation of the Framework Agreement and its Modalities.

Annex I to the Technical Arrangements for the Implementation of the OAU Framework Agreement and its Modalities (Demining activities) Annex II to the Technical Arrangements for the Implementation of the OAU Framework Agreement and its Modalities (Redeployment plans) Annex III to the Technical Arrangements for the Implementation of the OAU Framework Agreement and its Modalities (Local demilitarisation plans) Annex IV to the Technical Arrangements for the Implementation of the OAU

Framework Agreement and its Modalities (Implementation planning timeline)

Annexes to the Technical Arrangements for the Implementation of the OAU Framework Agreement and its Modalities

(Demining Activities)

ANNEX I TO THE TECHNICAL ARRANGEMENTS FOR THE IMPLEMENTATION OF THE OAU

FRAMEWORK AGREEMENT AND ITS MODALITIES

Demining activities include submission of the following to the peacekeeping mission:

- maps detailing dimension and exact location of all minefields;

- exact composition by type of mines and number of mines for each minefield;

- plan for clearing of all minefields;

- plan for marking minefields;

- plan for disposal of cleared mines;

- any other information needed for verification.

Peacekeeping mission will observe, verify and assist if necessary all demining activities.

ANNEX II TO THE TECHNICAL ARRANGEMENTS FOR THE IMPLEMENTATION OF THE OAU

FRAMEWORK AGREEMENT AND ITS MODALITIES

(Redpolyment plans)

Redeployment plans will include:

- current location of each unit to redeploy;

- size and composition of each unit;

- exact route each unit will utilize to redeploy;

- exact location each redeploying unit will redeploy to;

- start time of redeployment for each redeploying unit;

- estimated closure time for each redeploying unit;

- redeploying units are not authorized to deviate from the plan nor can they move form their new location unless approved by the peacekeeping mission;

- any other information needed to complete verification.

The Parties agree that redeployment will be completed within 14 days after the redeployment plans are approved by the peacekeeping mission.

The Parties agree to suspend any types of military flights in the vicinity of redeployment areas during the period of redeployment.

The Parties agree that the peacekeeping mission will observe and verify redeployment.

The peacekeeping mission will verify that the troops of one Party do not move into areas from which the other Party has redeployed.

ANNEX III TO THE TECHNICAL ARRANGEMENTS FOR THE IMPLEMENTATION OF THE OAU

FRAMEWORK AGREEMENT AND ITS MODALITIES

(Local Demilitarization Plans)

Local demilitarization plans will include:

- current location of each unit to demilitarize;

- size and composition of each unit;

- exact route each unit will utilize to demilitarize;

- exact location each demilitarizing unit will move to;

- movement start time of demilitarization for each unit;

- estimated closure time for each demilitarizing unit;

- demilitarizing units are not authorized to deviate from the plan nor can they move form their new location unless coordinated with the peacekeeping mission;

- any other information needed to complete verification.

The Parties agree that demilitarization will be completed within 7 days after the demilitarization plans are approved by the peacekeeping mission.

Deployment to original positions will commence upon the determination of the peacekeeping mission.

The Parties agree to suspend any types of military flights in the vicinity of demilitarization areas during the period of demilitarization.

The Parties agree that the peacekeeping mission will observe and verify demilitarization.

ANNEX IV TO THE TECHNICAL ARRANGEMENTS OF THE OAU FRAMEWORK AGREEMENT AND ITS MODALITIES

Implementation Planning Time-Line

D-Day:Signing of the Framework Agreement, Modalities and Technical Arrangements.

D+2: Cessation of hostilities as provided for in paragraph 2 of the Technical Arrangements.

D+3: Neutral Commission established.

Initiation of demining activities by the Parties.

D+4: Parties forward requests to the UN Secretary General.

D+5: Commencement of the work of the UN Cartographic Unit.

D+10: Appointment of OAU Representative.

D+14: Deployment by the OAU, with the support of the United Nations, of liaison officers/observers.

The Neutral Commission begins its work on the ground.

D+25: Establishment of the Follow-up Commission and the Military Coordination Commission.

Appointment of the Special Representative of the UN Secretary General.

Parties designate chief representatives to the Follow-up Commission and

Military Coordination Commission (one from each Party for each of the Commissions).

D+35: Neutral Commission submits its determination.

D+40: Neutral Commission's report released to the Parties.

D+45: Parties submit redeployment plans to the peacekeeping mission.

D+48: Redeployment plans approved by the peacekeeping mission.

D+49: Observers in position to observe and verify redeployment.

D+50: Commencement of redeployment of Eritrean forces.

D+64: Redeployment of Eritrean forces completed and verified by peacekeeping mission.

 Restoration of civilian administration by Ethiopia commences.

D+71: Restoration of civilian administration by Ethiopia completed.

 Redeployment of Ethiopian forces commences.

D+85: Redeployment of Ethiopian forces completed and verified by the peacekeeping mission.

 Restoration of civilian administration by Eritrea commences.

D+92: Restoration of civilian administration by Eritrea completed.

Establishement of an independent body to investigate the origins of the conflict.

D+185: Delimitation/demarcation completed unless extended at the request of the Cartographic Experts.

 Return of legitimate authorities completed, unless delimitation/demarcation has been extended.

Appendices

APPENDIX 4: AGREEMENT ON CESSATION OF HOSTILITIES BETWEEN ETHIOPIA AND ERITREA. ORGANISATION OF AFRICAN UNITY 18 JUNE 2000

Proposal of the OAU for an Agreement on Cessation of Hostilities Between the Government of the Federal Democratic Republic of Ethiopia and the Government of the State of Eritrea

Having taken part in the Proximity Talks called by the Organization of African Unity in Algiers from 29 May to 10 June 2000, under the Chairmanship of Algeria the Current Chair of the OAU and with the participation of its partners namely the United States and the European Union,

Committing themselves to the following principles:

- Resolution of the present crisis and any other dispute between them through peaceful and legal means in accordance with the principles enshrined in the charters of the OAU and the United Nations;

- Rejection of the use of force as a means of imposing solutions to disputes;

- Respect for the borders existing at independence as stated in resolution AHG/ Res 16(1) adopted by the OAU Summit in Cairo in 1964 and, in this regard, determine them on the basis of pertinent colonial treaties and applicable international law, making use, to that end, of technical means to demarcate the borders and, in case of controversy, resort to the appropriate mechanism of arbitration;

Reaffirming their acceptance of the OAU Framework Agreement and the Modalities for its Implementation which have been endorsed by the 35th ordinary session of the Assembly of Heads of State and Government, held in Algiers, Algeria from 12 to 14 July 1999, Taking into account the latest developments in this crisis,

Commit themselves to the following:

1. 1 - Immediate cessation of hostilities starting from the signature of this document. In particular the two Parties agree to the following: 1-1 cessation of all armed air and land attacks;

   1- 2 guarantee of the free movement and access of the Peacekeeping Mission and its supplies as required through the territories of the Parties; 1- 3 respect and protection of the members of the Peacekeeping Mission, its installations and equipment.

2. - A Peacekeeping Mission shall be deployed by the United Nations under the auspices of the OAU.

271

3.   - The mandate of the Peacekeeping Mission shall be:
     3-1 monitor the cessation of hostilities;
     3-2 monitor the redeployment of Ethiopian troops;
     3-3 ensure the observance of the security commitments agreed by the two
     Parties in this document, in particular those provided for in paragraph 14;

4.   -The size and the composition of the Peacekeeping Mission shall be adapted
     to the mission assigned to it and shall be determined by the Secretaries General
     of the United Nations and the OAU with the acceptance of the two Parties.

5.   -The Peacekeeping Mission shall terminate when the delimitation-
     demarcation process of the border has been completed.

6.   - A Military Co-ordination Commission shall be established by the OAU and
     the United Nations with agreement of the two Parties in order to facilitate the
     functions of the Peacekeeping Mission. It shall be composed of representatives
     of the two Parties and chaired by the leader of the Peacekeeping Mission.

7.   - The mandate of the Military Co-ordination Commission shall be to co-
     ordinate and resolve issues relating to the implementation of the mandate of
     the Peacekeeping Mission as defined in the present document. The Commission
     shall deal with military issues arising during the implementation period.

8.   - Upon the signing of the present document, both Parties shall conduct
     demining activities as soon as possible with a view to creating the conditions
     necessary for the deployment of the Peacekeeping Mission, the return of
     civilian administration and the return of population as well as the delimitation
     and demarcation of their common border. The Peacekeeping Mission, in
     conjunction with the United Nations Mine Action Service, will assist the Parties'
     demining efforts by providing technical advice and coordination. The Parties
     shall, as necessary, seek additional demining assistance from the Peacekeeping
     Mission.

9.   - Ethiopia shall submit redeployment plans for its troops from positions
     taken after 6 February 1999, and which were not under Ethiopian administration
     before 6 May 1998, to the Peacekeeping Mission. This redeployment shall be
     completed within two weeks after the deployment of the Peacekeeping Mission
     and verified by it.

10. - In accordance with the principle established in paragraph 3 of the Framework
     Agreement, it is understood that the redeployment of Ethiopian forces will
     not prejudice the final status of the contested areas, which will be determined
     at the end of the delimitation and demarcation of the border and, if need be,
     through an appropriate mechanism of arbitration.

11. - Upon verification of Ethiopian redeployment by the Peacekeeping Mission,

Eritrean civilian administration, including police and local militia, will be restored to prepare for the return of the population.

12. - In order to contribute to the reduction of tension and to the establishment of a climate of calm and confidence, as well as to create conditions conducive to a comprehensive and lasting settlement of the conflict through the delimitation and demarcation of the border, the Eritrean forces shall remain at a distance of 25 km (artillery range) from positions to which Ethiopian forces shall redeploy in accordance with paragraph 9 of this document. This zone of separation shall be referred to in this document as the "temporary security zone."

13. - The Eritrean forces at positions defined in paragraph 12 of this document, as well as Ethiopian forces at positions defined in paragraph 9 of this document, shall be monitored by the Peacekeeping Mission.

14. - Ethiopia commits itself not to move its troops beyond the positions it administered before 6 May 1998. Eritrea commits itself not to move its troops beyond the positions defined in paragraph 12 above. The OAU and the United Nations commit themselves to guarantee the respect for this commitment of the two Parties until the determination of the common border on the basis of pertinent colonial treaties and applicable international law, through delimitation/demarcation and in case of controversy, through the appropriate mechanism of arbitration. This guarantee shall be comprised of:

a) measures to be taken by the international community should one or both of the Parties violate this commitment, including appropriate measures to be taken under Chapter VII of the United Nations Charter by the UN Security Council;

b) actions by the Peacekeeping Mission to monitor key and sensitive areas of the temporary security zone through liaison officers at the division and regimental levels with Ethiopian and Eritrean units deployed at key points along the temporary security zone on their respective sides; regular patrols; reconnaissance missions; and challenge inspections throughout the temporary security zone coordinated through the Military Co-ordination Commission with the participation of liaison officers of the Parties as decided by the Chairman of the Military Co-ordination Commission;

c) deployment to and continuous monitoring by military units of the Peacekeeping Mission at posts in key and sensitive positions within the temporary security zone in order to monitor the implementation of the commitments made by both Parties in paragraphs 9 and 12 of this document;
d) periodic technical verification of the temporary security zone to help determine compliance with this document.

15.   - Upon the signature of the present document, the two Parties shall initiate separate requests to the Secretaries General of the OAU and the United Nations, as necessary, for assistance to implement this document.

For the Government of the Federal Democratic Republic Ethiopia
For the Government of the State of Eritrea

APPENDIX 5: AGREEMENT BETWEEN THE GOVERNMENT OF THE FEDERAL DEMOCRATIC REEPUBLIC OF ETHIOPIA AND THE GOVERNMENT OF THE STATE OF ERITREA 12 DECEMBER 2000

The Government of the Federal Democratic Republic of Ethiopia and the Government of the State of Eritrea (the "parties"),

Reaffirming their acceptance of the Organization of African Unity ("OAU") Framework Agreement and the Modalities for its Implementation, which have been endorsed by the 35th ordinary session of the Assembly of Heads of State and Government, held in Algiers, Algeria, from 12 to 14 July 1999,

Recommitting themselves to the Agreement on Cessation of Hostilities, signed in Algiers on 18 June 2000,

Welcoming the commitment of the OAU and United Nations, through their endorsement of the Framework Agreement and Agreement on Cessation of Hostilities, to work closely with the international community to mobilize resources for the resettlement of displaced persons, as well as rehabilitation and peace building in both countries,

Have agreed as follows:

Article 1

1. The parties shall permanently terminate military hostilities between themselves. Each party shall refrain from the threat or use of force against the other.

2. The parties shall respect and fully implement the provisions of the Agreement on Cessation of Hostilities.

Article 2

1. In fulfilling their obligations under international humanitarian law, including the 1949 Geneva Conventions relative to the protection of victims of armed conflict ("1949 Geneva Conventions"), and in cooperation with the International Committee of the Red Cross, the parties shall without delay release and repatriate all prisoners of war.

2. In fulfilling their obligations under international humanitarian law, including the 1949 Geneva Conventions, and in cooperation with the International Committee of the Red Cross, the parties shall without delay, release and repatriate or return to their last place of residence all other persons detained as a result of the armed conflict.

3.   The parties shall afford humane treatment to each other's nationals and persons of each other's national origin within their respective territories.

Article 3

1.   In order to determine the origins of the conflict, an investigation will be carried out on the incidents of 6 May 1998 and on any other incident prior to that date which could have contributed to a misunderstanding between the parties regarding their common border, including the incidents of July and August 1997.

2.   The investigation will be carried out by an independent, impartial body appointed by the Secretary General of the OAU, in consultation with the Secretary General of the United Nations and the two parties.

3.   The independent body will endeavor to submit its report to the Secretary General of the OAU in a timely fashion.

4.   The parties shall cooperate fully with the independent body.

5.   The Secretary General of the OAU will communicate a copy of the report to each of the two parties, which shall consider it in accordance with the letter and spirit of the Framework Agreement and the Modalities.

Article 4

1.   Consistent with the provisions of the Framework Agreement and the Agreement on Cessation of Hostilities, the parties reaffirm the principle of respect for the borders existing at independence as stated in resolution AHG/Res. 16(1) adopted by the OAU Summit in Cairo in 1964, and, in this regard, that they shall be determined on the basis of pertinent colonial treaties and applicable international law.

2.   The parties agree that a neutral Boundary Commission composed of five members shall be established with a mandate to delimit and demarcate the colonial treaty border based on pertinent colonial treaties (1900, 1902 and 1908) and applicable international law. The Commission shall not have the power to make decisions ex aequo et bono.

3.   The Commission shall be located in the Hague.

4.   Each party shall, by written notice to the United Nations Secretary General, appoint two commissioners within 45 days from the effective date of this Agreement, neither of whom shall be nationals or permanent residents of the party making the appointment. In the event that a party fails to name one or both of its party-appointed commissioners within the specified time, the Secretary-General of the United Nations shall make the appointment.

5. The president of the Commission shall be selected by the party-appointed commissioners or, failing their agreement within 30 days of the date of appointment of the latest party-appointed commissioner, by the Secretary-General of the United Nations after consultation with the parties. The president shall be neither a national nor permanent resieent of either party.

6. In the event of the death or resignation of a commissioner in the course of the proceedings, a substitute commissioner shall be appointed or chosen pursuant to the procedure set forth in this paragraph that was applicable to the appointment or choice of the commissioner being replaced.

7. The UN Cartographer shall serve as Secretary to the Commission and undertake such tasks as assigned to him by the Commission, making use of the technical expertise of the UN Cartographic Unit. The Commission may also engage the services of additional experts as it deems necessary

8. Within 45 days after the effective date of this Agreement, each party shall provide to the Secretary its claims and evidence relevant to the mandate of the Commission. These shall be provided to the other party by the Secretary.

9. After reviewing such evidence and within 45 days of its receipt, but not earlier than 15 days after the Commission is constituted, the Secretary shall transmit to the Commission and the parties any materials relevant to the mandate of the Commission as well as his findings identifying those portions of the border as to which there appears to be no dispute between the parties. The Secretary shall also transmit to the Commission all the claims and evidence presented by the parties.

10. With regard to those portions of the border about which there appears to be controversy, as well as any portions of the border identified pursuant to paragraph 9 with respect to which either party believes there to be controversy, the parties shall present their written and oral submissions and any additional evidence directly to the Commission, in accordance with its procedures.

11. The Commission shall adopt its own rules of procedure based upon the 1992 Permanent Court of Arbitration Optional Rules for Arbitrating Disputes Between Two States. Filing deadlines for the parties' written submissions shall be simultaneous rather than consecutive. All decisions of the Commission shall be made by a majority of the commissioners.

12. The Commission shall commence its work not more than 15 days after it is constituted and shall endeavor to make its decision concerning delimitation of the border within six months of its first meeting. The Commission shall take this objective into consideration when establishing its schedule. At its discretion, the Commission may extend this deadline.

13. Upon reaching a final decision regarding delimitation of the borders, the

Commission shall transmit its decision to the parties and Secretaries General of the OAU and the United Nations for publication, and the Commission shall arrange for expeditious demarcation.

14. The parties agree to cooperate with the Commission, its experts and other staff in all respects during the process of delimitation and demarcation, including the facilitation of access to territory they control. Each party shall accord to the Commission and its employees the same privileges and immunities as are accorded to diplomatic agents under the Vienna Convention on Diplomatic Relations.

15. The parties agree that the delimitation and demarcation determinations of the Commission shall be final and binding. Each party shall respect the border so determined, as well as territorial integrity and sovereignty of the other party.

16. Recognizing that the results of the delimitation and demarcation process are not yet known, the parties request the United Nations to facilitate resolution of problems which may arise due to the transfer of territorial control, including the consequences for individuals residing in previously disputed territory.

17. The expenses of the Commission shall be done equally by the two parties. To defray its expenses, the Commission may accept donations from the United Nations Trust Fund established under paragraph 8 of Security Council Resolution 1177 of 26 June 1998.

Article 5

1. Consistent with the Framework Agreement, in which the parties commit themselves to addressing the negative socio-economic impact of the crisis on the civilian population, including the impact on those persons who have been deported, a neutral Claims Commission shall be established. The mandate of the Commission is to decide through binding arbitration all claims for loss, damage or injury by one Government against the other, and by nationals (including both natural and juridical persons) of one party against the Government of the other party or entities owned or controlled by the other party that are (a) related to the conflict that was the subject of the Framework Agreement, the Modalities for its Implementation and the Cessation of Hostilities Agreement, and (b) result from violations of international humanitarian law, including the 1949 Geneva Conventions, or other violations of international law. The Commission shall not hear claims arising from the cost of military operations, preparing for military operations, or the use of force, except to the extent that such claims involve violations of international humanitarian law.

2. The Commission shall consist of five arbitrators. Each party shall, by written notice to the United Nations Secretary General, appoint two members within 45 days from the effective date of this agreement, neither of whom shall be nationals or permanent residents of the party making the appointment. In the event that a

party fails to name one or both of its party-appointed arbitrators within the specified time, the Secretary-General of the United Nations shall make the appointment.

3. The president of the Commission shall be selected by the party-appointed arbitrators or failing their agreement within 30 days of the date of appointment of the latest party-appointed arbitrator, by the Secretary-General of the United Nations after consultation with the parties. The president shall be neither a national not permanent resident of either party.

4. In the event of the death or resignation of a member of the Commission in the course of the proceedings, a substitute member shall be appointed or chosen pursuant to the procedure set forth in this paragraph that was applicable to the appointment or choice of the arbitrator being replaced.

5. The Commission shall be located in The Hague. At its discretion it may hold hearings and conduct investigations in the territory of either party, or at such other location as it deems expedient.

6. The Commission shall be empowered to employ such professional, administrative and clerical staff as it deems necessary to accomplish its work, including establishment of a Registry. The Commission may also retain consultants and experts to facilitate the expeditious completion of its work.

7. The Commission shall adopt its own rules of procedure based upon the 1992 Permanent Court of Arbitration Optional Rules for Arbitrating Disputes Between Two States. All decisions of the Commission shall be made by a majority of the commissioners.

8. Claims shall be submitted to the Commission by each of the parties on its own behalf and on behalf of its nationals, including both natural and juridical persons. All claims submitted to the Commission shall be filed no later than one year from the effective date of this agreement. Except for claims submitted to another mutually agreed settlement mechanism in accordance with paragraph 16 or filed in another forum prior to the effective date of this agreement, the Commission shall be the sole forum for adjudicating claims described in paragraph 1 or filed under paragraph 9 of this Article, and any such claims which could have been and were not submitted by that deadline shall be extinguished, in accordance with international law.

9. In appropriate cases, each party may file claims on behalf of persons of Ethiopian or Eritrean origin who may not be its nationals. Such claims shall be considered by the Commission on the same basis as claims submitted on behalf of that party's nationals.

10. In order to facilitate the expeditious resolution of these disputes, the Commission shall be authorized to adopt such methods of efficient case management and mass

claims processing as it deems appropriate, such as expedited procedures for processing claims and checking claims on a sample basis for further verification only if circumstances warrant.

11. Upon application of either of the parties, the Commission may decide to consider specific claims, or categories of claims, on a priority basis.

12. The Commission shall commence its work not more than 15 days after it is constituted and shall endeavor to complete its work within three years of the date when the period for filing claims closes pursuant to paragraph 8.

13. In considering claims, the Commission shall apply relevant rules of international law. The Commission shall not have the power to make decisions ex aequo et bono.

14. Interest, costs and fees may be awarded.

15. The expenses of the Commission shall be borne equally by the parties. Each party shall pay any invoice form the Commission within 30 days of its receipt.

16. The parties may agree at any time to settle outstanding claims, individually or by categories, through direct negotiation or by reference to another mutually agreed settlement mechanism.

17. Decisions and awards of the commission shall be final and binding. The parties agree to honor all decisions and to pay any monetary awards rendered against them promptly.

18. Each party shall accord to members of the Commission and its employees the privileges and immunities that are accorded to diplomatic agents under the Vienna Convention on Diplomatic Relations.

Article 6

1. This agreement shall enter into force on the date of signature.

2. The parties authorize the Secretary General of the OAU to register this agreement with the Secretariat of the United Nations in accordance with article 102(1) of the Charter of the United Nations.

DONE at [Algiers, Algeria] on the [12th] day of December, 2000, in duplicate, in the English language.

FOR THE GOVERNMENT OF THE FEDERAL DEMOCRATIC REPUBLIC OF ETHIOPIA:
[Prime Minister Meles Zenawi]
FOR THE GOVERNMENT OF THE STATE OF ERITREA:
[President Issaias Afewerki]

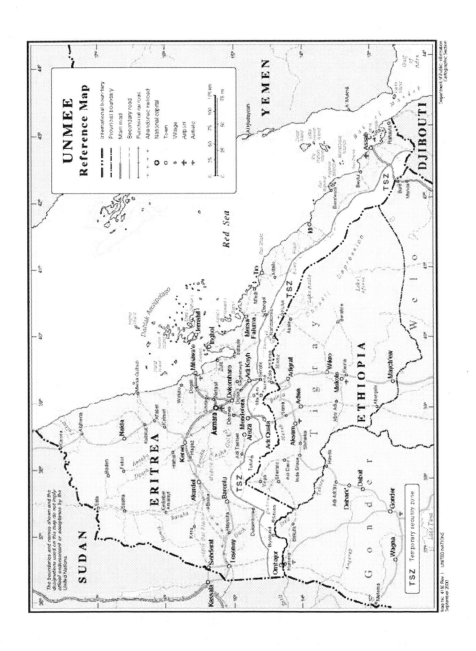

Note on confidential Unmee maps

The maps published here reveal Unmee's weekly military assessment of the situation as at 8 April 2002 for each of the three sectors covering the border between Ethiopia and Eritrea.

Given that they represent a snap shot of what prevailed at that particular point in time, the position of the troops as indicated on the maps do not necessarily reflect the current state of deployment. They nonetheless indicate the precise location of the Temporary Security Zone as understood by UNMEE. Also significant is the identification of a number of border towns not always found on other maps of the area. This is notably the case of Badme, which as can be seen on the Sector West Map remains beyond the traditional Ethiopian border, but inside territory under Ethiopian control, it is thus not covered by the Temporary Security Zone.

The editors would like to once again stress that none of the maps shown here were provided by any of the contributors to the volume.

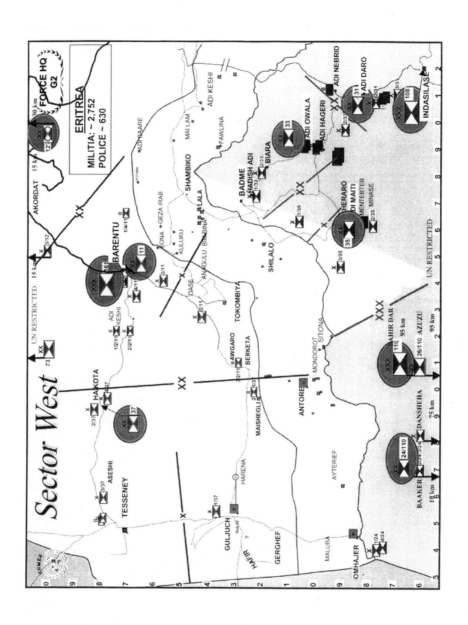

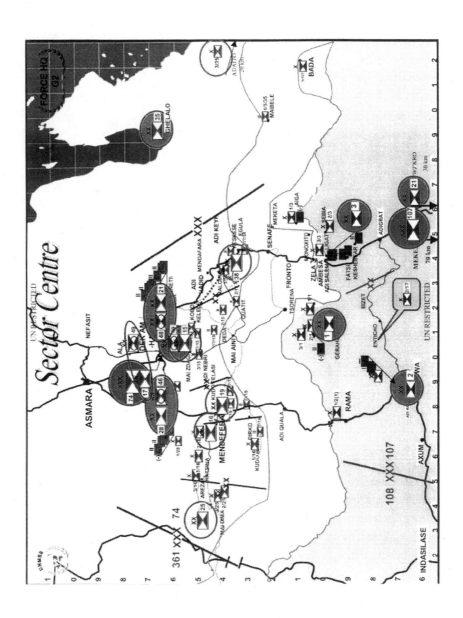

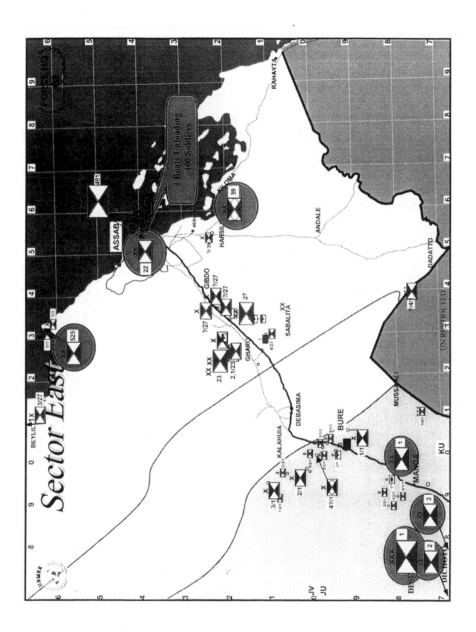

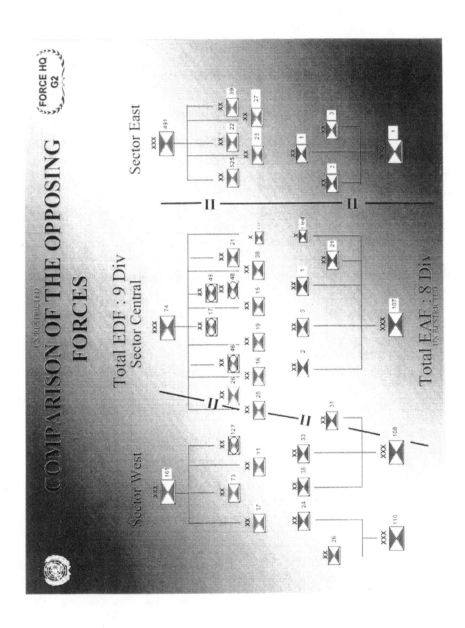

Notes on contributors

Lionel Cliffe has been working on and in Africa for over 40 years, and on the Horn for over 20. He is Emeritus Professor of Politics at Leeds University and received the Distinguished Africanist Award of the UK African Studies Association in 2002. He edited the volume Eritrea's Struggle for Self-Determination with Basil Davidson in 1990 and has written several other articles on both Eritrea and Ethiopia and on the Horn region. He conduct field research on food security in Eritrea both during and after the liberation war, and on land settlement problems in Ethiopia in 2001. He has been a frequent visitor to both countries during their war and subsequently.

Patrick Gilkes is a writer and broadcaster on the Horn of Africa. He has held a number of positions, including Senior Research Analyst, Africa Research Group, Foreign and Commonwealth Office, UK; Consultant - Save the Children Fund UK 1992-2000, Human Rights Watch 1993-1994; Deputy Head of Training, BBC World Service 1988-92; Head BBC Somali Language Service 1983-88 and Producer BBC Africa Service 1974-83. His publications include *War in the Horn – Conflict between Eritrea and Ethiopia*, with Martin Plaut, RIIA, 1999; *Conflict in Somalia and Ethiopia*, Wayland 1993; *The Dying Lion – Feudalism and Modernisation*, Freidman, 1974.

Dominique Jacquin-Berdal is Lecturer in International Relations at the London School of Economics and Political Science. Her research focuses on the Horn of Africa and she is the author of *Nationalism and Ethnicity in the Horn of Africa*, The Edwin Mellen Press, 2002.

Alexander Last did a BA in History at Manchester University before studying at the American University in Cairo. Between 1998 and 2003 was a correspondent for Reuters and the BBC in Asmara. Currently works for the BBC World Service in London.

Leenco Lata was a founding member of the Oromo Liberation Front (OLF) and served on the Front's executive bodies from its inception. As the Deputy Secretary-General of the OLF, he was a member of the Transitional Government that took power in Ethiopia in 1991. As such he worked closely with the current leaders in Ethiopia and Eritrea.

Ian Martin was Deputy Special Representative of the Secretary-General in the UN Mission in Ethiopia and Eritrea November 2000 - December 2001. Previously he was Special Representative of the Secretary-General for the East

Timor Popular Consultation, and also worked in Bosnia and Herzegovina, Rwanda and Haiti. He was Secretary General of Amnesty International 1986-92, and is now Vice President of the International Center for Transitional Justice.

Martin Plaut is Africa Editor with BBC World Service News. He was formerly Associate Fellow at the Royal Institute for International Affairs and Africa Secretary with the Labour Party. He has written widely on Africa and is co-author of *Power! Black workers, their unions and the struggle for freedom in South Africa.*

John Prendergast was part of the facilitation team behind the two-and-a-half-years U.S. effort to broker an end to the war between Ethiopia and Eritrea. He also served as a Special Advisor to the U.S. State Department focusing on conflict resolution in Africa and as Director of African Affairs at the National Security Council. Previously, John has worked for a variety of think tanks, UN agencies and NGOs in Africa and on African issues, including the U.S. Institute of Peace, Human Rights Watch, and UNICEF. He has written six books on Africa and published widely on U.S. foreign policy.

Richard Reid received his doctorate from School of Oriental & African Studies, London before becoming assistant Professor of History, University of Asmara, Eritrea where he remained between 1997 and 2002. Since then he has been lecturer in African and imperial history at University of Durham. He works on pre-colonial and modern eastern and northeastern African history, with particular interest in the culture and practice of warfare. Author of *Political Power in Pre-Colonial Buganda* (Oxford, 2002).

Philip Roessler is a doctoral student and Harrison Fellow in the Department of Government and Politics at the University of Maryland. His research focuses on globalisation and conflict in Africa.

David Styan teaches in Birkbeck College, London. He wrote extensively on the economies of Ethiopia and Eritrea during the 1990s.

Philip White is a freelance researcher/consultant with over 25 years experience working on issues of food security, conflict, disasters and rural/agricultural development, mainly in Africa. He has been involved in Eritrea and Ethiopia since 1987, when he was co-researcher on the Leeds University *Eritrea Food and Agricultural Production Assessment Study.*
Contact: philip@rauwhite.freeserve.co.uk

INDEX